STUDIES IN COMMONWEALTH POLITICS AND HISTORY

No. 2

General Editors: Professor W. H. MORRIS-JONES
Institute of Commonwealth Studies
University of London

Professor DENNIS AUSTIN
Department of Government
University of Manchester

Malaysia — New States in a New Nation

KV-553-846

DORSET INSTITUTE OF
HIGHER EDUCATION
LEARNING RESOURCES
CENTRE

CLC LIBRARY BOOK
R28955W0577

20. FEB. 1989

Malaysia — New States in a New Nation

Political Development of Sarawak and Sabah in Malaysia

WITHDRAWN

R. S. Milne

Department of
Political Science,
University of British Columbia

and

K. J. Ratnam

School of
Comparative Social Sciences
Universiti Sains Malaysi

FRANK CASS : LONDON

First published in 1974 in Great Britain by
FRANK CASS AND COMPANY LIMITED
67 Great Russell Street, London WC1B 3BT, England

and in United States of America by
FRANK CASS AND COMPANY LIMITED
c/o International Scholarly Book Services, Inc.
P.O. Box 4347, Portland, Oregon 97208

Copyright © 1974 R. S. Milne and K. J. Ratnam

ISBN 0 7146 2988 X

Library of Congress Catalog Card No. 72–92971

All rights reserved. No part of this publication may be reproduced in any form or by any means, electronic, mechanical, photocopying, recording or otherwise, without the prior permission of Frank Cass and Company Limited in writing.

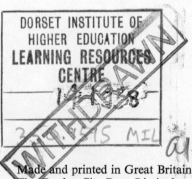

DORSET INSTITUTE OF
HIGHER EDUCATION
LEARNING RESOURCES
CENTRE
WITHDRAWN

Made and printed in Great Britain by
The Garden City Press Limited
Letchworth, Hertfordshire SG6 1JS

Contents

Map

Preface

The authors are particularly indebted to people, as opposed to books and documents, because much of their material was gathered from hundreds of interviews. It is impossible to thank all the two hundred persons concerned by name, but we should like to express our gratitude here for their frankness, patience, provision of information and hospitality. The degree of co-operation was extraordinarily high. To preserve confidentiality and avoid boredom, only a minute proportion of the information obtained is actually ascribed to individuals in the footnotes.

We wish to thank Zakaria Haji Ahmad for his services as a research assistant, Robert Jackson, Mansoor Marican, Diane Mauzy and John Wood for reading and commenting on portions of the manuscript, and Mr. Lim Hong Too of the University of Singapore Library for translations from Chinese newspapers. Financially, the project would have been impossible without support from the Asia Foundation, the Canada Council and the President's Research Fund, University of British Columbia. Within the Asia Foundation our special thanks are due to Lindley Sloan, John Sutter and Douglas Murray for their co-operation and friendly encouragement. We are doubly indebted to Professor W. H. Morris-Jones, in his capacity as joint editor of this series, and as Director of the Institute of Commonwealth Studies (University of London), for providing facilities for us during periods when we were in London. We also benefited from the help of several efficient typists, particularly Mrs. Lilian Wong, Cik Noorsalma Noorlajis and Mrs. Anne Barnes.

The period covered by the book is from just before the inclusion of Sarawak and Sabah (North Borneo) in Malaysia (1963) until the conclusion of state and parliamentary elections in Sarawak and the parliamentary elections in Sabah (mid-1970). However, one or two important developments which have occurred since then have been referred to briefly. In September 1973 Tan Sri Mohammed Fu'ad (Donald) Stephens was installed as Sabah's Head of State. Thus in 1973 he and Tun Mustapha had exchanged the positions they held ten years before.

A word is necessary on the use of proper names and on titles. "Enche" is the equivalent of "Mr." The spelling of this word has recently been changed to "Encik", but we were unable to make the necessary alterations as the manuscript was already with the printers when the new spelling system was introduced in mid-1972. "Tuan" is used instead of "Enche" before "Syed", a name borne by descendants of the Prophet, Muhammad, and before the title, "Haji", a title given to a Muslim who has made the pilgrimage to Mecca. "Dato" (which has been changed to "Datuk") is a title conferred by a state of Malaysia, and corresponds roughly to a British knighthood. Its equivalent, when conferred by the Head of State of the Federal Government, is "Tan Sri". A still higher federal title is "Tun". Dato, Tan Sri and Tun are all non-hereditary. On the other hand, "Tengku" (roughly equivalent to Prince) is hereditary. The old Malay title, "Datu", very common in Sarawak, is also hereditary. Persons whose names are prefixed by "Temenggong" or "Penghulu" are part of the Native Chiefs complex, described at the start of Chapter 6. In the index individuals are referred to by their most recent known titles, for example Tan Sri Temenggong Jugah, but in the text, where the reference is to a time before current titles were acquired, they are referred to as they were then known, for example as Temenggong Jugah.

According to terminology introduced after Malaysia was formed, the two Borneo territories combined are sometimes referred to as "East Malaysia", the former "Malaya" as "West Malaysia".

During the period covered by the book three Malaysian dollars were worth approximately one United States dollar.

R.S.M.
K.J.R.

Abbreviations

A.D.O.	ASSISTANT DISTRICT OFFICER
BARJASA	BARISAN RA'AYAT JATI SARAWAK
BUNAP	BORNEO UTARA NATIONAL PARTY
CCO	CLANDESTINE COMMUNIST ORGANIZATION
C.D.O.	COMMUNITY DEVELOPMENT OFFICER
D.D.O.	DIVISIONAL DEVELOPMENT OFFICER
D.O.	DISTRICT OFFICER
DP	DEMOCRATIC PARTY
FAMA	FEDERAL AGRICULTURAL MARKETING AUTHORITY
FIDA	FEDERAL INDUSTRIAL DEVELOPMENT AUTHORITY
FLDA	FEDERAL LAND DEVELOPMENT AUTHORITY
I.G.C.	INTER-GOVERNMENTAL COMMITTEE
MARA	MAJLIS AMANAH RA'AYAT
MCA	MALAYSIAN CHINESE ASSOCIATION
MIC	MALAYSIAN INDIAN CONGRESS
MIDFL	MALAYSIAN INDUSTRIAL FINANCE LIMITED
M.R.P.	MINOR RURAL PROJECT
NBCA	NORTH BORNEO CHINESE ASSOCIATION
N.C.	NATIVE CHIEF (Sabah)
O.K.K.	ORANG KAYA KAYA (Grade One Chief, Sabah)
O.T.	ORANG TUA (Headman, Sabah)
PANAS	PARTY NEGARA SARAWAK
PAP	PEOPLE'S ACTION PARTY
PM PARTY	PASOK MOMOGUN PARTY
PSC	PUBLIC SERVICE COMMISSION
SANAP	SABAH NATIONAL PARTY
SCA	SABAH CHINESE ASSOCIATION
SCA	SARAWAK CHINESE ASSOCIATION
S.D.O.	STATE DEVELOPMENT OFFICER
SNAP	SARAWAK NATIONAL PARTY
SUPP	SARAWAK UNITED PEOPLE'S PARTY

TUPP	TUGAU UNITED PEOPLE'S PARTY
UMNO	UNITED MALAYS' NATIONAL ORGANIZATION
UNKO	UNITED NATIONAL KADAZAN ORGANIZATION
UP	UNITED PARTY
UPKO	UNITED PASOKMOMOGUN KADAZAN ORGANIZATION
USIA	UNITED SABAH ISLAMIC ASSOCIATION
USNO	UNITED SABAH NATIONAL ORGANIZATION

DORSET INSTITUTE OF
HIGHER EDUCATION
LEARNING RESOURCES
CENTRE

1

Introduction

Sarawak and Sabah

Many books on political development can correctly assume that the reader has some basic knowledge of the country or countries under discussion. However, such an assumption about Sarawak or Sabah (until 1963 called North Borneo) might be incorrect. At times, indeed, the term Borneo has been used to indicate remoteness and unfamiliarity, as in the phrase, "the wild man of Borneo". On another occasion the territories were referred to as the "odds and ends of empire". The non-specialist reader, impressed by the numerical dominance of Indonesia in Southeast Asia, and by the huge population of nearby China, cannot be expected to know very much about territories with a total population of less than two million. Most of this short chapter, therefore, takes the form of a sketch of the history and social and economic conditions in the two states. A short bibliography is also given at the end of the book.

The bibliography includes a section on Malaya/Malaysia, which is necessary because this book studies a rather unusual form of the problem of political development. Sarawak and Sabah are not independent countries. In 1963 they ceased to be British colonies and became part of Malaysia, based on the previous Federation of Malaya but also including these two territories and, from 1963 until 1965, Singapore. So the political development under review is political development not in autonomous states but in two states of a federation, of which the nucleus, Malaya, had become an independent federation in 1957.

Malaya had not yet solved the problems of its own political development when its leaders became responsible also for guiding the political development of Sarawak and Sabah. There is, consequently, a continual interaction between the central government in Malaya in which about 85% of the population live, and the state governments in the two Borneo territories, separated from Malaya by water and by the usually correct assumption that the Borneo states are less developed. Important events in Malaya are bound to have repercussions in Sarawak and Sabah, although the reverse is not equally true. If there is a fall in the price of rubber, upon the export of which Malaysia's foreign exchange earnings chiefly depend, there may be a slowing down in the amount of finance available from the centre for the promotion of the Borneo states' development plans. And if there are severe inter-communal difficulties in Malaya, as there were immediately after the elections in May 1969, one consequence may be to retard political development in Sarawak and Sabah; in 1969 the effect was that the state and parliamentary elections in Sarawak and the parliamentary elections in Sabah were suspended. In this chapter, and throughout the book, political development is conceived of, not as an attribute of each Borneo state in a vacuum, but as a resultant of local happenings as influenced by the Federal Government and its agents.

The circumstances which led to the formation of Malaysia in 1963 are mentioned in Chapter 2. The birth of the new federation was not entirely smooth. Most opposition parties in Malaya opposed it, although the Alliance Government, which has been in power ever since Malaya became independent in 1957, won a convincing victory at the 1964 elections, with Malaysia as one of the main issues. There was also initial reluctance to join Malaysia in both Borneo territories, although most of the local elites had been won over by the time federation actually occurred. Two external complications at one and the same time threatened the new federation, but also indicated that, just because of the threat, it would be patriotic for its inhabitants to support it. Between the proposal to form Malaysia and its actual formation the Philippines revived a dormant claim to part of the territory of North Borneo (Sabah), and Indonesia embarked on a course of "Confrontation", a kind of cold war with occasional warm spells. These objections were temporarily met by a survey of political opinion in the two territories by a United Nations team in mid-1963, which showed that a majority of the population

EAST MALAYSIA

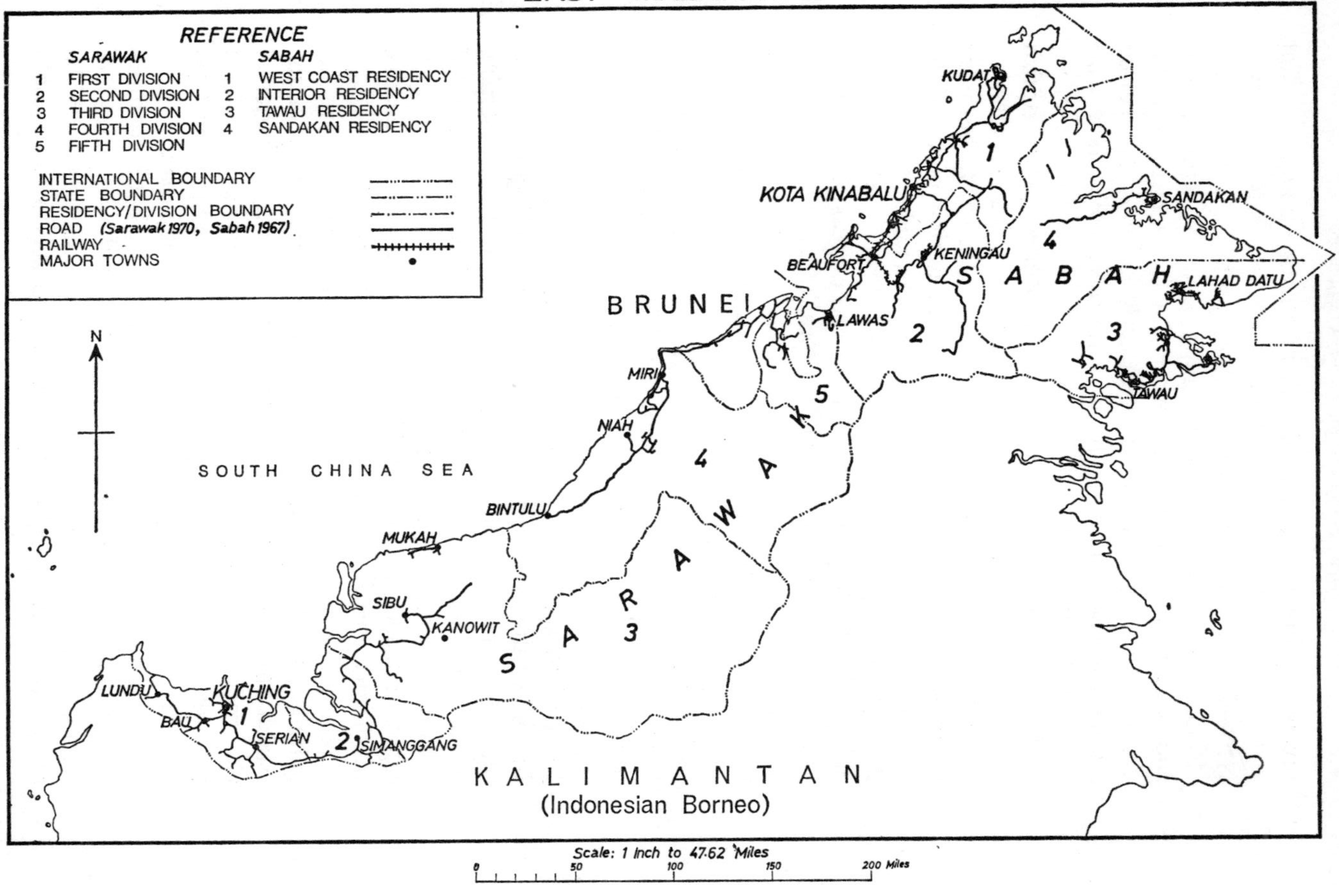

favoured joining Malaysia. But Confrontation continued, and absorbed the energies of Malaysian, British, Australian, and New Zealand troops until the fall of the Sukarno régime (1965), which was followed by a rapprochement with the new Indonesian rulers. The Philippine claim faded into the background, but was brought up again early in 1968. A separate section of the bibliography is concerned with these two external threats.

Between 1946 and 1963 both territories were British colonies. Their previous histories, however, were somewhat different. The north of the island of Borneo, where both are situated, was in effect a power vacuum during most of the nineteenth century. Much of the area was under the rule of the Sultan of Brunei or, on the east coast of what is now Sabah, the Sultan of Sulu. But in most areas the Sultans' jurisdictions were nominal, and the local representatives of the Sultans exercised their own rule, or misrule; the inland tribes, who were not Muslims, were in effect largely independent. The area was a cross-roads for incursions by European powers, and it was much a matter of chance that the colonial map later took the form it did, with the British established in the northern quarter of the island of Borneo (apart from the tiny British-protected enclave to which the once-great sultanate of Brunei had shrunk), while the rest of the island was Dutch. In this confused situation James Brooke, an English adventurer, won the gratitude of the Sultan of Brunei by helping to subdue a local revolt, and by 1841 had become Rajah of Sarawak. Subsequently the Brookes received both British recognition and protection, and, taking advantage of the chaotic conditions, greatly extended their original territory.

North Borneo had less glamorous beginnings, and was acquired through a series of concessions, culminating in the establishment, in 1882, of the British North Borneo (Chartered) Company. The argument that some of these concessions from the Sultan of Sulu were only leases, constitutes the main legal basis for the Philippine claim to some parts of Sabah.

Soon after the end of the Japanese occupation both territories were taken over directly by the British as colonies. The chief reason given was that the high cost of rehabilitation would be too great for the previous governments to bear and so would have to be assumed by the British Government. The change was accepted without much opposition in North Borneo, but in Sarawak, although the Rajah favoured it, some of his relatives and possible successors did not. Many of the elite opposed the change, especially some Malays who had been closely attached to Brooke rule and who had held important posts in the civil service. "Cession", as it was known, produced a split in the Malay community, which was still evident in 1963 when Malaysia was formed.

Apart from cession, the historical factors mentioned still are of importance. History, as well as geography, attracts some Sarawak Malays to the idea of rule by Brunei. Muslims in Sabah, also, may be influenced by having come from areas formerly under the domination of Brunei or Sulu. Conversely, some other groups, such as the Land Dayaks of Sarawak or the Dusuns of Sabah, may have heard tales from their parents or grandparents of the alleged iniquities, many years ago, of the agents of the Sultans of Brunei and this may have influenced their attitude to "Malays" in general.

Sarawak and Sabah, like Malaya, are both multi-racial societies. But, although Sarawak has only about one-ninth of the population of Malaya and Sabah about one-fifteenth, the racial pattern is more complex. In Malaya nearly all the population can be put under the broad headings of Malay (nearly 50%), Chinese (about 38%), and Indian and Pakistani (about 10%), leaving only about 2% of the population under "Others". But this is not so in either of the Borneo states. In mid-1967 the Sarawak population of about 900,000 could be split into the following broad groups: Malay, 18%; Melanau, 6%; Iban (Sea Dayak), 29%; Land Dayak, 8%; Chinese, 33%. But even then the remainder amounted to about 6%, which included quite important minorities in the politics of Sarawak, such as the Kenyans and Kayans.

The situation in Sabah in mid-1967 was similar. The population of just under 600,000 could be divided into: Kadazans (Dusuns), 30%; Muruts, 4%; Bajaus, 12%; Chinese, 22%; Other Indigenous, 18%; Others, 14%. Some Dusuns strongly disliked being described as Kadazans, and one authority (Rutter listed no fewer than six varieties of Inland Dusuns and nine varieties of Coast Dusuns. After the four main groupings are exhausted, nearly one-third of the population is left in the residual categories of "Other Indigenous" or "Others".

Politicians from Malaya found it difficult to believe that the differences between some of the groups in Sarawak or Sabah were really important, although the groups themselves obviously believed that they were. There was therefore a tendency to over-simplify the racial situation in the two states, as looked at from Malaya. For example, the Alliance Party organization, which in Malaya was based on a union of three racial parties, a dominant "indigenous" Malay party, a Chinese party, and an Indian party (UMNO, MCA and MIC), was difficult to apply in the Borneo states, without modifications. There was no single indigenous group which was as homogeneous as the Malays in Malaya; there were *several* indigenous groups. Should each "group" form a separate party in the Sarawak, or Sabah, Alliance, and who should have the final say on what should be counted as a "group"?

The broad racial breakdown by itself does not give much information of political value, unless it is supplemented by data on language and religion. Malay has often been described as the "lingua franca" of the area; this is correct, but knowledge of Malay was more widespread in Sabah than in Sarawak, also the Malay spoken in the Borneo territories was different from the Malay spoken in Malaya. Again, although each main racial group had its own language, and although the languages were often quite closely related to each other there were different varieties of, say, Iban or Dusun (Kadazan) spoken in different areas. A major issue, which directly affected federal-state relations in Sarawak in 1965, was whether in fact Iban was a separate language or only a variety of Malay. There were also, in each territory, several dialects of Chinese in use.

Religion is also basic to an understanding of the social and political life in each state. Just as Sabah had more Malay speakers than Sarawak, it also had more Muslims, approximately 38% compared with 23%. In Sarawak the Muslims were made up of all the Malays, some of the Melanaus and some smaller groups such as the Kedayans. In Sabah the Bajaus were the largest Muslim group, together with most of the "Other Indigenous", about 7% of the Kadazans, and the Indonesians (who formed a high proportion of the "Others"). The distinction, Muslim/non-Muslim, was a more important distinction than any other religious distinction, for instance than a division between Christian and non-Christian. Inter-marriage, for example between Chinese and non-Chinese, was much more common if the non-Chinese were not a Muslim than if he were. However, the lines between Muslims and non-Muslim were sometimes crossed by the adoption of a Chinese child by Malays who brought it up as a Muslim.

Religious differences were so decisive that in some instances they resulted in actual switches in racial categories. Many of the "Malays" in Sarawak were actually originally Melanaus or Land Dayaks. But when they were converted to Islam they began to describe themselves as "Malays", and this was how they came to be listed in the census. This example illustrates how tenuous racial divisions in the two states could be. But religion could also be a source of cleavage. The fact that the (Muslim) Malays formed the dominant group politically in Malaya made religion a key issue for non-Muslims in the Borneo states when the formation of Malaysia was being considered.

There were variations in the attitudes of Government towards the various races and also in their degrees of exposure to outside influences and modernization. In Sarawak the Malays were favoured for government jobs under the Brookes, because they had performed corresponding ruling functions before the Brookes arrived, and because, unlike the Iban, they were numerous in the original area of Brooke rule. The Iban were also high in the prestige scale, because of their large numbers and their reputation as warriors. The Iban who were nearest to the capital, Kuching, were the first to come under the Christian influence and to be exposed to education and modernization. In North Borneo the Chartered Company did not rely on any single group to the same extent as the Brookes relied on the Malays, but different ethnic groups had different stereotypes in the eyes of the British: Tuaran Dusuns, for example, were less "difficult" for the government to deal with than Dusuns from Papar; the West Coast Bajaus had the image of being good warriors and accomplished horsemen.

In each territory before 1963 the attitude of government

to the Chinese was equivocal. They were welcomed as hard workers, but their social life and system of education tended to be separate from that of the rest of the population. They were more literate than the other ethnic groups, among which an educated, as opposed to a traditional, elite was almost non-existent. The number of Chinese was too large for them to function merely as traders, as in some areas of Southeast Asia; at the same time, compared with non-Chinese, a smaller proportion of them worked on the land and a larger proportion lived in the towns and were engaged in trade. Different language groups of Chinese tended to concentrate in certain trades, and sometimes clan solidarity was weakened by business rivalry. In Sarawak by 1963 much of the Chinese population, especially the "young chauvinistic" town dwellers, was disaffected, and formed the hard-core opposition to Malaysia.

The reasons why the Chinese in Sabah were less alienated are hard to disentangle. In both states China exercised a powerful ancestral and cultural attraction, and under the Brookes, the Chartered Company, and the British, there was little attempt by government to integrate them into the life of other communities. After the formation of Malaysia measures taken to help the non-Chinese, for instance in civil service appointments, and in business, led to some Chinese resentment. However, there were reasons why alienation was greater in Sarawak than in Sabah: Sabah, when it was North Borneo, had a history of tougher control of immigration and of Communist infiltration in the schools, less stringent restrictions on Chinese legal ownership of land, and better job opportunities because of a more prosperous economy. In North Borneo, as compared with Sarawak, the Chinese had had more links with Hong Kong, which had a tradition of being non-political, than with "radical" Singapore. In the 1960s subversive movements in Sarawak, largely Chinese, led to government counter-measures which reinforced Chinese feelings of being excluded from the society. Examples included the calling in during April 1963 of all guns and ammunition from non-Natives (Chinese), no matter how non-subversive they were, and the controlled areas of Chinese resettlement (mentioned below) which, they considered, caused unnecessary hardship.

In both states the rôle of the Chinese is especially crucial, because their proportion in the population was expected to increase, mainly because of their higher birthrate. However, the 1970 census showed that their share of the population was less than estimated, only 30% in Sarawak and 21.3% in Sabah.

Political and constitutional advance were slow in both Sarawak and North Borneo; Sarawak's first political party was formed only in 1959, North Borneo's in 1961. Before the war each had begun to follow a "British" pattern of having a representative but non-elected body which gave advice to the Rajah (in North Borneo the Governor) plus a smaller advisory body, Supreme Council in Sarawak, Executive Council in North Borneo. Between 1946 and 1963 the pattern was continued of increasing the number of people on these bodies who represented groups, as distinct from the Government, and decreasing the proportion of official, government representatives. By the time Malaysia was formed Sarawak had a system which ensured that its top legislative and executive bodies roughly reflected, although indirectly, whatever approximation to the popular will existed. Directly-elected district councils elected Divisional Advisory Councils, which, in turn, elected more than half the members of the legislature, the Council Negri. The Council Negri chose half, five out of ten, of the members of the chief executive body, the Supreme Council. North Borneo was a little way behind, but by Malaysia Day its Executive Council and Legislative Council were chosen in a similar indirect way, via a "tier" system. However, even in 1963, unlike Sarawak, not all the members of its district councils were elected; some were nominated. In each territory the State legislative body was to be wholly directly elected in the first state elections held after Malaysia.

The slow pace of constitutional change under the British was attributable to several factors. There was no great demand for quick constitutional advance, except perhaps among those Chinese in Sarawak who were believed to be under Communist influence. Also, the British timetable for independence, if indeed they consciously had one, was much slower than it had been for Malaya. At a guess, until 1961 the British probably thought of Sarawak and North Borneo as being about twenty years "behind" Malaya. But soon after Malaysia was proposed in May 1961 it became clear that there was to be only a six-year difference in the British tenure of power as between Malaya (1957) and the Borneo territories (1963).

Economically, some indication of the Borneo states' lack of development compared with Malaya can be gathered from the figures for Gross National Product per head (1965) which were approximately: Malaya M$952; Sabah M$862; Sarawak M$737. But they do not bring out the full extent of the states' economic backwardness. After all, in the above figures Sabah is nearer to Malaya than it is to Sarawak. And both Sabah and Sarawak have a higher Gross National Product per head than, say, Thailand or the Philippines, which on other criteria are economically more developed. There are, however, some other relevant indices. Population was almost ten times as dense in Malaya as in the Borneo states. In 1960 the urban population ("urban" being defined, unusually, as an agglomeration of 3,000 people or more) was 15% in Sarawak and in North Borneo, less than half the corresponding percentage in Malaya. In each of the Borneo territories about 80% of the population (in 1960) was engaged in agriculture, forestry, or fishing, compared with about 60% in Malaya (1957). On the other hand, manufacturing and construction accounted for about 10% of the labour force in Malaya and only about 6% in the Borneo states, while the corresponding figures for trade, transport and other services were 30% and 13% respectively.

The "underdeveloped" nature of the Borneo states' economies may be seen from the nature of their exports. Sabah's principal export is logs, which account for over three-quarters of the value of her exports. Sarawak's principal exports are petroleum, logs, pepper, and rubber. If Sarawak's petroleum is excluded, the manufactured exports from each state are very small, although efforts are being made to build up exports of veneer, plywood and other wood products, as opposed to exporting logs. Above all, in both states, there was a shortage of human resources, particularly of people with education and skills.

Obviously, the main growth in industry and manufacturing is likely to occur in already relatively well-developed Malaya rather than in the Borneo states. But even in agriculture these states are comparatively underdeveloped. Only about 7% of the land area in Sarawak, and a rather smaller percentage in Sabah, is under settled cultivation, in comparison with about 17% in Malaya. This difference reflects a less severe pressure of population on land as well as a lack of communications and amenities which would permit more land to be cultivated more intensively by settlers.

In both states there is a tradition of shifting cultivation, which has become the basis of a whole way of life. In Sarawak shifting cultivation is found together with longhouses, although in Sabah it is sometimes not associated with them. Objectively, shifting cultivation is undesirable. Unless the cycle between crops is long enough (something like fifteen years), the soil is impoverished, and in any case the yield is lower than for settled cultivation carried on with the aid of irrigation and fertilizers. Also, the shifting population makes it impossible for the Government to provide amenities, for example education, which can be made available for concentrated settled communities.

In both states the government is trying to improve agricultural productivity. One method is through land settlement schemes, which combine the objective of promoting settled, as opposed to shifting, cultivation with providing training for those in the schemes through managers and supervisors who themselves have had training in agriculture.[1] Apart from actual training courses, agriculture extension workers are also active in both states. Other measures take the form of increasing the planting of *padi* to reduce dependence on imported rice, encouraging the planting of new types of crops, for example improved types of rubber, or switching from rubber to, say, oil palm in the interests of diversification. All of the above are reinforced by heavy expenditure on drainage and irrigation.

Other economic and social indicators will show that Sarawak and Sabah were "behind" Malaya at the time when Malaysia was formed. Although both Malaya and the Borneo states were "tropical", rainfall was heavier and the obstacles to communications more formidable in the latter. Rivers were numerous, and Sabah had a railway with a hundred miles of track, but roads were few. Roadmaking was difficult; the abundance of rivers and heavy rainfall were impediments, and so were swamps and mountains. Stone which could be used for roadmaking was scarce except in west Sarawak or the southeast of North Borneo. Since Malaysia air traffic has increased; six years after Malaysia in both territories civil air freight per head had more than doubled. But communications by other means take a long time. Correspondence from the Limbang District Council to the state government has to travel across the whole breadth of Sarawak; if it does not go by air, the sea route may take up to six weeks. Communications between Sarawak and Sabah are even more difficult. After Malaysia a scheme was considered for improving the quality of buffaloes in Sarawak by importing stock, but it was stated in the Sarawak Council Negri (Legislative Assembly) in June 1966 "that the transportation of buffaloes from Sabah to Sarawak has proved to be so difficult as to make purchases from that source almost impracticable". Road mileage grew rapidly after Malaysia was formed. By 1969 in Sarawak there were about thirty eight miles of road for every thousand square miles in the state, while the corresponding figure for Sabah (1968) was approximately fifty four. But the map on page 3 shows that there are still gaps, and some of the roads linking main centres, for instance Kuching and Sibu, were constructed only in the late 1960s.

In a wider sense of "communications", radio programmes were begun under British rule, although transmissions were made more complicated by the need to broadcast in a number of languages. The number of radio licences was almost static in Sarawak for the first six years after 1963, if allowance is made for the increase in the population; in 1969 it was only fifty three per thousand inhabitants. However, in longhouses one radio set might serve the needs of everyone, and there were also many "pirate" listeners in Sarawak who did not take out licences. In Sabah the number of licences grew one and a half times in the period 1963–8, to seventy five per thousand inhabitants. As in Sarawak, there were many "pirates", and the set given to each chief or headman was intended for communal use. Television did not start in Sabah until late 1971; it is not due to begin in Sarawak until 1975.

The number of telephones grew by roughly 60% in each state in the first half dozen years or so after Malaysia, reaching thirteen per thousand inhabitants in Sarawak (1969) and fifteen in Sabah (1968).

Newspaper circulation, except in the towns, was restricted by linguistic fragmentation, and also by illiteracy and delays in distribution. Almost all newspapers were in English or Chinese. Circulation is particularly hard to measure, because of differing degrees of "inflation". But in each state by the end of the 1960s it was roughly fifty five per thousand inhabitants.

Some other social and economic indices may be quoted. The number of inhabitants per physician was actually larger in Sarawak in 1969 (roughly 13,700) than in 1963. The Sabah 1968 figure, however (about 9,300), was a decided improvement on the 1963 one. In both states the proportion of the population between five and nineteen which went to primary or secondary school had increased quite markedly, 1963–8. However the percentage had increased more rapidly in Sabah (71 in 1968) than in Sarawak (50). Compared with Malaya, the most striking differences in indices were in literacy and in electricity consumption per head. According to the latest figures available, the percentage of the population over age ten which was literate in the Borneo states in 1960, roughly a quarter, was less than half the corresponding figure for Malaya in 1957. And, although electricity consumption per head had doubled in Sabah by 1968 (102 kilowatt hours) and grown by 50%, 1963–9, in Sarawak (to 88 kilowatt hours), it was nowhere near the Malayan figure. The 1968 electricity consumption per head in Malaya was three and a half times as great as in Sarawak and nearly three times as great as in Sabah.[2]

In the First Malaysia Plan, 1966–70, there was a concentration on the improvement of transport and communications, as well as on education, in the Borneo states, which is reflected in the figures in the table. Even in 1963 when Malaysia was formed, Sabah enjoyed a high rate of economic growth. And it is significant, for instance, that the *Second Malaysia Plan, 1971–1975* (p. 19, paragraph 75), found that, 1965–70, the Gross National Product at current prices grew by 11% per annum in Sabah and 8% per annum in Sarawak, a higher rate of increase than for Malaya. The faster rate of growth of the

Borneo states towards the end of this period reflected the deliberate decision of the Federal Government that in the First Malaysia Plan there would be a greater proportionate increase in public development expenditure in Sarawak and Sabah as compared with Malaya.

To summarize, the Borneo states presented a picture of an area with a lower standard of living, a less dense population, and more difficult communications, than Malaya. The prosperity which rubber and tin had brought to Malaya was absent, although there was a timber boom in Sabah, and it was hoped that when mineral resources, for example copper in Sabah, were developed, a general increase in wealth might follow. Politically, the development of institutions and pressures for independence from a political elite had come later than in Malaya. Only in the sphere of local government were the states, particularly Sarawak, in a sense more advanced than Malaya.[3]

In 1963 Sarawak and Sabah had different traditions and images, derived from their history, which had also an effect on their future. Sarawak had been somewhat sheltered economically by the Brookes, but their paternalism had not ruled out limited political advance. Under the British, local government on a multi-racial basis, local elections, and political parties were all launched. North Borneo had been slower to experiment constitutionally, but, having been run by a Company, had been more go-ahead economically. There was a greater emphasis on providing good communications and on the exploitation of natural resources than in Sarawak. Under the British, and later inside Malaysia, this policy was continued, as the data quoted above indicate. A particular form of exploitation in Sabah, which had great political significance, was the exploitation of timber.

As a guide to the reader, it may be helpful to outline the key political events in the two states from 1963 until 1970. In Sarawak the initial Alliance government was headed by an Iban, Dato Stephen Kalong Ningkan, leader of the Sarawak National Party (SNAP). However, the relations between the parties in the Alliance were not stable, and there were two revolts against Ningkan's leadership, described in Chapter 5, in 1965 and 1966. The second of these removed Ningkan as leader, the rebels having the support of the Federal Government. 1966–70 was a period of manoeuvring and indecision with a weak Alliance Government, headed by Dato Tawi Sli, facing the opposition of Ningkan's party, now out of the Alliance, and of the first party ever founded in Sarawak, the Communist-infiltrated Sarawak United People's Party (SUPP). In the Sarawak state elections of 1970 the Alliance won only half the seats. However, the leader of the mainly Muslim, Parti Bumiputera, Dato Haji Rahman Ya'akub, was appointed Chief Minister and, rather unexpectedly, formed a coalition between the Alliance Party and the SUPP.

In Sabah the first Chief Minister, Dato Donald Stephens, was the leader of the UNKO (United National Kadazan Organization). But the Sabah Alliance Party (which included all the political parties in the state) was as unstable as its Sarawak counterpart. A struggle developed between UNKO (later renamed UPKO) and the other main party in the Alliance, USNO (United Sabah National Organization), and between their respective leaders, Dato Stephens and Tun Datu Mustapha bin Datu Harun, the first Sabah Head of State. There were two Cabinet reshuffles in 1964; UPKO lost ground in both, and in the second Stephens was forced to give up the Chief Ministership to Peter Lo of the Sabah Chinese Association (SCA). After the state elections of 1967 Tun Mustapha, who had ceased to be Head of State and had re-entered politics, became Chief Minister, and UPKO was excluded from the Cabinet. For some months it seemed that UPKO would provide a rallying point for opposition. But at the end of 1967 Dato Stephens dissolved UPKO, and made his peace with Tun Mustapha, and Sabah was left without any opposition except for some rather loosely-organized Independents.

The Pattern of the Book

The book's aim is to study intensively politics in the states of Sarawak and Sabah, concentrating on the first seven years after the formation of Malaysia, 1963–1970, but also including some historical material. The main sources were books and pamphlets (the most important of which are listed in the bibliography); government and political party documents;

reports of debates in the legislature; newspapers; interviews. The last source was perhaps the most important. Over a hundred persons were interviewed, politicians, administrators, journalists, and others, some of them several times. The longest interview lasted approximately eleven hours. Field trips were made inside the two states, including accompanying some politicians during their election campaign tours. Interviews were not structured, in the sense that questionnaires were not used. But the same questions were put many times to different persons, and the answers compared. Answers provided the basis for additional questions, and so a cycle of question-answer-question-answer was built up. Care has been taken to preserve anonymity in appropriate cases. A minimum of footnotes has been used to indicate information derived from interviews, otherwise the book would have been even longer than it is.

Chapter 2 sets the political scene by describing the formation of Malaysia, and discussing consequent problems of federalism and nation building. An account is given of the conflict between state nationalism and Malaysian nationalism in Sarawak and Sabah.

Chapters 3 and 4 deal with the political process as revealed in the formation and functioning of political parties and with elections, particularly the 1967 state election in Sabah and the 1969–70 state and parliamentary elections in Sarawak. Chapter 5 contains a case study of the political process in Sarawak, based on the cabinet crises of 1965 and 1966, and a section on coalitions.

Chapter 6 deals with administration in the field and the way in which the former colonial structure was modified by the formation of parties and the rise of politicians. The chapter also describes the evolution of local government councils and of the machinery for rural development, and the relations between these and the administrative structure.

Chapter 7 considers certain aspects of the political process in greater detail: the strategies and "rules" of politics; the use of money, particularly money derived from timber; the relation between money and power; violence and combinations of money and violence.

The concluding chapter attempts to relate various notions

of "political development" to politics in Sarawak and Sabah. Several different concepts of political development, including "modernization", are examined, and possible conflicts and contradictions in these approaches are analysed. Many of the concepts are seen to be of limited utility, but those relating to social mobilization, political stability, and institutionalization are found to be of some value. An appendix provides data on political and other elites in the two states.

Throughout the book two interweaving and interacting themes are apparent. One is the changes resulting from the increasingly important role of politics and politicians in states which until 1963 had been colonies. Politics is, as it were, superimposed on administration. The other is the impact of the Federal Government. From 1963 onwards Sarawak and Sabah were changing because they were "new states". But they were also changing because they were new states in a new *nation*, Malaysia. These inter-related themes constitute the warp and the woof of the book.

2

Federalism and Nation-Building

This chapter seeks to analyse the relations between the Borneo states and the Federal Government for approximately the first seven years after federation. To what extent did the inhabitants of Sarawak and Sabah feel loyalty to Malaysia, to what extent did they come to regard themselves as belonging to a Malaysian nation?[1] This is not the same as asking if they were constitutionally or administratively part of Malaysia, or if federal government power was effectively exercised in these states. The emphasis is on the effect of federalism on nation-building, as opposed to state-building, an essentially cultural, as opposed to structural, problem.[2] Inside the new federal framework, what measures were taken to create a Malaysian nation? What was their impact on the embryonic "national" sentiments which existed in each of the Borneo States in 1963? The sequence is: to review the main issues raised when Malaysia was formed and the principal views expressed on them; to examine the premises on which the Federal Government acted in seeking to build Malaysia; to see what measures were adopted by the Federal Government to promote nation-building, and which gave rise to friction and why; to assess how successful the promotion of Malaysian nationalism had been by 1970 and how it had been aided or hampered by "state nationalism" inside the two states.

The Formation of Malaysia

After the end of the war in 1945 the chance to unify Malaya, Singapore, Brunei, North Borneo and Sarawak, was lost, although there would have been a good case for unification on economic grounds.[3]

There were several links between the various territories. A British official, the Commissioner General for South East Asia, had broad authority over the administration of all five territories; the Governor of Sarawak was also the High Commissioner for Brunei; the Governors of the territories met regularly in conference and so did certain committees; there was a single Judiciary for Sarawak, Sabah, and Brunei and a single Geological Department; there was also a common currency. In the late 1950s and early 1960s there were two important developments. Malaya became independent (1957),[4] and a Free Trade Agreement[5] was signed between Sarawak and North Borneo which was to come into effect over a period of years.

However, the proposal for a federation of the five territories, put forward by Tengku Abdul Rahman, the Prime Minister of Malaya, on 26 May 1961, went far beyond the existing arrangements, and came as a distinct surprise to the elites in the Borneo territories. There were good economic and other reasons for such a federation, as there had been in 1945. The pressure for a quick federation, however, arose from internal difficulties in Singapore. One way out was to form a union between Singapore and Malaya, but this would have caused the Malays in Malay to fear Chinese preponderance in such a union; a way to redress the balance was to form a wider union, which would include the three Borneo territories, Sarawak, North Borneo and Brunei. The Tengku's proposal along these lines was speedily taken up. Leaders of the five states concerned discussed the ideas at the Commonwealth Parliamentary Association Regional Meeting in Singapore, 1961. This was followed by: a Malaysia Solidarity Consultative Committee, which by February 1962 has issued a memorandum supporting Malaysia; a Commission of Enquiry (known after its Chairman as the "Cobbold Commission"), consisting of three British and two Malayan members, which ascertained the views of the inhabitants of North Borneo and Sarawak, and found them on the whole favourable to Malaysia; an Inter-Governmental Committee under Lord Lansdowne, which worked out detailed terms for union; finally, when the four states (excluding Brunei) and Britain had reached agreement, the Malaysia Act (1963) and other consequential legislation.[6]

Original reactions in the Borneo territories to the Malaysia proposals, with a few exceptions, were not enthusiastic. The doubts and reservations are revealed in the Cobbold Report, and are also indicated in Chapter 3. Quite apart from any ethnic reactions, or real or imagined memories of oppression by Brunei Malays, the idea of federation with Malaya and Singapore came as a shock. The territories were undeniably much less well-developed than Malaya, or Singapore; one comment was that they were twenty years behind,[7] another that they were forty years behind.[8] Suddenly the prospect of slow growth towards independence, under the paternalistic rule of the British, was replaced by a future in which it seemed that Sarawak and North Borneo would no longer be sheltered as they had been before. There was fear of an imminent unknown, which the inhabitants of the territories had not yet been prepared to meet.

It may seem remarkable that North Borneo and Sarawak agreed to join Malaysia. One reason was the absence of a feasible alternative. If Malaya was largely an unknown quantity for Sarawakians or North Borneans, Indonesia and the Philippines, which did not share a connection with Britain, were even more *terrae incognitae*, so political links with either of them were ruled out. What Native non-Muslims knew about Indonesia was not always favourable, for instance in Sarawak Temenggong Jugah's[9] impression was that it was run largely by the Communists. Another possibility, a federation of North Borneo, Sarawak and Brunei, originally found support in each of the three territories,[10] but some of the support was embarrassing. In Sarawak it came from the Communist-infiltrated Sarawak United People's Party. In Brunei it came from A. M. Azahari, leader of the Party Rakyat, who later instigated the Brunei rebellion of 1962. Independence of each territory separately was not seriously considered, although since then some countries with very small populations have become independent. An independent Sarawak would certainly have found it difficult to deal with Communist subversion without outside help. Most important of all, another possibility, perhaps the most attractive alternative to Malaysia, became increasingly unrealizable, namely that North Borneo and Sarawak could continue as British colonies.

The first response to the Malaysia proposal from British officials in the two territories had been "slightly chilly",[11] but it soon became evident that the British Government was favourable. Ever since Harold Macmillan's "Wind of Change Speech", early in 1960, the British Government had been receptive to possibilities of disengagement from its colonies. Later the Governor of North Borneo told the annual Conference of Chiefs, "When the day comes for this country to cease to be a colony of Britain you will need friends. Can you find better friends than the people of Malaya?"[12] The British case for "disengagement" was ably expressed by the Sarawak Attorney-General in September 1962. He suggested that it was not a breach of the moral obligations incurred by the British when they took over the country from the Brookes if the British Government "were to grant Sarawak independence as part of a Federation of Borneo States". Even if British rule were to continue (which was impracticable in the face of the increasing amount of anti-colonial sentiment expressed all over the world), this could only be for a few years, and when that time came Sarawak could not stand alone.[13] In a wider context is could be surmised that British forces would be withdrawn from the area, or that their size would be much reduced in the forseeable future. In that event even a union of Sarawak, Brunei and North Borneo would face defence problems. Indeed, one reason why Donald Stephens gave up his support for such a union was that some months after the Tengku's Malaysia proposal a British Conservative leader had told him that a withdrawal would occur by about 1972.[14]

There were certain positive attractions in joining Malaysia. Since 1957 the Malayan Government had shown good leadership and had achieved a high degree of racial harmony.[15] It was promised that the widely-admired rural development plans operating in Malaya would be extended to the Borneo States.[16] It was also agreed that finance would be made available by the Federal Government to pay for part of the cost of this development. Financial considerations were particularly appealing to Sarawak, which had a much less prosperous economy than North Borneo.

Because of the initial reluctance of the Borneo States to join Malaysia, concessions had to be made on the part of Malaya. Paradoxically, many were obtained because of the weakness of the Borneo States. Most were intended to protect the states from the full effects of their underdevelopment, as compared with Malaya. The issues on which particular groups in each territory felt most deeply can be gathered from an examination of the evidence given to the commission of Enquiry and summarized in its Report (the Cobbold Report). Here the issues are listed merely as an indication: language; education; constitutional guarantees; qualifications to be Head of State; ethnic composition of the civil service and the future expatriate civil servants; citizenship; religion; native privileges; immigration; representation in the federal parliament. In the first few years after Malaysia some of these issues, such as citizenship, aroused little or no controversy. Others gave rise to friction, and are analysed later in this chapter.

As a result of these concessions, the Constitution of Malaysia, altered in accordance with the Malaysia Act, was much more complex than the Constitution of Malaya. The Ninth Schedule of the Constitution, containing "Legislative Lists" had to be amended to include lists of state powers and concurrent powers which belonged only to the Borneo states, or to one of them, but not to the states of Malaya.[17] The Borneo states were also given special grants (Tenth Schedule Part IV). One of the grants given to Sabah, but not Sarawak, was based on "growth", a grant which until 1968 was to increase correspondingly as the net revenue derived by the federation from Sabah exceeded the net revenue which would have been so derived on certain assumptions in 1963.[18] The two states were also given additional sources of revenue, notably import duty and excise duty on petroleum products, export duty on timber, and fees from road transport licences. To pay for the cost of administering health services, Sabah was also given 30% of customs revenue with some exceptions, not already allocated to it under other headings.

The Federal Government concentrated on convincing the elite in the two territories of the advantages of joining Malaysia. As early as August 1961, Dato Stephens, Tun Mustapha and the Datu Bandar took "a good look round the country for themselves".[19] Speaking in Parliament on 16 October, 1961, the Tengku said that in the last few months there had been twelve delegations from the three territories, totalling 103 persons who had come to tour Malaya.[20] These visitors were well treated in Malaya, and were given presents, usually a

Parker pen, on their departure. At the same time prominent politicians from Malaya came to visit the Borneo territories. Among them was Dr. Lim Swee Aun, a cabinet minister who was particularly active and successful in persuading local Chinese that their counterparts in Malaya were well-off, and that it was in their interests to support the Malaysia plan. It is doubtful if the people of the territories, apart from the "leaders", rather narrowly defined, understood very clearly what was at stake. There may have been some exceptions. One Sarawak district officer wrote in his annual report:

> The proposal to form the Federal State of Malaysia stimulated longhouse discussion and not a little controversy. It took a great deal of patient explanation ... to translate a rather complicated idea into a simple and accurate picture of what the new form of State would be. It can be said that this was done successfully for later in the year when opinion had sufficiently crystallised it was Dayak opinion in the main that sought sufficient safeguards to ensure that Sarawak would not lose by joining Malaysia.[21]

At the same time much of the discussion on the proposal was in simple, not to say oversimplified terms, in which with varying degrees of ingenuity, joining Malaysia was compared to contracting a marriage. The Cobbold Report believed that there were three broad types of opinion on the Malaysia proposal; one definitely in favour, one decidedly opposed, and one in favour in principle but determined to have certain safeguards. However, perhaps Puan Tra Zahnder was nearer the mark when she listed a fourth type, who "appear to know nothing or little about Malaysia but agree to it because they have been told that Malaysia is good for them".[22]

Substantially, therefore, the support for Malaysia shown in the two territories at the local council elections of 1962 and 1963, took the form of support for local leaders, who had themselves been convinced of the desirability of Malaysia. But some local leaders, particularly the non-Muslim Natives, had accepted Malaysia only as a "package deal", containing unpalatable provisions, on condition that certain safeguards and benefits were included. The actual operation of the new federation brought to the surface some of the points of friction which previously had been hidden inside the package.

It has already been said that the Government of Malaya

found the idea of Malaysia attractive, partly because the territories, with a predominantly non-Chinese population, would in some sense help to balance, or offset, a union between Malaya and "Chinese" Singapore. Apart from this, two other objectives were important; the ending of colonialism in the Borneo territories, and prevention of the spread of Communism there. "The important aspect of the Malaysia ideal, as I see it, is that it will enable the Borneo territories to transform their present colonial status to self-government for themselves and absolute independence in Malaysia simultaneously, and baulk the Communist attempt to capture these territories."[23]

Evaluation of Federalism and Nation-Building

Understanding of the Malaysian federation may be deepened by applying various hypotheses. We might consider, for example, Etzioni's concept of "rates of exchange". In a union, he says, there is an exchange of various kinds of assets, which may be placed in three categories; "coercive", "utilitarian", and "identitive".[24] In the Malaysian context Malaya was, broadly speaking, exchanging two assets in the form of protection and economic aid in return for a third, a recognition of its leadership status by the Borneo states. This agrees with Etzioni's general hypothesis that the main interest of the elite units (i.e. the most powerful state in the proposed union) does not seem to consist in improving their utilitarian rates of exchange. There is, rather, an investment of utilitarian assets by the elite units in exchange for some symbolic (identitive) gratification, such as that gained from the status of leadership.[25]

To some degree Malaysia fits Riker's hypothesis of the central role of a "bargain" in the formation. At least two circumstances, according to him, encourage a willingness to strike the bargain. "1. The politicians who offer the bargain desire to expand their territorial control, usually either to meet an external military or diplomatic threat or to prepare for military or diplomatic aggression or aggrandisement. But, though they desire to expand, they are not able to do so by conquest, because of either military incapacity or ideological distaste. Hence, if they are to satisfy the desire to expand, they must offer concessions to the rulers of constituent units which is the essence of the federal bargain.... 2. The politicians who accept the bargain, giving up some independence for the sake of union, are willing to do so because of some external military-diplomatic threat or opportunity. Either they desire protection from an external threat or they desire to participate in the potential aggression of the federation. And furthermore the desire for either protection or participation outweighs any desire they may have for independence".[26]

However, in the Malaysian case, a few modifications must be made to ensure a fit for Riker's hypothesis. The threat perceived by the Malayan politicians who offered the bargain was not "the prospect of Indonesian conquest of Borneo and outlying islands"[27] except remotely; confrontation with Indonesia did not begin until after the bargain was offered by the Tengku. The external threat was from Communist infiltration from Singapore, backed at very long range from China. Paradoxically, this external threat was to be dealt with by making it internal, through merger with Singapore. There was also the possibility of apparently easy expansion, because, subject to conditions, the British were agreeable to transferring the Borneo territories. On the other hand, the Borneo politicians were not under any immediate external threat, although in the long run, when the British left the area, they would be defenceless against attack, for example, from Indonesia. Instead of the desire for protection outweighing the desire for independence, they were being offered a switch in protection (Malaya-backed-by-Britain instead of Britain) plus a certain measure of independence in a federal state, the ambiguous "independence through Malaysia".

Thomas M. Franck goes further than Riker; he analyses not only the conditions under which federations take place but also which goals and factors are needed to ensure successful federations. In the successful primary "Goal-Factor Type" of federation political federalism is given a supreme value and the goal is "federation for its own sake".[28] Apart from this, Franck makes an important point. Federations which are formed only for "tertiary" reasons (e.g. to achieve ethnic balance, obtain earlier independence, or because the colonial power wants to unload a commitment) are unlikely to last unless secondary factors come into play.[29] These secondary factors are: common language; similar values, culture; complementary economics; common colonial heritage; common enemies; common challenge. At first sight it might appear that the tertiary factors had been dominant in the creation of Malaysia. But, at least as regards the Borneo states, some secondary factors were already present,[30] and since 1963 the Federal Government has been active in promoting a common language and common values. The speed with which the Malaysian proposals were implemented and the complication resulting from the initial impetus to federation having come from Singapore, should not be allowed to obscure the fact that Malaya's union with the Borneo states does not fall into the category of "makeshift arrangements designed to facilitate the transition from colonialism to independence".[31] In the long term it was desirable that Sarawak and North Borneo should join with Malaya. Unfortunately, the process was rushed, which led to frictions between the Federal Government and the states which could have been partly avoided if the tempo of federating had been slower. The colonial power was not "wanting to join together the wrong peoples".[32] It was, however, implicated in joining the "right peoples" at too short notice.

Problems of Nation-building in Malaysia

It was not the intention of the Malayan government to replace one form of colonialism by another:

> When the Borneo territories become part of Malaysia, they will cease to be a colony of Britain . . . they will be partners of equal status, no more and no less than the other States now forming the Federation of Malaya. Where does he get the idea that by taking in the Borneo territories, we would colonize them? The days of imperialism are gone and it is not the intention of Malaya to perpetuate or revive them.[33]

These assurances were made in good faith; however, the inclusion of the two Borneo states posed problems of nation-building, and of federalism, quite different from those hitherto encountered in Malayia.[4] Apart from Malays, Malaya was made up ethnically almost entirely of Chinese, and in a broad sense "Indians", most of whom were descended from immigrants who had arrived less than a century previously. They were resistant to assimilation by reason of their claims to be heirs of great civilizations, and were largely impervious to conversion to Islam. The approach to nation-building of the Malayan Government from 1957–63 may be summarized as follows; "... (i) the Malays are predominant politically, but yet in a minority; (ii) the policy of the Malay-dominated Government is that the nation-building problem should be tackled through a long-term programme based on language and education; (iii) the Government is determined in the short run to preserve Malay dominance in certain spheres; along the lines of the 'bargain',[35] (iv) it has decided to move slowly in dismantling the existing pattern of communally-organized traditional rôles and interest groups and also of its own party structure."[36]

In the Borneo states, however, the level of development of the inhabitants, apart from the Chinese and a very small number of "Indians", may have seemed to the Federal Government to indicate a different policy on nation-building than that hitherto pursued in Malaya. In Sarawak almost a fifth of the population was actually "Malay". The appearance of the other indigenous inhabitants resembled that of the Malays of the peninsula more than that of Chinese or Indians. The Malay language was spoken widely throughout the two territories. The indigenous peoples of Borneo, unlike the Chinese and Indians, were not known to be heirs to any ancient, prestigious civilization, and some had proved to be amenable to conversion to Islam, whether spread from Brunei or Sulu. In the absence of deep knowledge of the Borneo territories, the closest analogy in the middle of some members of the Federal Government might have been with the Sakai and other aboriginal tribes in Malaya; yet such a comparison was bound to be widely resented by the more educated, among the indigenous peoples of Sarawak and Sabah. In 1963, therefore, the Federal Government was probably more impressed by the geographical, constitutional, and procedural impediments to nation-building in the Borneo states than by the human and cultural impediments. It almost certainly underestimated the refactory nature of the latter. When the Tengku visited Sarawak in July, 1961, his engaging personality proved attractive, but some of the content of his statements was injudicious.[37]

There is no really satisfactory way of categorizing the means used for nation-building in Malaysia. Policies overlap with people; for example, it may be difficult to decide which reactions to a Director of Education in a Borneo state occur because he is from Malaya and which occur because of the policies he is implementing. However, for convenience, in the following sections a broad division has been made between persons and organizations, on the one hand, and cultural policies on language and education on the other. Financial aspects of federalism and nation-building are then considered.

Under persons and organizations, four headings have been used: ministerial contacts; relations between federal and state parties; civil service contacts; and the impact of federal and state parties; civil service contacts; and the impact of federal organizations. It would be difficult to assess how far the knowledge gained from these contacts was on balance favourable or hostile to nation-building.[38] It will be clear from what follows that some contacts had unfavourable effects; it cannot be assumed that an increase in the number of state-federal contacts will automatically assist nation-building.[39]

Ministerial Contacts

The most obvious way in which regular personal contact between the states and the Federal Government can be maintained is through membership in the cabinet of politicians from the two states. There was formal provision for this in the shape of a Minister for Sarawak Affairs and a Minister for Sabah Affairs inside the Cabinet. The Sarawak post was held by Temenggong (later also Tan Sri) Jugah during the whole period. The Sabah equivalent post was held successively, with some intervals, by Dato Donald Stephens, Tun Mustapha, and Dato Ganie Gilong. In addition, a Sarawak politician, Dato Rahman Ya'akub, who had previously been an assistant minister, became a member of the Cabinet,[40] before returning to Sarawak as Chief Minister in July 1970. The importance of the two ministerial posts of Sarawak, and Sabah, Affairs would seem to depend very much on informal considerations. Indeed, the post of Minister of Sarawak Affairs (which preceded the creation of the corresponding Sabah post) was establishd, not as part of a nation-building programme, but for *ad hoc* reasons; a prestigeful position had to be found for Temenggong Jugah to make up for his not having been appointed Sarawak Head of State. Language difficulties seem to have set a limit to Jugah's effectiveness as a channel of communication between Sarawak and the Federal Government. Moreover, when Dato Rahman Ya'akub was in the Cabinet he was undoubtedly the main source of Cabinet information and advice on Sarawak.

Similarly, in Sabah the effectiveness of the Minister of Sabah Affairs as a channel of communication between federal and state governments has varied according to the confidence placed in him by the Federal Government; this, in turn, has been influenced by the nature of the relations between his party in Sabah and the Alliance Party in Malaya. There is no doubt, for instance, that as Minister of Sabah Affairs, Tun Mustapha had the confidence of the Federal Government to an extent that Donald Stephens never had.

Other contacts at ministerial level take place at regular meetings of Chief Ministers from the states and at those sessions of the Conference of Rulers which are attended by Chief Ministers. Individual state ministers also visit Malaya, just as individual federal ministers visit the Borneo states. Pre-eminent among the latter, 1963–70, was Tun Razak; his visits naturally were usually concerned with rural development, but because of the crucial importance of development and his own position as Deputy Prime Minister of Malaysia they obviously made a considerable contribution towards nation-building.

Federal—State Party Relations

"Malaysia has a federal system of government, and wherever there were federal systems of government difficulties between the States and the Centre were bound to occur. But we are lucky in Malaysia that except for one state (Kelantan) we have Alliance Government in all the states. This makes it easy to work."[41] This statement by Tun Ismail, a member of the Malaysian Cabinet, reflects the experience of the Alliance

Government in Malaya. But it also applied to the Borneo states, although with some limitations. "Alliance Government" in Sarawak or Sabah had to be understood in terms of the Sarawak Alliance Party or the Sabah Alliance Party, which was not always aligned with the party in Malay on all issues. Nevertheless, the later chapter on parties and elections indicates the wide scope of the contacts between the Alliance Party in Malaya and the Alliance Parties in the two states. Additionally, in the case of ministers it is difficult to distinguish, except analytically, between governmental links and party links. Dato Rahman Ya'akub, before becoming Chief Minister of Sarawak in July 1970, was a federal minister (previously an assistant minister) with governmental functions in the Borneo states. At the same time he was a member of the Alliance Party, and at one period, inside the Alliance Party, he was simultaneously a leading member of both UMNO and BARJASA/Bumiputera.[42] Even when appointed Chief Minister of Sarawak he envisaged a possible return to the Federal Government. "God willing, I shall return to the federal political arena later and place my service to the party as I have done in the past."[43]

Another interesting combination of state-federal and political-governmental aspects is Tuan Syed Kechik, a lawyer, who as a member of UMNO had been political secretary to the Minister of Information and Broadcasting, Senu bin Abdul Rahman. He played a role as intermediary of the Federal Government in Sarawak, and, later, was appointed political secretary to Tun Mustapha while the latter was Minister for Sabah Affairs. He was active in helping Tun Mustapha during the Sabah state elections in 1967, and, having become resident in Sabah, left UMNO and joined USNO, became a member of the USNO Central Executive Committee, and later Legal Adviser to USNO.[44] In 1967 he was appointed the first Director of the Sabah Foundation,[45] clearly a key job in the process of nation-building.

On particular occasions prominent Alliance politicians from Malaya played the role of intermediaries in contacting the Alliance Party (or one of its components) in Sarawak or Sabah, notably Dr. Lim Swee Aun, Enche Khir Johari or Enche Manickavasagam.

Apart from influential persons who functioned as intermediaries between the Malaysian Alliance Party (or UMNO) and a state, the top figures in the Malaysian Alliance, notably the Tengku and Tun Razak, naturally commanded the allegiance and deference of Alliance politicians from the Borneo states. During the parliamentary sessions such links would be reinforced when these leading figures had regular meetings with all Alliance M.P.s including those from Sarawak and Sabah.

The combined governmental-party influence of the federal Alliance Government was especially clear in the Sabah crises of 1964 and the Sarawak crises of 1965 and 1966, described in Chapter 5. During such crises the federal politicians naturally tended to stress their longer experience. As one member of the MCA rather bluntly asked a group of Sarawak Alliance politicians in 1966; "What do you know about politics? You have been at it for only three years, whereas we have been independent for ten years."

Relations between federal and state Alliance politicians were usually conducted with more finesse. But on the federal side they were sometimes carried on in such a way as to leave politicians from the Borneo states with the impression that there state's problems made little impact on federal politicians, unless there was "trouble" in a Borneo state. There were conspicuous exceptions to this generalization, notably Tun Razak's interest in development in the Borneo states. But, in spite of the available channels of information, sometimes knowledge of Borneo politics in Kuala Lumpur could best be decribed as sketchy. Most of the time federal politicians had other problems on their minds, and it required a real effort of the will to give the amount of attention to Sarawak and Sabah which politicians from these states thought they deserved.

Civil Service Contacts: Borneanization

Federal-state contacts at civil service level take the form partly of meetings of committees and of conferences. Perhaps the most important type of meetings is the State and Federal Relationships Committee, in which state secretaries and other state officers meet various senior central government officials;[46]

in 1968 it met in Sabah. Conferences have been extremely valuable when they have taken the form of seminars lasting several days. Most of the civil service seminars attended by officials from Sarawak and Sabah have been held in Kuala Lumpur. However, some have taken place in the Borneo states, including a particularly successful conference on agricultural development held in Sarawak in August, 1968; in the course of this seminar participants from West Malaysia were able to visit on the ground a land development scheme and a pepper-processing centre.

The civil services in Sarawak and Sabah have been arenas of conflict in federal-state relations and nation-building. The formation of Malaysia overlapped with the process of replacing "expatriate", mostly British, civil servants in the two states. In Malaya the process of "Malayanization" had raised several issues, notably the speed at which the operation should be carried out, and the question of which ethnic groups, Malay or non-Malay, would be the chief beneficiaries from the departure of the British. But in Sabah and Sarawak, the situation was more complex. The issues just mentioned were present, but with the added complication that there was no single equivalent of "the Malays"; in each territory there were several indigenous ethnic groups corresponding roughly to the Malays, which fell into the two broad sub-groups of Muslims and non-Muslims. Unlike Malaya, however, in the Borneo territories there was the additional possibility that when expatriate civil servants left, they might be replaced, not by local people people ("Borneanization"), but by civil servants from Malaya ("Malayanization").

During the first half-dozen years or so after September, 1963, progress was made in removing expatriate civil servants. Between 1964 and 1968 the number of expatriates in Division I in the Sabah state civil service fell from approximately[47] 165 to 120. The corresponding drop in Sarawak was from about 120 to 85. The decreases may not appear to be spectacular, but three points should be remembered. By 1968 the expatriates had been almost entirely removed from the commanding heights of administrative positions, whether in the state capital, at permanent secretary level, or in the field as Residents and D.O.s[48] Also, those who remained were nearly all on contract and not in permanent pensionable posts, as their predecessors had been. Most important of all, the supply of possible replacements from within the territories was extremely restricted. In 1960 North Borneo, if Europeans and other "non-local" persons are excluded, had only 1,280 persons who had completed a full secondary education, and 1,178 of these were Chinese; Sarawak had 2,282, of whom 2,107 were Chinese. The supply of University graduates was even scantier North Borneo had 119 "local" people who had completed University or Technical College, including 115 Chinese; Sarawak had 214, of whom 205 were Chinese.[49] The non-Chinese graduates from both territories in 1960 could be counted almost on the fingers of two hands.

Borneanization was already an issue before the formation of Malaysia. After Malaysia was proposed, crash measures were adopted to increase the supply of local civil servants. The whole educational system was expanded, training provisions were extended, and in some cases the formal educational qualifications for certain jobs were relaxed. At the top administrative level interim expedients were adopted which aimed to combine the retention of expatriates with giving local people status and administrative responsibility. In Sarawak the Residents were, on the whole, Borneanized before the permanent secretaries, but in three divisions they were given the aid of experienced expatriates as advisers. In Sabah, Borneanization at the top administrative level occurred first in the Secretariat rather than in the field. There was a scheme to prepare local people for taking over permanent secretaries' jobs by having each of them "understudy" the relevant number-two man as a supernumerary. More effectively, two or three expatriates were kept on in the Secretariat as "senior administrative officers" to plug any gaps resulting from the appointment of relatively inexperienced local permanent secretaries. In both states the most difficult posts to fill were those which required professional or technical qualifications plus some experience. It was just not possible to prepare local people for such posts by taking any short cuts; consequently even in 1969 many of the top jobs in, say, the Public Works Department, were filled by expatriates recruited on contract.

The Inter-Governmental Committee[50] saw the process of

replacing expatriates by local officers in somewhat rational and formal terms; it considered local expectations of employment and advancement, expatriate expectations of tenure, and the need to programme the handover so as not to destroy the efficiency of the services. But in practice the replacement process was influenced by other considerations. To some degree the expectations of locals and expatriates were in conflict, which led to an exaggeration of accomplishments and qualifications on the one hand, and to a rigid conviction of indispensability on the other. Also, the interests of the various local civil servants, and prospective civil servants, were not homogeneous. The education figures for 1960, cited above, showed that the Chinese in both territories were vastly better qualified in this respect than the Natives. Three years before Malaysia Day a Sarawak committee on the replacement of expatriates by local people made the obvious point, which also applied to North Borneo, that "it would not be in the best interests of Sarawak, or of the provision of racial harmony, if the service came to consist predominantly of representatives of any one race".[51] There was in fact provision for the protection of Natives in the new Sarawak and Sabah constitutions drawn up at the time of Malaysia. But the protection was not complete; beyond its limits, the quicker the expatriates were removed the greater the chances that a Chinese would be appointed to a vacancy.[52] However, if the expatriates' departures could be slowed down a little, the time could be used to train a Native to fill the post.

Even inside the category of "Natives" there were conflicts between the claims of different ethnic groups. In Sarawak, for example, since the days of the Brookes the Malays had been traditionally more prominent than other Natives in the civil service. And in 1960 they were educationally ahead of other Natives in the general population, although they were far behind the Chinese.[53] Ethnic considerations are still important in the civil service. It is widely assumed that Chief Ministers would favour their own ethnic groups appointments and promotions to top posts, whether the actual evidence bears out this assumption or not. Certainly, the political parties scrutinize such appointments very closely to see how they affect the ethnic balance.

A good example of the conflicting claims of various local groups to benefit from an appointment consists of the dispute over the appointment of a state secretary in Sabah in 1964.[54] This dispute was related to the "federal-state dispute" to the extent that the Chief Minister at that time, Dato Donald Stephens, had contrived to identify himself with "states rights", and the Chief of State, Tun Mustapha, had seemingly aligned himself with the policy of the Federal, Alliance Government.

Indeed, in both Sabah and Sarawak the expatriate question became, for a time, inextricably bound up with the conflict between a non-Muslim Native Chief Minister (Dato Stephens and Dato Ningkan, respectively) and the Federal Government. Before Malaysia was formed, the Tengku observed that now that most of the expatriates in the Borneo territories were familiar with Malaysia, they were "all for it".[55] Later, however, he became convinced that expatriates were unduly influencing the Chief Ministers of the two states. "The Tengku explained that until British officers in Sabah and Sarawak were replaced by Malaysians, it would not be possible to appoint more Borneo ministers (in the federal Cabinet)." In effect, the British were administering these states now. So by bringing in more ministers from the Borneo states "we will indirectly be bringing British influence into the Cabinet".[56] A month later he told the General Assembly of his party (UMNO) that the central government had made a mistake when it agreed that British officials should continue to serve in the Borneo states until they could be replaced by local men. The expatriates had failed to promote a sense of Malaysian unity. Under this influence the people of Sabah and Sarawak spoke of Malaya as if it were a different country, and regarded Malayan officials as new rulers come to interfere in their affairs.[57]

By 1966 a more acceptable government was in power in Sabah, but the Tengku continued his attack on the Sarawak expatriates. He asked the Sarawak Government to set up a Borneanization Committee, adding, "I am not happy that Sarawak still has an administration that is colonial in nature. I cannot do anything, because under the Inter-Governmental Committee Agreement it is not possible for the Central Government to bring the administration in Sarawak into line with the centre."[58] Expatriates were also accused of blocking nation-building in Sarawak,[59] of opposing the use of the National Language in the two states,[60] and of rude behaviour towards a federal minister in Sabah.[61] More generally, the influence of expatriates was alleged to be pervasively pernicious. For example, they were said not to give enough publicity to the fact that most of the money for roads, land settlement, and other forms of development, came from the Federal Government. They were also denounced for giving aid and comfort to politicians who were opposing the Federal Government, particularly during crises in federal-state relations.[62] Expatriates, naturally, could not defend themselves in public. The more sophisticated among them would have said that they were engaged in the thankless task of being intermediaries, trying to slow down a too sudden federal impact on the Borneo states, while also trying to reconcile the state governments to the reality of federal power. Actually, they were defended by those politicians in the two states who themselves were the joint objects of attack. In addition, however, offence always being more satisfying than defence, a vulnerable target was found on the other side in the form of those civil servants in the Borneo states who had come from Malaya. The charge was made that the expatriates were being got rid of in order to "Malayanize", not "Borneanize", the civil service.

With the formation of Malaysia the former civil service in both North Borneo/Sabah and Sarawak had been split. In each, that portion which dealt with the subjects allocated to the state in the new federation remained as the state civil service. The other portion, which was concerned with subjects that had now become federal, was transferred to the federal civil service. The schemes and conditions of service in the two portions were now different. The federal departments in Sarawak (or Sabah) were really of two types. One type contained posts like the Federal Secretary, Federal Finance Officer, and so on, which were created after Malaysia, and in fact formed an extension of the federal organization in the state. The other consisted of departments which had already been in existence in Sarawak before Malaysia Day, but whose functions had now come under federal responsibility, for instance the Customs Department. Some of the appointments made to the federal departments were of officials from West Malaysia.

While the Inter-Governmental Committee Report had guaranteed that Borneanization would be a first priority, there was no absolute guarantee that no Malayan would be appointed to any federal post in the Borneo states.[63]

The reaction against Malayan officials being appointed to the federal service jobs inside the two states was out of all proportion to the numbers involved. In 1966 there were only forty-one such officers in Sarawak and twelve in Sabah. In January 1968 there were only twenty-one in Sarawak and twelve in Sabah.[64] Part of the explanation for the violence of the reaction is that Malayans were also appointed to other jobs, not actually in the civil service but which the local population did not distinguish from the civil service, such as the Sabah Electricity Board.[65] Another important reason for opposition was that some of the Borneo posts involved were key posts from the point of view of national integration, for example those of Director of Radio Malaysia and of Director of Education.[66] Objections to such posts being held by a Malayan were especially strong from those in the Borneo territories who were opposed to the *policies* on national integration which the federal government was pursuing, or the speed at which these policies were being implemented. The reactions against such officers, as voiced by SNAP and UPKO, were substantially reactions against the reminder that federal officers gave of the federal presence and of the fact that Sarawak (Sabah), by ceasing to be a British colony, had not achieved complete independence, but only that limited degree of independence which can be enjoyed by a state in a federation. Against these "gut" reactions, reasoned explanations that the officers from Malaya were in the Borneo states only temporarily, until local people could be trained, or that such officers were reluctant to stay for a long time in Borneo but would much rather go back to West Malaysia, did not make much headway.

The post which attracted most criticism was that of Federal Secretary, or Deputy Federal Secretary.[67] The function of the newly-created Federal Secretary was described as that of liaison between federal officers in the state and the Federal Government.[68] Its creation was justified by the distance of the territories from West Malaysia and the need to effect a smooth transition after Malaysia was formed. On one interpretation, the Federal Secretary's job was not to exercise general control of federal departments in the state, although the heads of federal departments were expected to consult him. This description of the job came from a Federal Secretary who saw the post as transitional: "I hope that in the not too distant future a Federal Secretariat in Eastern Malaysia will no longer be needed."[69] But not all Federal Secretaries have taken this limited view of the intensity or the duration of their functions. Another expressed the opinion in an interview that the Federal Secretary should consciously work for the achievement of national integration, that integration would take a long time, and that therefore the job should also last for a long time.

Symbolically, therefore, the Federal Secretary was an obvious target for supporters of "states' rights". His presence "makes us Sabahans feel like a 'protectorate' State instead of an independent state within the Federation of Malaysia".[70] Perhaps the individual who succeeded in stirring up most controversy was Yeap Kee Aik, appointed Deputy Federal Secretary on Sabah at the time Malaysia was formed, who among other things was accused by the UPKO of "behaving like a colonial governor".[71] In Sarawak during the suspension of the elections, 1969–70, the Federal Secretary, Harun Ariffin, came under attack from the Chief Minister, Dato Tawi Sli. The Chief Minister complained about the fact that the State Operations Council was headed by the Federal Secretary, and not by himself, and said that in these circumstances the people of Sarawak could not be blamed for thinking that Sarawak was ruled by the Centre.[72]

Another type of official was sent to the Borneo states from Malaya for reasons quite unconnected with making good shortages of qualified officers in these states. There was an exchange scheme, mostly at District Officer level, intended to let officials from both East and West Malaysia see what conditions were like in the other part of Malaysia. A Malayan officer, for example, who in West Malaysia used his own car freely and then claimed a transport allowance, would have the difficulties of communication in Sarawak brought home to him in a direct way during his tour of duty. If in 1967 he had used his own car on the new Kuching-Simanggang road and had suffered several punctures, he would have understood why local officers were reluctant to use their own cars for such a journey. The scheme operated on only a small scale, however, because there were not many officers keen to make an exchange. Financial arrangements were not very attractive for the East Malaysians, and the West Malaysians did not relish being so far away from the centre of things and thought that living conditions in Borneo might be strange for their families.

The acrimonious controversy about expatriates and members of the federal civil service appointed to the Borneo states from Malaya obscured an important point. An integrated civil service, at least at the top levels, is an important factor in promoting *national* integration.[73] Ideally, this integrated service should comprise the senior administrative officials of the state civil service as well as of the federal civil service. There are obvious difficulties in securing complete "free trade" by exchanging administrative officials between the states and West Malaysia.[74] There are differences in conditions of service; psychological barriers to movement; fear that until more trained officials are available from the Borneo states the exchange may be a one-way traffic equivalent to "Malayanization". But until these problems are overcome, a potent instrument of national integration is being neglected.

The Impact of Federal Organization and Programmes

As a result of the formation of Malaysia there has been a federal impact on Sarawak and Sabah through the spread of programmes and organizations, hitherto confined to Malaya, to the two states. Outstanding among these was the development programme, described in Chapter 6. Development programmes existed in the two states before Malaysia, but their scope has now been greatly extended; they are financed mainly from federal sources, their co-ordination is carried on at federal level, and their administration in each territory is in the hands of the State Development Officer, who is stationed locally but who is a federal official. State Development Officers have encountered none of the public criticism which has been directed at Federal Secretaries, Deputy Federal Secretaries, Directors of

Education and Directors of Radio. Presumably they are popularly associated, not with federal attempts at integration through domination, but as distributors of federal financial benefits.[75]

Linked with the development organization is MARA (*Majlis Amanah Ra'ayat*) which extended its activities to the Borneo states in 1966. It has encouraged cottage industries, operated bus companies, carried on training courses and sent other people for training to Malaya, and has made loans to finance non-agricultural pursuits.[76] It has also tried to encourage people to buy shares, notably in the MARA Unit Trust. Other organizations established in Malaya have been slower to spread to the Borneo territories. The Federal Agricultural Marketing Authority (FAMA) established an office in Sabah only in March 1969. In Malaya the FLDA (Federal Land Development Authority) proved to be successful in encouraging settlement.[77] But the FLDA pattern does not operate at all in Sarawak, and was tried to only a very limited extent in Sabah. In each territory there were state schemes which offered greater attractions to the settler, and in Sarawak the complex nature of the land laws was an additional barrier. FIDA (Federal Industrial Development Authority) undertook an industrial survey in Sabah which was completed in 1969, and a Sarawak survey was announced in the following year.[78] MIDFL (Malaysian Industrial Development Finance Limited) has also operated in the Borneo territories. However, because of the concentration of industry in West Malaysia, MIDFL has also tended to concentrate most of its efforts there. By February 1968 it had contributed $3.5 million to various manufacturing enterprises in the Borneo states, but this was only about 5% of its total commitments in Malaysia. In April 1970, however, it was announced that in future it would invest about $10 million in the Borneo states every year.[79]

The federal armed forces stationed in Sarawak and Sabah played a rôle in modernization, as did British and other Commonwealth troops before them, through civic action programmes, notably road building. Because the troops were Malaysian such activities may also be considered as contributions towards nation-building. Another more direct attempt to further nation-building was the provision by the armed forces of part-time lecturers to help with National Language Weeks.[80]

These federal programmes and organizations undoubtedly affect the way of life of many people in Sarawak and Sabah. But the extent to which they have influenced nation-building is uncertain. To be sure, measures have been taken to make it clear that the benefits they confer derive largely from the Federal Government and from federal money. This point is often made when politicians on tour announce that a Minor Rural Project[81] will be given to a certain area. One of the purposes of "civic assemblies", held in both states is undoubtedly to underline the rôle of the Federal Government. The assemblies stress other issues, such as anti-communism, voting procedures at elections, health measures and so on, and introduce sometimes thinly-disguised party politics. But they also fulfil a nation-building function in spreading information about the Federal Government's share in development.

On the other hand, federal-state finance is not a simple subject, and at various times opposition parties have argued that the "federal" money which pays for certain benefits is really money which has come from the people of the state. Also, too crude propaganda in favour of MARA, FAMA and so on as federal organizations may create a boomerang effect. Some shrewd federal officials have been quick to see that state susceptibilities are tender, and that organizations such as MARA may initially be regarded with suspicion, just because they come "from outside".

A further cause of trouble is that the distribution of benefits from federal sources is very closely watched for signs of ethnic discrimination. This became a big issue at various times where the allocation of Minor Rural Projects was concerned. MARA is also subject to criticism because it was explicitly designed to help Natives, excluding Chinese.[82] In both states opposition parties have frequently stated, and MARA officials frequently denied, that it has tended to help Muslim Natives more than non-Muslim Natives. Some of the criticism seems to have been the result of a lack of knowledge of MARA's policies. A non-Muslim Native who was refused a loan to start a business might not be aware that MARA's aim was to encourage businesses already in existence rather than to start new ones; he might therefore, mistakenly, allege ethnic discrimination.

Language and Nation-Building: Education Policy

The two most obvious "cultural" aspects of nation-building consist of language and education. In Malaya, unless Parliament decided otherwise (which it did not)[83] English was due to lose its position as joint official language in 1967, leaving Malay as the sole official language. But the Malaysia Act extended until 1973 the period in which English could be used in the Borneo states for certain official purposes. These purposes included: (*a*) speeches in Parliament by members for or from a Borneo state; (*b*) in the Borneo Courts and in the Federal Court on appeals from a Borneo Court; (*c*) in the legislative assemblies of the states "or for other official purposes (including the official purposes of the Federal Government)".[84] Even after 1973 the use of English under (*b*) and (*c*), above could not be ended except by an enactment of the legislature of the Borneo state concerned.

There was no necessary inconsistency between these provisions and the fact that Malay was the National (as opposed to official) Language[85] for all Malaysia. Indeed the whole point of the provisions, on a rational interpretation, could have been that they provided time for those who did not already know Malay (the National Language) to learn it. Not all the inhabitants of the Borneo states were starting from scratch. Malay was a *lingua franca* in the region and had been extensively used for government purposes under the Brookes,[86] the North Borneo Company, and the British.

Measures were taken to promote the use of the National Language by National Language Weeks, during which there were performances of various kinds in the language as well as debating and oratorical competitions. It's use was also promoted via the radio. Malay announcements, time checks and songs were introduced in the non-Malay services. The total proportion of broadcasting time in Malay (or Indonesian) in each state was also increased. The proportion of broadcasting hours in Sarawak devoted to programmes in Malay was approximately 23% in both 1963 and 1969. But in the latter year another 3% of the total consisted of Forces Programmes in Malay, and there was an additional 8% listed under "Bahasa Malaysia, the National Language".[87] The same trend could be seen in Sabah, from 1963 to 1966, but only if "Malay" and "Indonesian" were taken together. The Malay proportion of hours broadcast was approximately the same in both years, 20%, but the Indonesian proportion rose from 12% to almost 20%.[88]

However, there were obstacles to a rational approach to such a delicate subject as language. Opposition to the National Language was probably greatest among Chinese, especially in Sarawak, who wished to have Chinese accepted as an official language.[89] But there was also resistance among Natives, especially those who were not Muslims. Before Malaysia "Kadazan" (the kind of Dusun used near Penampang) was fast becoming the standard Dusun language, a process that had been encouraged by broadcasting policy.[90] The important political leadership positions of the Kadazans in the UNKO (later UPKO) might have encouraged them to think of Kadazan as a potential state language. Supporters of the Kadazan language were "assimilationist" in so far as they wished to have Murut Programmes incorporated in the Kadazan section the state radio.[91] Some Ibans also believed that because they were the largest ethnic group in Sarawak, their language, when given the chance to develop, might become an official language. Iban programmes from Radio Sarawak were an important ingredient in Iban nationalism during the 1950s. In point of fact the sheer multiplicity of languages made it hardly possible for Kadazan and Iban to become official languages. If they had been granted such a status, this would have encouraged demands for a similar status for Chinese and perhaps also for other Native languages. But pride in Iban or Kadazan did show itself in a suspicion of federal government attempts to force the pace on Malay, and it strengthened the support for English, useful as a means of advancement, as the most practicable alternative.

The issue was aggravated by confusion between the status of Malay as the National Language (which it already was in all Malaysia) and its status as the official language in the Borneo territories (which it could not be, constitutionally, until 1973, and might not be even then). Most federal pronouncements were scrupulously correct on the issue; while urging the advantages of Malay as a means for promoting national unity, they showed understanding of the nature of the safeguards constitutionally provided until 1973 and beyond. But, whether because of confusion or enthusiasm, sometimes politicians spoke as if these safeguards did not exist. One Sarawak M.P., Che Ajibah binte Abol, said in 1964 that if the people of Sarawak did not make a start immediately on encouraging the use of the National Language, they would become "wall-flowers" in 1967 when Malay became the sole official language.[92] And in 1969 the Federal Education Minister, Enche Khir Johari referred to the steps being taken, such as National Language Weeks, to make Malay the sole official language in East Malaysia by 1973.[93]

The reaction against the possibility of Malay becoming the sole official language in 1973 was more violent in Sarawak than in Sabah. This may have been partly because the use of Malay was already more widespread in Sabah than in Sarawak in the early 1960s.[94] But the reaction probably arose mainly from the greater across-the-board resistance of the non-Muslim Natives in Sarawak to federal influence compared with their Sabah counterparts, based mainly on their constituting a higher proportion of the state's population. Dato Ningkan's objections to the Federal Government's methods of implementing the national language in Sarawak contributed, according to him, to the Tengku's dislike of him and to the 1966 constitutional crises in Sarawak.[95] The Tengku's view that there was no such thing as the Dyak language, "Dyak" being only a branch of the Malay language,[96] intensified Ningkan's opposition. He retorted by making a radio speech bound to wound the susceptibilities of the Federal Government suggesting in effect a change in federal policy to conform to Sarawak conditions. Since Sarawak would not be ready for a change in language policy before 1973, perhaps the change to Malay as the sole official language in Malaya should also be postponed until that date? Ningkan's successor as Chief Minister of Sarawak, Penghulu Tawi Sli, believed that "our only hope in binding the whole Malaysian people together is in having one National Language: without a National Language of our own, we cannot even truly call ourselves a Nation".[97] But he was firm on the importance of 1973 and the principle of state choice after that date. "The position about languages in our State is perfectly clear. Malay is the national language and English is an official language until 1973 and thereafter unless the Council Negri decides otherwise."[98] Before the 1970 elections in Sarawak it was not certain that English would cease to be an official language in Sarawak in 1973. However, the formation of a Government in July 1970, in which the Chief Minister was Dato Rahman Ya'akub and the dominant party was Bumiputera, has greatly strengthened the possibility that it will no longer be an official language after then.

In Sabah, on the other hand, where knowledge of Malay was more widespread in 1963, Tun Mustapha and other ministers made repeated announcements that it was state government policy to have *Bahasa Malaysia* as the only official language in 1973 or before. Implementation of this policy was accelerated after the dissolution of UPKO at the end of the 1967. Tun Mustapha frequently referred to one language as a means of creating national solidarity, especially in a multi-racial society.[99] These pronouncements were backed by attacks on government officers who ignored governmental directives to use *Bahasa Malaysia*, especially during National Language Month.[100] In September 1969, his policies were endorsed by a number of different ethnic communities, who declared their support of the state and central government in making *Bahasa Malaysia* a truly official language of the nation. Its use should be encouraged and radio programmes in Murut, Bajau, and Kadazan should be replaced by *Bahasa Malaysia* programmes.[101] A body with the express objective of promoting national integration through the study of a common language and culture, and *Badan Bahasa Sabah*, was formed in March 1970.[102]

The education issue was closely linked with the language issue. However, there was no actual mention of education in the Malaysia Act, although there was a provision in the Report of the Inter-Governmental Committee providing for some autonomy in education for the two states.[103] Education was a federal subject, but the current policy and system of administration of education in the two states was to remain under the state government until the Government agreed to a change. At the time when Malaysia was formed, the education systems in Sarawak and Sabah were similar in their degree of under-development; both had only just over half of the age group, 6–14, attending school. Beyond that, however, there were marked differences. In Sabah most of the Government primary schools and Native Voluntary primary schools (although not Mission, Chinese, or private primary schools) taught in the medium of Malay. Even in English and Chinese medium schools Malay was a compulsory subject, "though the lack of suitably qualified teachers has so far made it exceedingly difficult to implement this policy".[104] There were, however, no secondary schools teaching in the medium of Malay.

In Sarawak, not only were there no secondary schools teaching in the Malay medium, neither were there, strictly speaking, any primary schools teaching in Malay. Apart from Chinese primary schools, the rest used the medium of English, "though at present some native schools use the vernacular—Malay, Dyak, etc.,—to a varying extent in the lower primary classes, depending on the ability of the teacher in English".[105] Another feature distinguishing Sarawak from Sabah in 1963 was that Chinese education had recently suffered an upheaval. Communist influence and infiltration had penetrated some Chinese schools, and in 1961 the Government attempted to assert its control by announcing that the medium of instruction in secondary schools must be English if they were to qualify for Government financial aid.[106] The formation of Malaysia took place before the effects of this crisis in Chinese schools had died away.

An immediate consequence of Malaysia was to increase the amount of Malay being taught in both states. Even in Sarawak, which was behind Sabah, by the beginning of 1965 Malay classes had been set up in about three-quarters of the secondary schools and about a quarter of the primary schools.[107] In the first few years after Malaysia there was an acute shortage of persons qualified to teach Malay in both states. As the shortage was gradually being overcome, through provision of Malay courses for existing teachers and by ensuring that those who passed through Teachers' Training College were trained to teach in Malay, a contentious point of policy came into prominence in Sarawak; would the emphasis on teaching Malay end just with all the pupils being taught Malay, or would it be extended to a requirement that the medium of instruction in all schools should be Malay?

In the long run, no doubt the emphasis on Malay would tend to lead to this second conclusion. Dato Ningkan implied as much when in 1964 he opposed the adoption of Malay as the medium of instruction "for the time being", but went to say that until "such time as the people of Sarawak have caught up with our fellow citizens in Malaya and Singapore in the educational field, it is unrealistic for us to try to introduce Malay as a medium of instruction".[108] But how long was the long run? Non-Muslim Natives in Sarawak were unwilling to have the term defined by the Federal Government. The issue came to a head when in late 1964 there was agitation in Sarawak for the abolition of primary school fees, as had recently been decided on for Malaya. The Federal Minister of Education said bluntly that this was a matter not of dollars and cents but of principle: "If Sarawak, or for that matter Sabah, wished to enjoy a federal educational privilege, then she must be ready to reconsider the present I.G.C.'s provisions and conform to the national educational policy." At the same time he pointed out that this did not mean conversion of all schools to the national language overnight.[109]

With the appointment of a new Minister for Education, Khir Johari, early in 1965, the temperature cooled down, and in August 1965 Khir announced that there would be no primary school fees in the Borneo states from January 1966 for Government and Government-aided schools. There were no strings or conditions attached but there must be co-ordination and it was important to consider how the federal and state systems could be brought closer together.[110]

Less than a year afterwards the new Sarawak Chief Minister, Penghulu Tawi Sli asserted that English would remain the medium of instruction "until or unless the Government should decide differently. We have no plans to make any changes here."[111] The issue has remained quiescent after that, although in early 1969 the Minister mentioned that the Government was trying to speed the development of education in Sarawak so that it could be "the same as in West Malaysia".[112]

The increased tempo of replacing English by Malay in Malaya, announced in July, 1969,[113] was bound to have an effect in the Borneo states. It was obvious that Tun Mustapha, a dedicated promoter of the National Language, would follow the federal example quickly in the sphere of education. A policy along these lines was announced in December, 1969. From January, 1970 Sabah primary schools using English as a medium of instruction were to switch to *Bahasa Malaysia* as sole medium in the teaching of all subjects except English, beginning with Primary One classes. It was expected that by 1975 the medium of instruction for all primary classes would be in *Bahasa Malaysia.*[114]

The situation in Sarawak was initially different. For reasons previously discussed, before July 1970 it was unlikely that the political leaders in the Sarawak Alliance Government would encourage the use of Malay as a medium of instruction to the same degree as Tun Mustapha in Sabah. The situation changed dramatically when in July 1970 the federal Education Minister, Dato Rahman Ya'akub, became Chief Minister of Sarawak. Although he made no early pronouncement on the topic of education, it may be assumed that, after his appointment, education policy in Sarawak will be closer to that in Sabah and West Malaysia than it was before.[115]

Two other items should be mentioned briefly under the heading of education. One is the system of Adult Education classes operated by the federal Ministry of National and Rural Development, extended to the Borneo states after Malaysia. These classes have the major objective of helping to wipe out illiteracy, but they also have a nation-building aspect; "the people will be able to read and write and understand the basic machinery of Government and appreciate the intention of Government in carrying out its development plan and thereby they, too, will be able to contribute in making our development plan 100% successful"[116] In both territories the medium of instruction used is Malay. Non-Muslim Native parties have alleged that some of the teachers in these classes have been used as party workers.[117]

The Sabah Foundation, created by Tun Mustapha who is Chairman of the Board of Trustees for life, was set up in 1966 to provide education facilities for Sabah youth, mainly in the form of scholarships to secondary schools. It is financed partly by government grants and by the public but also by income from timber concessions.[118] An important function of the Foundation is to secure secondary school places in Malaya for Sabah children whom it supports financially. In 1969, 120 school places were secured, seventy-five in the Malay medium and forty-five in the English medium.[119] Among the objects of the Foundation, in a wide sense, are some which are explicitly designed to encourage nation-building: "to promote the healthy and harmonious growth of a truly Malaysian national consciousness characterized by multi-racial tolerance, good-will and understanding among all the Sabahans; to promote the gradual growth and synthesis of all cultures which exist in Sabah; to constantly protect the image of Malaysia and create a true Malaysian outlook among the people of Sabah"[120]

Finance, Federation and Nation-Building

Nation-building in Malaysia cannot be divorced from the financial aspects of federation. It was often remarked that Malaysia was a "package deal", and part of the package was that the Borneo states would be enabled to share in the prosperity of Malaya, and, in particular, in the fruits of Malaya's successful rural development schemes. Apart from the actual financial provisions in the Constitution, the Inter-Governmental Committee Report had referred to targets for development expenditures in the five years after Malaysia, $300 million for Sarawak and $200 million for Sabah.[121]

The economic inducements were important, not only as part of the "federal bargain" but also for the nation-building process. In the early years economic benefits might be expected to cushion some of the resistance to the cultural aspects of nation-building just discussed. Furthermore, governmental effectiveness contributes to legitimacy and therefore to nation-building.[122] Some aspects of effectiveness are analysed in the final chapter, but others, namely the financial benefits arising directly from Malaysia, will be mentioned here.

It is not easy to calculate what the direct economic benefits of joining Malaysia were for Sarawak and Sabah. Even the basic financial transactions are hard to understand. And some aspects, such as the formation of a Common Market, had indirect effects, for instance on the cost of living and on the future of manufacturing industry in the two states, which are hard to measure.

The balance sheet of transactions between the federal and the Borneo states is complex. Many of the figures quoted by politicians are not comparable. Among the many complications is the existence, in addition to ordinary budgets, of development budgets, both state and federal. Federal financial help to a state may take the form of a grant, or a loan, included in the state development budget, or of "direct" federal expenditure in the state. When a figure is quoted for the latter, sometimes the federal expenditure for defence and internal security is included, sometimes it is not. Another pitfall is that estimated development expenditure is always different from actual expenditure; in any given year a third or a quarter of the estimate may not be spent.[123] A very rough idea of the scope of federal financial benefits to the two states is given in Tables 8.1 and 8.2 of the *Annual Bulletin of Statistics*, Malaysia. From 1964 to 1969 Central Government revenue from Sabah was about $30 million a year less than Central Government expenditure on Sabah;[124] the corresponding Sarawak figure was about $70 million a year. There was an appreciable difference in the financial resources of the two states. Initially the ceiling for all non-defence expenditure in Sabah, whether spent by the federal or the state government and whether "development" expenditure or not, during the Five-Year Plan 1966–70, was $300 million, of which only $60 million would come from the state.[125] But financing the Five-Year Plan depended on factors such as the price of rubber and external aid to Malaysia, which by 1966 were not conducive to rapid development. Consequently the state government took over the responsibility for a large number of projects, originally intended to be financed by federal grants or loans. "We have accepted this rather heavy burden because it will mean rapid development for the state. In addition to this assumption of responsibility for previously federal-financed projects the state has considerably raised the original ceiling for development by embarking on several new state projects and expanding the scope of others."[126] So, by late 1968, the sources of finance for development in Sabah were substantially reversed. The total intended expenditure for the Five-Year Plan had increased to $346.9 million of which the state was to finance 74%, as compared with the 20% originally intended.

In Sarawak a high proportion of expenditure on development has come from federal sources; at the start of the five-year planning period the federal share was over 90%.[127] However, in the estimate for 1969 the state funds to be allocated to development were more than doubled; as in Sabah, some projects which had hitherto been financed from federal grants or loans, such as rural credit for the Sarawak Development Finance Corporation (SDFC), were now taken over by the state.[128] But this assumption of financial responsibility was on nothing like the same scale as in Sabah; development in Sarawak, 1966–70, was financed overwhelmingly from federal sources.

Undeniably the Borneo states, especially Sarawak, have derived great direct economic benefits from union with Malaya. The Federal Government lived up to the letter and the spirit of its financial commitments. But economic benefits are in a sense subjective. Not all the population of Sarawak and Sabah was fully aware of having benefited; some of the benefits would come only in the long term, as a result of investment. This was the rationale for minor rural projects, to provide quick proof of the economic advantages from Malaysia. In point of fact, these projects also raised problems of discrimination, and therefore led to some dissatisfaction.[129] In certain areas, also, people might complain of lack of development, although the signs of development around them were obvious. In one district a local official complained of lack of development since the end of British rule, although the number of schools had increased from twenty-eight to fifty-four in the past six years. At the same time local pride tended to resent too heavy-handed an emphasis on the financial benefits derived from Malaysia. There were unfavourable reactions when occasionally it was suggested that development might be "hampered", if an Alliance Government were not elected in one of the Borneo states, which almost amounted to a hint that in such an event development money might be reduced. The Tengku denied that this would happen (as did other federal politicians), but added that, in order to receive development aid, an Opposition-controlled state "must follow the Federal Government's policy and techniques in the implementation of projects to the letter".[130]

Estimates of financial benefits derived from Malaysia varied with the political position of the observer over time. Dato Ningkan, for instance, made different estimates of Sarawak's financial benefits from Malaysia when he was Chief Minister than he did when in Opposition. In 1965 he said that from the revenue collected in Sarawak the state could not even cover its recurrent expenditure, let alone social economic development, or defence expenditure.[131] But in 1967 his party, SNAP, alleged that the money which came from the Federal Government under the Development Plan was not a gift, but came "from the revenue of Sarawak". Sarawak "has or can raise a potential revenue of at least double that figure now being allocated to us for the development of our state".[132]

In one respect, namely increases in customs duties and taxes, the formation of Malaysia was perceived as disadvantageous in the two states. An important economic aspect of Malaysia concerned the Malaysian Common Market,[133] which was to come into existence by stages after public enquiries by a new Tariff Advisory Board which held its first enquiry in November 1964. By March 1966 goods of Malaysian origin with a few exceptions, were to be permitted to move freely without duty inside Malaysia.[134] Later, this freedom of movement inside Malaysia was to be extended to imported goods. At the same time, by stages, the import duties on imported goods were to be "harmonized" for different parts of Malaysia.

A common market was an important element in creating greatly increased trade between Malaya and the Borneo states. Between 1963 and 1968 imports to Sarawak from West Malaysia rose from approximately 1% of total imports to about 10%. Exports from Sarawak to West Malaysia in 1968 compared with 1963 remained roughly constant, at about 1½% of total exports (although 1964–7 on average they amounted to about 4%).[135] Similarly, in Sabah imports from West Malaysia had jumped from about 2% of all imports in 1963 to 16% of all imports in 1968.[136]

There were hostile reactions in the Borneo states, particularly Sabah, to the consequences of the measures to set up a common market. One immediate effect was a substantial rise in the price of over 100 "main items" in Sabah; it was alleged that by November 1965 the prices of some commodities in Sabah had risen by between 10 and 50 %.[137] The problems raised by higher import duties were extensively ventilated in the Press, as was the difficulty of obtaining regular supplies of goods produced in West Malaysia, which the new duties were designed to protect.

So great was the increase in the cost of living in Sabah that the Chief Minister set up an advisory committee on the subject in January 1966. It found that the increase in consumer prices in Sabah, 1963–6, was about 20%,[138] and listed a number of reasons for the increase, including the rise in import duties and high freight costs. However, it also alluded to factors associated with the boom in Sabah's economy, including high expenditures by government and individuals resulting from the great increases in timber exports. The Sabah Government was willing to try to contain rises in the cost of living by attempting to lower freight charges, improve communications, and keep down profits, but it was not agreeable to slowing down the tempo of development.[139] The effect of the boom on the cost of living in Sabah is illustrated by the fact that Sarawak, with a much lower tempo of development, experienced a much smaller increase in prices.[140]

Part of the resentment which accompanied the introduction of the common market derived from the obvious contrast between the losses to consumers in Sabah and the gains to manufacturers in Malaya. The contrast put a strain on the new, slender bonds of loyalty between the different parts of Malaysia. In this context there were obvious disadvantages to offset the economic advantages of development finance from Malaya. The divergence of interests between the small number of manufacturers in the Borneo states and their counterparts in Malaya was perhaps even more marked.

> In West Malaysia the locally made cigarettes are sold for 20 cents a packet while in East Malaysia the locally made cigarettes are sold for 40 cents per packet. Despite the difference in quality, the cheaper West Malaysia-made cigarettes, under the favourable terms of common market, would pour into East Malaysia market. Although this would help reduce the prices of cigarettes and relieve the high cost of living, the vitality of the five existing East Malaysia cigarette manufactures would be greatly frustrated.[141]

The prospect for the small number of Sarawak manufacturers in existence was no brighter. The Honorary Secretary of the Sarawak Manufacturers' Association gave a long list of the handicaps suffered by members of his association, including high costs of water and electricity and of converting land titles to a commercial basis, high freight charges, and delay by the Federal Industrial Development Authority (FIDA) on companies' applications for pioneer status.[142]

"Harmonization" in another sphere produced equally unpopular reactions in the Borneo states. The Inter-Governmental Committee Report had provided, in paragraph 24 (1), that increases in Federal taxation, should be imposed in graduated stages in Sarawak and Sabah. Eventually there should be equality of taxation between persons in similar financial circumstances within the different regions of Malaysia.[143] But increases in income tax for Sabah and Sarawak were imposed for 1966, and were followed by a number of other tax increases[144] applying to the whole of Malaysia. Taken in conjunction with higher import duties, they led to protests that the pace of harmonization was too rapid to be reconciled with the provisions for "gradual" harmonization referred to in the I.G.C. Report. One tax in particular was fought bitterly in Sabah, as well as in the Federal Parliament by Peter Lo, Sabah's Chief Minister.[145] The 1967 Federal budget provided that (state) timber royalties, and also the money paid for the right to extract timber under a licence or permit,[146] should no longer be deductible expenses for (federal) income tax purposes. The Sabah Chief Minister conceded that the federal government had lost income tax revenue, because of a recent increase in the state royalty rate. But he thought that the budget proposal amounted to double taxation of timber, on which Sabah's prosperity depended, and that the money should have been raised either by a direct grant payable by the state government or by a corresponding reduction in the level of federal expenditure in Sabah.[147]

There was also a feeling of injustice, because harmonization was not applied in the reverse direction. Trade licensing fees in the Borneo states were higher than corresponding fees in West Malaysia, and their continuation at that level was widely resented.[148]

The Federal Government's spending on development in Sarawak and Sabah preceded increases in taxation in the two states, as provided for in the Inter-Governmental Committee Report. The Tengku supported this procedure. He thought it important that the territories be made to feel that they were "members of the new nation" before being taxed.[149] This sequence accords with Etzioni's precept that, for a successful union, "substantial rewards for co-operation or progress towards amalgamation had to be timed so as to come before the imposition of burdens resulting from such progress towards amalgamation (union)".[150] However, there still were protests in the two states that the burdens on them had been increased too quickly, and that harmonization had not been sufficiently gradual.

In the short run, therefore, the perceived economic benefits from Malaysia were sometimes not as evident as the perceived economic losses. Moreover, if the non-financial ingredients of a package deal are unpalatable, the deal may be rejected even if the financial components are attractive. When arguing against Malaysia its opponents usually questioned the existence of the economic benefits, and took advantage of the complexities of the financial transactions involved to deny that there really were any net benefits. But, if pressed, opponents sometimes admitted the existence of the economic benefits but denied that they compensated for losses in other directions. "There is no doubt some economic advantage in a federation. But economic interest is not everything," argued Stephen Yong; an economic interest might be properly sacrificed for a political one.[151]

Constitutional Disputes

The account just given indicates that the process of nation-building in Malaysia did not proceed completely smoothly. The problems encountered will be seen more clearly if attention is given to two broad topics rather than to individual sectors of the nation-building process. The first of these is constitutional disputes, the second is the relation between state nationalism and Malaysian nationalism.

Sabah and Sarawak differed from the other states in

Malaysia because they had been allocated greater constitutional powers. But this was difficult for the Federal Government to grasp after six years' experience of dealing with states possessing only weak powers. Statements were made which did not adequately reflect the true constitutional position, including the remark that the states would be "partners of equal status, no more and no less than the other states now forming the Federation of Malaya".[152] Also, after Singapore's departure from Malaysia the Tengku was understandably upset over demands from the UPKO for renegotiation of Sabah's position in Malaysia. But when he remarked that "you can't just say that you wanted to be treated specially or be put into special position.... Everybody is the same in this federation",[153] he omitted to mention that there were some respects in which constitutionally Sarawak and Sabah were *not* in the same situation as the other states.

Constitutional relations[154] between federal and state governments may be considered under two main headings. In the first place, a few alleged specific breaches of the Constitution will be considered. SNAP, for example, maintained that, to its disadvantage, the Constitution was abused on a number of occasions. During the 1966 constitutional crisis, ran the allegations, wrong advice was given to the Sarawak Governor to persuade him to dismiss Dato Ningkan, and, after Ningkan's reinstatement by a Court decision, it was unconstitutional for the Governor to remove him via the machinery of the *Emergency (Federal Constitution and Constitution of Sarawak) Act, 1966*.[155] The courts upheld the validity of the Act and refused to reinstate Ningkan, but SNAP felt that they had been cheated by an abuse of the Constitution. They were confirmed in this view, and so was the SUPP, when the Sarawak state elections, which were due in October 1968 at the latest, were postponed so as to coincide with the state elections in Malaya (and with the federal Malayan elections) in May 1969. The opposition parties objected to the fact that the elections were delayed, maintaining that the official reasons given for delay were not the real reasons, namely that the Alliance feared defeat at the polls. They also objected to the delay being effected via a constitutional amendment in the Federal Parliament, where a two-thirds majority was easily obtained, as opposed to via legislation in the Council Negri where a two-thirds majority could not have been obtained.[156]

The suspension of the Sarawak state and federal elections in May 1969 was a rather more complex business. Not even the most militant member of SUPP or SNAP accused the Alliance of having deliberately staged the riots in Kuala Lumpur on 13 May in order to have an excuse for postponing the completion of the Sarawak elections. But, once the trouble in Kuala Lumpur had occurred, intelligence reports that elements responsible for the current disturbances in Malaya were also responsible for trying to cause trouble in Sarawak and Sabah were given as a reason for suspending the elections there.[157] SNAP issued a statement on the suspension, entitled "Democracy is dead"; "on the implications of the elections being suspended indefinitely, the SNAP spokesman queried whether the Federal Government intended to rule Sarawak indefinitely from Kuala Lumpur".[158] This was a reference to the setting up of a National Operations Council and State Operations Councils which had been given extensive powers during a period of national emergency. The Chief Minister of each state was made Chairman of the State Operations Council. But in Sarawak, from May 1969 until July 1970, the Chief Minister was not even a member of the State Operations Council, apparently on the ground that he was a candidate for election to the Council Negri, not a member of the Council Negri. The Chairman of the Sarawak State Operations Council was the Federal Secretary, although shortly after Dato Rahman Ya'akub became Chief Minister in July 1970 he was also made Chairman of the State Operations Council.

SUPP and SNAP gave assurances that no racial trouble would occur in Sarawak,[159] but no step was taken towards the resumption of the elections. Conceivably, considerations of what the likely result would be, may have influenced the Federal Government's decision on the continued suspension of the elections. But perhaps the most decisive reason for putting them off for just over a year was the feeling that there were so many vital problems to solve in Malaya (including internal party problems) that the, literally, peripheral problems of the Borneo states would have to wait at the end of the queue.

These were not the only instances of constitutional disputes between the Federal Government and the states. There were other prominent examples, including the controversy about the powers of the Head of State for Sabah when the office was occupied by Tun Mustapha.[160] Without examining these, a second heading under "constitutional relations" may be mentioned. Over and above any specific alleged breaches of the constitution in each state, opponents of nation-building on the Federal Government's terms and at the Federal Government's pace claimed that the general balance of state-federal power, envisaged during the bargaining before Malaysia was formed, had not been observed. They claimed that "the constitutional guarantee of local autonomy for these states was rather drastically and subtly undermined by a process of political intervention from Kuala Lumpur".[161] In Sabah the UPKO had grievances on topics, dealt with above, such as "Malayanization", language and so on, and on others which have not been discussed, immigration from West Malaysia[162] and religion. The UPKO was oppressed by the cumulative effect. "We are being forced to accept Malaysia as a unitary state and not a federation."[163] The whole grievance was greater than the sum of its parts; the Twenty Points added up to more than the sum of the individual points and soon acquired a symbolic significance. It was to this symbol particularly that the UPKO appealed to rally its followers and keep them united after the party had failed to win the 1967 state elections.[164]

In Sarawak Dato James Wong defended the sanctity of the Constitution, laying stress not on what he regarded as individual breaches, but on the cumulative effect. He mentioned that the Constitution had been violated twice in less than two years, and referred to a remark of Goldfinger's in a "James Bond" novel. "When you do it once, it is happenstance. When you do it the second time it is possibly coincidence. But if you do it a third time, it is enemy action." He went on to allege that if the Constitution was violated a third time, those who did it would be the enemy of the state and of the nation.[165] Symbolically, for him the Sarawak Constitution corresponded to the Twenty Points in Sabah.

State Nationalism and Malaysian Nationalism

Alternatively, state-federal conflicts may be looked at in terms of rival nationalisms. One of the complications of nation-building in Malaysia was that before 1963 a certain degree of national consciousness existed in Sarawak and to a lesser extent North Borneo, although this was still at a rather early stage. Even in Malaya it was not until comparatively recently that "Malays" and "Chinese" had come to be looked on as "structural entities".[166] Similarly, before 1963 very few useful generalizations could be made about, say, "the Iban" in Sarawak or "the Dusuns" in North Borneo. Pringle mentions the increasing ethnic awareness of the Iban under the Brookes,[167] but even in 1962 it was possible for the two newly-created Iban political parties to agree to recruit members from different geographical areas.[168] In 1963 the Sarawak Malays were still perhaps not as united as they had been before the split over cession in 1946.[169] In North Borneo there were clear lines of distinction between those Muslims whose ancestors had been under Brunei influence and those who had originated in Suluk-influenced areas. In 1963 the Christian Penampang group of Dusuns was only just assuming the leadership of a rather extensive range of other groups. In both states Chinese nationalism had fired the imagination of some younger Chinese but had not had so great an effect on the older generation.

The divisions between broad ethnic groups, such as Malays, Kadazans, Chinese, Land Dayaks and so on, are most obvious, perhaps, in economic relationships, in the ethnic membership and policies of political parties, and in competition for posts in the civil service. Calculations in terms of ethnic arithmetic and fears of ethnic domination are endemic. To give just one instance, a respected Chinese businessman in Kuching, who is on the fringe of politics, is firmly convinced that family planning policy in Sarawak is aimed mainly at lowering the Chinese birth rate in relation to the birth rates of other ethnic groups.

By 1963 it would have been hard to claim that there was such a thing as a North Borneo, or Sabah, sense of nationhood. The biggest single factor in stimulating such a sense was perhaps the Japanese occupation;[170] but probably it would be more accurate to say that current attitudes between races reflected toleration rather than any conscious sense of nationhood.[171] In Sarawak the situation was somewhat different. No doubt some of the much-praised racial harmony in Sarawak also reflected mainly toleration. However, the Brooke Rajahs had provided a focus for loyalty which was lacking in North Borneo, administered by a Chartered Company. Disraeli said of India, that you "can only act upon the opinion of Eastern nations through their imagination", and added that a "monarch was more likely to have this effect than a chartered company, however venerable and worthy".[172] Older politicians and civil servants in Sarawak frequently used the phrase, "in the Rajah's days" but no corresponding references were made in Sabah to the Chartered Company. The British also encouraged Sarawak nationalism when they started the practice of setting up racially-mixed local authorities in 1948.[173] The consequence was that by 1963 there was such a thing as "Sarawak nationalism" which made an appeal to some members of all major races in the country.

After Malaysia was formed, it became clear that nationalism in the Borneo states, particularly in Sarawak, would create problems for nation building in Malaysia. To some extent what appeared to be a deliberate assertion of state nationalism, as opposed to Malaysian nationalism, may have been nothing of the sort. It may simply have represented a time lag in getting used to a new idea, or have resulted from taking literally the phrase, "Independence through Malaysia". In rejecting the Philippines claim to Sabah in 1964 the Legislative Assembly referred to the "sovereignty of Sabah" as resting in "the people of Sabah".[174] Also, even if state nationalism, or "tribalism", exists, it may be possible to build on it rather than to try to eradicate it.[175] Essentially, this is what the Alliance Party tried to do in Malaya. But it is a different matter to try and build on an already existing, or embryonic, territorial nationalism which is itself multi-racial. It is true that the "level of integration", in a given unit may be too low to favour unification into a larger unit.[176] But it may also be too high; at any rate the level of integration in Sarawak seems to have been higher than the Federal Government thought it was.

Obviously, there may be conflict between building loyalties

at state level and building them at national level. SUPP and SNAP (especially after it went into opposition) were multi-racial parties, whcih operated without any racial divisions and so encouraged loyalty to Sarawak. But SNAP, and also SUPP until it became part of the Sarawak Coalition Government in July 1970, was decidedly critical of the way in which federal government policy affected Sarawak, and so the contribution to Malaysian nation building may have been negative. During the formation of Malaysia religion had been an important issue: after 1963 it remained important in determining policies and political allegiance. Viewed from Kuala Lumpur, the conversion of Kenyahs and Punans in Sarawak to Islam could be seen as promoting nation-building. However, in Sarawak such conversions could be regarded as splitting ethnic groups which had already acquired a group identity.[177] Religious conversions did not become a big issue until the United Sabah Islamic Association was formed in 1969. The appeal of USIA was largely in terms of "unity and solidarity". Between August, 1969 and January, 1971 there were 3,482 converts to Islam in Sabah.[178] These included prominent Native previously non-Muslim elites, notably Dato Stephens, a former Chief Minister, and Dato Ganie Gilong, a federal cabinet minister. USIA's activities were in line with the assimilative policies of the state government in other fields, notably language and education. Presumably the state government felt strong enough and determined enough to be sure that the net effect of its policies, in the long run at least, would be to promote nation-building.

More potent than state nationalism in Sabah and Sarawak was the growth of communalism, in the sense that communal sentiments were becoming more prominent and communal groups becoming larger and more inclusive: for example, Ibans as a whole were now being regarded as a communal group, not just Ibans in a particular area.[179] To some extent the Federal Government was right in thinking that Sabah or Sarawak nationalism was really largely Kadazan or Iban nationalism. The Kadazans and the Iban were, respectively, the largest groups in the two states when Malaysia was formed. In the absence of Malaysia, each might have hoped eventually to be the dominant group, either under the British or after they had gone. After the World War II the Kadazans "felt that their position in Sabah should be like the Malays in Malaya".[180] But, quite apart from the loss of support, especially in the Interior, which resulted from their insisting on the name Kadazan instead of Dusun, their estimates of their strength were unrealistic. Numerically they were much less important than the Malays in Malaya. They assumed, wrongly, in their electoral calculations that Kadazans formed more than half the electors and that they could win more than half the seats in the state Legislative Assembly. This arose from a gross under-estimate of the numbers of Chinese and Indonesian electors and of the Kadazan Muslims, who on religious grounds would be likely to support USNO. It took over four years for the party leaders to realise the arithmetical truth and to dissolve the party. Even then a crucial point was not mentioned. Dato Stephens was entirely correct in observing that "we are big in Sabah, but looking at the overall picture of the region we live in, we are small".[181] But he omitted to bring out the fact that even in Sabah the Kadazans were not a dominant political group.

In Sarawak, on the other hand, by reason of their actual numbers and their advantages from the electoral boundaries, the Iban were potentially the dominant political ethnic group. Their potential for dominance failed to be effective at the 1970 state election, only because of their fatal incapability to unite.[182]

Yet it would be wrong to say that Sarawak nationalism was entirely Iban nationalism in disguise. It is true that Dato Ningkan benefited from the rôle of martyr and champion of states' rights, which he increasingly assumed in his contests with the Federal Government. And his party, SNAP, which was originally basically an Iban party, used the slogan of "Sarawak for Sarawakians", which appealed to all Sarawak nationalists who wished to emphasize "independence" in the concept of "Independence through Malaysia". The most obvious indication that Sarawak nationalism was more than just Iban nationalism came from the attitude of some Malays in Sarawak. The Tengku, referring to British rule in the Borneo territories, had stated: "If they, who are people of a different race and from a different world, can do much for the people of the Borneo territories, sufficient to gain their confidence, how much more can we do for those who belong to the same ethnic group whom we regard as brothers in the same family."[183] But even among the Malays in the Borneo territories, to say nothing of the non-Malays, brotherhood did not automatically ensure harmony. The minor clashes which occurred in Kuching early in 1966 had "neither racial nor political overtones. The trouble was confined entirely to a number of Malaysian servicemen, not as well disciplined as they should be, and the Malay community in Kuching."[184] And the reaction against the posting of officials from Malaya to fill jobs in the federal civil service in the Borneo states was not purely a non-Malay reaction. It was a Malay (Dato Abang Othman) who expressed the hope that these, mostly Malay, federal officers "will not keep on continuing to regard themselves as somewhat superior, and by keeping themselves aloof they [sic] look somewhat like the former colonialists".[185]

In one important respect there was no conflict between state nationalism in Sabah and Sarawak, on the one hand, and Malaysian nationalism, on the other. In Sabah resistance to Indonesian Confrontation and to the Philippine claim for territory was opposed on the basis of loyalty to both Sabah and Malaysia.[186] Indeed, from 1968 on, some of the most vociferous support for resistance to the Philippines came from ex-UPKO members. In Sarawak, broadly speaking, both state nationalism and Malaysian nationalism were opposed to the Indonesians when Confrontation existed, and both types of nationalism were also behind government measures against Communist terrorists.

If nationalism at state level were so strong that it was irreconcilable with Malaysian nationalism, demands for secession would be the logical consequence. Even when Malaysia was being formed the Fourth Divisional Advisory Council of Sarawak had unanimously agreed that the state would have the right to secede,[187] but the Council Negri did not support this recommendation.

The secession issue was raised most plainly at the time of Singapore's exit from Malaysia. If Malaysia was a package deal, ran the argument, the contents of the package were radically changed when Singapore left. The racial balance was altered, and economically Sarawak and Sabah were deprived of the opportunity of benefiting from being able to buy Singapore goods without customs duties inside the common market. Indeed Lord Cobbold had endorsed the view that to join Malaysia was in the best interests of the Borneo territories only subject to the assumption that Singapore also joined the federation.[188] SUPP and MACHINDA called for a referendum in August 1965 to determine Sarawak's future, but the Chief Minister, Dato Ningkan, opposed this, stressing that Sarawak, unlike Singapore, was heavily dependent financially on the federal government.[189] In Sabah there was a delayed reaction from the UPKO when its leader, Dato Stephens, raised the question of a re-examination of the relations between Sabah and the Federal Government to take account of Singapore's departure from the federation.[190] UPKO seems to have been most concerned about renegotiating the federal bargain on the issues of immigration, customs duties, and state control of the police. Drafts stating the UPKO position were drawn up, but they were never finalized. Instead, a few weeks later Dato Stephens resigned from the federal Cabinet.

The question of renegotiation was again raised by the UPKO in the period between its loss of the state election and its dissolution, April–December 1967. It was explicitly linked to implementation of the Twenty Points, [191] and to proposals for a referendum to ensure their enforcement. However, after UPKO's dissolution, secession or even formal renegotiation ceased to be public political issues. In Sarawak, on the other hand, support for secession persisted. In 1965 an alternative to Malaysia was put forward quite openly; Stephen Yong of the SUPP revived the old proposal for a three-state Borneo federation (consisting of Sarawak, Sabah and Brunei) in August 1965.[192] Inside the SUPP there are different views on secession, or at least differences about the expression of such views. In SUPP Chan Siaw Hee, before his detention in 1968, was rather uncompromising in his stance on secession, although on his release he recognized that Malaysia was a *fait accompli*.[193] But the moderate leaders of the party, in a conference with the leaders of the Malaysian Alliance Party held shortly before the 1969 elections, agreed to accept Malaysia in principle. However, even after SUPP joined the state government in July 1970, presumably agreement in principle would not rule out later demands for secession, if it were not followed by concessions to the party on appropriate issues. The leader of SNAP, Dato Ningkan, has stated that the party "is irrevocably committed to a full support of Malaysia . . ."[194] Also, some of the party leaders, for example Dato James Wong, are deeply convinced that, for economic and security reasons, Sarawak must remain part of Malaysia. However, at grass roots level, SNAP support undoubtedly benefited from a strain of Iban nationalism which would not regret separation from the federation.

The Federal Government has repeatedly denounced any idea of secession. The denunciations were most severe shortly after the exit of Singapore when there seemed to be some danger of a chain reaction. "Once the logic of secession is admitted, there is no end except in anarchy".[195] The Federal Government argued that secession by Sabah or Sarawak would not be logical, and reinforced the point with some blunt speaking. Any who intend to secede, said the Tengku in a broadcast, "by force or by any other action will be regarded as rebels and traitors and we will deal with them as such".[196] Sabah and Sarawak would remain in Malaysia for ever.[197] Such statements were paralleled by pronouncements from other federal politicians. Constitutionally, a two-thirds majority in the Federal Parliament would be necessary for the separation of Sarawak and Sabah from Malaysia. Secession by force would be hard to achieve unless, possibly, the armed forces of the Federal Government were tied down by overwhelming obligation elsewhere, e.g. against Communists on the Thai border.

In West Malaysia there has been some dissatisfaction with the continuance of Malaysia, expressed, for instance, by pro-MCA businessmen and by some UMNO branches, because of the expenses of supporting the Borneo territories financially and receiving little in return. While the Tengku, the founder and "father" of Malaysia, remained Prime Minister, it was unlikely that this dissatisfaction would have much effect on federal government policy. But earlier speculations that Tun Razak, the Tengku's designated successor, might be more inclined to adopt a strict cost-benefit approach to Malaya's union with the Borneo states were not borne out. Tun Razak did not succeed the Tengku until September, 1970, and by that time there was a cogent additional reason for maintaining the union. The riots which followed the 1969 elections in West Malaysia had constituted such a threat to national unity that psychologically any possibility of a Borneo state being permitted to leave the federation became even more remote than before.

Sabah, from 1968 onwards, presented an interesting study of state-federal relations. With the collapse of the UPKO, open opposition to cultural assimilation almost ceased. But Tun Mustapha was carrying on a campaign, within Malaysia, in support of Sabah's state rights. When he was Head of State Tun Mustapha had deplored the action of the Chief Minister, Peter Lo, in taking Sabah's side against the Federal Government in open parliamentary debate; as a member of the Alliance Government. Enche Lo, he said, should have appealed to the Federal Government through private talks.[198] Later Tun Mustapha had denied allegations that he was a stooge of the Federal Government by claiming to be a stooge of the Malaysian nation.[199] However, once opposition to the USNO had crumbled, Tun Mustapha, while remaining devoted to the broad aim of achieving national unity in Malaysia through cultural means, such as language and education, became a staunch defender of states' rights on status and bread-and-butter issues. As undisputed ruler of Sabah, he championed the state *vis-à-vis* the Federal Government.[200]

In September, 1969 he unilaterally cancelled a projected British army exercise in Sabah, a decision in which the Federal Government, which constitutionally was the relevant authority, later concurred. Shortly afterwards he attacked a Federal Government proposal that immigration procedures into Sabah should be relaxed to make the admission of workers from West Malaysia easier, referring to the powers over immigration given to the state in the Malaysia Agreement. He condemned federal ministers who "come here to criticize our policies and our government without first knowing our country's background".[201] Sabah's rights could not have been defended more determinedly by the UPKO leaders in the days when they fought under the standard of the Twenty Points. Tun Mustapha did not hesitate to press for television for Sabah and for a new airport for Kota Kinabalu, and to attack the federal Economic Planning Unit for blocking these, and other, development projects in the state.[202] Television was particularly dear to Tun Mustapha, partly because of its potentialities for education and modernization, but also because of its importance in nation-building. "It would at the same time serve a very useful purpose in unifying the various races . . ."[203]

The most extraordinary feature of these demands by Tun Mustapha was that they were not demands that the centre should assume additional financial responsibilities in the state. Sabah was sufficiently well-off to have taken over a large share of the Federal Government's commitments for development in the state.[204] Tun Mustapha was quite willing that Sabah should pay for both television and the airport. What he wanted to change was the *priorities* of the central government on development by moving Sabah projects up from their existing place in the federal queue. On television the solution adopted seemed to amount to the Sabah state government's lending the necessary money to the Federal Government. The usual pattern of exchange, to use Etzioni's term,[205] was being reversed. Affluent Sabah under Tun Mustapha was willing to give utilitarian assets, money, to the Federal Government in exchange for identitive assets, the prestige of having television when it wanted it instead of when the Federal Government had planned that it should have it.[206]

Conclusion

This chapter has necessarily emphasized the frictions arising from federalism and attempted nation-building rather than the often unrecorded successes. The concept of Malaysia as a union of Malaya, Sarawak and North Borneo was entirely reasonable; it was made more difficult, however, by the speed with which the new federation was formed and by the dislocations resulting from Singapore's departure. By the terms of the Malaysia Act cultural measures favouring nation-building, mainly language and education, could operate effectively only in the long run, while opposition to them was very easily aroused in the short run. Economically, the benefits from

Malaysia, although considerable, were not quickly evident, and did not match the unrealistic expectations which had been stimulated. In both Sarawak and Sabah appeals to states' rights and state nationalism gained some support, but Sarawak nationalism was stronger for historical reasons, and the ethnic proportions of the population gave it a firmer base.

To counter these appeals and promote Malaysian nationalism the Federal Government used its armoury of constitutional weapons and also took advantage of party ties. By 1969, with the aid of Tun Mustapha's dominant personality, "integration" was being accelerated[207] in Sabah, although the Tun had evolved a personal version of "Sabah nationalism" which was not inconsistent with Malaysian nationalism. In Sarawak, until 1970, there was something like a stalemate, reflected in the postponement of the elections and the fluidity of party politics. Since the formation of the, Bumiputera-dominated, Alliance-SUPP coalition in July 1970 the situation has altered. Dato Rahman Ya'akub is an able and accomplished politician and enjoys the support of the Federal Government. From announcements made soon after the new state government was formed, the emphasis of his administration is on efficient government and economic development.[208] It would be wrong, however, to expect that the style of governing would resemble that of the Sabah state government. To be sure, shortly after his appointment as Chief Minister, Rahman Ya'akub said that Sabah was a "model state", whose development, government administration and solidarity should be followed by Sarawak.[209] But Rahman Ya'akub's personal style, deriving from a legal and intellectual background, is less frontal and more diplomatic than Tun Mustapha's. His policies in Sarawak during his first year of office, 1970–1, have been less directly "integrationist" than might have been expected. Moreover, although he has nearly solid support from the Muslims in Sarawak, the proportion of Muslims in the population is quite small, only just over 20%. Above all, the coalition state government formed in July, 1970 is dependent on SUPP participation. Differences between moderate and extreme SUPP members could eventually constitute a strain on the coalition and set a limited term to its life.

3

Political Parties

It is in the sphere of party politics that the changes which have recently occurred and are now occurring in Sabah and Sarawak are best highlighted. The many areas of our inquiry, ranging from specific issues such as federal-state relations to more general ones related to political development and the characteristics of the emerging political elites and their styles of politics, all receive some illumination here. Further, the activities and changing fortunes of the parties help us to understand some of the most striking consequences of the newness of competitive politics in the two territories and the accompanying instability and changes in group affiliations. The institutional as well as the popular bases of political power are still in their early stages of development and one of the main concerns in this chapter will be to look at the ways in which this has affected the organization and functioning of political parties.

Compared with the rest of Malaysia, a crucial feature of party politics in Sarawak and Sabah is its newness. The first political party in Sarawak was not formed until June 1959 and in Sabah not until August 1961, some three months after the announcement of the Malaysia proposal. These states have also had comparatively little experience of organized, competitive politics. The first elections to all local authorities in Sarawak were held only in 1959 and the state did not have a directly elected legislature until 1970. Sabah started even later, its first district council elections not being held until December 1962 although it subsequently went ahead of Sarawak by holding direct elections to its Legislative Assembly in April 1967. Needless to say, this newness of political parties, coupled with the rapid changes brought about by the creation of Malaysia, has had a profound influence in shaping the character of political activity in the two states. Given the rapid appearance, as well as the speedy disappearance, of many parties within a relatively short period, political alignments have remained fluid. Being uncertain about their support, parties have tended to be eccentric, or at least unashamedly opportunistic, in their attempts to form alliances, and the political framework has consequently been characterized by considerable instability. This has also complicated the attempts to find a proper groove for relations between the central and state governments, and, in the case of the ruling Alliance, for relations between state and national leaders.

The ethnic pattern in both Sarawak and Sabah was very different from that in Malaya, and this had a considerable effect on the party system. There was no single indigenous group in either state corresponding to the Malays, but several indigenous groups. Even when a "group" seemed to be distinctly marked off from others by having a common name, for example "Ibans" or "Dusuns", it was far from being homogeneous or cohesive. The non-indigenous population, on the other hand, was more homogeneous than in Malaya, because it consisted almost entirely of Chinese[1] rather than of Chinese and Indians. Nevertheless the proportion of non-indigenous people was smaller, and the rather direct opposition of "Malay" and "non-Malay" was not reproduced in either of the states.

If Malaysia had not been created, it is quite probable that political parties in the two territories would still have been established along communal lines. To be sure, the first three parties in Sarawak, which were formed before the Malaysia proposal was made by the Tengku in May 1961, were multi-ethnic by their constitutions. But in point of fact, they were already attracting members on a largely ethnic basis. Some non-Chinese left SUPP[2] because it was "too Chinese", in order to form PANAS; in turn, some members left PANAS because it was "too Malay". In Sabah the parties were actually formed *after* May 1961, although they existed embryonically before then.[3] It is therefore impossible to say whether or not they would have followed the lines they did, indicated in the next paragraph, if Malaysia had not come into existence. There was an ambivalent relationship between the men who became the leaders of the two main parties, Dato Stephens and Tun Mustapha. In the context of Malaysia, and with the federal government playing an important rôle, they were predominantly rivals. If Mayalsia had not been established, with fewer pressures to form parties quickly and to hold elections, the relation might have been less competitive and ethnic differences might have been played down.

As things turned out, in the context of Malaysia, the major parties in each state fall quite neatly into three categories: Native non-Muslim; Native Muslim; and non-Native.[4] The indigenous groups in each state are so numerous and so heterogeneous that they provided a poor basis for party divisions. Religion therefore is a better guide for distinguishing between the policies and sources of membership of the different Native parties, although no party constitution actually prescribed religion as a criterion for membership. In Sarawak in 1963 there were two Native non-Muslim parties, originally drawing support from different geographical areas, SNAP and Pesaka, and two Native Muslim parties, PANAS and BARJASA, which later joined together to form Parti Bumiputera. There was also an unequivocally Chinese party, the SCA (Sarawak Chinese Association) as well as the SUPP, which combined a strong appeal to Chinese[5] with a radical approach, not found in other Borneo parties. In Sabah in 1963 there were two Native non-Muslim parties, UNKO and Pasok Momogun, which soon coalesced. The single Native Muslim party was the USNO. There was a single Chinese party, which after some changes of name, was known as the Sabah Chinese Association.

Although the creation of Malaysia may not have had much effect on the kind of parties formed in the two states, it did have an influence on their relationships and on their fortunes. The larger, longer-established, and more experienced Alliance parties in Malaya helped to shape "Alliance" parties in Sarawak and Sabah,[6] although these structures, because of the different background, could not parallel exactly the structure in Malaya. The impact of being in Malaysia was also felt in another way. The Alliance Federal Government, in which the most important component was the United Malays' National Organization (UMNO), was concerned with the question of nation-building within the new federation.[7] It found that it could work best with, and place most trust in, those parties in the two states which shared its views on nation-building and on related issues such as language policy, education policy, and the employment of, mainly British, "expatriates" in the civil service. At the same time, on a party level, UMNO had close relations with Muslim parties in the two states. This is not to say that there was a complete identity of interest between Muslims in the Borneo states and Malays from Malaya.[8] But the position of the Native Muslim parties *vis à vis* other parties was obviously strengthened by the inclusion of Sarawak and Sabah in Malaysia. The Native Muslim party in Sabah, USNO became dominant *de facto* from 1965 on, and after 1967 was in an unassailable position, with Tun Mustapha as Chief Minister. It was not until 1970 that the Native Muslim party in Sarawak, Bumiputera, filled the Chief Minister's post. If Sarawak and Sabah had each been independent, it is unlikely that the Native Muslim parties would have done so well, considering that only about one-fifth and two-fifths of the respective populations were Muslims. However, Islam provided a good basis for discipline, which was lacking among the Native non-Muslim population.

Sarawak Parties: the SUPP

The first political party to be launched in Sarawak was the Sarawak United People's Party, or SUPP. The initiative in forming the party was taken by a group of moderate Chinese, led by Ong Kee Hui,[9] and the intention was that it should be a non-communal party with a mass base. It has been claimed that the proposal had first been discussed with the Governor, who, having initially given his approval, later became concerned that the immediate consequences of organized party activity might not altogether be beneficial to Sarawak. Undeterred by this change in official attitude, and claiming that their plans were now too far advanced to allow any reconsideration, the organizers of the SUPP inaugurated their party in June 1959. The history of the SUPP since then has both heartened and disappointed its original founders. On the one hand, as other parties emerged and groped their way in the political arena, the SUPP had no difficulty in establishing itself as the best organized and most disciplined party in the state, enjoying the widest and most stable support. But as the Malaysia proposal gained momentum, it found itself more and more isolated in the political scene.[10]

All the other parties (many of which had earlier expressed reservations about the proposal but which had soon abandoned their opposition to it), in an attempt to strengthen the Malaysian cause and safeguard their own future, joined forces to form a Malayan-type Alliance, dedicated to achieving outright victory for the pro-Malaysia forces at the forthcoming district council elections. Although it remained the single most powerful party in the state, the SUPP soon came to realize that it could not match the combined strength of the other parties. The 1963 district council elections were fought almost entirely on the single issue of Malaysia, and the SUPP was the only party which remained opposed to Sarawak's entry into the new federation. Considering the help which the other parties received from the Malayan Alliance,[11] and the way in which its own strength was blunted by the arrest of many of its workers for alleged communist subversion, the SUPP did well to receive almost one quarter of the votes and 116 seats, compared to the Alliance's just over one-third of the votes and 138 seats.

TABLE 3.1

Results of the Sarawak District Council Elections, 1963

Party	Votes won	Seats won
SUPP	45,493	116
PANAS	28,242	59
Alliance	56,896	138
Independents	55,061	116
	185,692	429

Given the intensive propaganda for and against the proposed Malaysia scheme, and the high degree of partisanship stimulated by the issue, one may be puzzled by the remarkable success of Independent candidates, as shown in the above table. The fact is that these candidates did not stand aloof from the main debate on Malaysia, and in most cases based their own campaigns on a pro- or anti-Malaysia platform.

Their decision not to stand on a party ticket was the result of other factors and did not reflect a refusal to be associated with the issues raised by the parties. For one thing most parties had barely become organized by the time elections were held, and, hampered by poor communications, had not extended their activities beyond the main centres of population. Consequently, in the more remote parts of the country (particularly in the Fourth and Fifth Divisions) these parties were in no position to select suitable candidates and launch a proper campaign. Further, because parties were a new phenomenon, there was also considerable doubt as to how the electorate would respond to particular labels. Intending candidates, who were often local notabilities, therefore found it much safer to run on their own credentials rather than risk the complication of a party ticket.[13] This reasoning was often accepted by the parties themselves and, once they felt satisfied that particular candidates of good standing belonged to their own camp, they saw no reason for putting up official candidates of their own, or for that matter, for encouraging other "Independent" candidates. In the case of the SUPP, however, there was one additional consideration. Some of its supporters who stood as Independents probably did so because they wanted to reduce the risk of being identified with subversion since the SUPP had by this time come under close scrutiny for Communist infiltration.

Apart from the political isolation already referred to and the growing influence of the extremists, the moderate leaders of the SUPP soon experienced another disappointment. This was the increasingly Chinese image which the party soon began to acquire and which undermined the earlier multi-racial hopes of the founders. This was perhaps a logical and unavoidable development. For one thing the leadership was Chinese, and the party could therefore have been expected to have more immediate appeal among members of that community; for another, with the subsequent emergence of Native-based parties, it was natural for the indigenous groups to turn to these parties rather than to the SUPP for representation.

To be fair, the SUPP's "Chineseness" has not really been reflected in its membership. At particular periods (even well after the formation of the other parties) its Native membership has equalled, or exceeded, its Chinese membership.[14] The figures in the following Table, extracted from the records kept at the party's head office, are quite revealing in this regard.

TABLE 3.2

Ethnic Composition (Chinese/Native) of SUPP Members, 1959–69

	CHINESE			NATIVE			
Year	Total from previous year[a]	New Members	End-of-year total	Total from previous year[a]	New Members	End-of-year total	Grand Total[a]
1959		3,421	3,421		206	206	3,627
1960	3,421	10,249	13,670	206	6,869	7,075	20,745
1961	13,670	10,596	24,266	7,075	10,171	17,246	41,512
1962	24,266	3,472	27,738	17,246	5,613	22,859	50,597
1963	27,738	208	27,946	22,859	929	23,788	51,734
1964	27,946	49	27,995	23,788	100	23,888	51,883
1965	27,995	20	28,015	23,888	59	23,947	51,962
1966	28,015	78	28,093	23,947	485	24,432	52,525
1967	28,093	294	28,387	24,432	7,407	31,839	60,226
1968	28,387	706	29,093	31,839	4,225	36,064	65,157
1969	29,093	*100	29,193	36,064	*2,131	38,195	67,388

* Up to 15th June, 1969.

(*a*) These figures do not take into account the resignations which took place each year, records of which were not available. There were, however, good reasons for believing that the rate of resignations was higher among Native than among Chinese members (see p. 77).

Although the party has also seen to it that Native members have occupied something like half the positions in the Central Working Committee,[15] Native members have seldom exercised much influence. The key positions at all levels have been occupied by Chinese and the party's most active workers have also invariably come from that community. The Native members have on the whole not participated actively in the party's affairs and have not been well organized: at party conferences for example, the Chinese have tended to show up in larger numbers and to dominate the proceedings.

Two factors stand above others in explaining the rapid infiltration of the SUPP by the Communists and their sympathisers, and the subsequent domination of many of the party's branches by the extreme left wing. To begin with, by being the first party to be organized in the state the SUPP became the first respectable front available to the underground communist movement. Having previously not had any legitimate avenues for political activity, and mindful of the considerable promise shown by the SUPP soon after its inauguration, the communist movement was naturally inclined to take advantage of this new opportunity to acquire a respectable cover and an organizational framework for its own activities. Secondly, the SUPP was also the only mass-based "Chinese" party in Sarawak and for this reason was especially attractive. As in Malaya, left-wing politics in Sarawak has been an essentially Chinese phenomenon. Thus, given the objective of infiltrating a popular, mass-based party and using it as a convenient vehicle, it was prudent to select a "host" organization which was also Chinese controlled: the activists would be less conspicuous in such an organization and their twin functions of promoting communist and Chinese interests could be more easily merged. In a predominantly Native party, on the other hand, in addition to the problem of anonymity, there would also have been the risk of separate communal interests coming into conflict; at the very least, there would have been a disinclination on the part of the Native members to allow Chinese to occupy positions of importance.

The communist infiltration of the SUPP may also have been facilitated by the disinclination on the part of the founders to be selective in admitting new members. As the leaders of the first party to be formed in the state, and anxious to establish their pre-eminence without delay, they probably gave the highest priority to recruiting as many members as possible without much regard to other factors. If they were aware of the interest which the Communists and their sympathizers were taking in the party, they probably felt that in the long run these groups would be less of a threat if they were within the SUPP, under their leadership, than if they had chosen to support some other party or to form a "front" association of their own. If properly utilized their dedication and organizational skills could give the SUPP an advantage over any future rival.

This infiltration and the ensuing attempt at domination by the left-wing soon led to two problems. First, the party became the object of constant surveillance by the Government and many of its activities were consequently circumscribed. In 1964 and 1965, at the height of Indonesian "confrontation", some of the party's branches were closed down by the Government because they had allegedly come under communist control.[16] In April 1965 the Government also banned the SUPP's leading publications. *Tuan Chin Pau* and *Sa'ati*, on the grounds that they had consistently adopted a stand that was aimed at serving the interests of the Communist movement in Sarawak. Expectedly, the party condemned the move and described the Central Government as "a dictator trying to stifle the voice of the opposition", while the Secretary-General expressed surprise "because there was at no time any official indication that *Sa'ati* had done anything wrong except voice the people's views".[17] Finally, the SUPP has also suffered from the periodic detention of some of its key activists at the grass-roots level, on grounds of alleged subversion. Higher officials have also been incarcerated on occasion, the most important of these being Chan Siaw Hee, the Assistant Secretary-General, who was detained in August 1968.[18] There is no denying that these detentions have damaged the party's organizational capacity and disrupted some of its activities, although it is conceivable that in some cases repressive action by the Government only served to strengthen the dedication of the more committed members. The net result of these detentions has been that the left wing has never been able to enjoy stable leadership and has found itself dependent on the moderate leaders of the party.

These repressive measures, and the considerable Government and party propaganda against the SUPP as a dangerous and disloyal force, must have discouraged many Natives (to whom the other half of the SUPP's activities, namely the promotion of Chinese interests, could not have had much appeal anyway) from joining it and must also have been responsible for the frequent resignation of Native members, particularly during the period of Indonesian "confrontation". During 1964 and 1965 there were many occasions when groups of Native members sent in common letters of resignation, which received wide publicity in the newspapers and through the Ministry of

Information. An interesting feature was that copies of these letters were almost invariably sent to the local police by those resigning.

Secondly, there has been continuing friction between the moderate and extremist wings of the SUPP. The highest positions have always been in the hands of the former group (led by Ong Kee Hui and Stephen Yong, the President and Secretary-General respectively), while the latter have often dominated the branch committees. On the whole the extremists have seemed anxious not to disturb this balance: it has given them influence at the grass roots level without destroying the credibility of the leadership's claim that the SUPP is a respectable organization fighting for legitimate causes. But they have not always refrained from using their strength to challenge the policies of the moderate leaders. The most serious confrontation took place in June 1965, over the decision to participate in the Malaysian Solidarity Convention, a gathering of several Malaysian opposition parties aimed at presenting a common front on certain vital issues notably the safeguarding of non-Malay interests.[19] The President and Secretary-General of the SUPP had decided that they would participate in the Convention, and had in fact attended the first meeting held in Singapore on 9 May, 1965. The left wing of the party, however, was opposed to this on the grounds that participation in the Convention signified acceptance of Malaysia and because it did not approve of the ideological position of many of the other participants.[20] At the Annual Central Committee meeting held in June, the moderate leaders were severely criticized for their action, and, failing to get a vote of confidence, resigned their positions and walked out of the meeting.[21] The extremists immediately elected their own interim Committee, but soon realised that without the moderate leaders the SUPP's future would be most uncertain. Efforts were therefore made to persuade the latter to return, and the compromise finally arrived at was that the SUPP would remain in the Convention for a trial period of three months, during which period it would fight for the inclusion of the Socialist Front and the Barisan Sosialis. Before this period was over, however, Singapore was separated from Malaysia and the Convention came to a speedy end.

Although this was the only occasion on which there was an open breach between the left wing and the moderate leaders, hostility between them has hardly been concealed. In March 1964, the Secretary-General issued a statement on behalf of the Central Working Committee dissociating the SUPP from all foreign and subversive elements, and pledging to defend Malaysia. The SUPP was committed to constitutional means, and would not seek political changes by force or arms. Warned the Secretary-General: "Any member found to be consorting with armed rebels or subversive elements seeking to overthrow the Government by illegal means will be dealt with severely."[22] The extremists must have been stung by this, but, in the climate then prevailing, were not in a position to respond. Later that year, however, they got some satisfaction when the SUPP announced its decision not to participate in the National Solidarity Week and instructed its members who were on Solidarity Week Committees to resign their positions.[23]

During interviews, it was common for representatives of the moderate and extremist groups to speak freely of their contrasting policies, and to hint at the inevitability of an eventual showdown. The left-wing strategy all along seems to have been based on the belief that if the SUPP were to come to power they would have no difficulty in taking over control, but that if it failed to win power, blame could easily be placed on the weakness of the moderate leaders. Another possibility is that the left-wing (or, more particularly, the Communists) has not relied too heavily on the SUPP's coming to power through electoral means and in fact has not been too keen on such a prospect because the longer the party was kept out of office the easier it would be to convince its supporters that parliamentary struggle was not worth adhering to. The moderate leaders, for their part, have always seen themselves to be in competition with the extremists for the loyalty of the masses.[24] On the one hand they have succeeded in retaining control over party policy, thereby safeguarding the SUPP's legitimacy within the political system; on the other, they have never been able fully to control the activities of their branches or to dislodge branch committees which in their opinion have behaved in a manner that was likely to embarrass or compromise the party. But Government action, such as detentions[25] and the closing down of branches, has often taken care of this problem although there has always been the risk that excessive repression would in the long run benefit the extremists by lending support to their argument about the futility of parliamentary struggle.[26]

The dominant image of the SUPP, then, has been a combined product of its leftness and its Chineseness. As pointed out earlier, this has given the party a narrower appeal than was originally hoped for by the founders. But it would be wrong to conclude that this has also weakened the party: although the scope of potential support has no doubt been adversely affected, this dual platform has guaranteed the SUPP a firmer base and a more committed following than it might have enjoyed had its net been cast wider. As the sole champion of left-wing causes, it has benefited from the dedicated support of countless workers whose ideological fervour is unmatched among the supporters of the other parties. Potentially, the only other source of equivalent support would have been through communal politics: had communal differences been pronounced it might have been possible for the other parties also to inspire a similar sense of mission among their supporters. But parties have tended not to be communally exclusive, and, although different parties have concentrated on different communal interests, they have all given varying degrees of emphasis of compromise on communal issues. The SUPP's success as a "Chinese" party has in fact been partly dependent on this. The Sarawak Chinese Association (SCA) the only explicitly Chinese party in the state and hence the SUPP's logical rival for Chinese support, has not been in a position to be uncompromising in its advocacy of Chinese interests because, as a member of the Alliance, its survival has depended partly on not alienating its partners.

The SUPP, on the other hand, has not been similarly inhibited, although, as a socialist party and as a party which has been keen not to become exclusively Chinese, it has had to commit itself to improving the living conditions of the indigenous population. The issues which have the greatest appeal among the Chinese, like multi-lingualism and the right (of Chinese) to own land, have therefore often been presented not as communal issues but rather as issues which relate to equality.

It is noteworthy that despite its left-wing appeal the SUPP has never conducted any propaganda against capitalists in the state. As wealth is associated with the Chinese, such propaganda could have helped to swell Native support; but by the same token it would have undermined Chinese solidarity, on which the party has relied more heavily. Further, some of the party's leaders (including Chan Siaw Hee) have themselves been well-to-do businessmen and anti-capitalist propaganda may not have appeared very convincing coming from them. Finally, the SUPP has probably been reluctant to cut off its links with potential sources of financial assistance, as this was bound to be of importance during elections.[27]

Perhaps even more surprising is the fact that the SUPP has never had a declared ideology. The problem clearly has been that different sections of the party have believed in different things and have been revolutionary to different degrees. One would have thought that the pressure to act on this matter would have arisen not from a belief that it would win votes, but rather from a wish by the more doctrinaire sections of the party to have a "pure" ideology. As far as the leaders have been concerned, however, the party has probably been enjoying too much support for them to risk losing votes by being unnecessarily specific about their commitments.

Following the inconclusive election of 1970, the SUPP was invited to form a coalition with the Alliance.[28] Such a development would have been almost unthinkable a few years earlier, and if the invitation was difficult to extend it was also difficult to accept. The Bumiputera-dominated Alliance, however, obviously was of the view that a coalition with the SUPP would be preferable to one with SNAP, especially since such a coalition would involve a working relationship with the top leadership of the SUPP, which was moderate. The SUPP leaders on the other hand must have felt that this was the only chance they would have of sharing power in a reasonably stable government (i.e. a Government that would not come into conflict with the national leadership), and, although they were aware that the move would be seen as a betrayal by the left-wing, were prepared to hope that they would have sufficient leverage in the new Government to be able to "deliver the goods" and to build up faith in democratic competition among their supporters.

PANAS, BARJASA and Bumiputera

The next two parties to be discussed, Party Negara Sarawak (PANAS) and Barisan Ra'ayat Jati Sarawak (BARJASA) in fact no longer exist, having merged in 1967 to form a single party called Parti Bumiputera. It would however be unwise and possibly also misleading to treat them as a single unit here, because the separate identities which the two parties had until their merger, and the different ways in which they responded to political changes, will help us in our understanding of a crucial period in Sarawak politics.

PANAS, formed in April 1960, was the second party to emerge in Sarawak. Like the SUPP it started off with hopes of becoming a broad-based multi-racial party, although its chief sponsors were predominantly Malays. With the formation of SNAP and Pesaka its potential support among Ibans declined very quickly and before long the party came to be regarded primarily as Malay-based, with the First Division as its main area of operation.[29] PANAS owed much of its early following to the popularity of its highly respected leader, the Datu Bandar, and the fact that it was the first party in Sarawak which openly adopted a strongly pro-Malaysia stand.[30]

With the inauguration of BARJASA in January 1962, PANAS found its strength further reduced because it now had to compete for Malay support as well. However, unlike the SUPP, it was initially saved from growing isolation, because all the parties formed after it soon became supporters of the Malaysia plan and decided to play down their differences in the interests of furthering a common cause. An Alliance Party, roughly on the Malayan pattern, was formed with PANAS, SNAP, PESAKA, BARJASA and the SCA as equal partners. But as the 1963 district council elections approached, and decisions had to be made about the apportioning of seats among the different partners, PANAS became increasingly concerned about the perceived disadvantages of this arrangement. For one thing, given its earlier hopes of becoming a "national" party competing for power against a sole opponent, the SUPP, it now felt frustrated at having to share its ambitions with its four partners in the Alliance. But even if they were prepared to accept this fate for their party, the leaders of Panas were probably disappointed at not being accepted as the senior spokesmen of the Alliance and at not being given any special say in party affairs. Worse, they were not even regarded as the chief representatives of the Malay community, having to share this privilege with the leaders of BARJASA, some of whom were using their links with national (Malay) leaders in Kuala Lumpur to advantage.

Matters finally came to a head shortly before the opening of the election campaign, when PANAS announced its decision to leave the Alliance. In making this announcement, however, the Chairman of the party, the Datu Bandar, was careful not to antagonize the Alliance by making any references to disagreements with his colleagues. Somewhat curiously, he argued that the move was in fact aimed at strengthening the pro-Malaysia vote. "We find it vital," he observed, "to struggle against the movement of the anti-Malaysia Sarawak United People's Party in the general election. Therefore it is necessary to withdraw from the Sarawak Alliance." Saying that his party would continue to maintain close ties with the Alliance, he continued: "It (PANAS) will not depart from adopting or following the policy of the Sarawak Alliance and to render any assistance required when necessary."[31] The Alliance, understandably, failed to be mollified by this reasoning and one of its leaders made it known that there had been disagreements on matters of organization, exacerbated by clashes of personality.[32] In a firmly-worded statement, the Alliance insisted that it was not prepared to have parties with one foot in the Alliance and the other foot outside. A resolution unanimously adopted by the Alliance Council declared: "Any political party that has withdrawn from the Sarawak Alliance is considered outside the Alliance and will be treated as such."[33] There was, in other words, no question of collaboration between the Alliance and PANAS during the elections.

In the event, PANAS won 59 district council seats out of 429. Not surprisingly, it was most successful in the First Division where it in fact emerged as the strongest single party, winning sixteen of the thirty four seats in the Divisional Advisory Council while fifteen went to the SUPP and three to the Alliance. Because of the workings of the tier system[34] PANAS could have obtained all ten of the First Division seats in Council Negri had it won an absolute majority of the Advisory Council seats in that Division; but the Alliance now held the balance. Because PANAS was pro-Malaysia, one might have expected the Alliance to overlook its differences with that party and to help it (against the SUPP) to gain the ten seats in question. At the very least, the Alliance and PANAS might have worked out an acceptable compromise to exclude the SUPP which was, after all, their common enemy. But as things turned out the two parties which eventually came to an agreement were PANAS and the SUPP, which decided to share the First Division (Council Negri) seats equally.

Soon afterwards, these parties announced their decision to form a common front at the state level; in a joint statement they also claimed that the attitude of the Sarawak people towards Malaysia had not been clearly demonstrated in the election and advocated the holding of a referendum under UN auspices on the subject before Malaysia was formed.[35] This was most unexpected given PANAS's earlier stand on Malaysia, particularly when one considers the Datu Bandar's justification, quoted above, for his party's decision to leave the Alliance. The move was also surprising because PANAS could easily have obtained a larger number of Council Negri seats (for the First Division) by reaching a pact with the Alliance.[36]

How then is one to explain PANAS's behaviour? One possible answer is that this was the only way of saving face following the Alliance's refusal to respond to any of the offers of co-operation. The first rebuff immediately after the split was perhaps only natural, under the circumstances, and in any case may have been influenced by the Alliance's determination to avoid any confusion during the election. But the offer of friendship was renewed after the election, when the Datu Bandar expressed his party's willingness to form a coalition with the Alliance. He also offered to rejoin the Alliance, provided it undertook to reorganize itself as to comprise a single

Malay party, a single Dayak party and a single Chinese party.[37] In an obvious attempt to strengthen his hand he also let it be known that his party was simultaneously considering the possibility of forming a coalition with the Independents. This strategy could have worked had the Alliance won fewer seats or had there been any real doubt that the vast majority of the Independents would in fact support the Alliance rather than any other party. It would certainly have worked if there had been any real possibility that the SUPP would otherwise have come to power by default. As things were, the Alliance was well aware that it was in full control of the situation and therefore had no special cause to make concessions to PANAS. In a statement issued the day after PANAS had extended its invitation the Chairman of the Alliance, Temenggong Jugah, made it clear that his party had no intention of collaborating with PANAS and that it would instead form a coalition with the Independents.[38]

Looking back at the whole episode, it seems that PANAS, realising the inevitability of a continuing decline in its influence, decided that leaving the Alliance was a worthwhile gamble. But this gamble must have been based on the assumption that the Alliance would not do well enough in the election to be able to form a Government without its (i.e. PANAS's) support. Such a situation would give PANAS far more influence than it could ever have hoped to achieve as one of the five component units of the Alliance. Needs to say, a more immediate (but related) consideration must have been the larger number of seats which PANAS could contest, and thereby win, by contesting the election separately.

Notwithstanding the manner in which events unfolded, the subsequent getting together of PANAS and the SUPP was still something which could not have been reasonably anticipated. In an editorial entitled "Shock in Sarawak", the *Straits Times* commented:

> It would call for a very considerable effort to produce anything quite as cynical as the agreement between the Sarawak United People's Party and Party Negara to come together in an attempt to form a coalition government or, failing that, a united opposition. One Left, the other Right, the two parties have also stood on opposite sides in the single issue that matters. SUPP holds, as

> it has held, the view that Malaysia is the creature of neo-colonialists. Party Negara has believed—but apparently no longer—Malaysia to be every Sarawakian's dream come true.... On the most charitable reading, it is pique that has driven Party Negara into the SUPP's embrace.[39]

On the other hand, there were reports of even greater cynicism on the part of the Alliance: it was alleged it had also explored the possibility of collaborating with the SUPP in the First Division so as to exclude PANAS. This allegation, made by an official of PANAS, was totally denied by the Alliance,[40] although some SUPP members confirmed it during interviews.[41]

These events did not, however, place PANAS unmistakably in the opposition camp. While the intense rivalry between it and its erstwhile Alliance partners continued within the state, its position at the national level did not reflect this. In January 1964 its leader, the Datu Bandar, was sworn in as Minister without Portfolio in the Central Government, making him one of the two Cabinet Ministers from his state. This was indeed an anomalous situation. The Alliance was in power both at the national level and in Sarawak. The component units of the Sarawak Alliance were admittedly different from those of the nationally dominant Alliance Party of Malaya, and internal rivalries within the former (or even between its components and those outside it) were therefore not paralleled at the national level. But nevertheless the Sarawak Alliance was a part of the Malaysian Alliance and, if party discipline meant anything at all, one would have expected the national leadership to ostracise local recalcitrants. And yet the national leaders took the unusual step of appointing to the Cabinet a person whose party sat in the Opposition benches at the state level. This could not have strengthened the morale and local standing of the Sarawak Alliance, and could even have been construed as a repudiation of the position taken by the local leadership. The factors that may have encouraged the national leaders to act in such a manner deserve some attention.

To begin with, the attitude in Kuala Lumpur may have been that as PANAS was still a supporter of the Central Government (while continuing to have its differences with the Sarawak Alliance), there was no need to pay too much attention to local squabbles: the issues on which PANAS had parted company with the Sarawak Alliance were purely local and did not involve any disagreement on national issues—indeed, on the most important national issue, Indonesian "confrontation", PANAS was (despite its joint statement with the SUPP immediately after the district council elections) firmly on the side of the Central Government and had in fact been the first party in Sarawak to welcome the formation of Malaysia.

Secondly, personal considerations may have been an important factor. The Datu Bandar was, after all, one of the most influential persons in Sarawak: in addition to being a person of considerable eminence within the Malay community he was also widely respected by others. His personal contribution to the pro-Malaysia cause was well known, and he had not at any point allowed his local disagreements with the Sarawak Alliance to influence his support for the Central Government or, equally important, for the Tengku. No national purpose could therefore have been compromised through his appointment.

Thirdly, there was some evidence that the Central Government (and the national Alliance leaders) saw the disagreements between PANAS and the Sarawak Alliance not only as local but also as temporary, brought on by electoral considerations. Throughout this period, and for some time previously, there had been moves to merge PANAS and BARJASA so that there would be a single, much stronger, Malay/Muslim party in the state.[42] This move was seen at different times as the forerunner of a more general plan to bring about a merger of all Native parties, as part of an attempt to set up a Sarawak branch of the Malayan UMNO,[43] and as nothing more than a move to avoid competition between the only two "Malay" parties in the state.

The concurrent moves to convert PANAS and BARJASA into a Sarawak branch of UMNO, and to bring about a wider merger of all the Native parties in the state, probably contributed to some of the uncertainty during this period not only because the objectives of the parties concerned were not identical but because there was no clear indication of (and therefore widespread suspicion about) how each plan would affect the balance of power within the State Alliance. The establishment of an UMNO branch could, it is true, have paved the way for the elimination of PANAS-BARJASA rivalry and also have helped to establish a more decisive pattern of leadership sustained by national leaders. On the other hand, there was also uneasiness about which local faction (i.e. BARJASA or PANAS leaders) would inherit the new party locally and use its influence to advantage. For the other Native parties, there was also the additional fear that a united Malay party, linked directly with UMNO, the dominant unit of the national Alliance, would exert an influence well beyond its electoral strength and also be the Trojan Horse that would bring greater Central Government (and Malay) control over the affairs of the state.

Although there were intermittent announcements, from 1963, by spokesmen of PANAS, BARJASA and UMNO, about the desirability and imminence of the establishment of a Sarawak branch of the UMNO, the event never materialized. Instead, aided by new local developments, PANAS and BARJASA merged in 1967 to form a new Sarawakian party, Parti Bumiputera.

An interesting aspect of the discussions concerning the creation of a Sarawak UMNO was the absence of any co-ordinated policy. Throughout the period under consideration, both PANAS and BARJASA gave the impression of conducting their negotiations separately with the UMNO in Kuala Lumpur and did not seem to place much emphasis on 'clearing the deck' locally by ironing out their differences. It was clear that mutual antagonism continued[44] and the proposal to dissolve and become reconstituted as a part of the UMNO seemed to be viewed by each party more as an opportunity for pleasing the UMNO, and thus for obtaining some local advantage,[45] than as a suitable way of expressing their common identity. In fact, it is entirely possible that the main initiative on this issue came not from Sarawak but from Kuala Lumpur. The formation of a Sarawak branch of the UMNO would have strengthened the political standing of the parent body and thereby enhanced its status as the premier political party in the country. Further, it is quite likely that, as rivalry between PANAS and BARJASA became intensified, UMNO grew concerned about bringing the two parties together not only to strengthen the Sarawak Alliance but also to promote Malay unity in the state.[46]

But what continued to be baffling was the tendency for PANAS not to view its proposed incorporation into UMNO as a move which would automatically affect its status in Sarawak. For example, in commenting on the matter in January 1964, the Datu Bandar had no doubt in his mind that as a segment of the UMNO his party would automatically become a part of the ruling Alliance Party at the national level; but this, according to him, meant that PANAS would only "most probably" join the ruling Sarawak Alliance and sit on the Government benches in the Council Negri. In other words, it was conceivable to him that his party would become a part of the national Alliance without becoming a part of the state Alliance, and sit on the Government benches (along with the members of the Sarawak Alliance) in Kuala Lumpur while sitting with the Opposition in Kuching.

It is a common view in Sarawak political circles that rivalries which originated over the cession issue immediately after World War II were responsible for the refusal of one section of the Malay community to join PANAS under the Datu Bandar's leadership and for their decision to band together under a separate political party, BARJASA. The Datu Bandar and other Malay leaders of PANAS had been strong supporters of the transfer of power from the Brookes to the British Government, while many BARJASA figures had been associated with anti-cession activities. Pro- and anti-cession feelings had caused a deep cleavage within the Malay community at the time (particularly among the elites) and the personal rivalries which then emerged have in many ways persisted to the present day.[47]

Although it is difficult to deny the relevance of the cession issue in discussing PANAS-BARJASA rivalry, it is worth noting that this was not used explicitly during the formation of BARJASA: many persons who joined that party had, however, earlier been active in Barisan Pemuda (Youth Front), a group which, in addition to fostering Malay nationalism,[48] also contained a core of anti-cessionists. There are, however, other factors which account for the differences between PANAS and BARJASA.

As will be explained later, communications were quite poor in Sarawak during the early years of party activity. Not only were different parts of the state physically isolated from each other, but there was also a relative absence of interest groups and professional classes with state-wide links which could have been utilized, if not for direct political organization, then at least to facilitate broader and better co-ordinated activities arising from interlocking social and personal ties. There was also no nationalist movement of any consequence which had brought politically relevant groups from different areas into meaningful contact and the net result was that the new political organizations which sprang up in different parts of the state initially remained compartmentalised. Even inter-communal links, let alone inter-communal activities, were poorly developed with little organized promotion of Iban, Malay and other interests on a state-wide scale. In other words, there was no stratum of elites, distributed throughout the state, with a history of common participation or with similar concerns and potential political efficacy, who could be tapped at short notice for organized political activity. In the light of these circumstances, other factors which encouraged the formation of BARJASA may now be briefly explored.

To begin with, PANAS's activities were by and large concentrated in the First Division, where most of its leaders came from, and where the majority of Malays were settled. This left the rival Malay faction in the First Division, other Malays in the remaining Divisions and the Melanaus (the vast majority of whom lived on the coastal areas of the Third Division and many of whom were Muslims) without an obvious political party to which they could belong. The Malays outside the First Division were not a cohesive group, and were not easy to cater for because of their wide geographic distribution; they therefore did not merit special attention. The first and the third groups mentioned above were therefore the ones which most easily lent themselves to political organization and BARJASA's leadership as well as support came primarily from these groups. The "dissident Malay" image of BARJASA was confirmed by the active participation of persons from the First Division who were known to be unwilling to make common political cause with the Datu Bandar; the "Melanau image", on the other hand, was strengthened by the prominence of two leading Melanaus, Rahman Ya'akub and Taib bin Mahmud, and by the party's initial strength in the coastal areas of the Third Division. These, however, were not distinct identities for very long because both Rahman Ya'akub and Taib were in fact Muslim Melanaus who increasingly identified themselves with the Malay community and because these leaders and the "dissident Malays" from the First Division had overlapping antipathies towards the leadership of PANAS. BARJASA leaders must have realized that an essentially Melanau identity would have seriously affected their party's potential influence; to be a serious contender in the political arena BARJASA also had to become an effective spokesman of the Malay community and this must have further encouraged Rahman Ya'akub and Taib to identify themselves as "Malay" leaders.[49]

By becoming recognized as a primarily Malay party, BARJASA could claim to represent a broader political base; equally important, this could give it easier access to and favoured treatment from the nationally dominant political elites in Kuala Lumpur, which in turn would give it greater leverage as a component unit of the Sarawak Alliance. PANAS's initial attempts to become a dominant multi-racial (although Malay-led) party helped to throw BARJASA's "Malay" identity into sharper focus, the presence of some non-Malays within its ranks notwithstanding.[50]

As long as PANAS remained within the Alliance, however, BARJASA could not stake a claim as the foremost representative of the Malay community in the Government. For this reason, the former's decision to leave the Alliance was indeed a godsend, and provided fresh opportunities not only to appeal for greater Malay support within Sarawak but also to forge special links with the national leaders in Kuala Lumpur. Thus, by the time PANAS returned to the Alliance, BARJASA had gained a firm foothold in the Sarawak Cabinet and established its credentials in the federal capital. When PANAS returned to the Alliance some of the old intra-Malay rivalries were also resumed, but because of BARJASA's improved position (and perhaps also because of the Datu Bandar's death in the meantime) PANAS was less able to compete effectively: it was less united and before long even began to lose some of its members to BARJASA.[51] However, as already mentioned, these rivalries were partially terminated when the two parties merged in 1967 to form Parti Bumiputera.

Because of its weakened discipline and the inability of its leaders to agree on major issues,[52] PANAS was already in some disarray by the time of its merger with BARJASA. The formation of the new party, Bumiputera, was therefore seen as a victory for BARJASA leaders and certainly helped to consolidate their position in the state. Dato Abang Othman, who had replaced his brother, the Datu Bandar, as the leader of PANAS, and his close associates were known to have lost their control of the party's Executive Committee, although the degree of public support enjoyed by them remained an open question. Immediately before the merger Dato Abang Othman left PANAS to join SNAP, and with him out of the way BARJASA leaders did not have much difficulty controlling the new party. Although great care was taken to divide positions in the Central Executive Committee of Bumiputera almost equally between ex-members of BARJASA and PANAS, the important thing was that most of the ex-PANAS members had already come under the influence of BARJASA leaders prior to the merger[53] and were therefore unlikely to pose any threat to people like Rahman Ya'akub and Taib. It is, however, significant that Bumiputera found it necessary to select not only its Executive Committee members but also its candidates in such a way as to give the impression of equality between ex-PANAS and ex-Bumiputera members: even if the leaders of the ex-PANAS group were willing to ignore old divisions, they had no guarantee at least until the first direct elections were completed in 1970, that their supporters (who had been told that the two parties were merging as equals) would not defect to another party if the impression had been given that they had surrendered to BARJASA.

From its inception Bumiputera has conducted a relentless two-pronged campaign aimed at unifying the Malay/Muslim community under its leadership and at establishing itself as the senior partner in the Sarawak Alliance. The first of these objectives was an important factor in bringing about a merger of its two antecedent bodies but the fact that no other Malay/Muslim-oriented party existed in the state did not mean that the battle was automatically won. As already pointed out, some of PANAS's leaders, including Dato Abang Othman, had joined SNAP, thereby giving that party some appeal among Malays; also in SNAP was Ainnie bin Dhoby, a young, energetic Malay leader who had previously been in BARJASA but had left it following disagreement with its leaders.[54]

Following Pesaka's decision in 1966 to admit Malays some prominent Malays had also joined that party and this meant that by the time Bumiputera was formally launched, although there was no organized Malay/Muslim rival there were enough Malay leaders in some of the other parties[55] to cause concern. These leaders were admittedly not strong enough in their parties to make either SNAP or Pesaka acceptable as spokesmen of the Malay community, but some of them had a sufficient personal following to deny, Bumiputera did have great success in establishing itself as the unquestioned leader of the Malay community, although in the process it alienated its chief partner in the Alliance, Pesaka, and ran the risk of losing any support it may have had among the non-Malay indigenous communities in certain crucial constituencies where because of the ethnic distribution of the electorate, it needed their votes in order to win.[57] Bumiputera's leaders were obviously of the opinion that these votes were in any event likely to be difficult to get, and must have decided that the advantages of a more explicitly Malay/Muslim orientation (i.e. of making Malay/Muslim support more certain) would more than offset the disadvantages of alienating the other indigenous communities. Some of the other calculations that may have gone into this decision are discussed later in this chapter, but two illustrations of Bumiputera's attitude may be helpful here.

In October 1968, during the initial stages of the intra-Alliance negotiations for seats in the elections scheduled for the following year. Bumiputera decided that it would be advantageous to enhance its own unity in order to prepare its rank-and-file for the difficulties that appeared to lie ahead. The reasons for this were quite understandable, and may well have included the apparent intransigence of Pesaka. What was significant, however, was that unlike Pesaka, Bumiputera showed a willingness to pull out all the stops at this early stage, thereby risking the chances of possible agreement with Pesaka[58] and endangering some of its own stated goals of inter-co-operation among the indigenous communities. In a circular from its Secretary-General to all local divisions it outlined in fairly blunt terms the conflict which existed within the Alliance as a result of the unwillingness of Pesaka and the SCA to concede that all seats in Malay, Melanau and Bidayuh (Land Dayak) areas should be given to Bumiputera candidates.

Although the SCA was included in the criticism, the attack was concentrated on Pesaka which, as a Native party, claimed to represent the Malays and Malanaus as well. Not surprisingly, it was this particular claim which most provoked Bumiputera. In this regard, the circular pointed out that Pesaka's refusal to give Bumiputera a clear run in the Malay seats was not only because of its exaggerated estimation of its own following, but because "there are one or two Malays in Pesaka who do not dare to stand (for elections) outside a Malay area. These are the people who caused trouble and wish to grab Parti Bumiputera seats in Malay areas".

The other important message in the circular was the call for communal solidarity. Saying that the party's objective was "to unite the Malays and the Bidayuhs", the circular pointed out that every effort would be made to oppose those who were attempting to "split our race". Referring specifically to Malay leaders in Pesaka, the circular warned: "at the time when we were uniting our race and struggle for our community, these people were never seen in the rural areas. But now that they *want seats*, they are coming to deliver sweet words and expressions. Remember, such characteristics are unbecoming of honest leadership, and if we submit to their pleas and promises, our race will be disintegrated and with ease these people will conduct their opportunistic politics." Promising that the party would "carry on the struggle to unite our race", the circular concluded by saying: "let us struggle for the unity of our race —Beware of those who will outplay us in their greed for seats".[59]

The circular was, admittedly, meant for internal party consumption and the leaders were somewhat taken aback when SNAP, which had obtained a copy, released it to the press, demanding that if the Alliance seriously believed in multi-racial objectives it should sack Taib from the Central Government and expel Bumiputera as a component unit. Earlier assertions of Alliance unity now became uncommonly difficult to sustain, and Pesaka, which felt most outraged, issued a statement in the name of the Alliance which insisted: "We would like to stress that the Bumiputera circular only reflects Inche Taib's own policy and not [that] of the Alliance. There is no political (and racial) upheaval, between the racial groups within the Sarawak Alliance as SNAP imagines."[60] But this episode clearly reflected, and contributed to, the rapid erosion of goodwill between Bumiputera and Pesaka, which culminated in their decision to field candidates against each other in the 1969/70 election. In commenting on Bumiputera's action in distributing the circular, one newspaper observed: "Though politics is dirty, yet being a component of the Alliance, Parti Bumiputera should adhere to its aims by working on a multi-racial policy. It should never become the promoter of dirty politics."[61]

The other example of Bumiputera's "Malay" posture was the announcement by Dato Rahman Ya'akub, at the height of the 1969 campaign, that his party would become a part of UMNO some time after the election.[62] This announcement, apparently made without any prior consultation with Bumiputera's partners in the Alliance[63], considerably annoyed Pesaka (and, to a lesser extent, the SCA) because it was seen as a major breach of Alliance discipline: if Bumiputera wanted to link up with the UMNO, this was bound to have repercussions within the Sarawak Alliance and Pesaka for one, as an indigenous party also claiming Malay support, may have wanted a say in the matter. The main objection, however, was not related to Bumiputera's failure to observe the normal courtesies, but was brought about instead by uncertainty about the likely political consequences. Pesaka's leaders were quite convinced that this was a move to strengthen and unify Bumiputera's support; although, as an Iban-based party, they may not have been unduly disturbed by this,[64] they were nevertheless afraid that the Alliance as a whole (and their own party in particular) would suffer if the Ibans (encouraged by SNAP) interpreted the move as a precursor of increased federal (and Malay) control. If Bumiputera were indeed to become a part of the UMNO, it was bound to have added leverage as a result of its federal connections; in any event Pesaka, as a member of a reconstituted Sarawak Alliance which included the dominant national party from West Malaysia, was not going to find it easy to explain to the Ibans that it was in fact a party which placed the highest priority on Iban and Sarawakian interests.

There were, however, also some mitigating factors which Pesaka was quick to recognize. It was believed, for example, that even if Rahman Ya'akub's proposal were to succeed in producing more solid Malay support for Bumiputera,[65] a natural corollary would be the alienation of any non-Malay/Muslim support which that party might have had, which in turn would benefit Pesaka in those constituencies where the two parties faced each other. Some Malay seats may have been lost in the process, but there was likely to be more than adequate compensation in the non-Malay majority seats. Even greater consolation was found in the fact that the proposal helped to vindicate Pesaka's decision to contest the election under its own symbol and to field candidates against Bumiputera. Had the Alliance been united at the time, the embarrassment would have been considerable for Pesaka; but it was well known that the party regarded Bumiputera as one of its "enemies" and it now felt less restrained in drumming up Iban support by using explicitly anti-Bumiputera, pro-Iban arguments.

Of all the parties in Sarawak, Bumiputera is the only one that has not come into serious conflict with the Central Government. Although the party has always been mindful of its local identity and the need to fit into the Sarawakian political milieu, its informal links with the UMNO, the participation of two of its leaders in the Federal Government and the belief that federal support would provide some form of insurance in the event of any local crisis, have all encouraged Bumiputera to incorporate federal priorities into its own policies and to be unafraid of the threat of local isolation. As already pointed out, the party was able to achieve greater internal unity (and communal solidarity) than any of its rivals, and this no doubt gave it an advantage during the first direct election concluded in 1970. Dato Rahman Ya'akub was also the only person from Sarawak to have achieved any national prominence,[66] and local Malays must have taken pride in his achievements and in his close association with national leaders like the Tengku and Tun Razak.[67] The other parties may sometimes have found this distasteful, but there was no denying his contribution to the political unification of the Sarawak Malay / Muslim community.

Although, like Pesaka, Bumiputera did not have the kind of financial support[68] or elaborate organization that SNAP seemed to thrive on, it was believed to have one advantage over these parties. Most of the adult education officers in the state, whose appointments came under the Central Government's Rural Development vote[69] were apparently Bumiputera supporters who had been nominated for appointments by their leaders. This enabled the party informally to "employ" a number of field officers who were well placed in their respective areas, without having to pay for them because they were receiving salaries as Adult Education Officers.

SNAP and Pesaka

The Sarawak National Party (SNAP) was formed in March 1961. Its leader, Stephen Kalong Ningkan, had earlier been a medical dresser in the Seria Oil field in Brunei, but had apparently followed events in Sarawak with considerable interest before returning to form his party. From its inception SNAP has been a multi-racial party and it is occasionally maintained by some of its leaders that the decision to form it was the result of their conviction that the SUPP and PANAS, while claiming to represent all the communities in Sarawak, were actually not sufficiently multi-racial either in their composition or outlook. Although this may not be entirely untrue, the point needs to be made that SNAP dissatisfaction with the multi-racialism of these two parties was focused on the fact that they did not give due weight to the Iban community. Thus, while the SUPP and PANAS were dominated by the Chinese and Malays respectively, SNAP sought to establish itself as a multi-racial party dominated by the Ibans, believing that this was necessary to prevent the Iban community from being submerged under the existing brands of multi-racialism.[70] As in the case of its predecessors, SNAP's commitment to multi-racialism was therefore also modified by a distinct communal bias. If this was a logical defensive move, there was also a positive commitment to Iban interests in the minds of people like Ningkan, and a firm belief that the Ibans should not be left behind in the scramble for political power.

SNAP's original area of operation was the Second Division, from where Ningkan himself came, although support for it was also expressed by some aspiring politicians in the Third Division. The facts of political life in Sarawak were certainly favourable to the party, because multi-racialism with an Iban base was more likely to be rewarding, electorally, than multi-racialism with either a Chinese or a Malay base. However, two important developments adversely affected the realization of this advantage. First, the Malaysian proposal, made only two months after the inauguration of SNAP, dominated the local political scene during this formative period in Sarawak politics and encouraged the existing parties (and those formed soon afterwards) to concentrate on strategies and alliances aimed at supporting or opposing the scheme. This affected not only the rivalries that may otherwise have emerged among these parties, but also the distinct local image which each of them may have wanted to project for future electoral purposes. A triangular contest involving the SUPP, PANAS and SNAP, all multi-racial but each with a different communal bias, did not materialize, because during the following year three other parties were formed appealing explicitly to different communal groups.[71]

Of these, the party which most seriously affected SNAP's own future was Party Pesaka, a staunchly Iban-based party which concentrated its efforts in the Third Division.[72] The advantage of having only one party to represent all Ibans must have been well known to the founders of Pesaka, but it was quite evident that the leaders of the Iban community in the Third Division (regarded by them as the Iban heartland) were not prepared to accept Second Division leadership. SNAP leaders, for their part, may have been afraid that the more numerous Third Division Ibans, if brought into their party *en masse*, might wrest the leadership from them and hand the party over to the more traditional leaders from the Third

Division. It was, however, commonly recognized that Iban strength should not be split and the two parties therefore agreed not to spread into each other's territory. Reminiscent of the agreement made in earlier days between the Anglican and Methodist missions in Sarawak, this meant that SNAP would confine its activities to the Second Division and Pesaka to the Third.

Needless to say, this innocent belief in the workability of a mutually beneficial gentlemen's agreement did not last very long. With the creation of Malaysia, one important incentive for unity not only between Pesaka and SNAP but within the Alliance generally, ceased to exist; further, the rivalries which soon emerged among these parties because of the struggle for positions in the Government (and, equally important, because of the uncertainty created by the overlapping claims which some of them made about the support which they enjoyed) led to dissatisfaction over the appropriateness of the existing arrangements and encouraged the view that outright competition might be the only acceptable way of resolving ambiguities. In SNAP's particular case, a clear (and early) solution was found for the compromise—conflict dilemma when the Ningkan crisis of 1966[73] gave the party no alternative but to leave the Alliance and join the ranks of the Opposition. This deprived it of some of the advantages which it had earlier enjoyed as the dominant unit in the state Government, but it also released it from its previous obligations and enabled it to expand its organization and activities without inhibitions. An immediate consequence was that the party took an independent, and somewhat uncompromising, stand on certain key issues, notably the need to safeguard state autonomy against encroachments from the national Alliance Government.

Another important result was that SNAP soon dedicated itself openly to undermining Pesaka's credentials as a worthwhile spokesman of the Iban community, and conducted an extensive campaign to recruit members and establish branches in the Third Division. On the multi-racial front, a new drive was made to establish the party as a major contender for Chinese support and this was helped by the fact that an earlier behind-the-scenes financier, Dato Wee Hood Teck, had by this time become openly identified with the party by becoming the Chairman of its Kuching branch.

In addition to the commitment to multi-racialism and to the need to broaden the base of electoral support, the fresh overtures to the Chinese community must also have been influenced by the knowledge that adequate finances (especially as the party was no longer in office) could not be obtained without increased support from the Chinese community. The Deputy President, Dato James Wong, himself a Chinese millionaire, was clearly not in a position to finance the party single-handedly through an indeterminate period in the opposition, especially since this was also expected to be the period of greatest activity.[74]

As far as the wealthy Chinese were concerned, the decision to give financial support to SNAP must have been influenced either by the favours which they had received when the party was in office or by expectations of future favours in the event of SNAP's return to power. As far as the Chinese electorate was concerned, however, it was clear that the SUPP was the preferred party. But SNAP was often regarded as a good second choice and this enabled it to win Chinese votes in constituencies where the SUPP was not a contender. To many, an Iban-dominated but multi-racial party like SNAP was obviously a better choice than an exclusively Chinese party like the SCA which was likely to be dominated by its more powerful partners in the Alliance. To this extent, a number of Chinese appeared to have been of the opinion that they could exert greater influence within SNAP than, through the SCA, within the Alliance. The Sarawak Alliance's commitments to the national Alliance and to the Central Government, which indicated a transplantation of Malaya-based communal bargains, must have been important in discouraging support for the SCA.

Under other circumstances, this appeal to the Chinese might have offended Iban feelings and led to serious problems in retaining, let alone increasing, Iban support. But SNAP was in fact able concurrently to rejuvenate Iban support, largely by playing upon fears of Central Government (and hence Malay) domination. It also appeared to have been successful in convincing its Iban supporters that the overtures to the Chinese were necessary to strengthen the Sarawakian movement which it spearheaded, and that there was no risk that it would cease to be an Iban-dominated party.

Especially after its ejection from office, a noteworthy feature of SNAP was its elaborate organizational structure supported, as already indicated, by substantial financial contributions from key individuals. Until the suspension of the election in 1969, the important thing about this organization was that it was a continually functioning one.

As in the case of the other parties, SNAP's organization is headed by a Central Executive Committee. This Committee, however, has been too unwieldy to function as an effective unit and most decisions have tended to be made by an inner caucus of five or six persons headed by Ningkan.[75] Branch Committees constitute the bottom rung of the administrative hierarchy, but the main burden of grass-roots activity has fallen not on them but on paid "field officers" whose numbers have varied from time to time depending on need and on the availability of funds.[76] Although most field officers have been directly employed and paid by the party from funds donated by wealthy backers, some individuals with their own resources (notably Dato James Wong, the Deputy President) have tended to appoint their own field officers and to pay for them out of their own pockets.

As the party's main task force on the ground field officers have been responsible for making regular estimates of support in different areas, for submitting reports on opposition activity and for alerting the party about local grievances and impending defections. They have also been responsible for communicating information about the party and its activities to the electorate. Every time the party's leaders make an important statement, it is immediately translated into other languages (but usually only Iban and/or Malay) and sent to the field officers who are expected to convey the information to the electorate within a week. Field officers also constitute the vast majority of party workers who are paid for their services, the other category being the small number of full-time secretarial and administrative staff in the headquarters and in some of the branches. In some cases the appointment has been used as a device to provide compensation for loss of salary or

DORSET INSTITUTE OF
HIGHER EDUCATION
LEARNING RESOURCES
CENTRE

previous employment as a result of commitment to the party,[77] or to attract persons of calibre and good local standing as full-time party workers; in other cases, however, the appointment has only been for part-time work and payment has taken the form of small allowances. Thus the salaries paid to field officers has varied considerably—from $30 per month, the sum given to certain low-level part-timers, to $2,000, the salary paid to Ningkan, Othman and Endawie. The distribution of SNAP's paid staff and field officers just prior to Dato Wee's resignation in 1968, is given below, by Division, ethnic group and salary range.

The ethnic distribution leaves no doubt about SNAP's orientation, although the relatively small number of Malays and Chinese may partly have been the result of Malay and, more particularly, Chinese, areas being more accessible and densely populated and therefore requiring less decentralization of party activity. Further, it has to be borne in mind that party work as a supplementary source of livelihood is more important among the Ibans (who are generally less well-off in terms of cash) than among the Chinese and Malays.

Thirty-six of the forty-eight Malays in the table were placed in separate "Malay sections". Considering the Party's multi-racial outlook and otherwise non-communal organization,[78] this probably indicates a tendency to regard the Malays, of all the communities, as falling outside the main stream of party activity. At the same time, although SNAP differed from the other parties (except SUPP) in being relatively multi-racial in its appeal, and in the size and cost of its field operations, the existence of Malay and Chinese field officers demonstrated what was also true for all parties, although maybe to a lesser degree: patron-client relationships within parties did not follow purely ethnic lines.[79]

In addition to its field officers, SNAP also had a small number of part-time "inspectors"[80] whose identity was kept secret from field officers and other rank-and-file party members. These inspectors were expected to check on the credentials of those wishing to become field officers and to keep a watch on their activities once they were selected: should they feel that a field officer was not diligent in his work, or if there were any suspicion that he might be an undercover agent for a rival

TABLE 3.3

SNAP Staff and Field Offices, Monthly Payments

Salary range $ / Race	1st Division			2nd Division			3rd Division			4th Division			5th Division*			Total
	I	M	C	I	M	C	I	M	C	I	M	C	I	M	C	
0–99	5	1	—	36	3	—	34	1	—	17	—	—	—	—	—	97
100–199	22	18	10	54	11	—	72	6	7	22	1	—	1	—	—	224
200–299	4	1	3	3	—	—	4	—	3	2	—	—	—	—	—	20
300–399	4	2	—	1	—	—	—	2	—	—	—	1	—	—	—	10
400–499	1	—	—	—	—	—	—	—	—	—	—	—	—	—	—	1
500–599	2	—	—	—	—	—	—	—	—	—	—	—	—	—	—	2
600–699	1	—	—	—	—	—	—	—	—	—	—	—	—	—	—	1
2,000	1	1	—	1	—	—	—	—	—	—	—	—	—	—	—	3
Total	39	23	13	96	14	0	100	9	10	41	1	1	1	0	0	358

I = Ibans and other non-Malay/non-Muslim indigenous groups. The vast majority in this category were in fact Ibans.
M = Malays
C = Chinese
* It is possible that field officers in the Fifth Division were paid not by the "party" but by Dato James Wong personally. This may explain why only one paid officer from that Division was officially listed.

party, they were supposed to report this immediately to higher authorities.

SNAP leaders often claim that, while their party's main Iban rival, Pesaka, attempts to increase its strength by winning over traditional leaders (right down to the *Penghulu* and *Tuai Rumah* level) they build their own strength by opening branches and by promoting a new, more directly political, elite. These leaders argue that party branches provide more scope for participation by younger Ibans, who are without the same respect for the traditional hierarchy that their parents had. SNAP considers its advantage to derive not only from the fact that its non-traditional activists are better suited to the rough and tumble of competitive politics than conservative traditional leaders, but from the fact that since most of them are young they also have a better capacity for vigorous campaigning because this involves a great deal of travelling in remote areas and is physically exhausting.[81] Equally important, in the eyes of SNAP leaders, was the fact that their party paid its workers regularly, while Pesaka (and the other parties) did not—at least not on any similar scale: people who were paid to do a job did it better, provided there was proper supervision, than those who vaguely promised their support and influence. Another reason often given for not relying heavily on traditional leaders was that they were generally disinclined to oppose the Government, something which SNAP had to take into consideration once it was pushed out of office.

In the light of these claims, it is surprising that of the 358 paid workers referred to above there were twenty-four *Penghulus* and forty-five *Tuai Rumahs*. One possible explanation is that although SNAP was intent on building up its strength outside the traditional structure it did not want to exclude traditional elites from the party community because there was nothing to be gained from such a move. In other words, the party and the traditional hierarchy may not have been seen as rival structures and it was probably not believed that the extra-traditional orientation of the former would be undermined in any way by recruiting amenable members of the latter for party work. In any event, it would have been self-defeating to believe that *Penghulus* and *Tuai Rumahs* could be ignored altogether, and if the party could compete with

Pesaka for their support while pursuing its other strategies, so much the better. What was also important was that Pesaka, not having an army of paid workers, had to rely more exclusively on existing elites whose sympathy and support could be obtained without regular payment and who may have felt a closer affinity to the party because its leaders included two *Temenggongs.*[82]

Those parties, like SNAP, which had been formed before the Tengku made his Malaysia proposal in May 1961 had hardly had time to formulate their long-term policies and strategies before it was realized that they did not have to take a stand on the issue of independence from the British. One aspect of "independence", however, remained to be resolved and has continued to command the attention of political parties in East Malaysia. This concerned the relationship between the East Malaysian states and the Central Government. Originally this found expression in the disinclination of many of the parties (including SNAP) to join Malaysia, although all but the hard core of the SUPP eventually abandoned their opposition. However, the issue has remained alive in the sense that there are still some misgivings in the two states about the nature and extent of state autonomy and the legitimate boundaries of federal control. SNAP's position on this controversy explains much of its popularity.[83]

Ningkan's brushes with the Central Government, and the resultant crises of 1965 and 1966, are discussed in Chapter 5. What is worth noting here is that many of his disagreements with the Central Government arose as a result of his unwillingness to permit any erosion of state autonomy, although his personal style and internal rivalries within the Alliance were important factors. However, there is no denying that when he cautioned the Central Government not to overlook the State Government's constitutional rights on matters like language, education and Borneanization, he was making a favourable impression locally (among the non-Muslim Natives as well as among the Chinese) and a most unfavourable impression in Kuala Lumpur. Whatever the merits of his case the point remains that when he was finally expelled from the Chief Ministership, he had no difficulty in persuading a large section of the Iban community that he had been victimized for wanting to protect the interests of the state and for wanting to prevent the political and cultural submission of the other indigenous communities by the Malays. Among the Chinese, Ningkan's image was boosted not only by his multi-racialism, but also by his attempts to stem federal (which to them meant Malay) control and by his stand on the Land Bills.[84]

During the period leading up to the 1969 election, SNAP relied heavily on its slogan: "Sarawak for Sarawakians". This slogan was clearly meant to highlight state identity and to raise the spectre of federal control in the event of an Alliance victory. Needless to say, it was also possible to give the slogan a secessionist interpretation, although allegations to this effect were always officially refuted: Ningkan for one was consistently careful in all his public statements to deny any secessionist intentions, although many of his detractors were of the opinion during the 1969 election campaign that both he and his party made no serious efforts to be unequivocal at the grass-roots level. Secession, it was felt, was in fact an attractive proposition for many Ibans and SNAP was believed to be cashing in on this without explicitly committing itself to the cause. The slogan could not officially have been forbidden as subversive, not only because there were insufficient legal grounds[85] but because such a move would almost certainly have been politically damaging to the Alliance: SNAP could then have told the electorate that the ruling party did not want Sarawak for the Sarawakians but for someone else. To some Malays the slogan was also communal because to them it was only an indirect way of saying "Sarawak for the Ibans"; Ibans were the politically dominant community and anti-central government slogans, it was felt, were either actually or potentially a cover for anti-Malay sentiments. The Chinese apparently appreciated this slogan because they were themselves fearful of Central Government control which would lessen their economic hold, and, in the case of Communist sympathizers, their scope for political subversion in Sarawak.

Although the initial surge of support for SNAP after the cabinet crisis of 1966 was highly Ningkan-centred, it was believed that by the time of the 1969 election the party, rather than Ningkan, had become the symbol of state identity. The view was also widely held that the leaders of the party were not unanimously of the opinion that Ningkan was the best leader available or that he should automatically become the Chief Minister in the event of a SNAP victory. Such disagreements as existed, however (apparently stemming from misgivings about Ningkan's personal style), were not brought into the open because Ningkan was still a valuable property in many areas and any major internal split could have damaged the party's image as a staunch, steadfast and united spokesman of Sarawakian interests. The only threat in this regard occurred in 1969 when Charles Ingka, the party's paid Executive Secretary and an important figure, openly challenged Ningkan's authority at a meeting of the Executive Committee held for the purpose of selecting candidates. In view of the impending election this was undoubtedly a crucial period for the party, and, although the disagreement was initially believed only to be over the selection of candidates, it soon became clear that Ingka had more general objectives in mind, like the removal of Ningkan as the party leader.

Ingka's own view was that Ningkan was not a fit person to lead the party at the election, not only because of his high-handedness and his unwillingness to place the party's interests before his own, but because he had become so unpopular that SNAP's chances at the election would suffer if he continued to be its head. Ingka took great pains during the controversy to make it clear that his loyalty lay with the party and that it was concern for its future that had motivated him to raise the issue. The other members of the Executive Committee, however, decided to back Ningkan: there was some evidence that not all of them approved of his leadership, but this was not the time for the party to switch horses. Ingka was expelled from the Executive Committee, and subsequently contested the election as an Independent candidate in Ningkan's constituency.[86] Rumour was rife throughout this period that he had been bought over by the Alliance to wreck SNAP from within; failing that, he was apparently expected to do his best to defeat Ningkan at the polls, so that even if his party won he would not become Chief Minister and there would be a better chance of its being persuaded to return to the Alliance.

No doubt remembering the events of 1966, and confident that even if they did not get a majority of seats no other party would, Ningkan and his associates soon took steps to prevent defections by successful candidates after the election, to ensure that their party would not lose its bargaining position during negotiations that might take place for the formation of a coalition government. Every candidate was required to sign two statements, one addressed to the Chairman of the party and the other to the Speaker of Council Negri, saying that he would automatically resign his seat if he were to leave his party. Although the leaders were aware that these statements might not be legally binding, they nevertheless felt that every effort should be made to keep the party (particularly its successful candidates) together after the election. A great deal of money and effort had gone into their bid to return to power, and they were not prepared to see the fruits of their labours go to others. They were only too aware that in a tight situation the Alliance would try to win over some of their assemblymen, and did not have sufficient confidence that these assemblymen would be immune to well-judged overtures. These fears, and the accompanying precautions, were all the more significant as indicators of the essentially opportunistic character of Sarawak politics, because SNAP, next to the SUPP, was believed to be the best organized and disciplined party in the state, fighting for an important cause.

Party Pesaka was formed in June 1962 and, as already mentioned, established its base in the Third Division. Among its prime movers were Jonathan Banggau and Penghulu Francis Umpau,[87] who had previously been in the SUPP and PANAS, respectively, but who had rapidly become disappointed by the reluctance of these parties to give due regard to Iban political strength. They did not consider SNAP an appropriate vehicle for realizing Iban aspirations, and were also disinclined to regard that party as capable of mobilizing and representing the more traditional Ibans in the Third Division. They soon obtained the support of the two persons who constituted the apex of the Iban and Kenyah traditional hierarchy, respectively, namely Temenggong Jugah and Temenggong Oyong Lawi Jau, who were both then in PANAS but who, like Umpau, had become disillusioned with that party because of its failure to give proper recognition to non-Muslim Native interests.[88] The two *Temenggongs*, especially Jugah, immediately used their weight by calling upon the *Penghulus* in the Third Division to follow them into the party and to join them in establishing their people as a major force in Sarawak politics. Jugah was elected as the party's President at its first meeting and Temenggong Oyong Lawi Jau was made one of the Vice-Presidents. There was, as expected, pronounced support from *Penghulus* in the Third Division, many of whom were appointed as Committee members, especially during the initial period. Among the office-holders, however, were also some established Iban businessmen and budding entrepreneurs, who subsequently helped to build the party's organization.

During the first four years of its life Pesaka confined its membership to the non-Malay indigenous communities in Sarawak. Although this still left the party with a wide variety of groups to represent, the exclusion of Malays and Chinese meant that the Ibans were in full control. The calculation, quite rightly, may have been that as the minor indigenous communities could not hope to form viable political parties of their own, they would prefer to align themselves with the Ibans, not only because they were the largest indigenous group but because many of these minor ethnic groups were also not Muslim and therefore were automatically inclined to seek Iban rather than Malay leadership.

The decision to exclude Chinese is also easily understandable. Multi-racialism, although a worthwhile objective for any Government of Sarawak, was not, for Pesaka, appropriate at the party level, because it could undermine the ability of the Ibans to assert themselves politically. The Chinese could, if they joined the party in sufficient numbers, modify its perspectives as an indigenous party and encourage it to adopt policies that may be inimical to the preservation of the rights and cultures of the indigenous communities.[89] This, it was believed, would be SNAP's ultimate fate.[90] There were also some historical grounds for antipathy towards the Chinese, arising from the hostilities which had emerged in earlier times outside Sibu in the Third Division following the influx of large numbers of Chinese into the area.[91]

In 1966, following the breakdown of its talks with BARJASA to form a single Native party, Pesaka altered its rules to admit Malays while continuing to exclude Chinese.

With this move Pesaka came to include all the indigenous communities within its fold, although there was no suggestion that Iban dominance would in any way be jeopardized. But the party continued to be easily distinguishable from SNAP, not only because of its more traditional outlook and its tendency to regard the Third Division as the centre of its operations, but by virtue of the fact that while SNAP was a *multi-racial* party with an Iban base, Pesaka was a *Native* party with an Iban base. Bumiputera, on the other hand, was a Native party with a Malay / Muslim base.

There were two important reasons behind the decision to admit Malays. First, Pesaka was becoming concerned that while its main rivals were all expanding into its territory and doing their best to steal its members, it was not able to retaliate by carrying the battle into its opponents' camps. The SNAP threat was being met partially by improving party organization and by setting up branches in other parts of the state while retaining the original Third Division base. But this was primarily intra-Iban competition and, if anything, only highlighted the contrast between Malay unity[92] and Iban disunity. Looking forward to the time when seats would have to be apportioned among the Alliance partners for the first direct election, Pesaka probably envisaged a situation where its bargaining position would be weakened if, for example, the new party that was expected to be formed as a result of a merger of BARJASA and PANAS were to insist on putting up a few Iban candidates in certain Iban-majority areas without its (i.e. Pesaka's) being able to respond by threatening to put up its own Malay candidates in Malay areas.

The second, but related, motive for admitting Malays seems to have been the desire to weaken the Malays by splitting them. As pointed out, Malay unity has always been viewed as a threat to Iban interests and it was felt that if Malays (particularly a few prominent ones) could be wooed into the party the Malay community might be incapable of such domination.[93] Thus the Pesaka view was that if the Malays saw their attempts at domination as something which involved a big risk (because the price of failure could be total exclusion from the Government and possibly also unfavourable treatment from an Iban-dominated Government), at least some of them would prefer not to take that risk and try instead to obtain security through co-operation with the others.

Pesaka's prize "catch" through this move was Wan Alwi, a lawyer and a potentially influential member of the Malay community, who had apparently chosen not to join Bumiputera because of poor personal relations with its leaders and because of his suspicion that he would not be allowed to achieve much prominence within that party. Pesaka was, needless to say, also mindful of the dangers of opening its doors to Malays and was careful not to provoke any fears among its members about a possible "Malay take-over". During the 1969 election campaign, SNAP in fact used this in an attempt to discredit Pesaka in some heavily Iban areas, but with doubtful results.[94] However, one disadvantage which Pesaka experienced in competing with SNAP was that its credentials as the leading Iban party became difficult to sustain after 1966, because of the circumstances under which SNAP was forced out of the Government and that party's subsequent ability to portray itself as the alleged victim of a Malay-dominated Central Government which had received the support of local intriguers among whom Pesaka leaders had been prominent.

Pesaka tried very hard to offset this disadvantage by giving emphasis to its Iban and Sarawakian orientation. Its subsequent conflicts with Bumiputera must have helped in this regard, but its leaders also took pains to identify themselves with local Sarawakian interests. For example, soon after his installation as Chief Minister, Penghulu Tawi Sli called upon the Central Government to use restraint in implementing the National Language in Sarawak, a view which he reiterated with greater force just before the election campaign in 1969 when he asserted that Sarawak's Council Negri should be the body to judge about the introduction of Malay as the sole official language, in accordance with the agreement reached in the Inter-Governmental Committee prior to the formation of Malaysia.[95] Ironically, some Pesaka leaders even saw some advantage for their party in SNAP's slogan of "Sarawak for Sarawakians", because they believed that this would strengthen their hand in their dealings with the Central Government, which, in order to neutralize SNAP's appeal, would have had to moderate federal control and refrain from undermining Pesaka's efforts to promote an independent image.

Another disadvantage which Pesaka had in competing with SNAP, especially after 1966, was financial. As already pointed out, following its expulsion from the Government SNAP had embarked on an ambitious programme of expansion, convinced that as there was already a popular wave of sympathy for it, a vigorous campaign without any let-up would put it back in the driver's seat after the election. This also appeared to have been the view of some of Sarawak's political financiers, who, either because of past or anticipated favours or because (as in the case of James Wong) they themselves belonged to the party, began contributing on an unprecedented scale. Contributing to SNAP was made attractive by the fact that in addition to its apparently good prospects it was a party which stood on its own and which therefore lent itself to easier manipulation.

Pesaka, on the other hand, was in a somewhat different position. To begin with, after 1966 its leaders had to cope with governmental responsibilities and renewed intra-Alliance rivalries, and therefore did not have the same amount of time for party work. In addition, potential backers were faced with a rather more complex situation, because they had to choose between supporting Pesaka and supporting its partners or even the Alliance as a whole. Some of these backers already had commitments to the SCA, of which they were members,[96] although they were willing to accept a wider Alliance responsibitily as well. The problem, however, was in deciding which of the two Alliance Native parties they should favour.[97] Pesaka, as an Iban party, should normally have had the advantage but this was not now the case, for two reasons.

First, it was not by any means the strongest party in the state and there were also good reasons for believing that it did not enjoy the support of the majority of Ibans. Even with good financial support, its chances at any election were at best uncertain. This, and the continuing doubts about the future unity of the Alliance, reduced Pesaka's appeal as an obvious choice for large-scale financial assistance.

Secondly, because most financiers regarded their contributions as a form of investment rather than as an expression of political commitment, they were aware that in order to get maximum benefit they should also win the concurrent gratitude of the ruling Alliance Party at National level. It was well known that Parti Bumiputera, two of whose leaders held Ministerial appointments in the Central Government,[98] was the national Alliance's (or, more particularly, UMNO's) preferred party in Sarawak. As the elections approached, Pesaka also appeared far less disciplined than Bumiputera because of internal disagreements over strategy stimulated, in part, by emerging leadership rivalries.[99] It increasingly isolated itself from its partners and finally decided to contest the election under its own symbol while Bumiputera and the SCA, which had moved closer to each other in the meantime, joined hands by not fielding candidates against each other and by campaigning jointly under the Alliance symbol. For these reasons, Pesaka failed to stimulate much enthusiasm among potential financiers and the situation reached a point where, at the height of the election campaign, Temenggong Jugah felt compelled to discuss his party's financial difficulties in public, apparently in the hope of obtaining fresh support.[100]

It would, however, be wrong to conclude that Pesaka was so poor as to be unable to meet its "normal" campaign expenses; the point is that, as in Sabah in 1967, these expenses had in fact reached "abnormal" proportions and Pesaka's difficulty was really in keeping pace with its opponents. The party did have some important backers who gave it significant help, but their donations were often made to individual candidates rather than to a centralized fund. As already pointed out, because of its traditional orientation (but partly also because of its financial difficulties) Pesaka always showed a preference for working through traditional elites and therefore did not rely to the same extent as SNAP on branches and paid workers. If an elaborate organization was expensive, there was also the fear that any attempt to build up a new corps of (party) elites in the field would lead to conflict between these elites and the established traditional leaders and thereby lead to local factionalism, loss of discipline, and, ultimately, defections. The general practice has been for important leaders of the party to make periodic visits to different crucial areas and to establish personal rapport with the local *Penghulus*. Visits by important people, it has been believed, both flatter and impress the *Penghulus* whose support, if won, is easily transmitted to the *Tuai Rumahs* in their area and finally to the voters.

While Pesaka has considered this a more reliable (and less expensive) way of building up support than depending on paid workers whose credentials are difficult to establish in a traditional setting, SNAP leaders often expressed the view, during interviews, that support based on local traditional elites was inherently fragile because *Penghulus*, like other people were often easily bought over by money. After 1965 Pesaka did make a serious effort to improve its grass-roots organization so as to broaden its base and meet the challenge posed by SNAP's increased activity, but this organization never became as extensive or important as SNAP's. Significantly, the persons who most strongly advocated this strategy and who subsequently took the responsibility for building up a decentralized organization were themselves people who did not belong to the traditional hierarchy, like Thomas Kana, who, like Ningkan, had earlier been a medical dresser in Seria and who was appointed Secretary-General of Pesaka in 1965.

The Sarawak Chinese Association

The Sarawak Chinese Association (the SCA) was founded in July 1962, that is, more than a year after the Malaysian proposal and three years after the formation of the SUPP. Both these factors had an important bearing on the party's early history and have continued to influence its scope and activities.

As the Sarawak Alliance took shape in 1962, it was evident that one of its main shortcomings would be the absence of any organized Chinese support. Not only was a well established Chinese component not readily available, but the SUPP, which virtually monopolized mass Chinese support at the time and which had gained control of local authorities in the urban areas at the district council elections held earlier, was actively anti-Malaysia in its stand. Thus, both the Malayan sponsors of the Malaysia plan and local Sarawakian Chinese who found it in their interest to support it, saw an urgent need to build up a new vehicle through which they could further their aims. This, however, meant that from the beginning the SCA's image was more pro-Malaysia than pro-Chinese. Much of the early stimulus for the party undoubtedly came from the Alliance in Malaya, notably the MCA, many of whose leaders played an active part in bringing about a Sarawakian replica of their own party.

By the time the Alliance was formed, the SUPP was the sole anti-Malaysia party in the state and it was unavoidable that its competition was more keenly felt by the SCA than by any of its partners. This was compounded by the fact that the SUPP, in addition to its success in stimulating anti-Malaysia sentiments among the Chinese, was also unequivocal in championing certain explicitly Chinese demands, such as those concerning the status of Chinese education and the opportunities for Chinese to own land. It is conceivable that, by being within the Alliance, the SCA was able to make representations which helped to secure certain safeguards for the Sarawak Chinese within the new federation. But because of its obligations to the other members of the Alliance, and its fear of alienating the national leadership, it could neither voice its views in public nor press its claims too forcefully. Indeed, it was even possible for the SUPP to claim that those concessions which were made to the Chinese were the result of its own representation although it did not find them adequate.[101]

Unlike its Sabahan counterpart and the Malayan Chinese Association (MCA), the Sarawak Association did not grow out of an antecedent welfare association which had acted as a custodian of Chinese interests. Thus it did not have any existing goodwill to build on, and also could not rely on the corporate support of the wealthier Chinese who, in Sabah and Malaya, had grouped themselves under the banner of the welfare associations which subsequently disbanded and gave their banner to the political parties which represented the Chinese in their respective territories. Rivalries among individual businessmen had therefore not been moderated by participation in common activity, and funds for the SCA in succeeding years therefore became more personalized in Sarawak than in Sabah and Malaya. The Chambers of Commerce, as chambers, did not have much impact on the fortunes of the SCA, because they were reluctant to take on any specific political commitment: this reluctance must have been strengthened by their knowledge of the SUPP's popularity, which meant that open support for the SCA would have lowered their prestige in the eyes of the Chinese population. At the same time overt support for the SUPP was likely to be inimical to business interests, partly because of the influence of the Central Government in economic affairs. In the event, although there were attempts by SCA and SUPP sympathizers to gain control of the chambers, this did not lead to any immediate pay-off for either party. It is perhaps for these reasons that the use of Chinese wealth for political purposes has been less disciplined (and more eccentric) in Sarawak than in Sabah or Malaya.[102]

Many of the original sponsors of the SCA had earlier belonged to either PANAS or the SUPP, but had left because of the former's increasingly Malay orientation and the latter's infiltration by left-wing elements. Soon after the new party was founded, however, it was taken over by Ling Beng Siew, one of Sarawak's wealthiest businessmen, whose offer of financial support was difficult to resist. His subsequent domination of the party was resented by many, who saw it as an obstacle to the recruitment of younger and more dedicated members into the party, but his position has by and large remained unchallenged.

The SCA's powerlessness to act as an effective spokesman of the Chinese community was demonstrated early in its life, when, because of the activities of Communist terrorists, the Government issued an order in 1963 compelling non-Natives (in effect, the Chinese) to hand over their firearms to the police. This order naturally brought into question the loyalty of the Chinese in general as opposed to the loyalty of the Chinese Communists in particular, and the SCA's protests[103] were shown to be of no avail. This may well have contributed to the party's poor showing in the district council elections held that year.[104] The SCA's weakness was also demonstrated on a more general issue, the right of Chinese to own land.[105] The issue was raised by the SCA in its 1963 election manifesto, but only in a restrained way. The party's view was that those who needed land most should be freely allowed to acquire it, and that when new land was opened up a "reasonable allocation" should be made available for Chinese. However, the land bills which were subsequently drafted to effect these changes (and which were introduced into the Council Negri by Dato Teo, an SCA member of the Cabinet) had to be withdrawn at the last moment because of intense opposition from at least two of the component units of the Alliance. As pointed out elsewhere[106] the opposition to these bills, when combined with the personal antagonisms among native leaders in the Alliance, resulted in a Cabinet crisis which nearly split the ruling Alliance Party and which showed up the SCA's ineffectiveness and (at least to many Chinese) lack of courage.

The SCA has not been any more aggressive, or successful, on the issue of Chinese language and Chinese education. The party's constitution states that one of its objects (the twelfth out of thirteen) is "to preserve and sustain the use and study of the Chinese language".[107] The 1969 election manifesto repeated this aim, but subordinated it in effect to endorsing the wider use of the national language:

> Our party supports all concrete efforts to introduce the use of the national language, because we firmly believe that the national language can go a long way to promote our racial unity. We realise that it is still premature to enforce the use of the national language as the sole official language at this juncture. In accordance with the Malaysia Agreement, this question will be decided by the Council Negri in 1973. In any event, our Party strongly advocates the wider use of the Chinese and Iban languages. As long as the SCA exists, survival of the Chinese education and language is assured.

In substance the SCA was supporting the then existing *status quo* in education in two important respects: the existing predominance of English as a medium of instruction in the secondary school; the programme for the extended use of Malay in schools. Yet the former of these had only two years before aroused great agitation among the Chinese. The "McLellan Report" proposals for converting Chinese secondary schools to the English medium had run into heavy opposition, and, although refusal to convert meant a heavy financial sacrifice, a substantial minority of the school did not convert.[108]

Compared with the Chinese in Sabah and Malaya, the Chinese in Sarawak are in the enviable position of now constituting the largest single community in their territory. And yet from the very beginning the Sarawak Chinese Association has been much weaker than its counterparts in Sabah and Malaya.[109] The reasons for this deserve some attention.

As already indicated, the SCA was singularly unfortunate in having come into existence after Chinese support had already been harnessed by another party, namely the SUPP. This disadvantage was reinforced by the party's unwillingness (or inability) to be more aggressive than its rival in fighting for Chinese causes. Although this was partly the result of its leaders' desire to remain in the good books of national leaders and of Native leaders of local political parties (for business reasons as well as for anticipated political benefit), the SCA's position within the Sarawak Alliance also made such a situation unavoidable.

The SCA's lack of electoral support has been well known to its partners[110] and this has prevented it from being able to bargain effectively within the Government. But at the same time Chinese voters have probably not been willing to support the party precisely because of its inability to bargain aggressively on their behalf. Given this dilemma, the SCA's policy right up to the election was to align itself with the strongest party within the Alliance. Originally this party was SNAP which was favourably disposed to the Chinese and whose leader, Dato Ningkan, was the first Chief Minister. After SNAP left the Alliance in 1966, SCA began supporting Pesaka which was the strongest party in the Council Negri. In early 1969, however, as the elections scheduled for May that year approached, the SCA appeared to move closer to Bumiputera, and by the time the elections were completed in 1970, was definitely closer to that party although it retained friendly links with Pesaka.[111] The circumstances which led to this shift are discussed in the next chapter,[112] but one aspect of it deserves mention here.

To most observers, as well as to many members of the SCA, there seemed little doubt in early 1969 that Pesaka would win more seats than Bumiputera, although it was commonly felt that neither party would do sufficiently well to form a Government either on its own or in combination with the SCA.[113] Under these circumstances, the most "rational" cause for the SCA would have been to maintain equal links with Pesaka and Bumiputera, or, if this was not possible, to cultivate closer ties with Pesaka. The former alternative was not easy because of the intense rivalry which developed between the two Native parties and which made strict neutrality difficult to maintain; further, the SCA was not able to persuade both its partners to surrender certain seats to it, and, because Bumiputera was more amenable in this regard, it had fewer quarrels with that party and was able to collaborate with it during the campaign. But in all likelihood this was not the only calculation which encouraged the SCA to drift closer to Bumiputera, since many of its members (including some prominent ones) continued to believe that it would be more prudent in the long run to back Pesaka than Bumiputera: these members reasoned that political power in Sarawak would unavoidably be Iban-based and that Pesaka was the only party within the Alliance which was capable of representing that base. Those whose views carried more weight, however, had other considerations in view. A few of them appeared more keen on establishing good relations with Malay leaders at the national level, and considered supporting Bumiputera a better way of achieving this than supporting Pesaka;[114] They may also have felt that in the likely event of an inconclusive result, the Central Government would use its influence to "promote" Bumiputera and give it control of the new Government.

For some time, particularly in 1967 and 1968, there appeared to be a possibility that internal weakness and fears of declining support would lead some groups within the SCA to break away and form a new party. In the opinion of these groups, change from within was ruled out because of the control which Dato Ling exercised over the party and his apparent unwillingness to allow others to influence its policies.[115] In addition, the party was run so much along personal lines[116] that there was in effect no "organization" for them to capture. Thus, while one of the common complaints against the SCA had been that it was too much under the influence of Kuala Lumpur and therefore incapable of representing Sarawakian Chinese interests, some of these individuals, although agreeing with this, felt that something could in fact be salvaged if Kuala Lumpur would only interfere more, and put pressure on existing leaders of the SCA to vacate their positions.

In August 1967, the then Secretary-General of the party, Dato Teo Kui Seng, himself suggested the formation of a new party which might attract some of the more energetic and dedicated members of the Chinese community and which might therefore present a more dynamic image. Despite the publicity it received, nothing immediately came of this suggestion but during the first half of 1968 concerted attempts were made by a group of "intellectuals"[117] to start a new party or at least, by threatening to do so, to force internal reforms within the SCA. This group was not in any way opposed to the idea of the SCA—i.e. a party like the MCA and the Sabah Chinese Association, non-socialist and working within the Alliance to represent Chinese interests. But it was decidedly of the opinion that the SCA as it was then constituted and run, was not capable of gathering enough support to be accepted as a worthwhile organization even when compared to its counterparts in Sabah and West Malaysia. Knowing only too well the difficulty of getting the party's bosses to relinquish their hold voluntarily, members of this group sought support for their plan from national leaders in Kuala Lumpur, including the leaders of the MCA.[118]

It was claimed that these leaders, as well as some Bumiputera leaders, fully sympathized with the aspirations of the group, and it was believed that pressure would soon be put on the leaders of the SCA to surrender their positions or risk the withdrawal of support both from the centre and from Native components of the Sarawak Alliance. When some of the national leaders visited Kuching, however, they were apparently talked out of this by Dato Ling and others who, in addition to warning against the dangers of handing the party over to amateurs, also threatened to withdraw all financial support if they were overthrown. In the final analysis, the latter threat was perhaps the crucial factor which prevented the "intellectuals" from going ahead with their plan. Even without firm assurances from Kuala Lumpur they may have been prepared to set up an alternative to the SCA, in the hope that by demonstrating greater support they would finally be able to establish their case. But they knew that without substantial financial support this would be difficult to achieve. The movement finally collapsed in late 1968, when a few of the more prominent members of the group were "bought over"[119] by Dato Ling, given employment in his business and appointed to subsidiary positions in the party.[120]

The failure of the "intellectuals" was partly also the result of the absence of a single common objective. Throughout the period in question, some of them continued to believe that the most realistic plan would be to reform the SCA from within, while others clearly set their sights on forming a new party. A third view was that those involved should constitute themselves into a pressure group, not affiliated to any party and giving support to individual candidates (SCA as well as others) who in their opinion stood for the right principles. When the movement finally collapsed, many simply opted out of politics while others, as just mentioned, chose to identify themselves firmly with the SCA. Significantly, none drifted into other parties.

One of the SCA's "strengths", if it can be called that, was that it was the only party that could help the Alliance to *claim* that it also represented the Chinese community. But this was not always enough to guarantee its participation in the Government, as shown by the ambiguous position in which it found itself immediately after the crisis which led to Ningkan's removal as Chief Minister.[121] The fear all along had been that if the SCA were to be excluded from the Cabinet (either because it failed to win seats or because of differences with its partners) the Chinese in Sarawak would be unrepresented in the state Government. The SCA had in fact repeatedly used this argument not only to get more support from the Chinese but also to justify its accommodationist stance within the Alliance. The real test, however, came after the election in 1970 when it was shown that neither the SCA nor its partners had sufficient strength to carry on ruling the state under the existing Alliance arrangement.[122] Had the SCA won more seats, it would have been possible for the Alliance to form a Government, and for the Chinese to be adequately represented in it; had either Bumiputera or Pesaka won more seats, the Alliance could still have continued in power and "carried" a weak SCA. But in the event the only logical, if unexpected, development was for the SUPP to be invited to form a coalition with the Alliance, and, because that party was essentially Chinese-led, for the SCA to be excluded from the new Cabinet while remaining in the Alliance. Some time before the election an SCA leader had expressed the opinion during an interview that although the SUPP was doing its best to take up issues with the Central Government, it was not likely to get anywhere because it was always "trying the front door" while the SCA resorted to subtler methods. Backdoor politics may indeed have been the only option available to the SCA, but it also made it easier for its partners, when the time came, to show it out through the backdoor, without much fuss, while welcoming the SUPP through the front.

Parties in Sabah

Political parties were even slower to develop in Sabah than in Sarawak. Not one party existed in the state at the time of the Tengku's Malaysia proposal in May 1961, but by the end of that year the two parties which subsequently dominated politics in the state (namely the United National Kadazan Organization and the United Sabah National Organization) had both come into existence; by the end of the following year a host of other parties had also sprung up and the Sabah Alliance had firmly been established. However, although the Malaysia plan served as a stimulus for the growth of political parties, some of the parties which emerged had already been conceived prior to the date of the Tengku's announcement.

The first fully-fledged political party to be inaugurated in Sabah was the United Kadazan National Organization, or UNKO, which was formally established in August 1961. It grew out of pre-existing Kadazan Associations, the first of which had been launched in Penampang in the mid-fifties.[123] The activities sponsored by these Associations were mainly educational and cultural, but it was evident from the beginning that their founders were not unaware of the future political implications of bringing the potentially "participant" section of the Kadazan community under a common organizational framework. Although explicitly political goals were excluded from the objectives of these Associations, it was well known that their leaders used this new opportunity to generate embryonic political activity by forging links which had previously not existed and by exchanging and propagating ideas about the welfare of their community and the future of their country. Among the founders of the Penampang Kadazan Association was Donald Stephens, a Kadazan Eurasian, who was subsequently to emerge as the undisputed leader of the Kadazan community. As the owner of one of Sabah's chief newspapers *The Sabah Times*,[124] he was able to give a great deal of publicity to, and thereby encourage support for, the Associations and subsequently the political party.

UNKO started off as a party which restricted its membership to persons of Kadazan descent. This may partly have been the result of its having grown out of the existing Kadazan Associations, but another factor may have been equally important. Sabah at this time had not had any experience of competitive politics, and Donald Stephens and his associates, sharing a common (if somewhat exaggerated) confidence in the numerical strength of the Kadazan community and its ability to establish political pre-eminence, may have felt that a party which monopolized Kadazan loyalties was bound to form the backbone of any future elected government. In this regard their aspirations were very similar to those of the Iban community in Sarawak. But the first party to emerge in Sarawak was the SUPP, which was Chinese-led, and this, together with its implicitly ideological orientation, might explain why it was multi-racial and not communally exclusive: the Chinese, unlike the Ibans (and the Kadazans in Sabah) could not seriously hope to achieve political dominance[125] and their only hope of influencing government policy was through co-operation with the important indigenous groups.

Despite their confidence, it was clear that UNKO's leaders erred seriously in limiting their membership to Kadazans. Their policy might have paid off in the long run if the parties which emerged subsequently had also sought distinct ethnic identities:[126] in such an event the UNKO, as the representative of the largest single ethnic group in the state (32% of the population in 1960), would have become the dominant partner in any coalition or would at least have been in a very strong bargaining position. However, the next party which in fact emerged was the USNO, which based itself not on any ethnic group but on the Muslim population, without excluding non-Muslim participation. Thus purely in terms of communal arithmetic UNKO was immediately out-manoeuvred because the Muslim population was more numerous (about 38% of the population in 1960) than the Kadazan population, and religious affinity was likely to be as potent as ethnic identity in stimulating party loyalties. Further, because USNO did not confine its membership to Muslims, it was also in a position to solicit some support from the non-Muslim groups, thereby reducing UNKO's potential influence among the non-Kadazan and non-Muslim groups and even threatening (although not too seriously, except possibly in the case of the small group of Kadazan Muslims) its claim to be the sole Kadazan spokesman in the state. As a Muslim-based party, USNO was also able to recruit its leadership from different ethnic groups, and this no doubt enabled it to compete more effectively with UNKO.

UNKO's second error lay in the choice of the word "Kadazan". Donald Stephens and his associates were strongly of the opinion that the term "Dusun" (plantation folk) which had previously been used to identify their community was a "colonial" legacy which conveyed the impression of a backward subject people. According to them the term "Kadazan" was the one which originally applied to their community and it was a matter of some importance that it be revived in order to encourage self-respect and new nationalist perspectives. Many "Dusuns", however, were equally insistent that the term "Kadazan" referred only to one branch of the larger Dusun group of people, a branch that was located in the Penampang-Papar area. To them the promotion of the new "Kadazan" identity was only an attempt by the more aggressive and better educated Penampang-Papar group to establish its own hegemony over the entire Dusun population. The fact that most of the original leaders of UNKO came from that area only helped to confirm their suspicions.[127]

Like many of the parties in Sarawak, UNKO was originally opposed to Sabah's entry into Malaysia, and its leaders actively explored the possibility of obtaining independence first, or of forming a federation embracing Sarawak, Sabah and Brunei, as alternatives to the Malaysia plan. However, like the leaders of SNAP (but unlike those of the SUPP) in Sarawak, they quickly reversed their stand on the issue and within six months were sufficiently impressed by the rewards of joining Malaysia and by the constitutional safeguards which the Malayan leaders promised to Sabah, to become enthusiastic supporters of the proposed federation.[128]

Dissatisfaction with UNKO's Kadazan identity and USNO's predominantly Muslim image led, in January 1962, to the formation of the United National Pasok Momogun Party (PM) under the leadership of Sundang, a prominent figure among the Kwijau group of Dusuns. At its inception Pasok Momogun (literally, "people of the country") appeared designed to serve two important purposes. First, it was to be the voice not only of those ethnic groups (notably the Muruts) which were excluded by UNKO and which, because they were not Muslim, would not have found USNO particularly congenial, but also of those Dusuns who disapproved of being labelled as Kadazans.[129] The party was nevertheless multi-racial in membership, although the bulk of its support came from Muruts and dissident Dusuns. The second justification for PM's formation was opposition to Malaysia. Sundang, who had earlier been Vice-Chairman of UNKO, was unhappy with that party's quick turnabout on the Malaysia issue, and was determined to find an alternative vehicle for the anti-Malaysia cause.

The view has also been held that PM's formation was meant to serve a third purpose, more important than the two just mentioned. From the very beginning, although the Native sponsors of the new party had their own personal, communal and Sabahan motivations, Chinese encouragement and financial backing were very much in evidence. Two nominally non-communal but overwhelmingly Chinese-dominated parties, the United Party (UP) and the Democratic Party (DP), formed almost immediately after PM, were seen making vigorous efforts to establish their influence over PM, the former through financial control and the latter through the promotion of closer political ties.[130] PM's financial dependence on a group of wealthy Chinese was indeed an open secret, and it has been alleged that this reflected a not very concealed attempt by the

Chinese business community to thwart the formation of Malaysia by undermining UNKO's Kadazan base, and by providing an alternative focus of allegiance for dissident Natives.[131]

If the leaders of the Chinese community were apprehensive about the formation of Malaysia and were willing to oppose it, they were also aware the Native opposition was more likely to be taken seriously. By October 1962, however, these Chinese leaders were themselves persuaded to abandon their opposition to Malaysia and in that month UP and DP merged to form the Borneo Utara National Party (BUNAP), which immediately became a member of the Sabah Alliance Party.[132] As UNKO was also a member of the Sabah Alliance, earlier antipathies between it and the erstwhile (Chinese) backers of PM were healed and PM suddenly found itself without support. Organizationally it had never fully got off the ground and even intra-party elections had not been properly held. After a period of uncertainty, when it became increasingly clear that it could not make any impression on the combined forces of the Alliance, PM took the only course available and merged with UNKO early in 1964, accepting Malaysia (which had been formed in September 1963) as a *fait accompli.*

In order to avoid the impression that the merger of the two parties was tantamount to the incorporation of PM into UNKO, it was agreed that the combined party would take on a new name, United Pasok Momogun Kadazan Organization (UPKO). Further, Sundang was elected as one of the deputy presidents and a few of his colleagues were given places on the executive committee. But the marriage was not entirely a happy one, for a variety of reasons. First, Sundang was disappointed that he was not made the sole Deputy-President of the party, but rather one of several: to him this was not an adequate way of giving due prominence to the ex-PM component of UPKO. Second, despite the adoption of a new name, the old controversy about the term "Kadazan" was not ended. Sundang's proposal at the time of merger was that the "K" in UPKO should stand for "Kinabalu" and not "Kadazan",[133] and he was apparently under the impression that although the matter had not been resolved at the time of the merger the issue was still open and a change was likely to be affected in due course. It soon became clear that the ex-UNKO wing had no such intention and this continued to be a source of friction. A related issue was the party's symbol, which is discussed in another chapter.[134]

Finally, personal relations between Sundang and the ex-UNKO leaders continued to be strained despite the merger of the two parties. Although, following the merger, Sundang had been appointed Deputy Chief Minister of the State Government, he never seemed convinced that he was fully accepted as a member of the team and felt that the other (i.e. ex-UNKO) leaders of the party were far from enthusiastic about his position in the Cabinet.[135] For these reasons, he did not show much dedication in campaigning for UPKO when the party most needed him, namely after open hostilities had broken out between it and USNO. It was even unclear whether he would stay with the party in the event of its breaking away from the Alliance, if it insisted on continuing to use the term "Kadazan" in its name. The ex-UNKO leaders, for their part, seemed genuinely disappointed with Sundang for his aloofness and for his failure to stand solidly behind the party. Specifically they blamed him for not contributing his share to the financial costs of running the party, particularly when deteriorating relations with USNO, combined with the need to prepare for the oncoming elections, made rapid expansion imperative.[136] It was also alleged that he did not take his Ministerial duties seriously, and that this reflected poorly on the party.

Although internal UPKO affairs were not characterized by harmonious relations between ex-UNKO and ex-PM leaders, conflicts between them never became public, and the party was able to project itself as a reasonably cohesive and well-disciplined group. This, however, was possible only because the ex-UNKO component was unmistakably dominant, leaving the ex-PM group with little room for manoeuvre, and because Donald Stephens and his immediate lieutenants were able to carry the party on their own.[137] One indication of their success was that they were gradually able to overcome the earlier prejudice against the term "Kadazan": by the time of the elections in 1967 not only had the name of the party ceased to be an important issue, but UPKO had already established itself as a champion of Kadazan nationalism with support from

"Dusun" groups throughout the state. In this it was no doubt helped by the negative appeal of USNO's Muslim image among the Kadazans, and by that party's apparent reluctance to champion what could be represented as Sabahan interests against federal intervention.

Because PM had been multi-racial and had had close links with Chinese financiers, but presumably also because the ex-UNKO leaders had themselves come to recognize the disadvantages of being communally exclusive, UPKO decided to open its doors to all races. With this move, the founders of UNKO once again gained the initiative[138] and established a broader electoral base than any other party. But this mid-course correction probably came too late to be effective. The Muslim population was already solidly behind USNO and the Chinese had already formed their own party, the SCA,[139] which was a member of the Alliance. Nevertheless, USNO could not now claim to be the dominant party and many Chinese, especially the younger and better educated ones who did not find SCA's style and orientation attractive, began to take a keen interest in UPKO. The latter development, however, also presented the party with some difficulties and was the first source of open disagreement with the SCA, which claimed that the spirit of the Alliance demanded that it be allowed to be the sole representative of the Chinese. This must have contributed to the SCA's disinclination to support UPKO in its subsequent rivalries with USNO.[140]

As already pointed out, USNO, which was inaugurated in December 1961, was the second party to emerge in Sabah. Like UNKO, it came into existence largely through the initiative of one man, Datu Mustapha bin Datu Harun, who, even more than Donald Stephens, established his unquestioned personal control over the party. A Suluk, Datu Mustapha had worked his way up from rather humble origins: having started life as a houseboy under a Resident, he subsequently became an office orderly, a clerk, and a sergeant, First Lieutenant and Captain in the anti-Japanese guerrilla movement, before being appointed Native Chief Grade II in 1945 and Native Chief Grade I in 1951. Thus, by the early 1950s he was already a prominent member of the traditional hierarchy in Sabah and was a widely respected figure especially within the Muslim community. In 1954, he also became a nominated member of the Legislative Council and two years later was appointed to the Executive Council. By the time he founded USNO he had in addition acquired considerable wealth through holdings in timber and copra. Knowing his experience and motivation few doubted that Datu Mustapha would become a dominant personality in Sabah politics. Given Stephen's own aspirations and his separate mobilization of the Kadazan community, it was perhaps also inevitable that something like a gladiatorial contest would emerge between the two.

Although, like UNKO, USNO grew out of pre-existing non-political organizations, its parentage was not as clear-cut. The various Muslim associations [141] which existed in the state did facilitate the launching of the new party, but there was no evidence that their founders had had the same expectations of them as did their counterparts in the Kadazan Associations, namely as forerunners of a future political movement. Nevertheless USNO undoubtedly benefited from the support it received from the Muslim associations, and this must have been particularly useful during the early stages when the party did not have its own organization to rely on.

From its inception, USNO was unequivocally in favour of Malaysia and, until UNKO's change of attitude in January 1962, was the sole champion of the pro-Malaysia cause in the state. Even after January 1962 it remained distinguishable from UNKO in its stand on the issue because, unlike the latter, it did not show any special concern for the safeguards which Sabah would enjoy in the new federation. On specific issues like language and religion it did not share UNKO's anxiety about the extension of Malayan policies to Sabah and if anything seemed to favour uniformity. In this regard its views were similar to those of PANAS and BARJASA in Sarawak, while UNKO's reflected a position which was similar to that of SNAP. Nor were the reasons for this difficult to understand. As a Muslim-based party, not only was USNO (like PANAS and BARJASA) spontaneously inclined to welcome the incorporation of Sabah into a larger unit where the Malay (Muslim) group would enjoy political pre-eminence, but its leaders were also aware that by joining Malaysia, their own position and that of the Muslim communities in Sabah would be elevated because they would now become identified with the group which wielded power at the national level. Left on their own, in an independent Sabah, they may not have been able to withstand the combined strength of the local non-Muslim groups, led by the Kadazans; in a separate federation of Sarawak, Sabah and Brunei, the Muslim groups would again have been outnumbered by the others, led by the Ibans and the Kadazans. Within Sabah, or within a Borneo federation, the Muslims may therefore have been doomed to a permanent minority status and they would not have been allowed to take much initiative in determining the cultural and political priorities in their environment. Viewed differently, one might argue that while the Kadazans (and Ibans), like the Malays in Malaya, had no rival pulls as far as their local identity was concerned, the Muslim groups had emotional (and cultural) ties with the politically dominant Malays in Malaya and their local loyalties were to that extent less exclusive.

As already pointed out, USNO, while being primarily a Muslim party,[142] was open to all Natives. Although the decision not to confine its ranks to any single community initially gave it an advantage over UNKO, it is worth noting that Islam did not always act as a denominator which guaranteed the Muslim community's total identification with the party. Perhaps because of Mustapha's own influence, a disproportionate number of persons who originally held office in the party were Suluks from the Kudat area, and, although attempts were subsequently made to include representatives from other ethnic groups and areas, the largest Muslim group, the Bajaus, were never adequately represented on the Executive Committee.[143] Although the Bajaus did not have any obvious claimants who were denied office, it was believed that they were not entirely satisfied with this state of affairs and there were rumours in 1964 that they contemplated forming their own cultural association with a view to exploring the possibility of promoting a separate political organization.

There were, however, two factors which mitigated against this and which therefore helped USNO to retain Bajau support. First, the value of Mustapha's leadership in the total Sabahan context was widely recognized by the Bajaus and they knew that he was the only person capable of acquiring political power for any section of the population (in this case the Muslim section) with which they could readily identify themselves. Added to this was the absence of any prominent personality within the Bajau community around whom support could be mobilized; in any event those Bajaus who might have been capable of striking out on their own[144] were solidly behind Mustapha.

Second, given UNKO's attempts to establish Kadazan hegemony, the only rational move for the Bajaus was to support a party which could establish a larger base than UNKO, and any attempt to sponsor a separate Bajau party would to this extent have been self-defeating. Even after UPKO was formed, with membership open to all communities, there was no risk of Bajau defections to that party because leadership by other Muslims (like the Suluks and Brunei Malays) was undoubtedly preferable to leadership by the (non-Muslim) Kadazans.

Because of its greater willingness to accept national policies and to identify with the national leadership, USNO was well placed to receive favoured treatment from national Alliance leaders and to "deliver the goods" to its clientele. Its leaders, like those of Parti Bumiputera in Sarawak, were quite happy to see their party in some respects as the local extension of the UMNO in Malaya and were inclined to regard UMNO leaders (especially the Tengku and Tun Razak) not only as the effective leaders of the Malaysian Alliance but also as the persons who signified the political dominance of "their community" at the national level. In promoting Islam and the national language they were not only strengthening their links with the UMNO and the Central Government, but were also giving tangible proof of enhancing the interests of their supporters and of securing a better treatment for them than for the other communities in the state.

Looking back at the evolution of parties in East Malaysia and particularly at conflicts and conflict resolution within the two Alliance parties, one is struck by the relative steadfastness of the Muslim-based parties (Bumiputera in Sarawak and USNO in Sabah) and the unwillingness of their leaders to waver from set policies. In contrast, the chief non-Muslim

Native parties (UPKO in Sabah and to a lesser extent SNAP in Sarawak)[145] repeatedly kept adjusting their postures, notably *vis-à-vis* the Central Government and the other ethnic groups in their states. The explanation for this is not difficult to find. Muslim leaders and their supporters, because they saw Malaysia as a Muslim-dominated country, (while they were in the minority in their own states) perceived a greater degree of congruence between national and state priorities than did their non-Muslim counterparts. They also did not have the same difficulties of effecting a compromise between their personal beliefs about the desirable state of affairs in their own states and the realities of Malaysian politics (including federal-state relations) because, at least on "ethnic" and cultural issues, the policies of the Central Government (dominated by UMNO) and the "majority" political status of the Muslim community at the national level favoured their own positions in their respective states. It was therefore not surprising that the Central Government and national Alliance leaders should have shown sympathy for, and on many crucial occasions given assistance to, these two parties and their leaders, particularly in their conflicts with their non-Muslim Native partners in their local Alliance parties.

The non-Muslim Native parties (particularly SNAP and Pesaka in Sarawak and UPKO in Sabah) and their leaders, on the other hand, always found it necessary to keep a careful balance between their personal or communal preferences on the one hand and politically viable positions on the other. To them their "natural" political advantage could be established and sustained only by isolating political life in their own states,[146] but at the same time they become increasingly aware of the need to acquiesce in, or even actively support, communally uncongenial and politically embarrassing policies, such as those on language and education, if they were to be accepted by national leaders, as members of the "ruling team".

Unable to steer a fixed course under these circumstances, the leaders of these parties settled on a policy of "playing things by ear", often alternating between protestations of support and admiration for national leaders like the Tengku and Tun Razak, and expressions of doubt and anxiety about national policies. Such a tactic, although it may have made the leaders of these parties appear indecisive and on occasion even insincere, might have succeeded had there been no alternative local group for the national leaders to nurture and support, but the presence of Parti Bumiputera (and before it BARJASA) in Sarawak and USNO in Sabah undoubtedly undermined the bargaining position of the non-Muslim Native parties. In Sarawak, Iban disunity (compounded by over-optimism) was a crucial factor which finally helped Bumiputera to gain the initiative, but in both states the support of the Chinese parties was crucial in bringing about a state of affairs favourable to the local Muslim-dominated parties as well as to the Central Government.

As in the case of Bumiputera, one specific way in which national policies and the sympathy of the Central Government helped the USNO was that persons sympathetic to it were appointed as adult education teachers. As all adult education was conducted in the national language, it was perhaps unavoidable that all those appointed should have been Malay or Malay-educated. Coincidentally, of course, persons belonging to this group were generally also pro-Bumiputera or pro-USNO, and these parties must have benefited from the influence which these teachers wielded in the rural areas. Other parties, however, did not believe that this was the full extent of the advantage enjoyed by Bumiputera and USNO in this regard. During interviews, it was frequently alleged that these two parties had in fact succeeded in appointing their own men as adult education teachers and that these teachers were actively involved in party work, thus saving money because they were paid out of Government funds. Parties like SNAP and UPKO, on the other hand, did not have similar opportunities; further, their workers were party men pure and simple and therefore could not enjoy the same prestige and influence as adult education teachers.[146a] Another tactic employed by USNO to enhance its prestige and to fit into the traditional society was to appoint, where possible, village headmen as its branch chairmen. In this it was similar to Pesaka in Sarawak, and no doubt Mustapha's own position as a pre-eminent Muslim Native Chief (like the status enjoyed by Jugah, who was a Temenggong), must have made things easier. Although Dato Mustapha and Dato Yassin, like Dato Stephens and Dato

Sundang of the UPKO, were men of considerable personal wealth who could have "carried" their party financially, USNO was fortunate in receiving substantial funds from wealthy Chinese, not only via the SCA, but also directly. As USNO-UPKO rivalry built up after 1964 resulting in increased party activity,[147] costs began to increase by leaps and bounds. The SCA, which had previously maintained a neutral position, gradually found itself more and more in the USNO camp, not only because of its own conflicts with UPKO but also because it became clear that USNO was the most likely party to receive the support of the Central Government. Although, privately, many SCA leaders may have sympathized with UPKO's stand on several crucial issues (like state autonomy, language and education) and may have themselves feared federal (and Malay) domination, as businessmen and as conservative Chinese they must have felt compelled to support the party which was favoured by the Central Government. An additional factor, discussed in Chapter 7, may have been that many of them had been unhappy about the timber policies of the Stephens Government which placed restrictions on big enterprises and which they saw as pro-Native and anti-Chinese.

In December 1967, following its failure at the election held in April that year, UPKO dramatically announced its decision to dissolve itself and to urge its members to join USNO. At the election USNO had won fourteen seats and UPKO twelve, while five seats had gone to the SCA and one to a Chinese Independent who had defeated Peter Lo, the Chief Minister, in the Elopura Constituency. Earlier rivalries with the SCA made it impossible for UPKO to persuade that party to abandon its special relationship with USNO, and this left Mustapha firmly in control of the situation.

Technically, the new government should have included all the Alliance partners, but Mustapha, understandably, was determined that a government headed by him should not include individuals who did not support his policies and who were likely to use every opportunity to oust him and his party from office. He therefore decided to form an interim Cabinet, comprising only those individuals who had been Ministers in the previous government,[148] leaving the door open for UPKO to come in on his terms.[149] UPKO, however, insisted on its right as an equal senior partner in the Alliance, and refused to allow USNO to run the new government in a manner that would give it a dominant status. When this was refused, it announced its decision in May to leave the Alliance and to form the Opposition.

For a time, UPKO's hopes were kept alive by the court action which had been initiated by Richard Yap, its candidate in Bengkoka-Banggi, who had alleged contraventions of the election laws by Mustapha and who was therefore asking for the election in his constituency to be declared null and void. But when Richard Yap withdrew his charges,[150] and when UPKO unity was badly damaged through the defection of Payar Juman, one of its successful candidates, and through rumours of other impending defections, it was clear that the party was not very likely to withstand the effects of a full term in the Opposition. Apparently there were also growing fears of how Mustapha would handle his political opponents, and UPKO's decision, although precipitous and startling,[151] was not entirely inexplicable. To be sure, attempts were first made to persuade USNO to agree to a merger of the two parties,[152] but when these failed even abject surrender was considered preferable to the painful process of gradual decimation.

Since the dissolution of UPKO, USNO has remained the only Native party in Sabah and has established a position of dominance and authority unparalleled elsewhere in Malaysia. Ex-UPKO members have been admitted only selectively, and Mustapha has taken great care to ensure that there is no threat either to his own position or to that of his "original" party.[153] There has been no discrimination against previous UPKO strongholds, for example in the distribution of development funds, but this has been on the clear understanding that anti-Government activities will not be tolerated.[154]

UPKO's decision to dissolve highlights a point that may be of general significance not only to Sabah but to East Malaysia generally. As competitive politics is new, a long-range view is not often taken of a political career, and it is not always appreciated that such a career may involve periods in office and periods out of office and yet remain rewarding. To many members of UPKO, for example, a five-year period in the

Opposition appeared futile not only because they had not witnessed the possibility of alternations in government, but because their own political careers were so short and all the parties and representative government so young that five years could not be seen in any historical or long-term political perspective. Further, many had entered politics as a means of material advancement, and the initial rewards enjoyed by those who were well placed only served to confirm this belief. This tended to produce exaggerated notions about the consequences of being in and out of office, and, in combination with the above point about the newness of politics, resulted in a desperate "all-or-nothing" view of elections.[155] In the case of persons like Donald Stephens, who spent a great deal of their own money in maintaining the party, an additional fear must have been that a continued financial commitment for a further five years might prove to be wasteful and unrealistic because there was not an adequate guarantee of appropriate rewards at the end. As already mentioned, they may also have considered it hopeless to continue leading an opposition party like UPKO as long as Mustapha was the Chief Minister.

The third major party to be formed in Sabah was the Sabah Chinese Association (SCA), which came into existence only in June 1965. Compared to USNO and UPKO it has not enjoyed an important position in Sabah politics, but has nevertheless retained a measure of influence, not only because it has been the sole organized spokesman of the Chinese community but also because its financial contribution has been useful to the Alliance. Prior to UPKO's dissolution the SCA's position was also artificially strengthened by its ability to tilt the balance in favour of either of the two main contenders, an enviable position which neither its Sarawak counterpart nor its parent body, the MCA in Malaya, has ever enjoyed. With UPKO's dissolution, however, Sabah had no further place for a "kingmaker" and the SCA, facing only the massive strength of USNO, has therefore lost all its bargaining power with the possible exception of its claim to represent Chinese interests.

Compared with UPKO and USNO, the SCA's origins were rather complex, involving a larger number of (political as well as non-political) antecedent organizations. As early as the middle of 1961, partly as a reaction to the Tengku's Malaysia proposal, certain wealthy Chinese began to explore the possibility of forming an organization to protect Chinese as well as business interests in the state. These leaders had serious misgivings about the Malaysia plan, fearing not only a curtailment of their business opportunities as a result of the greater regulation of economic activities by the Malaysian Government, but also the extension of Malayan policies on language and education, and of Malay political domination.[156] They could not, however, agree on the most appropriate way of organizing themselves as some preferred an explicitly political organization while others considered a non-political but well-disciplined body to be more likely to succeed under the existing circumstances. There was also minor disagreement about whether the organization to be formed should be exclusively Chinese or be open to all communities. Those favouring direct political activity and open membership went on to form two political parties, the United Party (UP) and the Democratic Party (DP), in early 1962, while the others got together to launch the North Borneo Chinese Association (NBCA), exclusively Chinese and nominally welfare-oriented, some six months later. There was, however, some overlap of membership between the two political parties on the one hand and the NBCA on the other.

Although they did not place any formal communal restrictions on membership, both UP and DP were, for all practical purposes, Chinese parties. The main distinction between them was that the former was primarily Sandakan based and was dominated by some of the most wealthy Chinese in the state, while the latter was identified with Jesselton (later called Kota Kinabalu) and included a larger proportion of the middle and upper-middle levels of the Chinese business community.[157] These differences, however, did not lead to any overt hostility between the two parties; nor was there much evidence that they were working at cross purpose. Nevertheless, it was quite clear, especially to MCA leaders in Kuala Lumpur,[158] that Chinese interests in these states (and no doubt their own potential influence as a parent body) could only suffer through internal divisions, and vigorous attempts were therefore made to bring about a merger of UP and DP. This merger finally took place in October 1962, the new (merged) party calling itself the Borneo Utara National Party (BUNAP), a name subsequently changed to Sabah National Party (SANAP). This, however, was not considered adequate to cement Chinese unity, and in mid-1965 SANAP merged with the non-political Sabah Chinese Association (SCA)[159] to form a new, exclusively Chinese party which took the latter's name. Not unexpectedly, this move was resisted by those in the original SCA who did not want to have any overt political affiliations and who may also have thought that bargaining on behalf of the Chinese community could be carried out more successfully through the combined efforts of an explicitly political and a non-political (but financially powerful) organization, remaining outside active controversy and not causing offence to others than through, for example, competition for seats in the State Legislature.

Personal rivalries between the leaders of SANAP and the original SCA were also believed to have complicated the merger. Resistance to merger was apparently spearheaded by the Sandakan branch of the SCA, which on one occasion was openly accused of sabotage by the President of the Sandakan Chinese Chamber of Commerce.[160] There was also some confusion about the legality of the SCA's decision to dissolve itself and to merge with SANAP to form a new political party. Some felt that the decision could be taken by the Central Executive Council, while others insisted that constitutionally every branch had the right to determine its own future.[161] For some weeks individual branches of the SCA carried on debating the issue, and a few continued actively to resist the merger. At one point there was even speculation that a new "Chinese Welfare Organization" would be formed which would take over the organization and functions of the original SCA.[162]

These misgivings and difficulties notwithstanding, the new SCA was without doubt a potentially stronger representative of the Chinese community than any of its antecedent bodies; it was also financially very sound because the original SCA, as a welfare association supported by the wealthier Chinese, had been a well-connected organization.[163] But a significant section of the Chinese community appeared to view the leadership of the party as unduly accommodationist in its dealings, not only with its Native partners in the Local Alliance, but also *vis-à-vis* the Central Government, and the SCA therefore was never able to speak with the same authority as its two Native partners in the Alliance.

Partly as a result of its more complex origins, but partly also because of clan conflicts, regional orientations (mainly Sandakan versus Kota Kinabalu, but in some cases also involving the Interior Residency) and personal rivalries among the leaders, the SCA's life has been marred by internal disputes and a lack of unity. The party had, after all, grown out of separate organizations which had come into existence precisely because their leaders could not agree on common policies and objectives. Within the SCA many of these earlier rivalries continued, aided by the fact that, unlike USNO and UPKO, no dominant leader was available to unite the party. In a sense, Peter Lo was able to remain in office as President only because his rivals and their supporters were aware that he possessed neither the financial resources nor the organized ground support that could enable him to establish his personal control over the party. He was also not initially identified with the major factions, which could not come to any agreement over the distribution of positions within the party, and was therefore promoted as a compromise candidate, but even then only through the intervention of Alliance leaders from Kuala Lumpur. USNO and UPKO, on the other hand, were almost entirely the products of the personal initiative of Mustapha and Stephens respectively, and there was literally no one in these parties who could match them either in public or intra-party support. USNO and UPKO were also financially dependent on these two leaders, and this made the position of these leaders unassailable.[164]

Clan rivalries within the SCA have centred mainly on conflicts between the Hakka and Teochew groups, each accusing the other of cliquishness and of attempts to gain dominance. The former, although representing the largest single group within the SCA (and within the Sabah Chinese population at large) was not the "toughest" group within the party, and in many ways did not have the same organizational control. Its leaders, Peter Lo and Pang Tet Tshung, did not appear to have the same skills in political in-fighting and in party organization as Khoo Siak Chiew, the leader of the Teochew group and Yeh Pao Tze, a Foochow businessman and newspaper owner, whose faction included not only his own clan but also a significant number of Cantonese.[165] The Lo-Pang faction was based mainly in Kota Kinabalu and the Khoo faction in Sandakan (with some strength in Kudat), while the Yeh group had roots in Kota Kinabalu as well as in the Interior. In 1969, according to one reliable estimate, the SCA Central Executive Committee contained seven members of the Lo-Pang group, eight members of the Khoo group and fifteen members of the Yeh group with six members remaining uncommitted.

Despite its internal problems, the Sabah Chinese Association has had more success than its Sarawak counterpart. As pointed out earlier, until UPKO's dissolution its position (especially within the Alliance) was considerably enhanced by its balancing rôle, which gave it a bargaining power which was out of proportion to its electoral potential.[166] Even in purely electoral terms, it has fared better than the Sarawak Chinese Association, although in this it has been favoured by external circumstances. For one thing, it has not had any equivalent of the SUPP to contend with.[167] It has, however, to be noted that the SCA's "good" showing in the 1967 state election (when it won five out of the six seats it contested) does not provide much evidence of its popularity among the Chinese. Opposition to it came mainly from a group of Chinese Independents who appealed more directly to Chinese interests, accusing the SCA of ineffectiveness and of having been too accommodating in its relations with the Native components of the Alliance and with the Central Government[168]. Although the combined vote of the SCA candidates was higher than that of the Independents, some of the seats contained a significant number of Muslim voters who, because USNO threw its weight behind the SCA, must have voted for that party's candidates. In all likelihood the SCA polled no more Chinese votes than the Independent candidates in 1967 despite the fact that the latter had organized themselves only just before the election.[169] The SCA's complete success in the Parliamentary election of 1969 (when all three of its candidates were returned), again did not provide any convincing evidence of its following among the Chinese. The group of Independents and their supporters who, after the 1967 election, had attempted to form a new party, had encountered various difficulties in achieving their goal; following the May 1969 riots in West Malaysia and the subsequent declaration of a state of emergency, some of their key members (including Yap Pak Leong, the sole successful Independent candidate in 1967) were detained under the Preventive Detention Ordinance. This effectively broke the back of their movement.

Despite its advantages *vis-à-vis* the Sarawak Chinese Association, the Sabah Chinese Association has had to face an issue on which its reputation (among the Chinese) has suffered. This has to do with the status awarded to the Chinese language. In mid-1965 a campaign was started by various Chinese societies and associations in West Malaysia (led by the Chinese Teachers' Association, with active support from the Chinese Chamber of Commerce) to make Chinese one of the official languages of the country. Although the ensuing debate was in many ways Malaya-centred, developments there are not of immediate relevance in the present discussion. It was, however, unavoidable that the issue should have spread to East Malaysia and the Chinese in Sabah, already dismayed by the moderation shown by MCA leaders in Kuala Lumpur (notably Tan Siew Sin) sprung to action when the Central Government in the height of the controversy decided to prohibit the use of the Chinese language in announcements made at airports in their state.

The issue received widespread publicity in Chinese newspapers in Sabah,[170] and SCA leaders, despite their promises to make representations on the matter and their appeals to the Chinese to unite behind them in order to strengthen their hand, soon found that they were not in a position to defy the MCA and the Central Government; they could not risk their own positions within the ruling group, particularly since there was every likelihood that they would also alienate USNO by taking a "Chinese-first" position. The issue, coming at a time when the merger of SANAP and the welfare-based SCA was being finalized, appeared to have done some early damage to the new party, especially when the powerful Sandakan Chinese Chambers of Commerce felt provoked in late September to launch a campaign inviting the office-bearers of the roughly thirty societies and associations in their town to sign a petition to the Head of State and the Chief Minister requesting that Chinese be made an official language.[171]

For its part, the SCA made an effort to retain some initiative on the matter (and, presumably also to forestall an internal crisis) by deciding at its general meeting earlier that month that one of its six objectives would be "to ensure that the Chinese language will receive equitable treatment and to take a reasonable stand in fighting for the Chinese language to be made one of the official languages in Sabah."[172] Despite various assurances by MCA and local SCA leaders about the liberal spirit in which Article 152 of the Constitution[173] would be interpreted by the Central Government, and warnings about the consequences of any "rash" actions, there continued to be some resentment among the Chinese in Sabah over the SCA's failure to take a less compromising stand. In the words of a reader whose letter was published in the *Borneo Times*,

> The so-called "Chinese leaders" of Sabah should have come out to speak their minds on this issue, but these "Chinese leaders" are keeping quiet about it. Even our neighbouring Sarawak leaders have come out to protest against this [the prohibition of airport announcements in Chinese] for Sabah, putting our Sabah leaders to shame. From this we can easily see that the Sabah "Chinese leaders" have only the wish to become high officials. . . . Other than this they are just useless. The Chinese truly have lost their face for having such "Chinese leaders".

The Alliance Formula in Sarawak and Sabah

The above discussion has dealt primarily with the sequence of party formation and with the basic attributes of individual parties in Sarawak and Sabah. It may now be useful to take a broader view of the subject and to explore in some detail what is perhaps the most crucial feature of party politics in the two states, namely the extent to which party activities have been affected by the prevailing ethnic divisions. A convenient way of doing this would be to look at the difficulties which the Alliance parties in these states have faced in accommodating rival communal interests. Such an approach would not have been very helpful in the case of West Malaysia, where the distribution of political power among the main ethnic groups is unambiguous and where the major rivalries, on ethnic issues, are found between the Alliance or its component units and opposition parties which appeal either to Malay or to non-Malay interests. In Sarawak and Sabah, on the other hand, political power is not associated with any single community; further, the main ethnic rivalries have tended to exist more within the Alliance than between the Alliance and parties outside it.[174] One may therefore begin this discussion by asking: why has the "Alliance formula",[175] so successful over a long period in West Malaysia, produced special difficulties in Sarawak and Sabah?

One obvious answer is that the formula is in fact quite different. True, the basic principle of different parties getting together under a common framework while retaining their separate identities has been followed in both territories. But the assumption in West Malaysia has been that the component units of the Alliance cater to mutually exclusive groups within the population and therefore do not compete with each other for members. To this extent the rivalry between them is clearly defined and relatively easy to institutionalize: the UMNO represents the Malays, the MCA the Chinese, and the MIC the Indians.

In Sarawak and Sabah, on the other hand, the chief partners were far from being rivals in this limited sense alone. Most of them also competed with each other for members and were by virtue of this involved in a further struggle to become the accepted spokesmen of their particular Native communities.[176] An important consequence of this was that, whereas in Malaya disagreements between the parties could be settled in the conference room, in Sarawak and Sabah they tended to be taken to the people for adjudication. For this reason, while the local branches of the component parties have complemented each others' activities in Malaya, it was inevitable that their counterparts in the Borneo territories should have engaged in mutually destructive activities. Needless to say, the leaders of these Borneo parties eyed their rivals with suspicion, fear and resentment. In contrast, the leaders of the UMNO, MCA and MIC in Malaya have had nothing to fear from each other, at least as far as their positions within their own parties have been concerned; indeed, they have often been only too keen to lend support to each other, knowing that this can do nothing but good to the Alliance, and, indirectly, to themselves.

Another related factor is that even ethnic interests have not been as clear-cut in Sarawak and Sabah as they have been for a long time in Malaya. In Malaya, each of the three major groups—the Malays, the Chinese and the Indians—has had its own distinct identity, reinforced at a number of different levels by different attributes: "race", language, religion, occupation, economic status, tradition and geographic concentration. Thus the Malay community coincides almost totally with the Muslim and Native Malay-speaking group, while the Chinese and Indians have their own languages and religious affiliations; the Malays are widely recognized as the economically depressed community; unlike the Chinese and the Indians the Malays also have a cultural and traditional continuity in the local context which is reflected, for example, by the continuing presence of, and official recognition given to, their traditional hierarchy headed by the Rulers; and, finally, the rural farming population of Malaya is predominantly Malay, while the urban population and the commercial and industrial sectors are heavily dominated by the non-Malays, particularly the Chinese. Admittedly, differences do exist *within* these major communities,[177] but these have been politically irrelevant in a context where differences *between* them have been so pronounced that they have dominated the political scene.

The plural societies of Sarawak and Sabah, on the other hand, have certain properties which are markedly different. Most of them stem from the fact that the indigenous population in each of these territories is itself highly heterogeneous. Quite apart from the point already made about the competition, within the Alliance, between different Native parties, the potential for a common sense of identity among the indigenous groups has also been hampered by ethnic and cultural diversities. To begin with, the indigenous population in both states comprises a number of distinct ethno-linguistic groups; although some groups are large enough to have aspirations of dominance, none is as powerful as the Malay community in Malaya. Further, even the internal cohesion of these major groups has been affected by the fact that they do not have attributes which reinforce each other; on the contrary, there is a definite criss-cossing of many of the major cleavages in these states. Thus, just as the viability of Kadazan nationalism and solidarity (and hence UPKO's potential appeal) was undermined by the fact that some Kadazans were Muslims and that even many of those who were not Muslims could not totally identify themselves with the predominantly Catholic, Penampang-bred leadership, the attractions of Islamic solidarity (and hence USNO's potential appeal) were modified by the fact that many Muslims had closer ethnic affinities with UPKO.

This problem of overlapping identities has been more pronounced in the case of smaller minorities, like the Melanaus and Land Dayaks in Sarawak. Dialect differences, even within the major groups, have constituted another barrier to communal solidarity. A non-Native example of internal communal cleavage worth mentioning here is the long-standing rivalry between the Hakkas and the Teochews in Sabah, which has had an important bearing on the weakness of the Sabah Chinese Association.

Even where ethnic or cultural identity has not been modified by overlapping cleavages, the sense of communal oneness has often not been developed to anything like the extent found in Malaya. Many factors account for this. To begin with, given poor communications and the recent arrival of competitive politics, long-standing parochialism and local loyalties have been difficult to dislodge even through the use of communal appeals. Which part of the state one is from is often as important as what community one belongs to, as testified by Pesaka's emergence as a party which sought to represent Third Division Ibans. But perhaps the most striking example of this was the difficulty which the UPKO had in persuading all Dusuns in Sabah to identify themselves as Kadazans and thus to accept a common identity. While part of the difficulty no doubt lay in the unwillingness of some groups to accept the "Kadazan" label as an appropriate one, it was also quite evident that the history of isolation and the parochialism which had grown out of it had led at least some of these groups to regard themselves as distinct sub-branches of the Dusun or Kadazan group.

Particularly during the initial stages, lack of knowledge about the political process may also have militated against the emergence of a strong sense of common destiny. It is also relevant that, compared with Malaya, there was very little history of communal organization, especially for political purposes, in Sarawak and Sabah. By the 1960s almost the entire electorate in Malaya was quite familiar with the communal implications of various major policy alternatives, and had been exposed for some time to attempts by various parties to mobilize support along communal lines. In Sarawak and Sabah, on the other hand, the vast majority at least of the indigenous population had had no experience of communal activity and of the rhetoric of communal politics. Although various cultural organizations had existed previously, these were not of much importance; further, there had been no crises to stimulate communal identification[178] (comparable say to the Malayan Union proposal in Malaya) and no competitive politics to provoke a sense of communal solidarity.

Even the relationship between the indigenous and non-indigenous populations in Sarawak and Sabah has been different from that in Malaya. Some of the factors mentioned above (such as the criss-crossing cleavages, the newness of competitive politics and the relative absence of constitutional crises involving communal issues) partly explain this. There are, however, other points which are also worth considering. In the first place, the non-indigenous population in Sarawak and Sabah is not as strong numerically as its counterpart in Malaya, and is therefore not viewed in the same light by the indigenous political leaders. Equally important is the fact that there is not the same rivalry between a dominant indigenous culture and immigrant cultures, as is found in Malaya. True, the basic differences between these cultures are profound, but then there is neither the equivalent of a single indigenous culture (like Malay culture in Malaya) nor the same commitment on the part of the indigenous communities to advance the status of their own cultures with a view to establishing them as the bases of national (or state) unification. Indeed, the leaders of the two main ethnic groups, Ibans and Kadazans, have often expressed their desire to see the continued use of English both in education and in administration. Some of them, as Christians, have also been keen to resist the extension of the advantages which Islam, as the national religion, enjoys in the Malayan states. For these reasons, the leaders of the major indigenous communities have often shown a willingness to associate themselves with the local Chinese in trying to avoid the full impact of Malay as the national language and Islam as the state religion. For the non-Malay, non-Muslim indigenous communities of East Malaysia, the basic cultural threat may be seen as coming not from the immigrant communities but from the new nation's now dominant indigenous community.

The point has already been made that the "Alliance formula", while containing certain common properties, has not been the same thing in East as in West Malaysia. The implications of this appear not to have been fully grasped either in Kuala Lumpur or in the East Malaysian states, and this has often led to inconsistent interpretations of the formula and its objectives. It was only natural that the Malayan Alliance, as the effective parent body, should have regarded itself, and been regarded by the East Malaysian Alliance parties, as an acceptable pan-Malaysian paradigm. But the kind of reference group behaviour which such an assumption encouraged in East Malaysia did not always encourage smooth relations either between the centre and the regions or among the component units in Sarawak or Sabah.

If the arrangement in Malaya had been seen as an alliance between the indigenous and non-indigenous communities, in which the former enjoyed a position of pre-eminence, an East Malaysian parallel would have called for the formation of an Alliance Party in each territory made up of two components —one to represent the indigenous population and another to represent the non-indigenous (in effect the Chinese) population. Under such an interpretation, the Malays in Malaya and the UMNO would have constituted the reference group for the indigenous communities of Sarawak and Sabah and their political parties. But, given the heterogeneity of the indigenous population and the circumstances under which the parties were formed,[179] this was not at any time a likely development although attempts were in fact made to bring the Native parties together. UPKO's decision to dissolve itself has now produced this situation in Sabah. But this was more a home-grown Sabahan contribution to the art of conflict-resolution than a product of the interpretation of the Alliance formula now being discussed. Had it seriously been believed that the Alliance formula required a single indigenous party, the merger should have taken place before the 1967 election rather than after it, when USNO-UPKO hostilities had reached unprecedented heights. In any event, there is as yet no clear evidence that the "merger" has been viewed by the supporters of both parties as the termination of all previous rivalries.

The Malayan Alliance could also have been viewed as a consortium representing the three main communities in West Malaysia, in which the party representing the dominant community assumed the role of senior partner. If communal identity had been seen primarily in ethnic terms, the equivalent state Alliance parties in East Malaysia would in all likelihood have comprised five units in Sarawak and four in Sabah[180] and would have been led by an Iban component in Sarawak and a Kadazan component in Sabah. In such a situation the Malays and the UMNO in Malaya would have constituted reference groups for the Iban and Kadazan communities, although in this case the scope for an exact parallel would have been modified by the fact that neither of the senior partners in East Malaysia could have claimed an overall majority status. Another problem, in the case of Sarawak, may have been that the Chinese were as numerous as the Iban community. This problem, however, would have been offset by the greater political power of the Iban community, mainly as a result of rural weightage,[181] and by the concessions which the Chinese, as an immigrant community, would have had to make.

Finally, the Malayan Alliance could have been seen as a partnership between Malays and non-Malays, with the UMNO, representing the Malays, as the senior partner. In the Malayan context this is no different from a partnership between the indigenous and non-indigenous communities, but even when seen solely in terms of the ethnic distribution of the population this is a realistic and viable proposition which makes good political sense.

Such an interpretation of the Alliance, however, cannot make the same political sense in East Malaysia, for the obvious reason that the Malays are by no means the dominant community there and also because the majority of people in the non-Malay category are also of indigenous stock. Nevertheless, this view of the Alliance (or, rather, a modified version of this view) has not by any means been totally absent either in Kuala Lumpur or among some of the component units of the Alliance in East Malaysia, and has in some ways been responsible for the confused relationships, not only between the national and state Alliance leaders but also among the leaders of the Alliance components in Sarawak and Sabah. On the one hand, as already pointed out, an Alliance between Malays and non-Malays in which the former dominated could have been established in Sarawak and Sabah only in open defiance of the realities of political life in these states—not only for the obvious demographic reasons, but also because Iban and Kadazan acquiescence would not have been forthcoming. At the same time, while the Ibans and Kadazans may have accepted the UMNO as an appropriate model for their own parties, they could not have regarded the Malays of Malaya as their effective reference group because they shared neither a common identity nor common objectives with the Malays. If anything, their shared status as indigenous peoples notwithstanding, they were apprehensive not only of Malayan but also of Malay domination and to this extent were keen to establish a separate pattern of dominance within their own states.

These views were not unknown to UMNO leaders in Malaya. They became aware that the arguments which had supported Malay political dominance in Malaya had to be reformulated so that in Sarawak and Sabah, as well as for Malaysia as a whole the claims of the "indigenous" communities would become the operational concept which justified the distribution of political power: hence the substitution of the term "bumiputera"[182] for "Malay" in the country's political vocabulary. But Malay political leaders were also acutely aware that bumiputera unity was not as easy to promote as Malay unity, because the indigenous groups in the Borneo states had different, and sometimes conflicting interests. The

Malays were beyond doubt Malaysia's dominant indigenous group and the only group capable of national political power. Under these circumstances, the obvious strategy for them was to assume a dual rôle: of a distinct and uniquely indigenous community *vis-à-vis* the non-Malays in Malaya, where political power resided and where issues were relatively well differentiated, and of the dominant indigenous community at the pan-Malaysian level. This, however, led to some ambivalence because there was some scope for Malay unity even at the pan-Malaysian level, and it was difficult to resist the opportunities that were available for establishing special links with the Malay community in East Malaysia while promoting a more general unity of the indigenous peoples. The Malay community in Sarawak perhaps constituted a sufficiently large minority for this to be a worthwhile proposition in that state, although there were great risks that the other Native communities would be alienated and therefore remove themselves from the area of indigenous unity. In Sabah, the Malay community was so small that it could make no real contribution to Malay unity; consequently, the dangers of alienating the other Native communities in that state far outweighed any advantages that Malay solidarity could have provided. However, the presence of cross-cutting cleavages which have complicated the transplantation of the Alliance formula and frustrated the sponsors of Native unity have also, in a curious way, enhanced the scope for UMNO leadership.

The common denominator in this regard has, of course, been Islam. If on the one hand the main indigenous groups in Sarawak and Sabah could not get together to form a stable partnership, let alone forge a common identity, at the state level, the Muslims among them were at least able to compensate for this by establishing a special relationship with the UMNO and thereby becoming a tributary of the main stream in Malaysian politics. Not constituting a majority in either of the two states these Muslim groups were aware that they could use their ties with the UMNO (and, through it, the Central Government) not only to detain greater leverage in local politics but also, when the need arose, to gain entry into the ranks of the national elite. In this regard, it is perhaps less than coincidental that the only two Native politicians from

Sarawak ever to have been given "functional" appointments in the Federal Government at Minister or Assistant Minister level have both been Muslims: Rahman Ya'akub and Abdul Taib bin Mahmud.[183] Both of them had been controversial figures at the state level, and had become the targets of Iban hostility. The only person from Sabah who has been rewarded with a similar "functional" appointment[184] is Ghani Gilong, who was once an UPKO leader. Although he was not a Muslim at the time of his appointment,[185] he was chosen only after UPKO's dissolution and after USNO dominance had firmly been established.

It would be wrong to assume that the forging of this common identity between the UMNO and the non-Malay Muslim groups in East Malaysia was in any significant way contrived. It is true that the exclusive characteristics of Malay identity in Malaya, if transplanted to East Malaysia, would not automatically have embraced the non-Malay Muslim groups of Sarawak and Sabah. But as the non-Malays of Malaya do not share any ethnic or cultural attributes with the Malays, there has been no need to dissect "Malay identity" with a view to identifying those segments which separate the Malays from the non-Malays. But Islam is undoubtedly a crucial component of Malay identity and is also an important source of communal solidarity. Thus, for the Malays of West Malaysia, the shift from a "Malay" to an "Islamic" focus in promoting communal identity at the pan-Malaysian level caused neither much confusion nor any political discomfort: on the one hand it did not in any way dilute the distinctiveness of their identity in Malaya; it also did not threaten their position as Malaysia's pre-eminent political group, because the Muslim communities of East Malaysia were neither sufficiently large nor sufficiently distinctive as a group to cause any concern in this regard. For the Muslims of East Malaysia, identification with the politically dominant Malay community of Malaya was, as pointed out, of obvious political advantage; it also did not threaten their own political identities because religion was an important basis of that identity and a crucial variable which set them apart from the other indigenous groups in their states. For the Alliance Parties of Sarawak and Sabah, however, this was not a very happy development: it added to the problems of party unity and discipline, exacerbated personal rivalries, undermined the chances of a common stand not only on federal-state relations but also on local issues, reduced the importance of domestic factors in determining the balance of power among the component units, and, for these reasons, provoked disaffection particularly among the larger non-Muslim indigenous groups.

The Alliance formula has also faced difficulties in Sarawak and Sabah because of the numerous problems that have accompanied the allocation of seats among the component units during elections.[186] True, this has also been a continuing problem in Malaya, but the boundaries of this problem have been relatively well defined there: "Malay" and "non-Malay" seats are easy to identify, and the only difficulty in assigning seats to Malay (UMNO) and non-Malay (MCA and MIC) candidates has been the further requirement of giving UMNO some additional seats in recognition of its senior status within the Alliance and as a confirmation of the Malay community's claim to political power. In Sarawak, and in Sabah until the dissolution of UPKO, on the other hand, the absence of a distinct politically dominant community, coupled with the fact that more than one party claimed to represent some major ethnic groups, meant that ethnic considerations could not provide decisive guidelines for the allocation of seats. This was aggravated by the fact that at the time of the first direct election in each territory, there were wildly conflicting claims by the various parties about the support which they enjoyed in different constituencies. As there were no ways of resolving these disagreements, it was also not possible to allocate seats on the basis of reliable estimates of party strength.

In Sarawak, another related problem has been the absence of anything that can even vaguely be identified as an acceptable hierarchy of leaders. Admittedly Temenggong Jugah's position as Chairman of the Alliance has never been questioned, but he has never been seriously regarded (mainly because of his educational shortcomings) as a possible leader of the Government. Ningkan, at least for a time, was able to exert some authority but, even in his case, misgivings about the appropriateness of having a SNAP Chief Minister, together with doubts about some of his personal qualities, always made him appear insecure in office. Tawi Sli, who replaced Ningkan as Chief Minister, was openly spoken of as a compromise candidate who, partly because he was nobody's serious rival and partly because he had neither the political drive nor the popular base that could enable him to entrench himself, was an ideal person to hold the fort while the real contenders manoeuvred behind the scenes. So pronounced was the absence of an accepted hierarchy (not only within the Alliance but even within the component units) that right up to the day of Rahman Ya'akub's appointment in July 1970, no one had a clear idea of who would become the Chief Minister if the Alliance won the election. The choice was not between two almost equally powerful contenders (as was the case in Sabah)[187]; the likely candidates ran into a good half a dozen, all of them apparently enjoying an equal chance.

The ways in which the introduction of competitive politics, involving the growth of political parties and the emergence of new elites with new roles, has affected the old administrative and traditional structures is discussed in Chapters 6 and 8. These structures, partly because their influence was territorially compartmentalized, were not very appropriate as instruments for the promotion of national identity and integration.[188] With the formation of parties and the advent of representative government, however, national (or, more precisely, Sarawakian and Sabahan) issues and symbols have come to assume a primary importance. Parochialism is being rapidly undermined, and parties and their spokesmen have been vigorous in emphasising the state of the crucial political unit.[189] To be sure, parties have also played up to local interests and primordial loyalties; but to the extent that they have all based their appeals on the importance of gaining control of the state government, one important consequence of their activities has been the broadening of earlier perspectives.

One can, however, also be less optimistic in evaluating these changes. It can be argued, with some justice, that what we have witnessed so far is not the ideal of a rapid transition from parochialism to state or national consciousness, but rather a transition from parochialism to a new sense of ethnicity. Thus, the primary concern of Ibans and Kadazans (the largest indigenous groups in Sarawak and Sabah, respectively) has now become the establishment of their own pre-eminence in the politics of their states. They have, to this extent, become less preoccupied with their immediate parochial units (e.g. long-house or village), but they have not in the process acquired a communally neutral concept of their states, let alone of the Malaysian nation. Similarly, the Chinese have now probably become more conscious of their status and future *as Chinese*; and the pro-Central Government stance of the two Muslim-dominated parties, Bumiputera and USNO, can also be seen largely in communal terms.[190]

But the distinction between "ethnicity" and "nationalism" is not entirely clear-cut in the case of the indigenous groups. For example, what the other groups in these states (or, for that matter, the neutral observer) my characterise as Iban or Kadazan ethnicity may easily be seen by the Ibans and Kadazans themselves as "nationalism" because they consider Sarawak and Sabah as "their" territories and therefore think that they should be the logical inheritors of power. At a different level it can also be argued that the Muslim communities in Sarawak and Sabah have vicariously identified with "Malay nationalism" in West Malaysia which is similar to the Iban or Kadazan nationalism just mentioned. Muslim "ethnicity" in East Malaysia, then, unlike its Iban and Kadazan counterparts, derives its strength and inspiration to some extent from external (i.e. West Malaysian) sources.

Finally, the continuing importance of Sarawakian and Sabahan as opposed to Malaysian national aspirations, and the fact that ethnic cleavages in East and West Malaysia do not overlap significantly, have resulted in a situation where party politics in Sarawak and Sabah remain outside the mainstream of Malaysian national politics. Apart from the common use of the "Alliance" label, no political party founded in either Sarawak or Sabah has any presence outside its own state, and no party which exists outside either state has any branches inside it. In other words, not only do East and West Malaysian parties not exist in each other's territories, but even within East Malaysia every political party is confined within the boundaries of its own state. If this situation were to continue, it must have some adverse implications for national integration. But for the time being this is partly counterbalanced by the fact that the Governments in both states have succeeded in working closely with the Central Government, and perhaps also by the fact that the parties which wield the greatest influence in these states (Bumiputera in Sarawak and USNO in Sabah) have close ties with UMNO and accept its leadership at the national level.

APPENDIX

Political Parties in Sarawak and Sabah and Names of Some Important Leaders

Sarawak

Parties in September 1963 (formation of Malaysia)

Name	Composition
Alliance Party (Government)	
SNAP (Sarawak National Party)	Mostly non-Muslim Natives
Pesaka (Parti Pesaka Anak Sarawak)	Non-Muslim Natives
BARJASA (Barisan Ra'ayat Jati Sarawak)	Mostly Malays
SCA (Sarawak Chinese Association)	Chinese
SUPP (Sarawak United People's Party)	Mixed, but leaders mostly Chinese
PANAS (Party Negara Sarawak)	Mixed, Malays predominant

Parties in July 1970 (state and parliamentary elections)

Name	Composition
Alliance Party (Government)	
Pesaka	Natives, mostly non-Muslim
Bumiputera	Mostly Malays (a union of BARJASA and PANAS)
SCA	Chinese
SUPP	Mixed, but leaders mostly Chinese
SNAP	Mixed, non-Muslim Natives Predominant

Some Important Party Leaders

SNAP—Dato Stephen Kalong Ningkan; Dato James Wong
Pesaka—Tan Sri Temenggong Jugah; Dato Tawi Sli
BARJASA—Dato Haji Abdul Rahman bin Ya'akub; Haji Taib bin Mahmud (both later Bumiputera)
SCA—Dato Ling Beng Siew; Dato Teo Kui Seng
SUPP—Dato Ong Kee Hui; Stephen Yong
PANAS—The Datu Bandar; Dato Abang Othman (later SNAP)

SABAH

Parties in September 1963 (*formation of Malaysia*)

Name	Composition
Alliance Party (Government)	
USNO (United Sabah National Organization)	Natives, mostly Muslim
UNKO (United National Kadazan Organization)	Mostly West Coast non-Muslim Natives
United National Pasok Momogun Party	Mostly Interior non-Muslim Natives
SANAP (Sabah National Party)	Chinese
Sabah Indian Congress	Indian

Parties in July 1970 (*state and parliamentary elections*)

Name	Composition
Alliance Party (Government)	
USNO	Natives. Contained many ex-UPKO members (UPKO, Pasokomogun Kadazan Organization, was a union between UNKO and Pasok Momogun)
SCA (Sabah Chinese Association)	Chinese (formed by a union of SANAP and the SCA, a Chinese welfare organization)
Sabah Indian Congress	Indian
Independents	A loose grouping with mainly Chinese support

Some Important Party Leaders

USNO—Tun Datu Haji Mustapha bin Datu Harun; Dato Harris bin Mohd. Salleh; Salleh Sulong; Dato Yassin

UNKO (later UPKO)—Dato Donald Stephens; Dato Ganie Gilong; Peter Mojuntin

United National Pasok Momogun Party (later UPKO)—Dato G. S. Sundang

SANAP (later SCA)—Dato Khoo Siak Chiew; Dato Pang Tet Tshung; Peter Lo

4

The Sabah State Election of 1967 and Sarawak State Election of 1969-70

The Sabah Election of 1967: Negotiations between the Parties

Given the background of hostility between the chief Alliance partners, USNO and UPKO, it was inevitable that fresh rivalry should have been stirred up by the approach of the first direct state election in 1967. Initially the outstanding issue revolved around the allocation of seats among the three partners, particularly between USNO and UPKO; as indicated in the last chapter, this was made particularly difficult by the absence not only of common assumptions about which communities "belonged" to which parties, but also of hard evidence[1] on which the demands of the parties could be judged.

Although claims and counter-claims about their strength and the number of seats which this warranted had been a feature of USNO-UPKO relations for some time before the election, it was not until February 1967 that the two parties, together with the SCA, decided to get down to the actual business of trying to apportion seats. It was initially believed by both parties that, in negotiating, they could base their claims on estimates of support prepared by their own workers. Indeed, in many instances USNO and UPKO had gone to the extent not only of going through the electoral registers with a view to determining the ethnic/religious composition of the electorates, and thereby of making their claims appear "logical", but also of getting voters to endorse statements saying that they would vote for them. But it was well known that these lists of supporters were quite unrealistic, and it was not long before the parties decided to abandon the idea of using them during the negotiations: questions of method and honesty aside, it became quite apparent that people had tended to inform each party which approached them that they were its supporters, as a result of which both parties had equally long lists of supporters, containing many of the same names!

Understandably, the negotiations were dominated by USNO and UPKO: The SCA was not in a position to stake a major claim of its own, but nevertheless enjoyed the position of being able to influence the outcome by supporting one or the other of the main contenders. It was clear from the beginning that its support went to the USNO, for reasons already explained in the last chapter.[2]

During the negotiations, which lasted five days, Tun Mustapha made it quite clear that his party did not accept the proposition that USNO and UPKO were evenly matched in the support they enjoyed. Although at one time the parties had been about equally powerful, this was probably an accurate assessment. UPKO's decline dated from about late 1965. Dato Stephens had resigned from the federal Cabinet following a rejection of UPKO's request for a re-examination of Sabah's position in Malaysia after Singapore left the federation. USNO and the SCA then forced him and Peter Mojuntin to resign from their positions as UPKO President and Secretary-General, respectively. Almost concurrently Tun Mustapha resigned as Head of State and, by returning to active politics, strengthened the USNO. Stephens' and Mojutin's resumption of their party jobs in December, 1966 was accompanied by a change of policy on the admission of Chinese to UPKO. Since early in 1964 Chinese members had been admitted, but this policy was resented by the SCA and had to be amended for UPKO to be allowed to fight the forthcoming elections as a member of the Alliance. Consequently, although Chinese already in the party could remain in it, they could not be candidates for party, or elective governmental, office.[3] In the forthcoming 1967 elections UPKO could gain substantial Chinese support only indirectly, via votes for Chinese Independent candidates.

Tun Mustapha's proposal was that USNO should be allocated candidates in 18 seats, UPKO in 8 and SCA in 6. Despite their earlier boasts about their strength, the proposal tabled by the UPKO leaders called for a distribution of 13-13-6. Officially, the two parties stuck to their positions and, in an attempt to break the deadlock, it was proposed (and apparently agreed) that there would be no contests in the nine constituencies over which there were no disagreements, while in the remaining twenty-three seats the parties would be free to put up candidates and engage in "friendly contests" against each other. Surprisingly, only one of the nine constituencies was given to UPKO, the remaining eight being shared equally between USNO and the SCA. But this agreement was short-lived. According to UPKO accounts, Mustapha informed the others the following day that his party had thought the matter over and did not favour the idea of "friendly contests" against each other: they would therefore insist on their original proposal.

In his informal discussions with Mustapha, Stephens had apparently indicated that a possible solution would be to maintain the status quo—that is, each party would be given the number of seats it already had in the Legislative Assembly. This would have meant 14 seats for USNO, 11 for UPKO and 7 for the SCA. Mustapha had been unprepared even to consider this, but now, as a last-minute concession, he agreed to give one extra seat to UPKO, resulting in a distribution of 17-9-6. Not surprisingly, this was quite unacceptable to UPKO, and the negotiations finally broke down. USNO and the SCA then decided not to field candidates in those constituencies which had been given to each other under the earlier no-contest agreement covering nine constituencies, believing that despite any subsequent development the candidates in these constituencies had the right to stand as "Alliance" candidates using the Alliance symbol.

UPKO, however, fielded a candidate in one of the four constituencies which had earlier been given to USNO, Bengkoka-Banggi, where Mustapha himself was the USNO candidate. But the party's efforts to explain this decision were not very convincing. On the one hand, it asserted that the no-contest agreement had been invalidated by the subsequent breakdown of the talks, and that each party was now on its own for the purposes of the election while continuing to remain within the Alliance. At the same time, UPKO leaders also claimed that it had not been their intention to contest in Bengkoka-Banggi and that a telegram sent to the candidate instructing him not to file his nomination had arrived too late.[4] In the remaining eight seats the candidates fielded by the Alliance parties (one from UPKO, three from USNO and four from the SCA) were either unopposed or were able to use the Alliance symbol in their campaigns against Independent candidates.

There are some points about the negotiations which need explanation. First, why was USNO not prepared to accept fewer than seventeen seats, when it lacked any concrete evidence to support its claims? It is, of course, possible that Mustapha and his colleagues had genuinely overestimated their own strength and the extent to which UPKO may have been damaged by the earlier upheavals which had resulted in the resignation of Stephens and Mojuntin as President and Secretary-General, respectively, of the party.[5] But two other explanations seem more plausible. First, Mustapha may have set his sights firmly on obtaining a majority of seats for USNO; although he had no reason to doubt the loyalty of the SCA, he presumably had no wish to see that party in the position of being able to tilt the balance in favour of UPKO by deciding to join forces with it at a later stage. By having a majority of seats he could also be more certain of the SCA's support and this would have put an end to the uncertainty which had characterized the preceding three and a half years of Alliance rule. But this was clearly a gamble, and, one might feel, a foolish one, because it would have been quite unreasonable to expect UPKO to agree to such a proposal.[6] The second explanation, however, shows some of the additional calculations that may have gone into this gamble.

By being tough and uncompromising and by appearing confident about his assessment of the outcome of the election, Mustapha may not only have been hoping that he could encourage UPKO to doubt its own earlier judgement and thus accept the number of seats offered instead of going through a difficult and costly campaign. He may also have hoped that, as the only alternative to accepting his proposal (and especially since it could not count on SCA support) UPKO would decide to leave the Alliance and contest the election on its own. Such an outcome would have served a wider purpose: there would have been no further threat to USNO, from within the Alliance, and this would also have cleared the way for national

Alliance leaders in Kuala Lumpur to campaign actively for USNO.[7] USNO's chances of getting a majority of seats would thus have been increased, and, with UPKO outside the Alliance there would have been less risk of the SCA holding the balance of power.

The next point about the negotiations which needs further clarification concerns the attitude of UPKO: why did it ask for only thirteen seats, which it later reduced (although not officially) to eleven, and why was it prepared to accept only one of the nine seats that were agreed on under the no-contest pact? One possibility is that, despite their own boasts, Stephens and his associates recognized that USNO and UPKO were evenly matched, and that an equal sharing of seats between the two parties would be the obvious solution to the existing problems. But the willingness to accept the status quo was rather more surprising, especially since it would have been seen as a clear admission that USNO was in fact the stronger of the two parties. It is, of course, conceivable that UPKO, uneasy at the thought of having to fight against the combined strength of USNO and the SCA, wanted to avoid conflict without at the same time disgracing itself: the status quo, presumably, represented the final point beyond which a serious loss of face would have been inevitable. It may also have been believed that, by being modest in its demands, UPKO would gain public sympathy (and, possibly, also some much needed sympathy from the Malayan Alliance) for having been reasonable during the negotiations, and that any blame for a failure to reach agreement would thereby fall on USNO.

It is, however, unlikely that UPKO's tactics were determined by these considerations alone. From interviews, it was quite evident that the party did not regard the allocation of seats as the final determinant of the relative positions of the three Alliance parties, or that, in conceding a larger number of of seats to USNO, UPKO would be abandoning its own hopes of dominating the future Government. If, on the one hand the party's leaders showed an unexpected concern for the unity of the Alliance, on the other they also harboured hopes that a number of USNO and SCA candidates would be defeated by Independents and that together with the Independents they would be able to form a Government which excluded both

USNO and the SCA. Indeed, it was rumoured that some of the Independent candidates would in fact be covertly sponsored by UPKO (in areas not contested by UPKO), and that their campaigns would be devoted to attacking the USNO and, in some cases, the SCA. Given the degree of partisanship stimulated by the unconcealed rivalry between USNO and UPKO, and the consequent channeling of support to these parties individually rather than to the Alliance as a whole, such a manoeuvre would not have required UPKO openly to denounce its partners in the constituencies concerned: its supporters would not have required much open persuasion or public canvassing by UPKO to cast their votes against USNO and SCA candidates. Even if such a plan had not been contemplated by UPKO, its leaders could at least have hoped that some Independents would defeat USNO and (more probably) SCA candidates, and later join forces with them provided their combined strength could produce a majority. It is certainly true that of the Independent candidates who later emerged, those who stood the best chances of winning would have welcomed such a move.

Finally, one may also be a little puzzled by the idea of "friendly contests" which featured temporarily during the negotiations. The idea was apparently floated by UPKO,[8] and, in the light of that party's overall strategy, one is not surprised that it was willing to accept the distribution of 4-4-1 under the no-contest agreement. The proposal, if accepted, would have kept the Alliance nominally intact and thereby facilitated a more even contest between the different parties, without intervention from national leaders. It also would not have prevented UPKO from supporting Independent candidates even in these agreed constituencies. It was probably on realizing this that USNO changed its mind about the proposal. Mustapha must have decided that he would not be coaxed into abandoning what was probably his original aim: either of getting a clear majority for his own party or, as an alternative, of making things so difficult for UPKO that it would decide to leave the Alliance. In the event he achieved neither objective. No allocation was agreed upon, and UPKO, only too aware of the consequences of breaking away from the Alliance, decided that it would rather face the combined (but necessarily blunted, as there was no clear break) strength of USNO and the SCA than allow the Malayan Alliance to intervene on behalf of these parties, although a clear break might have been useful in making the issues more clear-cut.

The Candidates, Sabah 1967

On nomination day, 82 candidates came forward to contest the election. One of these, the UPKO candidate in Lahad Datu, was disqualified on the technical ground that his registration number had been entered incorrectly in his nomination form. Of the remaining 81 candidates, 25 were from USNO, 24 from UPKO and 6 from the SCA, while 26 were Independents. 2 USNO candidates were returned unopposed, in Usukan and Merotai. In the other thirty constituencies the line-up of candidates was as follows:

TABLE 4.1

Line-up of Candidates in the Sabah State Election of 1967

	Straight Fights	Three-cornered	Four-cornered	Five-cornered	Six-cornered
USNO-UPKO	16				
SCA-UPKO	1				
USNO-Independents	2				
'Alliance'-Independents	2				
USNO-UPKO-Independents		3			
USNO-UPKO-Independents			2		
Alliance-Independents			1		
SCA-UPKO-Independents				1	
UPKO-Independents				1	
'Alliance'-Independents					1
Total	21	3	3	2	1

Of considerable interest was the fact that Stephens himself was not one of UPKO's candidates. His intention not to contest had apparently been made clear during the negotiation over seats, and had been known by the inner circle of the party. It was, nevertheless, a surprising decision. The most charitable explanation, that given by the party, was that this was part of the attempt to bolster Alliance unity (by removing the only real challenge to Mustapha's authority) and to show the other partners how keen UPKO was to co-operate with them. This, however, does not explain why Stephens did not change his mind after all efforts at compromise had failed. The answer probably lies in the fact that those he most hoped to impress by his reasonableness and loyalty were not USNO and the SCA, but the Central Government and the Malaysian Alliance, particularly the Tengku. In this context, it is worth noting that he had already been offered (and had accepted) the post of High Commissioner to Canada,[9] and a decision to become a candidate (which clearly would have indicated a desire to become the Chief Minister) would not have been received too well by the Central Government. Stephens had apparently requested that the appointment should not be made public until after the election, presumably because he feared that this might damage his party's morale by showing that he could not be counted on to lead it for much longer. He may also have felt that the announcement could harm him (and his party's) image as the champion of Sabahan rights and as the only bulwark against Central Government control. In the event, the announcement was made in the middle of the campaign and was resented by Stephens and his associates as a breach of trust and an attempt to produce the very results which they had feared.

It was also the firm belief of many people (including most UPKO leaders) that had UPKO emerged with a majority, Stephens would be found a seat in the Assembly (most probably through a by-election in a safe constituency, brought on by the resignation of the successful candidate) and then become the Chief Minister. In view of his Canadian appointment and his general determination not to offend the national leaders, it seems logical that he should not have desired a personal re-entry into the political scene without some guarantee that this would pay suitable dividends. There was also a further advantage in that, by not being a candidate himself, he was much freer than Mustapha to participate in the general campaign, for example by travelling more extensively and by putting his time and effort to more general use. But some felt that this also had an important drawback because the party's morale may have suffered when it was found that the leader was himself not in the fight.

The Election Campaign, Sabah 1967

Although one saw the expenditure of a great deal of energy and money by the parties and their candidates, the actual campaign was not characterized by any lively debate over issues on which the different contenders held different views. Two reasons may be given for this. First, all three parties which contested the election were members of the Alliance, and although there were obvious differences among them, none was prepared to pursue these differences in a manner that could jeopardize its position within the Alliance. The best example in this regard was UPKO, which, in addition to having to face the combined force of the other two parties, also held different views on important matters like federal-state relations, education policy, religion, and so on. However, although there may have been some advantages in breaking away from the Alliance and thereby obtaining greater freedom of action and better opportunities for throwing issues into sharper focus, UPKO, as already pointed out, chose to retain its formal links with its partners, because not to have done so would have exposed it to the combined assault not only of the USNO and the SCA but also of the Alliance in West Malaysia.[10] Thus, there was no equivalent in Sabah of the campaigns subsequently conducted in Sarawak by SNAP and the SUPP, which (because they were not in the Alliance) were able to be rather more forthright in presenting their views to the electorate. But UPKO may have felt that there was no great need for it to conduct such a campaign openly because it had already been active earlier in demanding a re-examination of the terms of Sabah's entry into Malaysia.

The second reason for the relative absence of lively, clear-cut issues during the campaign was that both USNO and UPKO seemed to believe that their policies were already known and that basic communal differences in the society would ultimately determine the pattern of voting and thereby constitute alternatives to "policies" in the strict sense. After all, active competition between the two parties had already been going on for about three years, and, as elections had been considered imminent since 1965, serious campaigning had already been going on for some time. These parties may therefore have felt that the actual period of formal campaigning should most appropriately be used for a "holding operation", without raising new issues that might only complicate the situation. The only new factor which could turn "committed" voters into "floating" voters was, of course, money, and this may explain why, despite their convictions about their "natural" appeal among different sections of the population, both parties found it necessary to spend lavishly.[11]

A good part of the effort put in by the parties and the candidates was of a "public relations" kind, and involved an attempt to show the electorate that they were good guardians of the public interest. A high premium was therefore placed simply on "being seen" during the campaign, and candidates and their workers were therefore encouraged to travel frequently to all parts of their constituencies. This was perhaps meant only to reassure the voters that they had someone to rely on and that earlier promises would not be forgotten, but as the campaign progressed it also became necessary to keep regular checks on opposition activity and to retain a competitive position on "treating", so as to ensure that there would not be any leakage of existing goodwill. These visits were also used to confirm that names were correctly entered in the electoral registers, to tell people which polling districts they belonged to and where their polling stations were located, and generally to educate the voters on polling procedure.

An interesting feature of the campaign was the emphasis given to party symbols and the way in which these symbols assumed an importance of their own as a result of lively discussions that took place about the merits and demerits of the actual objects portrayed. *Symbols*, therefore, were transformed to *issues*, often generating intense and, for all practical purposes, serious controversy.[12] On the more conventional plane USNO, using its favoured position with the leaders of the national ruling party, urged voters to support it if they wanted rapid development because this was not possible without the goodwill and generosity of the Central Government. To drive home this point, it repeatedly accused UPKO of undermining the unity of the Alliance in Sabah and of complicating relations with the Central Government. The leaders of UPKO were described as unreliable and ambitious, and in this connection

Donald Stephens' failure to get along with his Alliance partners and with the Central Government during his tenure as Chief Minister received wide publicity.[13] Among the non-Kadazan groups, a point repeatedly used was that UPKO, for all its talk of Native unity (and, on various occasions, of multi-racialism), was in fact a party based on Kadazan chauvinism which, if allowed to come to power, would ignore the other indigenous communities. Indeed, USNO even did its best to undermine UPKO's credentials among the "Kadazans". The argument here was that the attempt to unite all Dusuns under a common "Kadazan" label was only an attempt by the Penampang-Paper-based Kadazan branch of the Dusun group to dominate the others and that the other Dusun groups should resist any such manipulation. Mustapha, for one, continually appealed for "Dusun" support, obviously in an attempt to isolate the "Kadazan" leadership of UKPO and to split the ranks of the "Dusun" community.

As a Muslim-led party USNO also used religious appeal among the Bajaus and the other Muslim groups, and obtained the services of numerous religious teachers during its campaign. The party was aware that this would be counter-productive among the non-Muslim groups and the religious theme was therefore not emphasised among these groups. But this was not enough to make USNO acceptable to groups like the Kadazans and the Muruts, who, partly through UPKO propaganda but partly also because of USNO's own actions and pronouncements, were disinclined to regard it as an acceptable spokesman of their interests. USNO, however, was not prepared to abandon its Muslim image in order to compete more effectively with UPKO in non-Muslim areas, because by doing so it would have risked the solid support it received from Muslim groups.

Finally, USNO gave a great deal of personal prominence to its leader during the election. Throughout the campaign, voters were urged to support Tun Mustapha, the only person capable of uniting the population and of running a Government that would be consistent in its policies. Very often at rallies a documentary film was shown about his life, emphasizing his commitment to economic development and recalling his contribution to the creation of Malaysia and his subsequent role as Sabah's first Head of State and then Federal Minister for Sabah Affairs. The clear message was that by supporting USNO the people would be placing themselves in safe hands.

UPKO's efforts were concentrated primarily in the non-Muslim areas, although the party fielded candidates in Muslim-majority areas as well. Its main argument in its non-Muslim strongholds was that USNO in collaboration with the politically dominant Malay community in Malaya, was attempting to establish Muslim dominance in Sabah. In some of the less sophisticated parts of the state, candidates and party workers apparently warned voters during informal discussions that if USNO were to come to power non-Muslims would be forced to embrace Islam, which in practical terms meant they had to undergo circumcision and cease eating pork.[14] UPKO also accused its opponent of toeing the federal line and promised that, if returned to power, it would define in clear terms the area of state autonomy (along the lines of the "twenty points" agreed upon at the time of Sabah's entry into Malaysia). At the grass roots level, it emphasized its dedication to preserving the cultural identity of Sabah, and to resisting the imposition of federal policies on language, education and religion. Some attention was also given to the need to prevent Malayans from taking over important administrative posts previously held by expatriate officials, and from taking advantage of land development schemes being opened up in Sabah: these, it was felt, should be reserved for Sabahans.

Throughout the campaign, UPKO was somewhat hindered by the fact that while it promised change and criticized the shortcomings of the Government, it was itself a part of the ruling party, with seats in the Cabinet. Nevertheless it did portray itself as an alternative Government, and in doing so attacked those aspects of administration and Government policy which it claimed were not to its liking; it also emphasized its isolation within the Government as a result of the collaboration between USNO and the SCA. In a sense all it could ask for legitimately was a further strengthening of its position within the Alliance, so that its own priorities would not be sabotaged. And yet it also presented itself as an alternative to "the Alliance", in that it harboured hopes of going it alone if given an overall majority, or at least of being able to dictate terms to its partners after the election. The decision to remain within the Alliance having been taken, there was little else it could do; but this tactic also gave USNO and the SCA ample opportunity to question its criticisms of "the Government", since Stephens had been the first Alliance Chief Minister and after his removal from that post (when he became the Federal Minister for Sabah Affairs, in which capacity he was a member of the Central Government) other members of his party had occupied positions in the State Cabinet, including the post of Deputy Chief Minister. Indeed, USNO was able to point out that it was UPKO's obstructionist attitude which had immobilized the Government and that as the only major party which had not filled the post of Chief Minister it (USNO) deserved the least blame for any failures to date; it was therefore also the obvious choice if the voters desired a more dedicated and better disciplined Government.

One specific charge which UPKO levelled against USNO was that Mustapha was using official facilities—including a Government helicopter—to campaign and that this contravened the election laws: not only was the use of such facilities improper, but the helicopter's fuel costs alone, regardless of whether they were borne by the Government, far exceeded the legal limit placed on campaign expenditure.[15] Another UPKO allegation was that Mustapha used federal civil servants to help his campaign. The complaint, however, was not formally lodged with the Election Commission.

Like USNO, UPKO placed a great deal of emphasis on the achievements and personal qualities of its leader. Although he was not himself a candidate, Stephens' photograph was often in party posters and leaflets. The *Sabah Times*, owned by him and used as the party's unofficial organ, gave him greater publicity than to any of the party's candidates, and Stephens himself travelled extensively throughout the election period to work for his party. There was no doubt that among UPKO supporters his visit constituted the highlight of the campaign in those areas which were on his itinerary, and every effort was made to give him a warm and appreciative welcome. As pointed out later in this chapter,[16] areas which were not fortunate enough to receive him were treated to recorded speeches by him, which were taken by candidates and party workers on their tours.

Not surprisingly, the SCA's campaign was based on the need to preserve Chinese unity: faced with opposition from a group of Chinese Independents,[17] it argued that the Chinese, not having the strength for independent action, could not afford to let their ranks be split because they would then lose their leverage in local politics. If there were Chinese unity in the face of Native disunity (as reflected by the rivalry between USNO and UPKO), the Chinese could always exercise an influence out of proportion to their numerical strength. Admittedly there was nothing new in this argument; there was also nothing new in the SCA's other methods of campaigning, and considerable reliance was placed on ancillary organizations (like the clan associations and Chambers of Commerce), the personal connections enjoyed by the more prominent candidates, and money.

As the campaign progressed it became clear to the SCA that it had two specific tasks: to discredit the Independents as trustworthy spokesmen of the Chinese community, and to encourage Chinese in constituencies not contested by the SCA to support USNO rather than UPKO. The first of these is self-explanatory; the second was important because the party had to shoulder some responsibilities as a result of its special relationship with USNO: not only did it wish to see USNO defeat UPKO, but it was aware that, given its shaky position among the Chinese, it needed USNO's assistance to get Muslim support in its own constituencies so that it did not have to rely on Chinese votes alone. Another reason for attacking UPKO was that it had forged close links with the Independent candidates who, if the opportunity arose, were expected to support that party in order to give it a majority of the Leglislative Assembly. In this connection UPKO's alleged anti-Chinese attitudes were given wide publicity. and this, it was hoped, would also cast doubts on the reliability of the Independent candidates. All these arguments were forcefully presented in a lengthy article which appeared in the *Overseas Chinese Daily News* the day before polling commenced, which also attacked Stephens and the wealthy Chinese backers of the Independent candidates (notably Kwan Jui Ming) of furthering their own interests through collaborating with the departed colonialists. The article (written by a member of the staff of the newspaper) was headed "British Overseas Propertied Bloc Instigates Stephens to Struggle for Power", and deserves to be quoted at length because of the great variety of issues openly raised in it. No attempt has been made to alter the wording or style of the following translation, which was obtained from local sources in Jesselton.

> Through the good offices of the White Chinese capitalists led by Kwan Jui Ming and using the English-educated [Chinese] Independent elements as instruments, he [Stephens] is to engage himself in suppressing the national capitalists from raising their heads and in weakening the Chinese cultural and economic position. For a certain length of time prior to the handing over of political power, the British carefully spotted a talent among the Legislative Council members nominated by the Colonialists who would be able to protect British interests hereafter and went all-out to cultivate him for taking up the responsibility of political leadership in future. At the time, Donald Stephens was a favourite child under Sir Goode [the British Governor] that he was to play an active part in politics as if a quasi Minister in the Legislative Council in readiness to become the chosen Chief Minister in the days to come. To be a Minister is of secondary importance. But the Chief Minister will be the main figure who holds the greatest power. In view of the fact that Donald has British blood in his veins and is related to the British as well as that he has also had an excellent foundation of English education, the British thus made the choice of Donald Stephens and painstakingly trained him how to be obedient and taught him the British way of divide-and-rule. In order to win the favour of Donald Stephens the Colonialist Goode first of all approved to give him a timber concession so as to provide him with sinews, reared him as a political leader imbued with an idea of greater Kadazanism and then asked him to form a political party in readiness to assume the British rôle in the Government.... In collaborating with Holley [the State Secretary] who had the control of state affairs, Stephens, the Chief Minister, had the authority which surpassed the decisive power of the Alliance National Council and ignored the collective responsibility of the Alliance Cabinet. Datu Mustapha, the only opponent who could confront Stephens in the political arena was bestowed with the honour as the Head of the State in order to freeze him at the post. Whilst Stephens

was the Chief Minister, the number of British officers was not only not reduced, the Sabahanization of civil service was also not introduced into practice, but on the contrary, the number of British officers was continuously on the increase.... His policy was no other than to leave the jobs to the British for the time being in order to prevent Chinese from taking up the British posts in the Administrative Offices of the Government. (This is why he has been called anti-Chinese.... During the colonial régime his own younger brother named Ben Stephens was merely a Health Inspector of the Town Board and then all of a sudden became a Resident. During the 8 months when he was in office, it was top priority for practically every Government office to engage the Kadazans to fill up vacancies. In the choice of awarding scholarships, although it has been specified that the Natives have the privilege of priority, the successful ones were largely Kadazans including those whose academic qualifications are far below standard while Chinese students with distinguishing records were rejected outright. (Here again is another case of anti-Chinese).... In addition, he allotted more land and timber concessions to the Natives. In fact the ones who got the benefits were local leaders of Kadazans.... In fact, the timbers were being utilized as capital for political activities of local leaders of Kadazans while other Natives were complaining such unequal deal. Mr. Stephens' adherents seized the opportunity to arouse and encourage other natives to join the rank and file of the Kadazans so that they could get the benefit.... At the time, partisans of the Pasokmomugun and USNO had the desire to leave their parties and consequently a good number of them joined the membership of the United National Kadazan Organization (UNKO) led by Mr. Stephens.... The agreement reached to solve the first political crisis was directed at the above-mentioned Mr. Stephens' autocracy under the brood of the British.... This agreement was aimed at thwarting Mr. Stephens' wish to use "Sabahan" for interpreting the original residents of Sabah in order to cultivate a concept of GREATER KADAZANISM and to prejudice against other races. Haven't the readers very often come across in Mr. Stephens' English newspaper items charging that Tun Mustapha has come from Sulu, Chinese from Tongshan, and Malays from Brunei? Thus one can very well tell what is the status of our Chinese, Suluks and Malays in the Eyes of Mr. Stephens.... Among the Government civil servants, the most senior one was Leong Ah Khoon ... then Lam Ting Kong and John Dusing in succession. Both USNO and SANAP strongly maintained that the most senior one must be appointed to fill the vacancy but Mr. Stephens contrarily objected. The case had almost brought about another political crisis. The USNO and SANAP finally were so considerate that they agreed to appoint Dusing as the State Secretary (because the former two are Chinese).... On the evening of General Elections, Mr. Stephens asked a British named Lutter (his father-in-law) to come to Sabah in the capacity of Manager of *Sabah Times*. Through the good offices of this man, the British propertied bloc wished to carry out the "Holley Plan". It was hoped that Mr. Stephens would make use of [the UPKO's] Greater Kadazanism to create a situation on the eve of General Elections as if they were subject to Malay oppression in order to excite non-Malay sympathy and support besides he would rally public support to form a multi-racial political party in order to divide the Chinese so as to achieve his objective of reinstatement to office. Under the colonial regime, Kwan's family was one which enjoyed special timber concessions similar (to that of) the British. Kwan Jui Ming who was once called a White Chinese by the Democratic Party has for long been an intimate friend of Mr. Stephens'. With British pull, Mr. Stephens went all out to help Mr. Kwan raise his head in politics, but it is a pity that this person has been of not much use. Ever since the formation of various racial associations the United Party, up to the Sabah National Party, he remained insignificant.... In this General Elections, Mr. Stephens conspired with Mr. Kwan, a member of the SCA, to subvert SCA.... When the readers read the *Borneo Times* operated by Kwan Jui Ming nowadays, isn't it devoted itself in conducting free-of-charge vigorous propaganda for the "independent" candidates under Mr. Stephens' control? In the most conspicuous columns are published unreasonably attacks against the SCA by Chong and Yap [Chong Thain Voon and Yap Pak Leong, the two most prominent Chinese Independents who stood in Sandakan] with their statements which have no intrinsic value at all.... Man Woo Loong and Company and office of the Cheng Kee Timber Company, all managed by Kwan Jui Ming, are located in the same building. The propaganda posters of Chong Tain Vun's an Independent candidate, were fastened inside the show window of Man Woo Loong so that they could not be torn off by other people. However, when the propaganda articles of Khoo Siak Chiew's, the post Vice-President of the SCA in which Mr. Kwan is a member, were put up on the glasses outside the Man Woo Loong Building, they were immediately torn off by Mr. Kwan's men and the glasses were washed clean without any trace.... Mr. Kwan, the leader, other timber merchants and members of the propertied class have long formed themselves into a bloc by pooling their manpower and wealth together to give Khoo Siak Chiew a complete knockout in the political field so as to avenge Mr. Kwan's repeated political failures. It is hoped that Mr. Stephens will be reinstated to form a colonial puppet government in order to fulfil the British wish and to enjoy special timber privileges with the British. . . . Your reporter strongly supports the SCA. Whether the SCA is healthy or unhealthy every Chinese has a responsibility. Those things which are unwholesome should be improved. To knock it down is a way to be a victim to those who wish to form a puppet government, isn't it? . . . [Sir William Goode] taught Mr. Stephen how to cope with Chinese by first of all suppressing the development of Chinese schools without additional classes and simultaneously frustrating Chinese economic development and restricting opportunities for Chinese to raise their heads in the political arena. . . . Propaganda articles for independent candidates in Jesselton were being sent from Sandakan. The Independents were flying in a group back and forth. Their fund for election campaign must be plentiful, isn't it? The UPKO killed a cow today, held a "Tapai Cocktail"[18] tomorrow and chartered planes and cars now and then. Where have they got the money? You are able to tell without thinking. . . . Voters! right in front of your eyes at present are two courses and two political ideological lines for you to choose. One is to build up a Sabah State Government of the Independent Malaysia with the Alliance of USNO and SCA in power. One is to establish a puppet government under the control of UPKO and the Independents with British support behind the scenes. . . .

There is one aspect of the campaign which deserves special comment. This concerns the use of force and intimidation[19] to persuade voters to support or not to support particular parties especially USNO and UPKO. Almost every person interviewed during and immediately after the election drew attention to this, often citing incidents when candidates, party workers and supporters were made the victims of the strong-arm methods of their opponents. Occasionally there were also accounts, often in the form of boasts, of how one's own skill in mobilizing superior forces had forestalled any sinister activity by one's rivals. There is no doubt that minor incidents were very much a feature of the election, or that there was a prevailing atmosphere of tension. But the tensions were noteworthy only in the Kudat area, and even then only during the closing stages of the campaign. This needs to be explained.

To begin with, the main prestige fight was in one of the constituencies in the Kudat area: Bengkoka-Banggi, where Mustapha was opposed by Richard Yap. Considerable resources were therefore poured into this constituency and it was unavoidable that the heat of the campaign there should have carried over into the neighbouring areas. Secondly, these constituencies polled late under the system of staggered voting, and this made it possible for USNO and UPKO to deploy scores of dedicated party workers from constituencies where the election was over, particularly their strongholds, to these areas. Thus, several landrover-loads of UPKO activists were exported from Penampang to the Kudat area, while groups of USNO supporters (mainly Bajaus) migrated north from the environs of Kota Belud. These "Crusaders" (as one UPKO interviewee jocularly referred to his group) were apparently often armed (mainly with knives of various sorts although a few carried shotguns) and carried with them all the apprehension and excitement of going to the frontline of the battlefield. Tension and sporadic attempts at intimidation were inevitable, but an important point is that these did not reflect the eruption of any intense local factionalism or the mobilization of rival gangs within the constituencies concerned. This was almost entirely the work of the large number of outsiders who had gone to the area to boost morale and to "prevent" the intimidation of their supporters. They went there expecting trouble, and, in confronting each other, were bound to create it. But the trouble they created seldom reached alarming proportions: there were certainly no deaths and even cases of serious injury were few and far between.

The large number of incidents referred to in the course of interviews were more often than not confined to these outsiders, although one was aware that the sense of adventure stimulated by the campaign, and the attempts by party workers to impress their candidates about the risks to which they were exposed, may have resulted in some of the accounts being exaggerated. It was difficult to verify these accounts but the following statements by candidates, reproduced from field notes, were typical of those received during interviews. (In these statements, "X" refers to the candidates' own party and "Y" to the rival party.)

(*a*) "One night, a group of seventeen Y thugs visited a pro-X longhouse where there were about fifty people. When confronted by me, they claimed that they had come for food and rest. The atmosphere was very tense and many of the women started crying while the men appeared frightened. I asked the people in the longhouse which party they supported, and they all said that they supported X. I then asked the Y men to leave, and told them that they had no business with our people. There was very nearly a fight, but luckily a police field force which was in the area arrived on the scene.

We then realised that there were another fifty men, all armed with *parangs* [knives] who were hidden in the bushes. The police disarmed them and also took away my pistol. I had told the police that I would surrender my pistol only if they agreed to post guards outside the longhouse. They did, and everybody had a good night's rest."

(*b*) "In every polling district (in the constituency in question) my supporters were assembled in one place the night before polling, and were kept under guard. The next morning they were escorted to the polling stations in groups, with guards in front and at the back. This made the people feel secure."

(*c*) "During the last week of the campaign about 600 —— (name of ethnic group) from —— (the name of an area) came into my constituency. When I saw the first wave of about fifty arrive, I felt helpless and thought that their presence and activities would undo all the work I had put in during the campaign. In fact, I broke down and wept. I felt much better when, a few days later, —— and —— (the party's two leading figures) arrived with a gang of supporters from —— (the name of an area). Although there was a great deal of tension during the following days, no real fights took place. But my party's candidate in —— (a nearby constituency) was beaten up in his constituency. He was dragged out of his landrover by two or three chaps and punched. He landed up in hospital."

(*d*) "On polling day, about fifty of my supporters were made drunk by Y workers. They were lured into the jungle on their way to the polling stations and given brandy and beer after being told that they must have made a mistake because their polling day was the following day. One of the *orang tuas*[19] told me that he had not cast his vote because he was too drunk."

(*e*) "Two Chinese shopkeepers to whom I had given outboard motors and who were strongly pro-X at the beginning of the campaign were threatened by —— (the leader of the rival party) and returned the outboard motors to me. They later campaigned actively for my opponent. On polling day one of them even refused to sell food and drink to me and my men and we had to go without food the whole day. On one occasion an *orang tua* was kidnapped by Y workers just before I visited his kampong. He later escaped, and told me that they had concealed him under a blanket when I passed the house where Y workers were gathered."

But there was also another (and in this case decidedly beneficial) aspect of the "crusades" which is worthy of comment. After their return, many of those who had been to the north (as well as to the other parts of the state) became the centres of attention in their own local communities not only because of the stories which they had to tell about their own experiences but also because of the interesting accounts which they had of the people in the areas they had visited—how they spoke the same language but with local variations, what their methods of cultivation were, how food and styles of cooking were similar or different, what the terrain was like, and so on. Often seats were found in the returning landrovers for party supporters from the areas visited, and they in turn went home with accounts of life in the more developed parts of the state. Listening to some of these accounts, and observing the reactions to them, one was forcefully reminded of the implications of having "poor communications" even in a territory the size of Sabah, and of some of the unexpected by-products of party politics and elections.

The Sarawak Election of 1969-70: Allocation of Seats in the Alliance

As in Sabah, the approach of the first direct election in Sarawak led to fresh rivalries within the Alliance, mainly over the allocation of seats. Here again, negotiations were complicated by the inherent weakness of the Alliance structure, the background of the mounting competition among the different partners, and by the absence of any clear-cut and mutually acceptable criteria: the Native components of the Alliance claimed overlapping membership and support, and were also unable to use previous performance as a guide because direct elections to the Council Negri or to Parliament had not been held before and because, since the indirect elections of 1963, major changes had taken place as a result of SNAP's departure from the Alliance, the merger of BARJASA and PANAS, Pesaka's decision to accept Malay members, the incorporation of the large number of Independents who had won in 1963 into different parties, and the expansion of all the parties (which had barely got off the ground in 1963) into territories previously not penetrated politically.

If anything could have been learned from the Sabah experience, it was that negotiations over the allocation of seats to candidates should be initiated as long before an election as possible. By delaying things to the end the Alliance partners should have been aware that they would be inviting confusion and mutual acrimony during the crucial pre-election period. Another consideration was that it would have been wise to reach agreement before relations between the parties got worse; it might even have been hoped that, if such agreement were reached well in advance, there might have been a halt to the increasing rivalries between the parties, because an important source of these rivalries, the competition for seats, would have been removed. The question of timing, however, appeared to be the only lesson learned from the Sabah experiences, and, although negotiations commenced as early as July 1968 (for the elections originally scheduled for mid-1969), the chances of agreement did not appear to have been enhanced and rivalries between the parties continued unabated.

A "logical" procedure would have been to allocate Muslim majority or Muslim plurality seats to Bumiputera, Iban majority/plurality seats to Pesaka and Chinese majority/plurality seats to the SCA. But this was not acceptable to the different parties for different reasons: to Bumiputera because it also claimed Land Dayak support and therefore wanted all seats with a Malay-Melanau-Land Dayak majority; to Pesaka because it considered itself the spokesmen of all non-Malay indigenous peoples and not of the Ibans only; to the SCA because Chinese-majority seats were not generally regarded as winnable seats (owing to the SUPP's greater popularity among the Chinese) and the party therefore needed some non-Chinese-majority seats and the active support of its partners in order to win a few seats. As far as the Native parties were concerned, there were also other complications not related to ethnic factors. Bumiputera, for example, felt that it had a legitimate claim over a certain seat which did not have a Malay-Melanau-Land Dayak majority but which had earlier been an area of PANAS strength. Similarly, Pesaka was strongly of the opinion that although the ethnic principle (i.e. the principle of giving parties communally appropriate seats) was a good guideline, party strength and the merits of individual candidates should also be taken into consideration. Accordingly, it argued that where it had a Malay candidate who had a wider following in a particular constituency than anyone who could be put up by Bumiputera, the seat should be given to it because this would enhance the chances of Alliance success.

The most controversial seats in this regard were Sebandi, Saribas and Kelaka. Kelaka, familiar ground to Wan Alwi, Pesaka's leading Malay figure, perhaps provides the best example of the conflict between the two parties. Bumiputera was adamant that, as a Malay majority constituency where Pesaka strength had not previously been demonstrated, it should automatically be regarded as a Bumiputera seat; if Pesaka considered Wan Alwi important enough, it should find him an Iban seat because, if he had any aspirations of becoming a Malay leader, he should have joined Bumiputera and not Pesaka. Pesaka, on the other hand, encouraged by Wan Alwi's own refusal to budge on the issue, was equally unprepared to make any concession and there was no way of resolving the deadlock. In the event both parties fielded candidates in the constituency and Wan Alwi was returned.[20]

According to their own versions of the ethnic principle, Bumiputera thought that it should be given eighteen of the forty-eight seats, while Pesaka thought it should be given about twenty-eight and Bumiputera eleven or twelve. After a period of uncertainty and intensive bargaining, a closed-door meeting was held between representatives of the three Alliance parties, at which Tun Razak was present. At this meeting, the partners were asked to consider a proposal (which had apparently emanated from the national Alliance leaders in Kuala Lumpur and not from any of the local contenders in Sarawak) that the seats should be divided as follows: twenty-two for Pesaka, fifteen for Bumiputera and eleven for the SCA. Pesaka leaders expressed some reservations, and this led to a private discussion between them and Tun Razak, during which he made it clear that this was a fair compromise and that Pesaka would do well to accept it. There was no evidence that Pesaka actually rejected the proposal at this meeting, although no formal, binding agreement was reached. It seemed, however, that while Bumiputera, the SCA and Tun Razak left the meeting thinking the matter had been settled, Pesaka continued to harbour hopes of getting more seats and thought the door was still open for further negotiations.

During the ensuing weeks it was clear that different leaders had different ideas of what had transpired. Some of the Bumiputera leaders who were interviewed seemed to think that they had been given fifteen seats,[21] and that these included the Malay-majority seats over which there had been disagreement; Pesaka leaders appeared convinced that they had not committed themselves to anything and denied that they had given up their claim to certain Malay seats; SCA leaders, like their Bumiputera counterparts, asserted that the numbers had been agreed on but that it was still up to Tun Razak to decide which party would get the controversial Malay seats.[22]

Before long, there was a perceptible shift in the main substance of the controversy: disagreement no longer seemed to be about the numbers which had been agreed upon but rather about what these numbers referred to. Bumiputera had no doubts that it had been given fifteen seats, Pesaka twenty-two and the SCA eleven, and that the identity of these seats had been spelled out. Pesaka, on the other hand, preferred to believe that fifteen seats had been given to the Malays, twenty-two to the Dayaks and fifteen to the Chinese, and that it was now up to the Alliance to find the most appropriate candidates belonging to these ethnic groups, not necessarily from the parties dominated by these groups. This left the door open for Pesaka to press its claim in certain Malay seats, and the party even offered Bumiputera certain Iban seats in exchange for them: Bumiputera would have none of this, and instead explored the possibility of reaching agreement with Pesaka on avoiding contests in those constituencies where one or the other party had no ambitions, and on having friendly contests in the others, so that some semblance of Alliance unity could be preserved. But this did not receive a sympathetic hearing because by this time Pesaka seemed more keen on competing with Bumiputera than on co-operating with it, convinced perhaps that an anti-Bumiputera stance would help its chances in Iban areas. However, for a while it seemed possible that Pesaka would be prepared to entertain the compromise proposed by Bumiputera, but there were rumours that its real intention was to subvert any agreement by sponsoring its own "Independent" candidates and by actively supporting them in constituencies given to Bumiputera. The final break came in March 1969, when it was decided that the members of the Alliance would have a free-for-all while nominally remaining within the Alliance and thereby distinguishing themselves from the other parties.[23] Even this was an achievement under the circumstances, because during the final stages of the conflict there was a possibility that either Pesaka or Bumiputera would sever all links with its partners.[24]

Before the negotiations finally broke down there was another issue which achieved some prominence. Perhaps in anticipation of the final outcome (but also because it wanted to project its own local, Iban image in any case) Pesaka had made preparations to use its own symbol (rather than the Alliance symbol) during the campaign. Bumiputera, when it came to know of this, felt that this was totally unacceptable as it made a mockery of the links which were believed to exist among the Alliance partners. It also argued that Pesaka had already agreed at a meeting in Kuala Lumpur to use the Alliance symbol, and Rahman Ya'akub claimed that if Pesaka went ahead with its plans it would have to leave the Alliance. Anticipating a break-up of the Alliance, Ningkan was quick to encourage Pesaka by inviting it to join forces with SNAP so as to launch a combined battle against Bumiputera.[25] But Pesaka somehow appeared convinced that it was capable of winning a majority of seats, and therefore preferred to pursue its conflict with Bumiputera on its own.

The matter was finally referred to the Malaysian Alliance Council in Kuala Lumpur, which decided in Pesaka's favour presumably in an effort to keep the Alliance going in any form for the time being. The national leaders may also have accepted the view that by using its own symbol Pesaka would be able to compete more effectively with SNAP as an Iban party; in addition they may have felt that in the event of Pesaka's leaving the Alliance as a result of its not being allowed to use its own symbol, the chances of an Alliance victory (or even of an Alliance-led coalition after the election) would have been hopelessly reduced. But doubts about Pesaka's intentions must have continued because long after the campaign had commenced Temenggong Jugah, after a visit to Kuala Lumpur, found it necessary to reiterate that his party was still in the Alliance. According to him, "The Tengku was under the impression that we were no longer in the Sarawak Alliance. But now he is very happy at our assurance."[26] Subsequently there was a denial that Pesaka intended to form a Government with the SUPP after the election.[27]

Having succeeded in its attempt to use its own symbol, which it hailed as a victory against Bumiputera,[28] Pesaka showed itself to be somewhat disingenuous when it subsequently protested in strong terms against its partner's decision to use the Alliance symbol.[29] Its view was that Bumiputera should also use its own symbol because the Alliance party as such was not fielding any candidates. On this issue, however, it failed to get the support of national leaders, and Bumiputera and the SCA (which did not field any candidates against each other) were allowed to campaign under the Alliance symbol.

The SCA, like its Sabah counterpart, was not actively involved in the controversies during this period, knowing that it had much less opportunity than either of its partners to strike out on its own. Its future, like Bumiputera's and USNO's (in Sabah) clearly lay in remaining within the Alliance, but unlike these parties (but very much like the Sabah Chinese Association) it could not rely on any decisive intervention in its favour from Kuala Lumpur. However, while the SCA in Sabah, the only Chinese party in that state, had good reasons for believing that as long as the two Native parties existed separately it would have great bargaining power because they were evenly balanced and needed its support in order to achieve dominance, the Sarawak Chinese Association could not contemplate a similar rôle with equal confidence. This was partly because it was already a minority party among the Chinese, but partly also because the political alternatives in Sarawak were not unavoidably confined within the boundaries of the Alliance Party as constituted at any given time.[30] As things turned out, the SCA, like its sister organization in Sabah joined hands with the Muslim-dominated party in the state although, unlike its counterpart, it continued to have friendly relations with the non-Muslim party (Pesaka) throughout the campaign.[31] The decision to side with Bumiputera, like the Sabah Chinese Association's decision to side with USNO, must no doubt have been influenced by the fact that, not having a strong foothold locally, it was advantageous to show a preference that would be well received in Kuala Lumpur.

The presence of other parties outside the Alliance framework also had a bearing on the strategies adopted by Bumiputera and Pesaka. On the one hand, the certainty of an Alliance victory could not be entertained, and these parties therefore had an additional variable to consider in weighing the advantages and disadvantages of conflict between themselves. On the other, precisely for this reason Pesaka, for example, found it attractive to keep its options open (by remaining within the Alliance while competing openly with Bumiputera) so as to give itself greater manoeuvrability in forming a coalition Government after the election, in the event that no single party (or even the Alliance as a whole) obtained a majority. A coalition with SNAP, for example, might have been well worth exploring, as it would have guaranteed Iban domination; but there was no need to prepare for this in advance because there was no way of predicting the outcome of the election. Pesaka, however, appeared convinced that whatever the outcome it would be the pivot of the next Government because no other party could form a Government without it and because every party would regard it as its first choice for a partner. (It was thus believed that SNAP's) differences with Bumiputera and the SUPP were greater than its differences with Pesaka, that Bumiputera had less in common with SNAP and the SUPP than with Pesaka, and that the SUPP would find Pesaka a far more congenial partner than either SNA or Bumiputera.

Bumiputera, on the other hand, could not have believed in early 1969 that it could have the same options after the election, because Iban hostility, coupled with the fact that the SUPP was regarded as lying outside the area of national consensus,[32] would have left it with no potential allies except the SCA, the weakest party in the state. For this reason it was clearly in Bumiputera's interests to limit Pesaka's freedom of choice by binding it to its Alliance commitments. It was not, however, prepared to pay an unreasonable price in order to achieve this because in such a case it could not have gained much even from an Alliance victory. Thus, while in Sabah the unwillingness to compromise was due partly to USNO's and UPKO's belief that they would win outright, in Sarawak Pesaka was reluctant to reach a settlement because it knew that other (possibly more attractive) options might emerge after the election.

On nomination day, 225 candidates put themselves forward for election in the forty-eight state constituencies. Of these 47 were from SNAP, 40 from the SUPP, 37 from Pesaka, 22 from Bumiputera and 11 from the SCA,[33] while 68 stood as Independents. The remarkable thing about the line-up was, of course, the large number of candidates contesting; an average of 4.7 per constituency. There was not a single constituency where there was a straight fight between two candidates, while there were seven six-cornered fights, three seven-cornered fights and one eight-cornered fight. There were twenty constituencies where candidates from more than one Alliance party stood, eighteen of which involved contests between Pesaka and Bumiputera (including Sebandi, Saribas and Kelaka) and two of which involved contests between Pesaka and the SCA.

Campaign issues in Sarawak

The issues which dominated the campaign contained no surprises, and reflected the rivalries already described among the different parties. Most of the parties issued elaborate manifestoes which were printed in full in the local newspapers, although their length, the range of topics covered in them[34] and the fact that many of the items were common to most or all parties[35] must have made them confusing to the majority of voters.[36] To be sure, there were also certain distinctive features of each manifesto which brought out the core commitments of the party concerned. Thus the SUPP, which had originally been anti-Malaysia but which had subsequently been persuaded to modify its stand,[37] kept faith with its left wing by raising the issue, although not in a manner that could provoke the wrath of the Central Government. Its manifesto made it clear that the party supported the "concept of Malaysia", but went on to express reservations about the way in which the federation had been created[38] and promised to fight for a re-examination of the terms of entry: "certain terms and conditions whereby Sarawak became part of Malaysia require to be re-examined so that the natural aspirations of the people of Sarawak will be realized. The SUPP will seek to attain this by constitutional means." The party was clearly aware that on the question of state autonomy it had a serious rival in SNAP, which also presented itself as a champion of Sarawak's interests and which in addition could point to its own alleged victimization by the Central Government when Ningkan was deposed as Chief Minister. Referring to SNAP's slogan in the course of an election broadcast, Stephen Yong, the SUPP's Secretary-General, took pains to neutralize that party's appeal on this issue by saying that his party also believed in "Sarawak for Sarawakians" but that unlike SNAP, which wanted to stick to the letter of the London Agreement, it wanted to change the existing terms because that was the only meaningful way of safeguarding Sarawakian interests. Using local analogies, the SUPP's President, Ong Kee Hui, explained his party's conception of the ideal federal arrangement at an election rally as follows:

> Malaya was a federation of eleven states. It is like a longhouse with 11 doors or "pintu". The Malaysia plan envisaged the joining on to this 11-door longhouse four more families, i.e. four more "pintu", namely the people of Singapore, Brunei, Sabah and Sarawak. We in the SUPP agree with the idea that

> these countries should live closer together and form one community or village. We think however that it would be more feasible if we do not actually join on to the longhouse of Malaya but move and build our own house near to Malaya so that we can be in one village, like a Malay kampong. We think that this will prevent any differences of race, culture or religion among our united population from causing any friction or quarrel, and at the same time, ensure our security and mutual co-operation.[39]

The SUPP's manifesto was also unique in that it was the only one which explicitly referred to socialism and socialist planning as the solution to Sarawak's problems. Although, like SNAP, the party also gave a great deal of emphasis to multi-racialism both in its manifesto and in the cause of electioneering,[40] it was nevertheless careful to express support for Malay as the National language. Thus in discussing education policy the manifesto declared: "The SUPP will encourage and foster the free and unhampered development of the language and culture of all races in Sarawak. While acknowledging the need for [the] development of a national language, Malay, the SUPP considers that no restriction should be placed on the use of the other languages in common usage such as English, Chinese, Iban and other native languages." Finally, and for entirely understandable reasons, the SUPP was also alone in raising the question of political detainees. This was an issue on which the party had to take a stand, not only because it was believed to be of critical importance by the left wing but also because failure to have done so would have exposed the moderate leadership to accusations of betrayal; there may also have been a withdrawal of support by some of the party's most active workers whose services were believed to be vital for success, particularly in the Chinese areas.[41] In its manifesto the party therefore declared: "those who are now detained under the Emergency Regulations should be given the right to clear themselves of any charges under which they are detained before an independent and impartial tribunal of jurists. Those found innocent should be released or given an opportunity to be rehabilitated so that they can take their rightful places in society once again as loyal citizens of the country."

True to its reputation, the SUPP conducted one of the best organized campaigns during the election, with a fair degree of centralized financing and direction. Its leaders, perhaps more than their counterparts in any of the other parties, travelled a great deal outside their own constituencies, in order to co-ordinate the election effort and to augment the party's activities, particularly in the Iban areas.[42] During interviews leaders of other parties often maintained that the SUPP conducted a dishonest campaign in that it promised different (and sometimes conflicting) things to Chinese and Iban voters. (It was, for example, alleged that when addressing the Chinese the party presented itself as a distinctively Chinese movement, dedicated to improving the status of Chinese education and enlarging the opportunities for the Chinese to acquire land from the Natives; in talking to Ibans, on the other hand, it posed as a champion of Native rights and a vehicle for the establishment of Iban dominance in Sarawak politics.[43] SUPP leaders, however, denied this charge and maintained that while there was some difference in the way in which they campaigned among the Chinese and Ibans, this was only a difference in emphasis which no party could avoid because different people were interested in different things.

As already mentioned, the main thrust of SNAP's campaign was the promise to safeguard the integrity of the state within the federation. Especially in Iban and Chinese areas it relied heavily on its slogan "Sarawak for Sarawakians" because this implied vigilance against increasing Malay influence and control. The party placed a great deal of emphasis on the need to preserve the sanctity of the Constitution because its view (unlike the SUPP's) was that while the Malaysia Agreement provided adequate safeguards for the state these had gradually been eroded through federal intervention. Ningkan and the other leaders were, however, only too aware of the risks of courting federal displeasure by being equivocal on their commitment to Malaysia[44] and, although they promised "the dawn of a more meaningful independence", they took care to emphasize in their manifesto that if elected they intended "to co-operate wholeheartedly with the Federal Government for the development and betterment of Sarawak". This co-operation, however, had to be "based on a true spirit of understanding and sincerity and mutual respect for State Autonomy and State Rights as provided in the State and Federal Constitutions and the London Agreement". When, soon after the commencement of the campaign, a Federal Minister warned that Sarawak might face the same fate as Kelantan[45] if it did not return the Alliance to power, SNAP was the first party to react by rebuking him for his threat and by telling him that the voters of Sarawak were not likely to be intimidated by his remarks.[46]

Although multi-racialism received more attention from SNAP than from any other party,[47] it was also evident that its leaders were mindful of the dangers of advocating complete equality: no party based on indigenous (in this case Iban) votes, however multi-racial in outlook, could avoid giving explicit support to the constitutionally-backed policy of allowing special privileges to the indigenous communities. Thus, while stressing multi-racialism, SNAP's manifesto also took care to elaborate on the issue: "Although SNAP is committed to a multi-racial policy, SNAP still subscribes to the constitutional provision whereby the special privileges of the natives are enshrined in order to help . . . the under privileged natives."

On language and education, the party did not even refer to the national language in its manifesto, and showed its clear preference for English when it observed: "SNAP believes that in view of the development in Sarawak in the field of learning . . . it is necessary to retain the English language as a medium of communication and for official use for the foreseeable future . . . SNAP further believes in the liberal use of other languages and pledges to promote these languages in their respective institutions of learning."

As far as the actual campaign was concerned, SNAP's multi-racialism did not by any means result in the projection of a well-integrated, communally neutral image, especially at the constituency level. Although most candidates extolled the virtues of multi-racialism and often attacked the Alliance for perpetuating racial politics in Sarawak, there was no denying a distinct communal edge to most of the local campaigns. Thus Iban candidates campaigning in Iban areas left their audiences in no doubt that SNAP was essentially an Iban-based party and that no other party was equally capable of promoting distinctly Iban interests. Some of these candidates, judging from their remarks during personal interviews, obviously also harboured anti-Malay sentiments[48] and it is very likely that these were communicated to the electorate.

R Malay candidates, on the other hand, while also pointing to the advantages of multi-racialism,[49] presented themselves essentially as desirable leaders of the Malay community. Some of them had previously belonged to BARJASA or PANAS, and were now facing candidates from Bumiputera. Because Bumiputera's Malay identity could not easily be denied, these SNAP candidates therefore concentrated their attack on that party's policies and leaders. The common theme appeared to be that Bumiputera spoke only for the "extremist" Malays in the state who were prepared to sacrifice inter-communal R harmony (and, indirectly, Malay interests) in order to pursue their communal goals. If Malays identified themselves with these policies they would have only themselves to blame if the other communities decided not to co-operate with them. // This would certainly happen if any support were given to Dato Rahman Ya'akub's plan to merge Bumiputera with the UMNO in Malaya.

The severest attacks, however, were aimed personally at Rahman Ya'akub and Abdul Taib, who were invariably portrayed as ambitious men who would go to any lengths to achieve their own goals. Not only were they not acceptable to the leaders of the other communities, particularly the Ibans, but they also had no right to speak as leaders of the Malay community.[50] Knowing the appeal that Bumiputera would have as a result of its association with Malay dominance at the national level, these SNAP candidates sought to offset this by appealing to local sentiments. In this regard, a great deal of prominence was given to an earlier statement by the Tengku that plans were being made to send people from Malaya as settlers to Sarawak. This was bound to undermine the opportunities available to Sarawakians (including Sarawakian Malays) and Bumiputera was not likely to express any reservations on this matter.[51]

Given its almost obsessive concern for organization, it was not surprising that SNAP should have set up an elaborate headquarters in Kuching with a prominent Iban[52] as its full-time head. But this office seemed to have very few responsibilities for co-ordinating the campaign and served instead merely as a centre which helped to prepare and distribute publicity material and which liaised with the Election Commission, Radio Malaysia Sarawak and the police as the occasion arose. The striking thing about SNAP's campaign was, in fact, its decentralized nature. Apart from the centralized handling of printed material and, to some extent, money,[53] the party's candidates were allowed on the whole to fend for themselves. It may have been felt that the groundwork had already been completed long before the election and that all that was required of candidates was for them simply to hold the fort with the help of their local organizations during the actual period of campaign.[54] Two other factors, however, will have to be taken into account.

First, Ningkan himself was pinned down to his own constituency as a result of Ingka's decision to stand against him and was therefore unable to spend much time in other areas to help bolster up the party's overall campaign. As this was the first direct election, even the party's other leaders did not have sufficient confidence in their own chances to allow themselves to be organized into a team of top-level campaigners who would travel to all parts of the state. This was no doubt also influenced by the poor communications in Sarawak and by the fact that outside the few urban areas settlements were both small and scattered. Thus, in travelling in the non-urban constituencies a leader often had to spend a great deal of time (and physical effort) to reach a series of small settlements, one or two at a time. Under these circumstances, even a person who was prepared to spend a few days campaigning outside his own constituency could not hope to have much impact, because the ratio of time spent to voters contacted would have been extremely unattractive.

Second, SNAP probably erred in fielding as many as forty-seven candidates for the forty-eight state seats.[55] The party had no hope of winning many of these seats, but may have felt that by contesting in almost every constituency and by putting up communally "appropriate" candidates in many of them, it could show not only that it was the strongest party and the only one capable of winning an outright majority, but also that it was the most multi-racial party in the state. But there was no doubt that SNAP spread itself too thin in order to prove this, and its capacity to organize a tightly-run campaign with a greater concentration of expenditure in the winnable seats must have suffered.

Pesaka, in its published propaganda and in its election broadcasts, steered clear of attacking its partners and identified itself firmly with the state and national Alliance Parties. It wholeheartedly supported the formation of Malaysia and expressed no reservations about Sarawak's experiences within the federation. Indeed, its manifesto made it clear that the importance of the election lay in the fact that it gave the people of Sarawak an opportunity "to prove to the world that the people here wanted Malaysia, still do and will continue to accept it as a far-sighted and wise move". The party pledged loyalty to Malaysia and promised to "rally behind the Central Government in defence of the Nation's territorial integrity and sovereignty". While claiming that it was "the senior partner in the Alliance", Pesaka also pledged "to work closely with other component parties in the Sarawak Alliance" and promised that together with Bumiputera and the SCA it would serve as "a mouthpiece of the truly loyal and dedicated people of Sarawak who crave for peace, prosperity and security". It saw the need for a "strong Central Government" catering for matters such as external affairs and internal security, as contained in the Inter-Governmental Committee Report and the Malaysia Agreement and expressed support for the use of the national language in the state and "the continuation of English as the official language unless and until the Council Negri votes to the contrary". The rights of the indigenous communities were stressed in the manifesto, although the party also pointedly urged the Government (obviously forgetting its claim to be the "senior partner" in the existing Alliance Government) to create an "office for non-Muslim Native Affairs".[56]

Given the escalating conflict between Pesaka and Bumiputera (and, to a lesser extent, the SCA), it was not surprising to find that this demonstration of Alliance solidarity was at best superficial and was not sustained in the course of the actual campaign, especially at the grass-roots level. About half of Pesaka's candidates were, after all, facing Bumiputera opponents and this, reinforced by the intense bickering between the leaders of the two parties particularly during the period leading up to the campaign, easily encouraged explicit anti-Bumiputera activity. The main argument used against Bumiputera was its alleged unwillingness to recognize Iban dominance and its unfounded claim that it also represented some non-Muslim indigenous groups, notably the Land Dayaks. Although Pesaka's irritation was influenced largely by inter-party rivalries and by antipathy towards the leaders of Bumiputera, there was also some evidence, particularly among its Iban candidates, of anti-Malay feelings and of a conviction that not only Bumiputera but the Malay community as a whole were unwilling to recognize (let alone abide by) the local rules of the political game: as Sarawakians Malays were not altogether reliable and were not likely to be congenial partners because they were more attracted by their new status as members of the nationally dominant community than by their Sarawakian identity. Some anti-Chinese sentiments were also evident, provoked partly by resentment of the influence which the Chinese seemed to wield through their superior economic status, and partly by indigenous nationalist aspirations.

If SNAP spread itself too thin by fielding too many candidates, Pesaka committed that same error and also waged its battle on too many fronts and did not concentrate on building up a distinctive image. As an Iban-based party it was in the awkward position of having to do battle with SNAP, and, knowing the latter's appeal among the Ibans, could do no better than to attack its overcommitment to multi-racialism (as opposed to the promotion of Iban, or at least Native, interests) and to give a "responsible Government-irresponsible Opposition" construction to Pesaka-SNAP differences. As a component of the ruling Alliance, it was in the equally awkward position of having to campaign with the same vigour against its own partners, and, in the process, of echoing some of the charges made against these parties by its other opponents.[57] As a result Pesaka, more than any other party, appeared to lack a positive image, and was not likely to be an obvious beneficiary of either the pro-Government or the anti-Government vote.

Bumiputera's campaign, as already implied, was the most direct and least confusing. It did not equivocate on too many issues, and, although it fielded candidates outside the Malay-majority areas, it clearly concentrated its efforts in the Malay constituencies and ran a campaign that was distinctly Malay-Muslim oriented. Unlike SNAP and Pesaka, and more than the SUPP,[58] it knew that it had no serious rival for the votes of the community it represented first and foremost, and ran a campaign that was intended primarily to prevent any leakage of Malay votes to other parties either as a result of the personal standing of their candidates or as a result of a flagging interest in communal solidarity. The party's message was clear: there was no dichotomy between national and local interests, and Bumiputera was the only party which enjoyed the confidence of the national (Malay) leaders; the Malay community in Sarawak was a part of the nation's politically dominant community, and there was no reason whatsoever for its members to suffer from a minority complex. The names of national leaders featured prominently in the campaign and all posters and banners displayed by the party contained the photograph of the Tengku and/or the slogan: "Sukong Tengku" (support Tengku).[59] The names of local leaders were not involved to any great extent and even Rahman Ya'akub was portrayed primarily as the Tengku's protégé;[60] he was, however, given some personal prominence both in published materials as well as informally during local campaigns, and his achievements in promoting Islam were selected for special mention.

The SCA, not having much known support and clearly regarded as the least important partner in the Alliance, generally refrained from striking out on its own and emphasized instead its Alliance identity. Although two of its state candidates faced opponents from Pesaka it was careful throughout the campaign not to issue any statements against that party and its leaders. Indeed, SCA's top leaders went out of their way to maintain cordial relations with Pesaka—some of them to the point of contributing generously to Pesaka funds although this often took the form of support for individual candidates. Some of the general statements in the SCA's manifesto were in fact an exact reproduction of the statements contained in Pesaka's own manifesto,[61] and SCA candidates and workers freely shared the Alliance Headquarters and its facilities with their Pesaka counterparts.[62] However, a special relationship did develop between the SCA and Bumiputera during the campaign, as a result of their not fielding candidates against each other. Its scope was somewhat limited (compared, for example, to the bond which emerged during the 1967 election in Sabah between USNO and the SCA there), but Bumiputera did make serious efforts to mobilize Malay support for SCA candidates in constituencies where the Malay vote was substantial; similarly, the SCA gave every assistance to Bumiputera candidates in areas where the Chinese vote was important.

The most notable example of this co-operation was in Kuching Barat, a Malay-majority constituency, where the local Bumiputera organization provided considerable support for the SCA candidate, Cheng Yew Kiew, by organizing meetings and by accompanying him on his tours. Even the Federal Minister for Education, Mohamad Khir Johari, during a visit to Kuching went out of his way to urge Bumiputera members to support the SCA candidate.[63] Expectedly, the opposition parties did their best to discredit Bumiputera in the eyes of its supporters by accusing it of betraying the Malay community: if Bumiputera was serious about looking after the interests of the Malays and about strengthening Malay representation, why did it not field its own candidate in Kuching Barat? But these attempts to undermine Bumiputera unity did not have much success, and the party's explanation that it was only exchanging its own support in Kuching Barat for SCA support in other constituencies seemed to have been accepted. Against most expectations, the SCA candidate in this constituency did in fact win the election.[64]

Significantly Bumiputera support was less efficacious in another constituency (Tarat), where, although the SCA candidate was more prominent (Dato Teo was a member of the State Cabinet), Land Dayaks rather than Malays constituted the largest community. Obviously Bumiputera did not have the same disciplined support among the Land Dayaks as among the Malays, in spite of its claims during the negotiations for seats.

Despite the emphasis given to its Alliance connections the SCA was also aware that it had to make certain commitments as a distinctly Chinese party, so as to retain at least some initiative in its competition with the SUPP. To the business community (which was almost entirely Chinese and whose members were often influential in clan associations, school management boards and Chinese welfare associations) it promised, in its manifesto, "tax holidays" for pioneer industries as a way of encouraging local investment, and the abolition of trade licensing fees "in order to lessen the burdens of our business community". On the more general, but extremely sensitive issue of education, it undertook to "look into the delicate problem of degrees awarded to Sarawakians by the Nanyang and Taiwan Universities [because] an opportunity should be offered to this group of intellectuals to serve the country and to play a rôle in our nation building". The party did not, however, advocate the establishment of Chinese as an official language and took exactly the same position as Pesaka on the language issue.

Methods of Campaigning in Sarawak: the Suspension of the Election: Violence

An accusation levelled against the Alliance (particularly the SCA) was that its candidates intimidated voters by telling them that the government had ways of knowing whom they voted for.[65] It was believed that certain candidates "proved" this to some voters by showing them that they knew their personal particulars (such as their identity card numbers), which made the voters doubt their own anonymity. A less subtle method was apparently to warn voters that if they supported an opposition party they would run the risk of being arrested. According to those who made these allegations, threats of this kind were used primarily among the Chinese. In this connection, it has to be borne in mind that security operations (accompanied by curfews in some areas) were stepped up during the period when the election was suspended, and Chinese areas (notably areas where the SUPP was strong) were the ones most affected. These threats, if indeed they were made, were presumably aimed at encouraging defections from the SUPP, or at least at discouraging intending SUPP voters from casting their votes.[66] Some SUPP members were in fact detained during this period and one of its candidates, who had apparently gone underground, was killed.[67] The most serious case of violence, however, occurred after the election had been resumed, when three members of a polling team were killed and four others injured in an ambush by communist terrorists near Sarikei in the Third Division.[68]

Another accusation made against the Alliance (particularly Bumiputera) by SNAP and the SUPP was that its Ministers were using Government facilities during their campaigns. The most severe criticism of this kind was made by James Wong, Vice-President of SNAP, who accused Rahman Ya'akub of using not only Government transport and Information Department loudspeakers but also senior civil servants during his campaign tours. He was adamant that this was not a proper use of government facilities and called on those responsible for ensuring that the election was conducted fairly, to put a stop to the practice.[69] Rahman Ya'akub, however, could not see any merit in the accusation, and replied: "I use Government facilities wherever I go. He [James Wong] has forgotten that I am a minister. Perhaps Dato Wong cannot make a distinction between a political government and a colonial government. As a minister I have to go around explaining to the people the policy of the government, the party in power."[70]

As already indicated, the election in Sarawak, originally scheduled for May 1969, was suspended following the outbreak of communal riots in West Malaysia and the subsequent declaration of a state of emergency.[71] The suspension lasted slightly over a year, and campaigning was prohibited by law during that period. This prohibition however was difficult to enforce at all levels, and although parties were effectively prevented from holding rallies and from campaigning in the open, there was simply no way of controlling all forms of communication between them and the electorate. The typical activity consisted of casual visits to various parts of their constituencies by candidates and their workers (who could always claim that they were visiting friends or relatives), during which election issues were discussed and kept alive, and information was gathered about fluctuations in support. Even this activity was very much toned down, and there was certainly nothing to match the excitement of the pre-suspension period. If, on the one hand, candidates felt secure in the knowledge that the chances of detection were remote outside the urban areas, they were also keen not to attract any undue attention to themselves by travelling too frequently or by becoming involved in the kind of overt campaigning that could lead to complaints from their opponents. As long as they did not think that their rivals were stealing an advantage, most candidates in fact seemed relieved that they did not have to keep up the pace which they had been compelled to set before the suspension. Many of them (as well as the parties generally) also seemed genuinely pleased that the law prohibited the expenditure of any money on canvassing, and, although some forms of spending continued, probably used this argument to turn down numerous requests for assistance from people claiming to be their supporters.

It is difficult to speculate with any confidence on the ways in which the suspension may have affected the chances of the different parties. SNAP and SUPP spokesmen who were interviewed just before the election was resumed in 1970, were almost unanimous that the suspension had worked to their advantage; in their view, the suspension had only further discredited the Government because it was seen as a plot to delay the victory of the opposition parties: the rioting, after all, had been confined to West Malaysia and there was no justification for halting the democratic process in Sarawak. At the same time it is also conceivable that opposition parties were even more dependent than the Alliance on keeping issues alive, and therefore on conducting a campaign which did not have any let-up; the Alliance, on the other hand, could always associate itself with government expenditure. Further, the Government was always likely to enjoy an advantage because of the authority it possessed, and deference and obedience may have been reinforced rather than undermined as a result of the suspension. In other words, while "the Government" was always present, at least notionally, the opposition needed to thrust itself forward more forcefully in order to make its own presence felt and to stimulate and sustain a rival commitment.

SNAP may have suffered particularly in this regard: it was

in the opposition, had relied more heavily than any other party on building support through frenetic activity and vast expenditure, and did not have any strong links with the traditional hierarchy which could have stood it in good stead during the period of suspension. Also relevant in this regard is the fact that, while party activities were curtailed during this period, Ministers and other government officers continued to make tours in their official capacities and to announce that funds would be spent on new development projects. There was, however, some ambiguity about Pesaka's position in this connection. On the one hand it claimed to be the premier party in the Alliance and may therefore have been regarded, at least by the Ibans, as the Government of the day. On the other, its Chief Minister was excluded from the State Operations Council[72] and it behaved as an opposition party when it joined forces with SNAP and the SUPP to demand the resumption of the election.[73]

As far as Bumiputera was concerned, it is quite conceivable that those who disapproved of the suspension held it particularly responsible because of its special links with the Central Government. But if this damaged the party's standing, it was only among its non-Malay followers, because the Malay community was exposed to other countervailing factors. It was, for example, felt by some people that the riots in West Malaysia had provided further incentives for communal solidarity among the Malays in Sarawak, not only because these riots were communal but because the Malays now feared threats to their political supremacy. Malay supremacy had to be demonstrated afresh, because it was no longer taken for granted by the others. Further, any doubts about Rahman Ya'akub's personal qualities (an issue which had featured prominently in the opposition campaigns) were now dispelled because he performed with distinction in this climate. Following his appointment as the new Minister for Education in the Central Government, he had achieved fame by reorganizing the West Malaysian educational system so as to give the Malay language unquestioned supremacy. The tremendous respect which he suddenly commanded among the Malays in Malaya as a patriot and as a man of courage and integrity undoubtedly boosted not only his own personal standing but also that of his party among the Malay community in Sarawak. Finally, it was also believed that Bumiputera campaigned indirectly more vigorously than any of the other parties during the suspension, via religious elites and adult education teachers.

When the election was resumed, it was made very clear to the parties that no fresh compaigning would be allowed: in other words, it was only the Election Commission which resumed its activities, while the parties, for all practical purposes, were expected to allow themselves to be judged on the campaigns which they had conducted a year previously. *The Emergency (Essential Provisions) Ordinance* No. 32, 1970, which laid down these rules, prohibited, among other things: (*a*) "The convening or organizing or assisting in doing so of any type of public meeting, procession or demonstration for the purpose of gaining votes or support"; (*b*) "The interviewing of members of the public for the purpose of the election" (including house-to-house visits either for the purpose of campaigning or for the purpose of issuing polling cards); and (*c*) "The making of statements of a political nature to the press". Candidates were, however, allowed to set up polling booths to assist voters, provided they conformed to certain requirements. As already pointed out, although these restrictions did in fact curtail party activities, not all forms of campaigning were effectively prevented, particularly in the rural areas.

The election campaign in Sarawak in 1969 was characterized by much less violence (or threats of violence) than was evident in Sabah in 1967. Admittedly, terrorist activities by communist elements, during the period when the election was suspended, did result in Sarawak's experiencing a larger number of violent incidents, resulting in several injuries and even some deaths; to this extent it may be argued that Sarawak in fact underwent a more pronounced period of instability arising from organized violence. But unlike the situation in Sabah this instability was not directly related to inter-party rivalries or to the heat generated by the election campaign. The incidents also did not involve workers or supporters of rival parties, and those responsible for them were condemned as anti-national elements by the leaders of all parties.[74]

One reason for the less charged atmosphere in Sarawak, and

for the relative absence of tense situations arising from the elections may have been the fact that party rivalries were more complex in that state. While in Sabah the contest took the form of a direct confrontation between two evenly-balanced opponents, each looking for dominance, the parties in Sarawak had several enemies to contend with simultaneously and were also aware that in all likelihood they would have to co-operate with other parties after the election, because no single party appeared likely to obtain a majority. Further, while the inevitability of a coalition was widely recognized, there was considerable uncertainty about its composition. One might almost say that none of the major parties considered any of the others as its automatic partner in a coalition, although some combinations (for example SNAP and Bumiputera) were clearly out of the question.

Another possible reason for the more orderly campaign in Sarawak was the fact that there were no equivalents of Kota Belud and Penampang in that state. These two areas in Sabah, as pointed out earlier, were intensely committed to USNO and UPKO respectively, and provided a ready supply of enthusiastic supporters who travelled to other parts of the state to campaign for their candidates. It meant something to be one of the "Penampang boys" or "Kota Belud boys", because this carried a reputation and conveyed identification with the core of the party. In Sarawak, on the other hand, there were no areas where any party enjoyed a similar overwhelming concentration of support, and which therefore had party workers available for "export". The fact that the pattern of party rivalries was more complex may have been partly responsible for this, especially since the Ibans, the dominant group, were not solidly behind any single party.

Finally, the potential for violence in Sarawak must have been considerably reduced as a result of the declaration of the state of emergency in 1969 and the accompanying suspension of the election. As campaigning was not permitted when the election was resumed in 1970, there was also very little likelihood of a reactivation of partisan activity. Further, because the results were all announced on the same day, there was not the same anxiety as had been experienced in Sabah about the outcome in those constituencies which polled last.

DORSET INSTITUTE OF
HIGHER EDUCATION
LEARNING RESOURCES
CENTRE

Features of Campaigning in Sabah and Sarawak. Expenditures

An interesting feature of the campaigns both in Sabah (1967) and Sarawak (1970) was the use by various candidates of modern gadgets to impress the voters. In Sabah, Polaroid cameras were put to good use by a number of candidates who took them along on their constituency tours. It was common practice for these candidates, after talking to the voters,[75] to invite them to be photographed. This particular ceremony was often the highlight of the proceedings, and stimulated great excitement among those present. Those being photographed were almost invariably asked to hold the candidates' election posters before them, and in this way each candidate was able to leave behind an appropriate memento of his visit. The accompanying scenes were often chaotic as those assembled did not always understand the working of a camera and some tended to stand well outside the angle covered, or even behind the cameraman.[76] The Polaroid's instant products were received with great jubilation and the candidates may have been justified in believing that this was a less strenuous way than any other of establishing a personal bond with some voters. Indeed, so popular was this activity that on various occasions during the campaign Polaroid film was not available in Jesselton, and some candidates had to make special arrangements to obtain it from elsewhere.

Another potent gadget, both in Sarawak and Sabah, was the tape recorder. Candidates often used these to record statements made by individual members of small groups whom they addressed, and these were played back immediately with great effect. When candidates stopped overnight in any settlement, they usually had to stay up until the early hours of the morning eating and drinking with the people who had assembled to meet them, listening to local complaints and giving advice on voting procedures. These (sometimes all-night) sessions, held in the homes of individuals or in longhouses, were generally completely unstructured: as the evening wore on, numerous conversations would be going on at the same time, some would be asleep while others (in the Kadazan areas of Sabah) would beat gong rhythms which would encourage some of those present to dance. These "meetings", it appeared, were often regarded by those present merely as a good excuse for a minor feast or celebration. In the course of such evenings, some candidates often took the opportunity to ask a few of those present to make speeches or to sing and these were recorded and played back at the end of each person's turn. Occasionally (in some Kadazan areas) the local "priestess" would be asked to record a religious chant, into which good wishes for the candidate and the importance of voting for him were generously woven in. In Sabah, several UPKO candidates and party workers also took along tape-recorded messages from Donald Stephens which were played to captive audiences in the more remote parts of the state which Stephens himself could not visit.

Particularly in Sabah, the parties spent a great deal of effort in educating the voters on election procedure. To be sure, the Election Commission and the Information Department considered this a part of their official responsibility, but the political parties also did their part. In the course of their visits to villages and longhouses, candidates and party workers often took pains to ensure that the voters knew which polling districts they belonged to, where their polling stations were located and the date and time of polling.[77] They also spent a great deal of time telling people what they should do after entering the polling station and how they should mark their ballot papers.[78] Often elaborate mock elections were conducted, with the "voters" celebrating the "victory" of their candidate after the anxiously-awaited "result" had been announced.[79] Candidates and party workers felt that while these mock elections helped to educate the voters, the simulated victories also helped to boost morale among their supporters.

Both in Sarawak and in Sabah polling was staggered over a few weeks because given poor communications and the shortage of trained manpower, the Election Commission could not supervise voting in all areas simultaneously or even within a few days. In poorly developed constituencies the same polling teams had to travel from one locality to another conducting the election on different days or at different times of the same day. Despite this attempt to overcome the difficulties posed by poor communications, many voters had to travel long distances on foot in order to cast their votes, because they lived in relative isolation and it would not have been feasible for polling teams to visit them. Thus, although there was a general willingness on the part of the Election Commission to take polling booths to the voters when necessary, those who lived in very small and scattered settlements were not always able to cast their votes conveniently. There was, however, no evidence that they were discouraged by this.

Compared with the 1967 state election in Sabah, one major difference in the administration of the election in Sarawak in 1969–70 was the fact that the votes were not counted until polling had been completed in all constituencies.[80] This may well have been the result of a lesson learned in Sabah in 1967, when votes were counted in each constituency as soon as polling was completed and the results were announced while voting was still taking place in other constituencies. This contributed to the tension which developed in the areas which polled last (because both USNO and UPKO knew that the last few seats could tilt the balance either way), and it may also have been felt that voters in constituencies which polled last may have been influenced by the results that were already known.

Reference is made in another chapter to the relationship between financial interests and party politics in Sarawak and Sabah.[81] The reasons for which individual millionaires and their financial empires have become involved in politics are also discussed in that chapter, but it may be useful to make some reference here to the ways in which money was used, rather than obtained, by the parties during their election campaigns.

To begin with, if lavish expenditure was facilitated by the mere availability of money from highly concentrated (and politically involved) sources, there were also some reasons why parties in East Malaysia were more dependent on money than, say, their West Malaysian counterparts. The most important of these was perhaps the poorly-developed system of communications, which resulted in high expenditure on transport. Many areas were accessible only by river and it was therefore necessary for parties to purchase or rent boats.[82] Both in Sabah and Sarawak, boats and outboard motors (and in Sarawak, just before polling, fuel as well) were in extremely short supply towards the end of the campaigns because whatever was available had been purchased or rented in advance by the transport-hungry parties and candidates. In some cases sabotage, rather than need, seems to have been the motivating factor, because certain wealthier candidates (or candidates with wealthy backers) purchased or rented more boats and outboard motors than they needed for their own use, just to make sure that their opponents would be disadvantaged by not having adequate transport facilities.[83] Even when boats were not required, parties tended to spend a fair amount on transport because landrovers were the only vehicles that could be used on the main tracks outside the developed areas. In Sabah, both USNO and UPKO spent substantial sums in purchasing or renting landrovers, not only for this reason but because many of their candidates lived outside their own constituencies and therefore had to commute frequently between their homes and various points in their constituencies.[84] Further, because most of the parties did not have well-developed local units outside the heavily settled areas, the candidates and their workers had to do a great deal of travelling themselves in order to cultivate the support of the electorate.

Poor communications and inadequate local organization were not, however the factors most responsible for the high cost of electioneering in East Malaysia, although they explain in part why costs tended to be higher in these states than in the states of West Malaysia. Widespread (and often lavish) treating of voters perhaps accounted for a larger percentage of the money spent during the campaigns and the scale on which this took place was without parallel anywhere in West Malaysia. No doubt the mere availability of money as a result of the willingness of some extremely wealthy persons to finance political activity was largely responsible for this. But there were also other contributory factors which need to be considered. Although party rivalries were reasonably clear-cut, direct elections had not been held previously and the parties had not been well organized when the indirect elections were held in 1962 and 1963. Thus, there was not much clear evidence of how support was likely to be distributed, especially since the dominant parties did not have exclusive and consistent communal images. This meant that, to be safe, parties had to outbid each other in doing favours to the electorate and the easiest and most tangible way seemed to be to give treats, and, whenever necessary, cash. It was extremely common for candidates, when visiting their constituencies, to provide feasts for their supporters: in the non-Muslim indigenous areas of both states, large quantities of liquor were provided at these feasts—generally only the local rice wine but, not infrequently, imported brandy and beer as well.[85]

In this connection, candidates in both states appeared also to have been subjected to a great deal of intimidation. When visiting their constituencies they were continually badgered for payments by (sometimes self-appointed) party-workers, who claimed that in the candidate's absence they had done so many days' work for him or that they had had to treat others on the candidate's behalf. Some shrewd persons (particularly those with some authority, like *Tuai Rumahs* and *Penghulus*) merely announced that they had been offered money by another party or its candidate and that they had refused it only because they preferred to support the candidate who was then visiting them and who, they were sure, would give them at least what they had been offered by the rival party. Given pressures of this kind some candidates could not be blamed for their reluctance to visit their own constituencies because they simply could not meet the numerous requests for money. Some frankly admitted how they lived in constant fear of their voters for this reason, and did not conceal their disgust for the greed of the people whose support they were courting.

In the course of the campaigns in the two territories, two kinds of expenditure seemed to emerge at the constituency level, one reasonably structured and the other almost completely haphazard. Structured expenditure involved allocations for transport, payment of regular workers, the purchase of boats and outboard motors for *Penghulus* or local chiefs or in the name of the party,[86] and, in some respects, planned (i.e. anticipated) treating of voters by candidates during their constituency tours. Haphazard spending usually took the form of payment on the spot to people who claimed one or more of the following: that they had been canvassing privately; that they were being offered money by a rival party; that they had belonged to a rival party but were prepared to defect; that they were hard-up and could use a few dollars for which they would be grateful. Some items, like payments to local elites and even the treating of voters, belonged in fact to a mixed category because, although the candidates had some prior estimates of their commitments, they also had to make adjustments in the course of the campaign depending on the activities of their opponents.

In some keenly contested constituencies (particularly those which involved prestige fights between two prominent candidates) the amount of money spent on the electorate escalated to unbelievable proportions and it was commonly asserted that in some of these constituencies many voters had more money in their hands during the election than they had previously possessed at any given time in their lives.[87] In the words of some candidates the election was "better than Christmas" for the majority of voters, and a not inappropriate remark was that it also provided a more effective way of redistributing wealth (at least during the campaign) than any form of taxation the Government could devise. In true Christmas fashion, the voters also spent their windfall in a frenzy, mainly on items which were for immediate consumption, like canned foods: to this extent, the people who benefited most from this "distribution" of wealth were probably the shopkeepers.

In both states, especially towards the end of the campaigns, many candidates found a partial solution to the spiralling costs by promising a variety of things to their voters in the event of their being elected. In many cases the promise was only a delayed financial reward: that money would be given after the election if the candidate won. Other promises included the appointment of certain persons as chiefs or *Penghulus*, the allocation of land to different individuals, and the giving of new outboard motors, boats or landrovers to helpful persons. Many candidates were fully aware that they could not keep these promises, and some successful candidates in Sabah found themselves in the unusual position of having to hide from their own supporters after the results were announced and of escaping to Jesselton at the first opportunity. At the moment of victory, they felt they would have been much safer in the company of their opponents' supporters than in that of their own! For weeks after the 1967 election in Sabah, the USNO and UPKO headquarters in Jesselton were full of party supporters from all over the state claiming payment for a variety of things.

Finally, the fact that the period of campaigning was somewhat longer in Sarawak and Sabah than in West Malaysia must also have contributed to the high expenditure. In Sabah (1967) there were fifty days between nomination day and the final day of polling[88] while in Sarawak under the original schedule there were to be sixty-five days. This meant that expenditure had to be maintained over a longer period of time. Transportation costs and the money spent on treating voters were therefore more likely to escalate than in West Malaysia particularly because, in the absence of any established or familiar rhythm of expenditure, the "standard" tended to be set by the most aggressive spenders.[89]

Newspapers and the Elections

An important difference between the election campaigns in Sabah and Sarawak arose from the fact that in the former the major newspapers were directly owned by the leaders of the different political parties and were used during the election as vehicles for party propaganda. The *Sabah Times*, owned by Dato Donald Stephens, conducted a vigorous campaign on behalf of UPKO which included not only publicity for its leader, candidates and policies but also criticism of USNO and its ambitions. It also gave more prominence than any of the other English language newspapers to the Chinese Independent candidates, who, it was hoped, would join forces with UPKO after the election. This participation by the *Sabah Times* in the conflict between UPKO and USNO had in fact commenced much earlier, and had included the publication of regular cartoons which poked fun at USNO and Tun Mustapha.[90] This was intensified with the approach of the election, and the newspaper left its readers in no doubt that it functioned as an arm of UPKO. Similarly the *Kinabalu Times*, owned by Mustapha, worked hard for USNO and also gave favourable coverage to the SCA, while on the whole ignoring UPKO. The *Daily Express*, owned by Yeh Pao Tze, a Vice-President of the SCA, expectedly devoted more space to the SCA and its

TABLE 4.2

Space Devoted to Individual Political Parties by the Sabah Times, Kinabalu Times *and* Daily Express *during the Sabah Election Campaign, 1967*

Newspaper	Column inches (excluding headlines, photographs and editorials) devoted to: USNO	UPKO	SCA	Independents	Editorial column inches devoted to the election (number of editorials in parenthesis)
*Sabah Times**	235.1	2,245.8	49.4	456.3	616.0 (39)
Kinabalu Times	1,582.0	168.5	201.1	16.7	309.7 (34)
Daily Express†	495.3	363.1	238.8	171.4	546.9 (33)

* The *Sabah Times* also devoted 135.8 column inches to the "Alliance" and its candidates, but most of this was about the SCA, since the four candidates who stood on the Alliance ticket were all from the SCA.

† The following issues of the *Daily Express* were unobtainable: 25–7 March, 3 April.

candidates than either of the other two newspapers, and also showed a clear bias for USNO over UPKO. The following table indicates the total number of column inches (excluding headlines and photographs) devoted by each of these newspapers to the three parties between nomination day and the final day of polling (i.e. between 9 March and 28 April, 1967, except Sundays). In reading the table, one has to bear in mind that each newspaper gave only favourable coverage to its "own" party while the space devoted to its opponents (i.e. UPKO in the case of the *Kinabalu Times* and *Daily Express*, and USNO and the SCA in the case of the *Sabah Times*) also included unfavourable comment.

Each newspaper also showed its bias in the photographs which it published during this period, as shown in the following table:

TABLE 4.3

Publication of Photographs of Political Leaders by the Sabah Times, Kinabalu Times, *and* Daily Express *during the Sabah Election Campaign, 1967*

	Newspapers		
Photographs of:	*Sabah Times*	*Kinabalu Times*	*Daily Express**
Stephens	24	2	1
Other UPKO leaders	44	2	2
Mustapha	1	10	6
Other USNO leaders	10	19	8
SCA leaders	14	10	18†
Independents	9	1	6

* The following issues of the *Daily Express* were unobtainable: 25–7 March, 3 April.

† Seven of Khoo Siak Chiew, four of Pang Tet Tshung, three of Peter Lo, and four of others.

In Sarawak, on the other hand, there was no newspaper which was directly owned by prominent politicians, although the *Utusan Sarawak*, a Malay paper, was unequivocally pro-Bumiputera and gave that party special prominence throughout the campaign. The *Vanguard*, and its Chinese equivalent, the *Sarawak Vanguard*, were owned by an Independent member of the outgoing Council Negri,[91] but neither consistently supported any single party although some believed that its reports showed an anti-Bumiputera bias.[92] On the whole, the Sabah pattern found no parallel in Sarawak, and, although a great deal of space was given to the election, the contentious sections were usually confined to the readers' columns. During the election the Sarawak newspapers threw themselves open as forums for public debate and a great deal of space was taken up by party officials, candidates and private individuals who took the opportunity to attack or defend particular candidates or parties and their viewpoints.

APPENDIX

Elections in Sabah and Sarawak[93]

Sabah

The first district council elections in North Borneo, held in late 1962 and early 1963, covered rather over 80% of the adult population. There were four main parties in the Alliance at the time, excluding the small Sabah Indian Congress. At the elections they were not faced by any rival parties, but numerous Independents stood, and in 49 out of 137 wards there were contests between parties which were inside the Alliance. The seats won by the Alliance were: USNO, 53; UNKO, 39; Pasok Momogun, 12; SANAP (BUNP), 27. Six seats were won by Independents. In the West Coast Residency and the Interior Residency USNO and UNKO were of roughly equal strength. Pasok Momogun's support was concentrated in the Interior Residency. In the Tawau Residency USNO did very much better than UNKO. The SANAP candidates polled highest in the towns where there was a heavy concentration of Chinese electors. A further series of district council elections was held in April, 1964 for the rural district councils of Tawau and Sandakan. There were no contests between Alliance candidates, although some Independents stood and were defeated; 13 USNO and 8 SANAP candidates were returned.

These elections decided the composition of the Sabah Legislative Assembly via a tier system with indirect voting. In April, 1967, however, direct elections were held for the state assembly. In effect, the line-up was USNO and the SCA (Sabah Chinese Association, the successor to SANAP) versus the UPKO (formed by the union of the UNKO and Pasok Momogun) and a group of Chinese Independents. Table 4.4 summarizes the voting, and gives some indication of its ethnic character;

TABLE 4.4

Sabah State Election, 1967; Votes, Seats, and Ethnic Composition of the Electorate[94]

Votes Won(%)				Seats Won			
USNO	UPKO	SCA	INDS	USNO	UPKO	SCA	INDS
40.8	40.8	9.4	9.0	14	12	5	1

Ethnic Composition of the Electorate (%)

BAJAU ETC: (Muslim)	KADAZAN	MURUT	CHINESE
38	36	6	20

There was a close relation between the proportion of Kadazans and Muruts in the electorate and the UPKO vote. Similarly, the USNO vote was derived largely from the vote of the Bajaus and the other Muslim Natives.[95] Indeed the results of eighteen out of the twenty-one contests between USNO and UPKO could have been predicted on the basis of the ethnic composition of the electorates. The Chinese Independents probably won a slightly higher proportion of the Chinese vote than did the SCA. However, the SCA candidates were helped by the fact that there were more Bajau etc. than Kadazan and Murut electors in the seats where they fought Chinese Independents. Consequently, five SCA candidates, but only one Chinese Independent candidate, were elected.

The first direct parliamentary elections in Sabah were not completed until June 1970. The Alliance (USNO and SCA) won eleven of the sixteen seats unopposed; all of these were won by USNO candidates. In the other five seats, USNO was victorious in two, SCA in three, against Independent opposition. The average Independent share of the valid vote was about 28%, a worse performance than for the corresponding state seats in 1967. The increasing tendency towards a *de facto* one-party state was continued at the 1971 state elections, when all the seats were won by the Alliance; the few Independents who filed forms were disqualified for having filled them in improperly.

Sarawak

The district council elections held in 1963, just before the formation of Malaysia, were the first after the general establishment of parties in Sarawak. The Alliance (SNAP, Pesaka, BARJASA and the SCA) faced the opposition of SUPP, PANAS (which had previously been inside the Alliance) and Independents. The parties had a mainly ethnic appeal. The Malays were attracted either to BARJASA, inside the Alliance, or to PANAS outside it. Similarly, SUPP in opposition and, less successfully, the SCA in the Alliance, were contenders for the Chinese vote. The two parties which drew mainly on non-Muslim Native support, SNAP and Pesaka, were both inside the Alliance. The main qualification to this generalization is that SUPP, with a broadly socialist appeal, had some attraction for Natives as well as Chinese. As shown in Table 3.1 above,[96] the Alliance won more votes and seats than any other group, but it was closely followed by the Independent candidates and by SUPP. PANAS received only half as many votes as the Alliance, and was weak outside the First Division. Inside the Alliance the strength of the respective component parties was, in descending order, SNAP, Pesaka, BARJASA, SCA.

The first direct elections to the Sarawak state legislature (Council Negri) and for Sarawak members of the Federal Parliament were held in 1970. The pattern of contending parties was confusing. The Alliance in the shape of Bumiputera (formed by the union of BARJASA and PANAS), Pesaka, and the SCA, was opposed by SNAP and SUPP. The ethnic vote situation was therefore different from 1963. In 1970 the Malay vote was no longer divided between two parties, but was substantially concentrated on Bumiputera. The Native non-Muslim vote was split between SNAP and Pesaka; SCA took a small share of the Chinese vote away from SUPP. The complexity of the voting pattern was increased because the Alliance had failed to come to an agreement on the division of seats, so in some constituencies Pesaka was fighting a candidate from either Bumiputera or the SCA, its fellow-members in the Alliance.

Table 4.5 reflects a broad pattern of ethnic voting, but only if some qualifications are borne in mind. A high proportion of the SCA vote was provided by Malay/Muslim electors (as was the Sabah Chinese Association vote in the Sabah 1967 state elections). Consequently the Malays in the electorate, broadly speaking, gave their votes to Bumiputera, to the SCA or to Malay Independents. The Chinese vote was cast mostly for SUPP, and to a lesser extent for the SCA and for Chinese Independents. The non-Muslim Native parties, SNAP and Pesaka, had a large share of "their" expected ethnic vote. But SUPP undoubtedly received a substantial number of "Other Native" votes, as well as some Muslim votes, proving that it had more than a merely ethnic appeal. In terms of seats SNAP and Pesaka, the "Dayak parties", suffered by fighting each other and so splitting the "Other Native" vote. They won only twenty state seats between them, in spite of the fact that in

TABLE 4.5

Sarawak Elections, 1970: Seats and Votes Won by the Parties; Ethnic Composition of the Electorate

Party	Parliamentary Election		State Election		Ethnic composition of the Electorate (%)	
	Votes won (%)	Seats won	Votes won (%)	Seats won		
SUPP	30.2	5	28.9	12	Chinese	28
SCA	4.4	2	10.6	3		
Bumiputera	17.3	5	14.8	12	Malay[a]	26
Pesaka	12.7	3	13.1	8		
SNAP	26.8	9	24.5	12	Other Native	46
Independents	8.5[b]	—	8.1	1[c]		

[a] Including Melanau.
[b] Roughly one quarter to Chinese Independents, one quarter to Malay Independents, one half to "Other Native" Independents.
[c] After the election he switched to Pesaka.

twenty-three out of the forty-eight seats the "Other Native" population had an absolute majority, while in another five it had a relative majority.[97] SUPP lost representation because it was a party with its main strength in the urban areas, where the constituencies had a higher number of electors than average. Consequently it failed to gain as large a percentage of seats as of votes.

5

The Politics of Manoeuvre and Negotiation

The previous chapter examined relations between politicians and their supporters; the theme of the present chapter is manoeuvres and negotiations among politicians. There are two parts to the chapter. The first deals with cabinet crises in Sarawak and, to a lesser extent, Sabah. The second is concerned with the formation of coalitions in the two states.

The Sarawak Cabinet Crisis, 1965 and 1966

The Sarawak cabinet crises of mid-1965 and mid-1966 reflected on the surface the impact of particular issues, notably the land question and Dato Stephen Kalong Ningkan's retention of the chief ministership, respectively. Actually they were manifestations of deeper tensions and antagonisms, between particular personalities, between the various political parties in Sarawak, between some parties and the government in Sarawak on the one hand, and the Alliance Party and the Federal Government in Kuala Lumpur on the other.

The immediate occasion of the 1965 cabinet crisis was the introduction of land legislation by the Sarawak Government. At first sight it might seem odd that Sarawak, with a population density of about seventeen persons to the square mile, should have a "land problem". Nevertheless, there was a problem, or rather two interrelated problems. How could the land which was cultivated by Natives be worked most efficiently? How could the existing land law be modified to permit more Chinese to acquire and use land legally? The first question hinges largely on the replacement of shifting cultivation by settled cultivation. This topic was mentioned in the first chapter of this book, but it is linked to the question of providing more land for the Chinese, in so far as more efficient use of land by Natives would have the effect of increasing the amount of land available for Chinese.

Under the Brookes there was no apparent shortage of land, and there was no attempt at codification of land law. The efforts of the Brookes were confined to preserving the right of Natives to the land, as against the Chinese, and to curbing Iban occupation of land at the expense of less aggressive groups.[1] In the period when Sarawak was a Crown Colony there was some codification, for example by the Land Code of 1958, but the resulting classification was by no means a model of clarification.[2] The code divided land into the following categories: Mixed Zone Land; Native Area Land; Interior Area Land.[3] Only Mixed Zone Land could be acquired by the Chinese. This did not mean that *all* Mixed Zone Land was available to Chinese, less than a quarter of it was actually available to them,[4] equivalent to about 2% of all the land in Sarawak. The remainder was unsuitable for agriculture or was held by Natives under customary tenure. During British rule Chinese demands for land became acute and vociferous.

The Report of the 1962 Land Committee considered that the provisions of the 1958 Land Code were unduly restrictive, and proposed, among other things, that Natives should be allowed to dispose of their land subject to the approval of the Resident.[5]

The 1962 Land Committee was a "technical" committee, consisting of expatriates.[6] But there were also pressing "political" reasons, after Sarawak became part of Malaysia, for reforming the land law. The hold of the SUPP over the Chinese vote could be broken only by the Sarawak Alliance Government's offering some really materially attractive proposal to a substantial number of Chinese, such as greater opportunities for owning land.[7] Some land settlement schemes were in existence by the end of 1964 but on much too small a scale to provide any effective political inducement.[8]

Early in 1965 it appeared that a number of demands could be met by changing the law on land. On the one hand, there was a tremendous Chinese demand for land. This was already taking the form of the Chinese acquiring as much Mixed Zone Land as they could get. There were also many Chinese occupying land by agreement with the Native owners, who lacked any legal title to the land and could be dispossessed after having occupied it for even as much as twenty years: they desired the security which would come from legal ownership. The number of Chinese families who wanted to acquire a legal title to land was probably between 10,000 and 15,000. On the other hand, there were many Natives who were willing to sell. Some were poor Natives who would probably have spent the purchase price on consumption goods. However, there were a few well-off Natives who wanted to sell part of their landholdings and use the proceeds for capital investment to develop their remaining holdings. On the face of it, well-drafted land legislation could solve several problems at once. If Chinese were allowed to buy land from Natives, their land hunger would be satisfied and their political disaffection reduced; moreover, because of their efficiency as farmers, the general level of productivity would be raised. The unhealthy concentration of Chinese in a few areas would be mitigated and their interaction with other racial groups would be stepped up. The Natives would acquire much-needed capital to invest in the remainder of their holdings. In the longer term, more intensive farming of land by Natives would provide a larger tax base and would reduce the cost of health, education, and welfare services, because they would be provided for a concentrated, rather than a scattered, population.

However, the apparent simplicity of such a change in the law encountered obstacles, which in the end proved insurmountable. The nature of the Chinese demand for land was not homogeneous. Some was for land in particular areas; for example, at that time few Chinese from the First Division were willing to move to the Fifth Division in order to acquire land. Also, not all Chinese who wanted to buy land wanted it in order to cultivate it themselves. Some wished to buy and then sell at a profit. Nor did the legislation take full account of the attachment of the Natives to their land. To some extent objections to making it possible for Chinese to buy land were rational; it was all too likely that some Natives would sell all the land they had and would be left without any resources.[9] But, beyond that, the attachment of Natives to their land was such that that almost no protective clauses or safeguards could weaken it, at least in the short run. Such an attachment to the land had been reinforced by Brooke policy, and memorably in the last speech of Rajah Charles Brooke to the Council Negri when he was in his mid-eighties:

> There may be others who may appear after my time with soft and smiling countenances to deprive you of what I solemnly and truly consider to be your right and that is THE LAND. It is your inheritance which, if once lost, no amount of money could ever recover. After my life the future will remain with you to be independent and free citizens, or be a humbled and inferior class without pride in yourselves or in your race. You must choose between the two, the owner or master on one side or the dependant and coolie on the other.[10]

In 1965, even if Native leaders' objections could have been overcome by giving them assurances that the rights of the Natives were not being betrayed, this would not have removed opposition to the bills. Many politicians wished to use opposition to the bills to achieve another goal, the removal of Dato Ningkan as Chief Minister.

The Minister for Natural Resources, Dato Teo (SCA), started to prepare land legislation in the summer of 1964. The main motive behind it was suggested earlier; to make more land available to Chinese thus reducing Chinese disaffection. The provisions of the bills[11] which were eventually drafted followed the lines of the Land Committee's 1962 Report. The legal titles of individual Natives, many of whom held land under customary rights, were to be clarified, and the rigid barriers against the sale of land by Natives to non-Natives were to be modified. The Minister had spent a year studying the land question, including a week's consultation with a New Zealand lawyer who had long experience in the subject. He had considered having the bills translated into Iban and also having the Attorney General make trips round the country explaining them. Neither of these schemes was actually carried out, although attempts were made to explain the broad outlines of the bills to district councils. This was unfortunate, because an important objection by Natives was that the bills should have been explained patiently over a long period at grass-roots level. More specifically, when the bills were discussed briefly in the Alliance Council at the beginning of April, Pesaka complained that they did not contain provisions for appeal to any authority higher than the Resident on land transfers. Other objections were spelled out in a Pesaka letter, signed by Temenggong Jugah, sent to the Chief Minister and dated April 8; the bills made alienation of land to non-Natives in Mixed Zone areas too easy, and the case for abolishing the existing land classification schemes had not been made out. The two fundamental points made about the bills were: that Natives were not yet sufficiently educated to make wise use of the money they would receive from selling land; that there would be a dangerous concentration of land in the hands of a few buyers.

According to one version of events, BARJASA did not voice any objections to the bills when they were brought up in the Alliance Council or in Cabinet. Another version is that the BARJASA leaders did voice objections similar to Pesaka's, but were under the impression that the bills would be amended to meet their wishes. One long-term factor that BARJASA had to take into account was that the bills might strengthen non-Muslim Natives too much for the comfort of the Muslims. The Malays and other Muslims lived mostly near the coast, and would be little affected by the land bills. But if inland non-Muslim Natives who sold land really did manage to develop their remaining land successfully, the delicate racial balance might be altered to the disadvantage of the Malays.

About the same time as the bills were brought up in the Alliance Council they were also studied by an informal group of elite politicians and civil servants, which included both Malay and non-Malay Natives. The group was not satisfied that the safeguards provided for Natives in the bills, as explained by Dato Teo and the Attorney General, were adequate.

It would be wrong, however, to think that the opposition to the bills arose because this guarantee or that safeguard had not been provided. Part of Pesaka's[12] opposition to the bills, and also some of the opposition in the other Native parties, lay in the deep Native attachment to the land, unshakable by rational argument, referred to earlier. This attachment was clearly revealed in the issues which some Native leaders,[13] such as Penghulu Tawi Sli[14] and Thomas Kana[15] emphasized when talking to their followers at grass-roots level. Linked to the

Native attachment to the land was a negative feeling towards Chinese who might be expected to benefit from the bills, and, particularly in BARJASA, towards well-off SCA leaders in that category. There was also a feeling that the Government had not done enough to promote Native (particularly Malay) development, and that Native votes might therefore be captured by SUPP or MACHINDA.

Some of the opposition did not arise from the nature of the bills themselves, but because the introduction of the bills provided a good opportunity for political manoeuvre. An important motive was to undermine Dato Ningkan's position as Chief Minister and perhaps remove him from office. Some of the younger elements in Pesaka wished the party to assume more prominence in the Government, and felt that it was unjust that the party was completely unrepresented in the state Cabinet. These elements in Pesaka, together with the BARJASA leaders, had the idea of forming a Native Alliance, from which SNAP, which had some Chinese members, would be excluded. The exact shape the Alliance would assume and its relation to UMNO, were unclear, but for the time being the Native Alliance concept provided a useful rallying point against the land bills and Ningkan.

The actual sequence of events during the crisis is as confusing to the political analyst as it no doubt was to the participants. Dato Teo had made some alterations in the bills, indeed their introduction in the Council Negri was postponed for seven weeks. However, the changes he made were not yet satisfactory to the critics of the bills, although he genuinely believed that they were. The bills' opponents were surprised and outraged when the bills were introduced in what they thought was a substantially unamended form. Dato Teo was equally surprised and outraged when the Chief Minister told him to withdraw what he (Teo) regarded as satisfactorily-amended bills at the last minute (11 May). The immediate opposition to the introduction of the bills took the shape of an agreement to set up a Native Alliance, consisting of BARJASA, Pesaka and PANAS,[16] and the resignation of BARJASA and Pesaka from the Sarawak Alliance.[17]

Dato Ningkan tried to meet the onslaught by inviting PANAS leaders to rejoin the Alliance and accept seats in the Cabinet;

however, they refused and stood by the Native Alliance. To have accepted Cabinet seats at that stage would have seemed in the eyes of the Malays to be taking advantage of the removal of the two BARJASA members from the Cabinet. Ningkan, after taking expatriate advice, also increased the rewards at his disposal in the form of jobs by passing a bill through the Council Negri (11 May), eliminating the *ex-officio* members of the Cabinet and increasing the other membership correspondingly by three. Pesaka support was vital to Ningkan, because it was the party with the most Council Negri seats; it was also, if the situation was well-handled, the party most likely to rally to the help of SNAP, which was, after all, the other Iban party.

The key figure in Pesaka was Temenggong Jugah, who was also chairman of the Sarawak Alliance. He had had little or nothing to do with the early stages of the negotiations between Pesaka, BARJASA and PANAS for the formation of a Native Alliance. This was the work of the younger leaders in Pesaka, such as Thomas Kana and Jonathan Bangau. Indeed it is doubtful if the Temenggong was fully informed of what was going on. Once the land bills had been dropped, it was obvious that Jugah was not prepared to break up Iban solidarity by opposing Ningkan. As soon as the land bills were taken off the Council Negri Order Paper he wrote to Ningkan withdrawing Pesaka's resignation from the Alliance. Presumably referring to his signature to the agreement for the Native Alliance, he said (15 May) that any statements should be ignored which "purported to be made by me which may be interpreted to mean a split between Dayaks and between the races". He also accused Taib (BARJASA) of trying to split Dayak unity.[18] The Temenggong's stand in favour of Ningkan was strengthened by the intervention of Dato Ling Beng Siew, Chairman of the SCA, after a dramatic and dangerous flight in an open helicopter, and also, according to a BARJASA account, by conversations with a highly-placed expatriate civil servant and with a prominent Chinese member of SNAP.

On 15 May the Temenggong was evidently speaking for himself rather than for Pesaka. However, on 16 May Dato Ningkan felt sufficiently confident to accept the BARJASA letter of resignation and at the same time to dismiss the two

BARJASA Cabinet members, Abdul Taib and Awang Hipni. This came as a great surprise to Taib. He and Ningkan had given an apparently friendly joint interview to the Press on 13 May, and Taib had assumed that the crisis was over once the land bills had been shelved. On the other hand, the BARJASA letter of resignation had not been withdrawn, nor had it been publicly stated that the Native Alliance, with its anti-SNAP and anti-Ningkan implications, had been dropped. Ningkan chose to continue the battle from his Sarawak base, declining to attend a conference with the Tengku in Kuala Lumpur on BARJASA's withdrawal from the Sarawak Alliance. Instead, non-Malay Native solidarity was symbolized by a meeting of Ningkan and Jugah with other leaders, including Temenggong Oyong and Pengarahs Jinggut and Banyang in Sibu (20 May). By 22 May Pesaka had followed Temenggong Jugah's lead; on that day he announced that the party had withdrawn from the Native Alliance.

The revolt against Dato Ningkan failed, but the result was a draw rather than a victory for the Chief Minister. It is true that the idea of a Native Alliance was dropped, at least for the time being, but the land bills had also been withdrawn. The "package deal" arrived at to end this particular crisis, also provided for the admission of two members of Pesaka into Cabinet, Penghulu Francis Umpau and Tajang Laing, and one member of PANAS, Abang Othman; it also included the return of the two BARJASA members who had been dismissed by Dato Ningkan, Taib and Awang Hipni. Additionally, the idea of a Native Alliance was not to be revived.

The end of the crisis therefore found Dato Ningkan and his chief local opponent, Taib, still confronting each other in the Cabinet. Although the important group in Pesaka who had helped to forge the Native Alliance had wanted Ningkan removed from the Chief Ministership, this did not hold good for Jugah. Also, there was little pressure from Kuala Lumpur for Ningkan to resign at this time; confrontation with Indonesia was still at its height, and government instability could be dangerous.[19] However, an important member of the Federal Government is reported to have suggested that BARJASA should not be left out of the new Cabinet, which implied that Taib should be re-admitted. This suggestion was accompanied by the rumoured prospect that Taib might soon be given a federal appointment outside Sarawak.

The second cabinet crisis, which followed almost a year later, revealed, if there were any doubt on the matter, that land was only one of several issues which could lead to a split in the Sarawak Alliance. Curiously, one new issue consisted precisely in the fact that this was the *second* crisis, or the second phase of an "endemic crisis". Pesaka and BARJASA leaders had, in addition to the old issues, the new issue of revenge for their frustration of the previous year. Some ominously referred to "the Anniversary" to indicate the planned target date for that revenge.

Other issues emerged which had not been prominent in the previous crisis, notably the timing of the introduction of Malay as the National Language in Sarawak and the pace at which expatriate officers should leave the civil service in Sarawak.[20] On both of these issues the Federal Government wished to move quicker than Dato Ningkan's government. This did not produce any noticeable division of views between SNAP and Pesaka, but it widened the gap, if that were possible, between SNAP and BARJASA, and crystallized mutual hostility between the Federal Government and Ningkan.

Previous issues were still alive. There were continuing complaints that development was not helping the Natives enough in particular areas. By the beginning of 1966 Taib was once more publicly raising the question of an alliance of native parties. Nothing came of the proposals; the more limited objective of a merger of PANAS and BARJASA into a single party was nearly achieved in March, but was rejected by the PANAS Central Executive Committee on 6 April.

The Native Alliance theme was repeated in a speech made "across the river" from Kuching by Ghaffar bin Baba, the Chief Minister of Malacca, on 19 May.[21] The Native Alliance question was also linked to development. There was a feeling that Native interests in development were being subordinated to Chinese interests, an emotion similar to that which had been aroused against the land bills. One consequence of this was to sharpen antagonism towards Dato Ningkan, who was thought to be "too much in the hands of the Chinese". Ningkan was not passive in the face of the efforts to form a Native Alliance against him. Inside SNAP there was a drive to increase Land Dayak membership, mostly in the First Division and in Kuching itself to build a strong branch with mainly Chinese membership, and with the wealthy Dato Wee Hood Teck as Chairman. This reinforced the image of SNAP as being "too Chinese" in the eyes of those who wanted a Native Alliance.[22] Ningkan also attempted to win friends in another quarter by referring favourably in public to Ong Kee Hui, the chairman of SUPP.

Personalities became relevant as well as issues. There were complaints of Dato Ningkan's egoism and temper and of his lavish display of money.[23] These are not fatal disqualifications in a politician,[24] but they add to the vulnerability of one who is under fire from other directions. The Tengku was also involved in a clash of personalities, partly because of the heat generated on the issues of language and expatriates in the civil service previously mentioned. His involvement was deepened when Dato Ningkan somewhat bluntly made a reference to the Tengku's age and to the desirability of his retirement.[25]

Finally there were two circumstances which were different from the previous year, and which clearly had a great effect on the outcome of the crisis. Confrontation had ceased and with it the need not to "rock the boat" by a drastic change in the composition of the government. Also Temenggong Jugah was no longer committed to the support of Dato Ningkan, because of such incidents as the Mason affair, and possibly because of continued persuasion by the "new men" in Pesaka such as Jonathan Bangau and because of the influence of Kuala Lumpur. Whatever the reason, shortly before the second crisis came to the surface, Jugah warned Ningkan that the only way in which a crisis could be avoided was by Ningkan's leaving the Chief Minister's post and perhaps also the Cabinet.

The 1966 crisis cannot be said to have begun at any definite date. For the sake of convenience it might be reckoned as having started on June 12 when Dato Ningkan, for the second time, dismissed Taib from the Cabinet, saying that he had no confidence in him and that he and others were trying to topple his government. Even if Taib had not been dismissed, in all likelihood the crisis would still have taken place. The only effect of the dismissal was probably to advance slightly the timing of the moves against Ningkan. Cynical observers of Sarawak politics might have gathered that a crisis was in the air simply from the fact that so many public denials were made that any split existed in the government.

The tactics adopted by the anti-Ningkan forces were slightly different from those used a year before. The *parties* in the government did not resign from it, but the remaining Pesaka and BARJASA *ministers*, who were left after Taib's dismissal, resigned on 13 June.[26] The strategy which had been carried only half way in 1965, the collection of signatures on an anti-Ningkan petition, was used again and pressed to a conclusion. Twenty-one signatures were collected against Ningkan,[27] and the signatories, who had gone to Kuala Lumpur, sent a telegram to him asking for his immediate resignation. They also announced that they would not attend the Council Negri meeting due to begin the next day (June 14).

An atmosphere of melodrama surrounds the visit of the Council Negri members to Kuala Lumpur and their return. Opponents of the Pesaka-BARJASA coup allege that pressure was exercised on members, and that on their return to Kuching they were kept incommunicado, and consultations were held with the police about their protection. For good measure, some sources add that an SCA member was also summoned to Kuala Lumpur, and that when he decided not to sign the petition he had difficulty in finding his trousers before leaving for Singapore. The promoters of the coup deny that pressure was used, and say that protection was necessary against attempts at bribery by Dato Ningkan and maybe even against physical violence. One of them also suggested that his phone was tapped by the British during this period, because he had heard crackling noises and cocks crowing on his line.

Dato Ningkan refused to resign, but on 14 June the Tengku announced that he had conferred with the Governor and the Governor would tell Ningkan to go. The Tengku explained that a letter had been sent to him, as head of the Malaysian Alliance Party, by a majority[28] of Council Negri members saying that they had no confidence in Ningkan. But he added "I do not sack." Hence the need to confer with the Governor. However, the Tengku as Head of the Alliance, had the power to choose Alliance chief ministers. Two names were submitted to him from Sarawak (presumably by the Pesaka-BARJASA group), Penghulu Francis Umpau and Penghulu Tawi Sli.[29] The Tengku chose the latter and his choice was endorsed by the Malaysian Alliance Party National Council. A last attempt was made to induce Ningkan to resign by Tun Ismail, the Minister for Home Affairs, who, along with Khaw Kai Boh, visited Alliance leaders in Kuching on 16 June. But there was no room left for compromise by this time. Ningkan requested a dissolution from the Governor, but was refused; there would have been some difficulty in granting it because the constituencies for direct Council Negri elections had not yet been delimited. He refused to resign, to the great astonishment of his opponents. The Governor, convinced by the arguments of the Malaysian Alliance National Council, dismissed him and his Cabinet on 17 June, and on the same day appointed Tawi Sli as Chief Minister.

The constitutional repercussions did not end there. Ningkan took legal proceedings to secure reinstatement on the ground that his dismissal by the Governor was *ultra vires*. The Governor, his argument ran, could remove him from office only if a vote of the Council Negri itself had shown that he had lost the confidence of that body. He won his case and was reinstated as Chief Minister,[30] but found that his victory was barren. He did not meet the Council Negri, in spite of numerous demands for a meeting by his opponents, because he could not avoid being defeated there unless he could persuade some Alliance members to defect.[31] On the other hand, the Governor did not accede to his request for immediate Council Negri elections. The political atmosphere was tense, and there were reports of attempted bribery or even of threats to use physical force on politicians.[32] The Federal Government broke the impasse, to Ningkan's disadvantage, by amending the constitution to give the Governor of Sarawak the power to summon the Council Negri to meet.[33] The Governor speedily made use of this power, and a vote of no confidence in the Ningkan government was passed (23 September). On the next day the Governor once again dismissed Dato Ningkan from the Chief Ministership and appointed Penghulu Tawi Sli in his place.

After Dato Ningkan's first removal from office there was a

new alignment of parties which continued after the Tawi Sli government took over again after Ningkan's brief reinstatement. SNAP left the Alliance on 3 June, and now only four parties remained in it. But, additionally, a shift in power had apparently taken place. Pesaka and BARJASA, the coup promoters had gained in power. PANAS and the SCA, which in the early stages of the crisis had both supported Ningkan, lost strength. PANAS had split, and although the majority of its executive and members remained in the party, there were some important defections to SNAP, notably its chairman, Dato Abang Othman. The SCA at one point was nearly excluded from the cabinet for having been a "traitor", because on 15 June its executive committee had asked the Tengku to withdraw its demand for Ningkan's resignation. Its previous member in the Cabinet was Dato Teo, who had introduced the land bills, and, as has been indicated earlier, the Pesaka-BARJASA coup organizers were not too sympathetic to the demands of those Chinese who were represented by the SCA. An effort was made to "punish" the SCA (and perhaps weaken its future bargaining power) by offering a Cabinet post to Leong Ho Yuen (MACHINDA). This offer was made several times, once at least along with the offer of another cabinet post to MACHINDA. The obvious assumption was that, if MACHINDA accepted, the SCA would be left out of the Cabinet. The offer was refused and the Alliance turned again to the SCA which had switched its support to the Alliance. There was a good deal of haggling but eventually there were two SCA members in the Cabinet, Dato Teo (Minister for Communications and Works), and Ling Beng Siong (Minister of State). The SCA-Pesaka relationship was symbiotic, each needed the other.[34] Also, Dato Teo was important as one of the few possible competent "working ministers".[35] However, the SCA had lost the key Forestry portfolio, previously held by Dato Teo, which, now combined with "Development", went to Taib (BARJASA).[36]

This brief account of the two crises may serve as the basis for certain hypotheses. First, during this period the policies of the parties and the personalities in them tended to favour some political party combinations and to discourage others. There was constant tension between BARJASA and PANAS resulting from the nature of the parties' original recruits, and they were not able to unite in a single party (Bumiputera) until PANAS had been split by defections some time after the end of the second crisis. In the early 1960s relations between Pesaka and SNAP were good, as was shown by the amicable agreement to share out spheres of interest in the third and second divisions, respectively. Later they deteriorated at the higher levels because of the rise of some new men in Pesaka and the party's dissatisfaction with the progress of development and its lack of Cabinet posts. But the "older style" Pesaka leaders, such as Temenggong Jugah, were still during the first crisis susceptible to appeals to Iban solidarity. Antagonism between the two mainly Iban parties was strengthened by Pesaka's tactical alliance with BARJASA. SNAP and BARJASA leaders were so mutually hostile that they could not work together. On the other hand, attempts to unite Pesaka and BARJASA into a single party were not acceptable to Pesaka, especially if the new party were to be part of UMNO. The SCA, in its party alignment, wanted to reproduce the Malayan situation by playing an "MCA" role to the local equivalent of UMNO. But what was the local equivalent of UMNO? At first the question did not arise, because out of the four Native parties only the relatively weak PANAS was not in the Alliance, and the SCA did not have to choose which of the other parties to support, because they were all in the Alliance. But the question had to be answered in the course of the two crises.

In the first crisis the SCA backed SNAP, and exerted its influence on Temenggong Jugah also to back SNAP. This was a decision to preserve the status quo and to support the party which had introduced the "pro-Chinese" land bills. In the second crisis the impulse originally was to do the same. But later the SCA switched to follow Pesaka, on the premise that the SCA should always be represented in the Alliance in order best to protect Chinese interests. The "rule" for the SCA seemed to be: (1) obtain representation in the government; (2) inside the government form a special link with the Native party which can do most for the SCA.

Until it joined the government in July 1970, in the shifting party alliances in Sarawak the SUPP was considered to be "outside the game" in its existing form, just as, for a long time

Communist parties were excluded from government coalitions in France and Italy. Only if the moderate leadership could be detached from the remainder could a purified SUPP be considered as a possible partner. Apart from its brief tactical alliance with PANAS in 1963, perhaps the only time before 1970 when the SUPP as a whole had a prospect of allying with a major party, or parties, was during the second crisis. When the twenty-one signatories of the anti-Ningkan petition were in Kuala Lumpur Ningkan could have asked for a vote of confidence in the Council Negri which was meeting at the time. With SUPP support he could have won all or most of the votes of the twenty-one members who attended.[37] If he won all of them, the vote at the next meeting of the Council Negri would have been 21–21 if no further changes took place. He also had good prospects of persuading some of the twenty-one who had visited Kuala Lumpur to come over to his side, for instance by offering them Cabinet jobs, as was indicated by the precautions taken to keep them protected from his attentions on their return to Sarawak. However, unless Dato Ningkan's powers of persuasion had proved to be very efficacious indeed, the continued success of this strategy would have depended on the kind of arrangement or alliance that he could have made with SUPP. The moderate SUPP leaders, at least initially, offered their backing without making any conditions and without asking for any representation in the Cabinet. But the more extreme section of the party would have supported SNAP only in exchange for the release of all political detainees and if SNAP had agreed to make a determined attempt to withdraw from Malaysia. Consequently a SUPP alliance would have given Ningkan a breathing space, but his next steps on the tightrope would have needed extraordinarily skilled footwork.

Another hypothesis is that, in the absence of clearly defined rules and precedents about the relations between party and government, each contestant simply chose the most favourable terrain on each occasion. This was literally true in Ningkan's general preference for Sarawak as the field of battle while his opponents on the whole preferred Kuala Lumpur. It was also true figuratively, as is shown by the tactics used during the second crisis. Up to the time when Ningkan was first replaced by Tawi Sli, the former was relying on the power he had as Chief Minister to control rewards and deprivations, including the power to make Cabinet appointments and dismissals. His opponents relied on the support of the Malaysian Alliance Party machinery, including the rôle of the Tengku in that machinery, and on the Tengku's influence in persuading the Sarawak Governor that he legally could, and immediately should, dismiss Ningkan.

After Ningkan had been temporarily restored as Chief Minister both he and his opponents were seeking to use those weapons which, respectively, lay most conveniently to hand. Ningkan relied on the Court decision which had reinstated him, and beyond that on the prospect of new elections to the Council Negri. The Tawi Sli "alternative government" desired an early meeting of the existing Council Negri in which it believed it could destroy the Ningkan government by a vote of no confidence; when Ningkan refused to summon the Council Negri the device of having the Federal Parliament change the constitution was brought into play.

The Sarawak Alliance National Council never developed into an effective forum for discussing the policies of the Sarawak Alliance. When it first came into existence it did not even have established voting procedures. During the 1966 crisis Ningkan tried unsuccessfully to have a meeting of the Council called, no doubt expecting to be supported by the votes of three out of five parties represented. Even if the Council had met, PANAS and the SCA might still have changed sides, as they actually did in the end, and voted against Ningkan. In any case a Sarawak Alliance National Council vote could have been got round by winning the support of individual PANAS and SCA members of the Council Negri in preparation for a vote of no confidence in that body.

Finally, there seems to have been a difference between the two crises in the use of money as a weapon. In the first crisis few or no financial inducements were held out in order to acquire or retain support. Perhaps this is because the land bills, although they became symbolically invested with more significance than their intrinsic importance warranted, still constituted an issue which determined allegiances and which made recourse to money unnecessary. The second crisis, on the other hand, assumed the form of an embittered power struggle between personalities, and each side alleged that the other offered vast sums of money to strategically-placed individuals in order to win that struggle.

The account which had just been given underlines the importance of the role played by the Federal Government. In each crisis there were discussions between politicians in the Sarawak Alliance Party and politicians in the Malaysian Alliance Party which did not have the approval of the Sarawak Alliance Party as a whole. In each crisis BARJASA and Pesaka, with the aid of the leaders in the Malaysian Alliance Party, were preparing a coup to take over power in the Sarawak Alliance.[38]

In the second crisis members of the Federal Government, in their capacity as leaders of the Malaysian Alliance Party, were also deeply involved in the implementation of the coup as well as in planning it. Given that the Sarawak Alliance Party was a component of the Malaysian Alliance Party, and given that the leaders of the latter had close links with the leaders of some of the parties in the former, what actually happened was not too surprising. When the Tengku, talking of the events during the beginning of the second crisis, observed that he and his colleagues were "powerless" to take any action,[39] he was surely speaking in a strictly constitutional sense. Taib's description of "Kuala Lumpur influence" in a Council Negri speech is perhaps a little more illuminating:

> There has been a suggestion, rather sinister I would say, that we (the members of the Tawi Sli government) are merely stooges of Kuala Lumpur, that Kuala Lumpur is our master. In our political thinking, Sir, this kind of relationship of servants and masters in the political circle doesn't operate at all in Malaysia. If there is anything that is operating in this kind of relationship then it would be between Mao Tze Tung and his cadres, with Mao Tze Tung as master.[40]

This analogy probably overemphasizes the rôle of ideology in Malaysian politics. But certainly the prestige of the Alliance leaders in Kuala Lumpur, and particularly of the "heaven-sent" Tengku, had a dominant effect on some less experienced and less sophisticated Sarawak politicians.

The fact remains that, however "influence from Kuala Lumpur" is defined and however it was exercised, in the second crisis a majority of the Council Negri members of the Sarawak Alliance Party were in favour of a change of government. Influence from Kuala Lumpur operated only through the linkage of a substantial body of local support. The second crisis seemed to be more Kuala Lumpur-inspired than it actually was. This is because the coup organizers[41] chose to operate through the Malaysian Alliance Party national machinery in Kuala Lumpur rather than through the Council Negri in Sarawak. Why, if the coup organizers had a majority, or nearly a majority, in the Council Negri did they not attend the Council meeting on 14 June, 1966, instead of boycotting it, and vote the Ningkan government out through a motion of no confidence? The main reason seems to be that in such a situation the coup organizers could not really be sure that they could achieve a majority in the Council Negri. They had a great, maybe even an excessive, respect for Dato Ningkan's powers of inducing defections, or redefections, as well as fear of his "temper".[42]

Apart from this consideration, the sequence followed in the second crisis, the replacement of Ningkan by Sli *before* a meeting of Council Negri,[43] could actually have affected the result of a vote in the Council Negri. Members might have hesitated to vote against Ningkan *as* Chief Minister, although they would not have hesitated to vote for Tawi Sli *once he had become* Chief Minister.[44] So the sequence which followed was understandable, although its legal basis was shaky.[45] Another reason given for the procedure which was adopted was that "inspired" demonstrations in Kuching, which actually occurred on a small scale, would have been intensified and might have resulted in racial violence. A final reason for seeking a solution outside Sarawak was that the choice of a successor to Ningkan could thus be limited to persons approved by the coup promoters. If the succession had been determined locally, it is possible that another nominee might have been selected, possibly Dato Endawie or Dato James Wong, both of SNAP.

Although there were good reasons why the climax of the June 1966 coup should be staged in Kuala Lumpur rather than in Kuching, the procedure which was used had the undoubted effect of producing an anti-Federal Government reaction and of writing a convincing script for Dato Ningkan's appealing rôle as the defender of "Sarawak nationalism".[46]

A Comparison with Sabah: the Sabah Cabinet Crisis of 1964

Sabah also had two cabinet crises soon after the formation of Malaysia, the second resulting, as in Sarawak, in the Chief Minister's being replaced by a member of a different party. A short comparison may serve to bring out some of the differences in the political strengths of the respective government parties in the two states.

The first Sabah crisis,[47] which reached its peak in June, 1964, was precipitated by announcements from the Sabah Head of State, Datu Mustapha early in the year that he was about to resign from his post.[48] The reasons behind his decision were described as "personal", however, it was apparent that USNO and UPKO were engaged in a fiercely competitive struggle to win the forthcoming elections. Pronouncements on when the elections should be held, debates on whether they should be direct or indirect and how many seats would be allocated to each party, rumours of a merger between the two parties, and UPKO's attempts to improve its position by recruiting Chinese members,[49] all contributed to a tense atmosphere.[50] In June representatives of the three Sabah parties went to Kuala Lumpur and conferred with the Tengku and other Alliance leaders. The agreement reached did not represent any dramatic shift in power within the Cabinet. However, the changes that were made were all disadvantageous to UPKO: an USNO Cabinet member received the newly created post of Deputy Chief Minister; the new position of Finance Minister was given to SANAP; the sensitive Natural Resources portfolio (which carried with it responsibility for timber policy) was taken from an UPKO man and given to a new Cabinet member, who did not belong to any of the constituent parties of the Alliance, Thomas Jayasuriya. Native parties were not to recruit Chinese, nor was SANAP to recruit Natives.

The December, 1964 crisis was more serious, because it arose from a direct confrontation between Tun Mustapha[51] and Dato Stephens. The immediate issue concerned the appointment of the first non-expatriate state secretary. Stephens wished to appoint John Dusing, a Kadazan,[52] but Mustapha delayed approval of the recommendation. In the course of the dispute the whole question of the constitutional relationship between the Chief Minister and the Head of State was raised. There was a direct clash of opinion between Stephens and the Tengku. The former maintained that, although he was bound to "consult" the Head of State, "consultation" did not mean "approval". The Tengku referred to an agreement among all parties that, when Tun Mustapha was appointed, he was to retain some party status as well as the usual constitutional status.[53] Again deputations from the Sabah parties went to Kuala Lumpur, where the Tengku once again acted as mediator. The meeting resulted in UPKO's losing the Chief Ministership (31 December, 1964). Dato Stephens switched to the post of Minister for Sabah Affairs and was succeeded as Chief Minister by Peter Lo (SANAP), the current Federal Minister without Portfolio. UPKO's compensations for the loss of this important post were not so great as they looked on paper. Stephens's new assignment was important only if the holder's relations with members of the Federal Cabinet and with the Malaysian Alliance were close and cordial.[54] The Deputy Chief Ministership was given to Dato Sundang (UPKO), but he was a less active politician than Stephens and had a smaller following. UPKO maintained its quota of three posts in the state Cabinet through the device of making Jayasuriya a member of the party.[55] But, although he kept the Natural Resources portfolio, this did not give UPKO control over timber; quite apart from Jayasuriya's concern for protecting the public interest, the Cabinet as a whole was now too aware of the benefits to be derived from timber to leave timber policy to the responsible minister.

There are certain obvious similarities between the Sabah and the Sarawak cabinet crises. In each state the first crisis did not result in a change of Chief Minister, but the second crisis did. And, in each state, the new Chief Minister who took over after the second crisis was a "compromise" or transitional candidate, paving the way in Sabah for Tun Mustapha, in Sarawak for Dato Rahman Ya'akub. In each state, federal influence was apparent, mainly through the medium of the Malaysian Alliance Party. The contrasts between the two sets of crises, however, were more evident. The Sarawak crises were more dramatic, were conducted in a more open and fluid setting, and called forth a more extensive repertoire of ploys and counterploys. In Sarawak Dato Ningkan, in his fight to retain office, dismissed ministers, and the Federal Government eventually used its emergency powers. The second Sarawak crisis was marked by threats of violence, by persuasion, including financial persuasion, by petitions, by splits and switches and by prospects of splits and switches. While Dato Stephens fought only verbally against the two Cabinet reshuffles decided on in Kuala Lumpur, Ningkan did not even consent to go to Kuala Lumpur for discussions with the Tengku and the Malaysian Alliance.

Some of the difference in the courses pursued by Ningkan and Stephens was no doubt based on personalities. Ningkan was a fighter, while Stephens had to face as an opponent the determined Tun Mustapha. Additionally, however, the situation in Sarawak was more fluid than in Sabah. To counter the initial opposition of BARJASA and the "new men" of Pesaka, Ningkan could still hope for support from other sources,—from the more traditional members of Pesaka, from the SCA, from PANAS, or even from SUPP. Moreover, Ningkan was an Iban, and at the first direct elections any likely distribution of constituency boundaries would result in a majority of seats being preponderantly Iban. Stephens had no possible corresponding sources of support. He was opposed by USNO, and by the time of the second crisis it was clear that he had also alienated SANAP.[56] Unrealistically, he may have hoped to win at the first direct elections,[57] but no preparations had yet been made for holding these. Consequently UPKO acquiesced in having its power reduced in each of the two 1964 crises, good examples of its policy of "conciliation" which alternated with its policy of "defiance",—to the confusion of its supporters.[58]

Coalitions: the size principle

In a multi-party system elections alone do not decide the composition of governments; the nature of the coalitions formed between elections is also decisive. The "size principle" has been stated by Riker in various ways. However, in terms of the "real world", the principle is as follows: "In social situations similar to *n*-person, zero-sum games with side-payments, participants create coalitions just as large as they believe will ensure winning and no larger".[59] The rationale of limiting the size of coalitions is simply that if, as entailed by the zero-sum provision, the size of the "cake" is indeed fixed, then, the smaller the size of a successful coalition, the greater the "payoff" to each member of the winning group. Applying the principle to coalitions of political parties in Sarawak and Sabah leads to the conclusion that parties in Sarawak seemed to act quite often as if motivated by the size principle, but that in Sabah its operation was less obvious.

The Sarawak Coalition of 1970

In Sarawak, one might have thought, the existence of the SUPP which could command about a quarter of the vote, would have simplified the situation and led all the other main parties to form a coalition against it. This was indeed the situation in 1962–3 before PANAS broke away from the Alliance and before SNAP left it. But in 1963 the other Alliance parties allowed PANAS to leave the coalition rather than accede to its demands for more seats in the forthcoming district elections, and in 1966 some other members of the Alliance were quite happy to see SNAP, and not just its leader Dato Ningkan, leave the Alliance. A few months before the start of the state elections in 1969, the two main parties in the Alliance, Pesaka and Bumiputera, seemed to be almost oblivious of the strength of the opposition. Pesaka made no serious attempt to reach an accord with SNAP to prevent the vote-splitting which would result from their fighting each other in predominantly Iban seats. Nor did Pesaka and Bumiputera come to an agreement to avoid putting up candidates to fight each other in certain seats, even although both were in the Alliance. It seemed hard to believe that the Alliance, given the weakness of the third component, the SCA, could be certain of winning a majority against SNAP and SUPP. To some degree Pesaka's intransigence might be attributed to optimism (less than SNAP's, but also less firmly-grounded) that it could win an absolute majority over all other parties. With hindsight, it might be guessed that Bumiputera was relying, not on the Alliance winning an absolute majority, but on its own skill in being able so to manage things after the election as to achieve a winning minimum coalition.

The results of the 1970 Sarawak state elections made possible a wide range of different coalitions of parties. The Alliance as currently constituted was just short of a majority,[60] so the obvious course of continuing with an unchanged combination of government parties was ruled out. Another solution, to admit SNAP back into the Alliance was not possible. Such a solution might have been acceptable to Pesaka, if only the question of whether SNAP or Pesaka should provide the Chief Minister could have been agreed upon. But it was not acceptable to Bumiputera, and Bumiputera, contrary to many expectations, had won the largest number of seats in the Alliance. Once it had been decided to appoint Dato Rahman Ya'akub as Chief Minister,[61] it was most unlikely that SNAP would be seriously considered as a partner. The friction between SNAP and BARJASA (before it combined with PANAS to form Bumiputera), and in particular the friction between Dato Ningkan on the one hand and Dato Rahman Ya'akub and Taib on the other, had been so great[62] that any other combination would be preferred by the new Chief Minister. A likely combination was a SUPP-SNAP-Pesaka government, and the three parties concerned held talks on this, along with the SCA, immediately after the election. For about two years it had been recognized as possible that SUPP might join the government after the elections. Such an outcome was apparently acceptable to the Federal Government; the conversations between the UMNO leaders and the SUPP leaders in Kuala Lumpur in February, 1969, a few months before the elections were begun, which ended in SUPP accepting Malaysia in principle and in the party's being allowed to conduct its campaign without hindrance, clearly envisaged such a possibility.

The reservations about a SUPP-SNAP-Pesaka government mainly came not from SNAP or even from Pesaka (with the notable exception of Tan Sri Jugah, who preferred Dato James Wong's proposal for an all-party government), but from SUPP.

It distrusted Pesaka as an ill-disciplined party, which could not be relied on. It had also been antagonized by the coolness which SNAP had shown towards its overtures for working together during the 1966 cabinet crisis,[63] and to possible arrangements for the two parties not opposing each other during the 1969–70 elections. SUPP, as a realistic party, was also sceptical of the amount of power that a SUPP-SNAP-Pesaka government would be permitted to wield. The State Operations Council was still in existence, headed by the Federal Secretary. If Bumiputera, the only Malay party, was not represented in the government, would the emergency regulations be lifted and parliamentary government return in Sarawak? Would the Chief Minister be permitted to take over the SOC chairmanship from the Federal Secretary? And when would the SOC be abolished or its functions reduced? Furthermore, if the only Malay party were excluded, might there not be a fear of Malay violence?[64]

The coalition which was actually formed was between Bumiputera and SUPP, as major partners, and Pesaka and the SCA, as minor partners. Parallel with the SUPP-SNAP-Pesaka talks, discussions took place between Bumiputera and SUPP. SUPP leaders, anxious to join the government after so many years in opposition, chose the coalition with Bumiputera as a major partner rather than the coalition with SNAP and Pesaka.[65] SUPP's objections to the latter coalition have just been indicated. The coalition it actually chose raised problems also. It differed from the *ad hoc* arrangement arrived at between SUPP and PANAS in 1963,[66] which did not bring with it any responsibility for governing. How could a party which had been infiltrated, and which contained some extreme socialists and some extreme Chinese chauvinists, work comfortably with a Malay party, whose policy was closely in line with the Federal Government's? In its agreement with Bumiputera, SUPP stipulated that it should have a Deputy Chief Minister appointed (Stephen Yong), that it should have equal control over policies and cabinet appointments with Bumiputera, and that the policies contained in its Election Manifesto should be implemented. Apparently these concerned principally the trial of detainees, the easing of restrictions over areas which were "controlled" because of a high incidence of

Communist subversion, education policy and land policy. All of these might prove difficult to implement. The first two were federal, not state, issues. Any benefits to Chinese education might conflict with the Federal Government's policy which the new Chief Minister had previously pursued as federal Minister of Education.[67]

In spite of these difficulties the SUPP preferred to work with Bumiputera, which it knew was a well-disciplined party. The discipline of its own more radical members might be tested by the mere fact of the coalition with the apparently ideologically distant Bumiputera. One SUPP stipulation may have been designed partly to reassure such members; it made a firm condition before entering the Government that the SCA should not be given any seats in the Cabinet. The notion of a coalition with SUPP was not new to Bumiputera leaders. Some of them had envisaged it even before the 1969 elections began. They admired SUPP as a party which resembled their own as being "disciplined". After the 1970 elections an important reason why Bumiputera, and the Federal Government, favoured a coalition with SUPP was that the party's five (federal) parliamentary seats could be crucial for securing the two-thirds parliamentary majority necessary for effecting desired constitutional changes.

The principle of a minimum winning coalition was applied in several ways in the formation of the new Sarawak Government in July 1970. A coalition of all parties, the previous Alliance plus both SUPP and SNAP, although favoured by Dato James Wong, was avoided. Apart from the problems of personal conflict which a government containing both Bumiputera and SNAP would have raised, such a government would have infringed the minimum winning coalition principle. A comparison of successive statements on this issue is revealing. The possibility of all parties being included in the government was mentioned by Tun Razak immediately after the election results were announced.[68] But these statements were made at a time when it was not certain that Pesaka (which was holding conversations with SNAP and SUPP) would back the new government. However, on 7 July a member of Pesaka, Penghulu Abok bin Jalin, was sworn in as a minister along with Dato Rahman Ya'akub as Chief Minister and

Stephen Yong as Deputy Chief Minister,[69] and on 8 July Pesaka issued a statement saying that it was still in the Alliance that it fully supported the coalition government.[70] By 11 July there was no longer any question of SNAP's being admitted. Tun Razak said "he did not think it was necessary to get SNAP into the Grand Alliance. 'We have enough support in Parliament as well as in the Sarawak Council Negri,' he added. "Furthermore, I did not think we can get the whole lot of them in although we may get a few".[71] The prospect of an all-party coalition was therefore held out only long enough to secure the adhesion of Pesaka, or of sufficient individual members of Pesaka or SNAP, to the new government to constitute a safe majority. There was apparently no compelling policy of forming an all-party coalition.

In another sense the coalition chosen was also "minimum". The rewards offered Pesaka were just sufficient to keep the party, or several individual members of it, in the government. Tan Sri Jugah was assured of his continuation as Minister of Sarawak Affairs and the party was given two Cabinet posts. But the persons appointed to these posts, Penghulu Abok as a minister and later, Simon Dembab anak Maja as a Deputy Chief Minister, were not selected by the party itself; they were chosen by the Chief Minister, and the party later acquiesced. Nor was the party a signatory to the agreement between Bumiputera and the SUPP. The party was *in* the government, but was not an equal partner in it. Because of the condition made by the SUPP, the SCA, in spite of its closeness to Bumiputera in fighting the election, was in an even worse position. It did not sign the Bumiputera-SUPP agreement, and it was excluded from the Cabinet altogether. No doubt Bumiputera and the SUPP, with the largest number of seats in the new coalition, were entitled to a larger payoff than either Pesaka or the SCA. But it seemed that their payoffs were disproportionately large, even when this was taken into account. The SCA was receiving less that "its share" because the SUPP was in a position to exact such a condition. Pesaka received less than "its share", partly as a "punishment" for having flirted with SNAP and SUPP.

Coalitions in Sabah. Representation of Ethnic Groups

At first sight the size principle does not seem to have had much influence on the formation of coalitions in Sabah. After the formation of Malaysia all the parties were included in the Government except for a period in 1967 between the time when UPKO went into opposition and the time it dissolved.[72] This is more suggestive of a *rival* of the size principle, the "unanimity principle". According to Adrian and Press, it can be stated in this way: "Among members of a group capable of direct communication with one another, the dynamics of intra-group interaction produces pressures for decisions of the group to be formally unanimous".[73] The authors say that such pressure for unanimity is likely to be found only in very small groups. To some extent the key to the apparent discrepancy might be that, in one sense, the group of Sabah leaders was very small; as far as the native parties, the USNO and the UPKO were concerned, the two leaders, Tun Mustapha and Dato Stephens, respectively, had tight control over their own parties and the two had close personal relations. Another reason, no doubt, was historical. In Sarawak the SUPP was formed before the parties which later constituted the Sarawak Alliance Party. But the Sabah parties were formed only after the Tengku advocated the creation of Malaysia. In Sarawak, because of the previous existence of the well-organized SUPP, the adoption of an "Alliance pattern" simply meant that there had to be at least one component of the Alliance to represent each major ethnic group; the SUPP and other parties might exist as well. But in Sabah, with no parties previously in existence, once the early shufflings and amalgamations were over, the Alliance pattern turned out differently. There was indeed an Alliance party for each major ethnic group (very broadly defined), but there were no other rival parties.

Other factors helped to favour a Sabah coalition embracing all parties. One was the belief that the resources of Sabah, especially timber, were boundless, so that the zero-sum condition was often not perceived as applying. Of course the assumption of unlimited resources was not correct, but it was only gradually recognized as incorrect, mainly by politicians below the first rank, who became dissatisfied at the discrepancy between their payoffs and the payoffs of the top politicians.

After the dissolution of the UPKO in late 1967, which was followed by ex-UPKO members' attempts to join the USNO, Tun Mustapha was faced with the situation so well summarized by Riker:

> When a coalition includes everybody, the winners gain nothing simply because there are no losers. Note: It must be assumed—and this is a highly significant assumption—that the members of a winning coalition have control over additional entries to their coalition. If they have no such control, all losers could invariably join the winners and thereby both produce a valueless coalition of the whole and nullify the winners' victory.[74]

Yet, given the pressures which the USNO and the SCA had been placing on the UPKO, notably by inducing UPKO assemblymen to defect, what would have been the consequences of a refusal by Tun Mustapha to accept ex-UPKO members into his party? There would have been a strong likelihood of violence and a disruption of Sabah's reputation for racial harmony. The fear of such an occurrence must have been present in Tun Mustapha's mind. This suggests that the zero-sum condition did not quite apply, and that the situation was indeed such that "the amount of individual payoff may *increase* as the size of the group increases".[75]

To put the point in another way, the USNO leaders might have lost more from the possible violence resulting from refusing to include ex-UPKO men in a "coalition", through granting them USNO membership, than they stood to lose by including them and distributing some rewards to them.[76] And yet, by the mere process of dissolving their party and seeking to join the USNO, were the ex-UPKO men automatically to become "winners" instead of "losers" and to qualify for all the rewards of winners? Tun Mustapha compromised. Dato Stephens became a High Commissioner, as had previously been proposed, and Dato Ganie Gilong became Minister for Sabah Affairs in the federal cabinet. Two other ex-UPKO politicians became political secretaries to Sabah ministers. But none of the ex-UPKO politicians became state ministers, except Payar Juman, the original defector from UPKO to USNO, who would certainly not have been selected as a minister by his UPKO colleagues.[77] The rewards of joining USNO were therefore limited. Ex-UPKO politicians became "winners", as well as USNO politicians. But some winners were less equal than others.

Another benefit which USNO gained from the admission of ex-UPKO members was that the transaction reduced its dependence on the Sabah Chinese Association, its other main partner in the Alliance. Its having to share some of the cake with ex-UPKO politicians was partly offset by its diminished need to share with the SCA. This gain was illustrated by the fact that after mid-1969 the SCA, in the person of Dato Khoo, lost the Deputy Chief Minister post, which was abolished.

One other factor may have predisposed Tun Mustapha to favour a coalition which included ex-UPKO members. In his analysis of side-payments Riker argues that there may be a tendency for leaders to overspend, in the sense that they may pay out more to win a victory than it is objectively worth.[78] Side payments are not necessarily made in money, and some of the categories specified by Riker have an intangible quality. However, the 1967 Sabah state elections were expensive in money terms, and in occupying the time and energies of leaders. In estimating the benefits of a coalition the possibility of avoiding such heavy expenditure in the future must have seemed most attractive.

A final point requires explanation. Why did the USNO in Sabah in 1967, and Bumiputera and SUPP in Sarawak in 1970, go to the trouble of adding to what was already, numerically, a sufficient winning coalition? USNO did this in 1967 by attempting to persuade UPKO assemblymen to defect, their first success being with Inche Payar Juman. Bumiputera and SUPP did the same in 1970 by inducing two individual Pesaka members to join the Cabinet. To some extent probably the USNO was motivated by a simple desire to assert its ascendancy. To Bumiputera, and SUPP, no doubt the inclusion of at least some Pesaka members of Council Negri was an insurance against the SCA, angered by SUPP's entry into the Government and its own exclusion from the Cabinet, threatening to pull out of the Government. Beyond this, however, in both instances there was probably a desire to have a *representative* Cabinet, containing in Sabah Kadazan, in Sarawak Iban, membership. The principle of the Alliance pattern that all major ethnic groups should be represented in the Government and the Cabinet had taken firm root in the minds of politicians.

In both states, then, the minimum-winning-coalition principle was applied to some extent. In one way the principle was given an extended interpretation. The December 1967 (Sabah) and July 1970 (Sarawak) coalitions were also "minimum" in the sense that the parties dominating the respective coalitions did distribute some payoff to the weaker partners but only a *minimum* payoff.

6

Administration in the Field: Local Government Councils: Development Machinery

Administratively, Sarawak now has five divisions and twenty districts, Sabah four residencies and twenty districts.[1] But there is no short way of describing governmental structures in the field and what they do. When new structures were introduced the old structures were left, although in a modified form. When the Brooke régime and the British North Borneo Company set up an administrative framework consisting of Residents, District Officers (D.O.s) and so on, they also expanded and institutionalized the existing rudimentary system of headmen or chiefs. Similarly, after World War II when elected local bodies were created, the chiefs and headmen, the Residents and the District Officers, still remained. This complex structure had to cope with three severe sources of strain within the space of a few years: the transition from being a British colony to being a state of Malaysia; the rapid growth of party politics; a much quicker tempo of economic development, especially in the rural areas.

Headmen and Chiefs, Sarawak

In Sarawak the Brookes developed their own version of indirect rule. They employed agencies which, apart from any powers deriving from statutory enactment or appointment, brought to the service of the Administration an authority derived from their traditional status in the community.[2] A civil service was introduced, consisting of European officials such as Residents and District Officers, reinforced by Native administrative officials. The effect was to change the working of the previous, truly "indigenous", element. Generally speaking, village headmen or their equivalent, had not traditionally possessed any autocratic powers over the members of their villages, or longhouses.[3] But their functions were now institutionalized, spread over a wider area, and fitted into a hierarchy of "indigenous" rule which paralleled the new civil service hierarchy.

"The "indigenous rule" hierarchy, which remained in Sarawak when Brooke rule replaced rule by Brunei, was not uniform. Just as the Brookes "allowed the various races to be governed by their own customary laws or 'adat', save only in a few cases . . .",[4] so they allowed for some diversity in the native administrative machinery. Groups in flat coastal areas, such as the Malays, which practised relatively intensive cultivation, were more concentrated geographically than groups inland which practised shifting cultivation, such as the Iban; consequently *Tuah Kampong* exercised influence over a wider area than the lowest member of the Iban hierarchy, the *Tuai Rumah*. The, non-indigenous, Chinese were also fitted into the pattern. As a result the formal structure for the major ethnic groups was eventually something like the following:

TABLE 6.1

Sarawak: System of Headmen and Chiefs established by the Brookes and still in existence, 1969[5]

Ethnic Group	Village (longhouse) Headman	Head (chief) of larger area
Malays, including Melanaus	*Tuah Kampong*	
Iban, etc.	*Tuai Rumah*	*Penghulu*
Land Dayaks	*Tua Kampong*	*Orang Kaya Pemancha*
Chinese	Area Headman (*Kapitan China*)	

During Brooke rule two other higher levels were created for non-Muslim Natives, "Temenggong" and, below that, "Pengarah". Presumably the intention was to manufacture an equivalent of the Malay *Datus*, originally hereditary, under the Brookes appointed for life, and now not appointed at all. At the time when Malaysia came into existence there were two *Temenggongs* (Jugah and Oyong) and four *Pengarahs*, there are now four and ten, respectively. The appointments since Malaysia were made principally in order to gain political support. The functions of *Temenggongs* and *Pengarahs* are negligible. Tan Sri Temenggong Jugah's duties as a *Temenggong* do not suffer from his preoccupation with his business interests, his being Minister for Sarawak Affairs, or his work as a party leader, because these duties are in effect non-existent. It is perhaps suggestive that even those deeply involved in the governmental process in Sarawak have to think for some time before they can say how many *Temenggongs* and *Pengarahs* there are. Certainly the senior *Temenggongs*, Temenggongs (Tan Sri) Jugah, and Oyong, are politically influential apart from being *Temenggongs*. The other *Temenggongs* are not very influential politically, even though they are *Temenggongs*.

The whole "chiefs and headmen complex", then, consists of four *Temenggongs*, ten *Pengarahs*, about three hundred *Penghulus* etc. and about two thousand *Tuai Rumah* (heads of longhouses) or their equivalent. The *Tuai Rumah* are not paid, but receive allowances when they travel on official business. *Penghulus* etc. are paid an average in salary and allowances together of about $130 to $150 a month, *Pengarahs* and *Temenggongs* somewhat more. Originally all were appointed by the Government but only after taking some account of local feeling.

The job of the headman may be indicated by two brief summaries, one applying to an Iban community, the other to a Land Dayak community. The functions of the Iban *Tuai Rumah* are both internal and external. Inside the community he is required to settle disputes. Externally, he is an intermediary between the community and the administrative system, and is often made responsible for implementing government policies. To carry out these functions satisfactorily, he must have, a sound knowledge of *adat* (customary law), impartiality, good power of judgement in handling disputes, and an ability to use words.[6] Among the Land Dayaks, the headman's rôle is said to have five aspects. He initiates village action, usually by summoning a meeting to discuss a project which has been proposed. Secondly, he presides at meetings and sums up the opinion which emerges there in the form of a definite decision. Third, he acts as the mouthpiece of the Government, appealing to the people at village meetings to do what is required of them. Fourthly, he acts, sometimes rather ineffectively, "as general director of such activities as are decided upon," for example, having Government property moved to another village. The headman "usually confines himself to very general directions and issues specific instructions only when he does not expect them to meet with objections. . . . This situation does not mean that a headman is without considerable influence. There is still scope for strength of personality, but it must produce results by persuasion and persistency rather than by dictation." Fifth, in an informal way, he helps to settle disputes.[7]

These functions in a modified form are also performed by *Penghulus*, or their equivalent. The emphasis is very much on the judicial rôle, on the interpretation and application of *adat*; formerly they were also responsible for tax collection. Indeed one Sarawak Cabinet Minister, when asked what important things *Penghulus* did apart from questions of *adat*, gave the example of dealing with marital disputes, which actually comes under *adat*. *Penghulus* also have the less precisely-defined rôle, which is nevertheless important for modernization, of acting as a link between Government and the people. The number of *Penghulus* etc. in an area cannot be increased unless the number of houses, or longhouse "doors", justifies it.

Headmen and Chiefs, Sabah

Before the coming of the British, in the shape of the Chartered Company, the various groups in North Borneo also had their village headmen. In the coastal areas the nobles, under various names, of the Courts of Brunei and Sulu over the villages in a predatory but fitful way. There was no regular system of chiefs who were hierarchical superiors of headmen.[8] As in Sarawak, the British did not impose complete uniformity for all ethnic groups, but a pattern emerged with headmen on a lower tier and Native Chiefs on a higher tier. The nomenclature is more standardized than in Sarawak. The headman originally known as *Orang Tua*, in 1966 became the *Ketuah Kampong*. The highest grade of Chief was designated a District Chief (*Orang Kaya Kaya*).

Under the British and indigenous functions of headmen

were supplemented by new functions which were required by the government in order to make the native element work smoothly with the "civil service" element. Chiefs were appointed by the Governor and headmen by the Resident, although the wishes of the local population were given great consideration.[9] When a headman died or resigned the Native Chief usually made recommendations for a successor. In some areas there was an increasing tendency for the position of headman to become hereditary. Chiefs were appointed from a variety of sources, notably from ex-policemen.[10] Chiefs and headmen were responsible for the maintenance of order in their territory, and it was their duty "generally to assist all Government Officers in the execution of their duties". They also had judicial functions in the Native Courts.[11] The duties of a headman, and the qualities required in order to be a good headman, were similar to those of their counterparts in Sarawak.

A few years ago the functions of Chiefs in Sabah were summarized as follows:

(1) to administer Native Law and Custom, through the Native Court;
(2) to exercise certain statutory powers under a number of ordinances;
(3) to act as the agents of the Government, in carrying out the policies of the Government amongst the Native people;
(4) to act as contact and information media, as a link between the Government and the Native population.[12]

In 1969 there was an establishment of 21 District Chiefs and 67 Native Chiefs. Their pay ranged from about $400 a month to $150 a month. Their legal position is anomalous; although they are full time pensionable government officers, they are not categorized and placed in one of the "divisions" of the Public Service, as other government officers are. There are also nearly 1,300 *Ketuah Kampong* (headmen), who until 1968 did not receive any regular pay, although they were given bonuses and awards. In July 1968 a change was made in the method of appointing and promoting chiefs and headmen. Previously the power to appoint chiefs had belonged to the State Public Service Commission but had been delegated to the State Secretary. The power to appoint *Ketuah Kampong* was vested in the Resident. Under the new legislation, appointments to both positions are made by the Public Service Commission.[13] In fact the PSC will act on the advice of a board, the Rural Administration Committee, consisting of senior chiefs. Other changes were made in 1968. In a few main centres, the chiefs were given office facilities and clerical help; the basic pay of *Ketuah Kampong* was standardized at the figure of $10 per month plus travelling allowances. It was also announced that uniforms would be issued to chiefs and *Ketuah Kampong*.[14]

These changes might be regarded as possible first steps in a very long process of "rationalizing" the system of chiefs and headmen by cutting down their numbers, setting certain minimum standards for appointment, such as literacy, and making them more efficient.

Sabah has one institution which has no counterpart in Sarawak, a yearly Native Chiefs Conference. This originated in the 1930s under the title of "Native Chiefs Advisory Council", its membership being confined to O.K.K.s, that is, grade one chiefs. Among the reasons advanced for creating it was that such a meeting would "enhance the prestige of those attending it and increase their sense of responsibility."[16] It was revived after the war, has a new title, and now is open to all grades of chief. However, in the last few years the demands articulated at the Conference have been, to say the least, particularistic.[17]

Chiefs and Politics

In both Sarawak and Sabah headmen and chiefs have become involved in party politics. Parties were eager to recruit them, and the possible rewards from political activity were large compared with their existing salaries and allowances. The consequences have been awkward. Headmen, or chiefs, are frequently exhorted to be loyal to the Government in power, but they may find it hard to draw the line between loyalty to the Government and loyalty to the party, or parties, which constitutes the Government. "Politicization" also undermines the administrative rôle of chiefs and headmen. They can no longer be looked up to with respect as independent and trustworthy. They may also be grossly inefficient, as was one Sabah Native Chief in 1966, "who drinks all day and does not work", but who was left undisturbed in his job because he was a source of political support for one of the government parties.

In retrospect, it may seem that this involvement in party politics was unavoidable. Theoretically it would have been possible in either territory for the Government to try to prohibit chiefs and headmen from joining or helping political parties. However, the Government did not do this, and so it was possible for chiefs and headmen to run in district council or state elections and, if successful, fill an elected position in a legislative body as well as an appointed position in the native hierarchy. This was not necessarily regrettable; it probably eased the transition from older structures to newer structures. But it meant that chiefs, or their equivalents, who also became members of elected bodies were nearly always elected on a party ticket, and therefore were clearly involved in politics. However, there would still have been an involvement in politics even if chiefs had been prohibited from seeking elective office. Competitive politics was new in both territories, communications were bad, and literacy and political sophistication were not high. Consequently, traditional authorities such as chiefs and headmen had great influence, especially on older electors inside their own areas.

In the Sabah state elections of 1967 the parties were aware of this influence, and a high proportion of election expenditure in rural areas was devoted to buying over chiefs and headmen in their capacity as opinion leaders. In Sarawak different parties have different priorities; Pesaka, for example, gave more attention to winning over chiefs and headmen than did SNAP.[18] Yet no party could ignore the influence of these people or neglect trying to win their support, whether by persuasion, intimidation, money or timber concessions.

In Sarawak, for *Penghulus* and their equivalent[19] the method of election was formalized in 1957.[20] The first time they were elected for a five-year term; if they give satisfactory service, their appointment was extended by the Supreme Council on the recommendation of the D.O. or the Resident. The election procedures are simpler than those for other elections. Nominations of candidates are made in advance, there is a secret ballot, the counting of the votes is witnessed by an official person, such as an administrative officer. The electors consist of heads of families, but only among the Malays, Melanaus, Ibans, and Land Dayaks. This was established after an election took place in Belaga, a Kenyah area in the Third Division. A candidate who supported the SUPP was elected by heads of families, but there were protests that this procedure violated Kenyah custom where the gap between the "high born" aristocracy and the remainder of the people is very wide.[21] A Minister, Tajang Laing, himself a Kenyah, intervened. After the same candidate had won a second time and by a larger majority in a ballot by heads of families, it was ruled that the correct procedure should be for the *Tuai Rumah* (who were almost certain to be high-born) to select one of themselves as *Penghulu*. This was done, and it is now the standard procedure for the "minority races".[22]

From about 1963 onwards the majority of elections for *Penghulu* have been contested on a party political basis. However, although parties have become active in these elections, they have not yet succeeded in organizing for them to the same extent as other elections. The personality of the candidates is relatively more important in *Penghulus*' elections. There is a tendency, for instance, to vote for a man from one's immediate area, partly because he may be better known, but also partly because, if elected, he will be more easily accessible if his help is required. One sign that the parties have not yet succeeded in organizing for these elections very thoroughly is that they seldom put up only one candidate. Even the SUPP sometimes fails to restrict its candidates to a single man. The other parties find it even more difficult to apply party discipline in this sphere; in 1967 in a Land Dayak area election for *Penghulu* there were thirteen Pesaka candidates and five SNAP.

One effect of the politicization of the *Penghulus* and their equivalent has been that litigants have been unwilling to go before a Native Court containing a *Penghulu* whom they know to belong to a different political party from their own. This has tended to increase the load of magisterial duties carried by District Officers and Sarawak Administrative Officers.

In Sabah the Native Chiefs Conference of 1964 considered that chiefs should be given time to disengage themselves from politics. Five years from then would be the appropriate time for complete disengagement, though some might disengage earlier. "They felt that their people in the *kampongs* still need to be looked after politically and by five years' time they hoped that they could look after themselves with full understanding about politics." This pious resolution referred, of course, only to chiefs running for election to district councils or to the state legislature. It did not explain how in the wider sense they could be disengaged from politics.

Actually, from 1963 onwards, chiefs and headmen in Sabah were deeply involved in politics. The criteria for the creation of additional chiefs or headmen were not as strictly laid down as in Sarawak, and there was constant pressure from parties for extra appointments[23] in areas where they were strong. This occurred at a time when, on an objective view, the numbers of chiefs and headmen should probably have been somewhat reduced. In areas such as Kudat and Kiulu the appointment of a chief to fill an existing vacancy was delayed because of the conflicting claims of opposing political factions. To fill some *Ketuah Kampong* vacancies chiefs were making recommendations to D.O.s based on political grounds rather than on merit. The 1967 state elections made things even worse. During the campaign many chiefs and headmen spent their time working for the party of their choice to the detriment of their official duties. And immediately after the election it was extremely difficult for the new Government to cut down on "politicization" of the chiefs because it owed its victory partly to their political efforts.

However, with the dissolution of the UPKO at the end of 1967 there was a change, and the chiefs in Sabah became more "rationalized"; after political competition was reduced, the office became less politically significant and acquired certain "rational" civil service characteristics. In Sarawak where political competition was acute, and where some chiefs were elected, the office tended to become more "political" up to the 1970 election. After the election it might be expected that, at least for a time, the degree of "politicization" would drop.

District Officers and Residents: Origins

The hierarchy of chiefs and headmen, as instituted by the Brookes and the British North Borneo Company, was linked with a corresponding hierarchy of District Officers and Residents. The native administrative organization did not report direct to the Secretariat in the capital but through the District Officer and Resident. The latter, after the pattern originated in British India, were generalists, not only in respect of their comprehensive administrative powers, but also in the sense that they also acted as magistrates.[24]

The qualities required for administrative officers recruited by the British North Borneo Company or the Brooke Rajahs were therefore unspecialized and difficult to define, except in rather old-world Imperial terms. The British North Borneo Company recruited its cadet officers by an interview with a Selection Board and not by competitive examination. The personal interview method enabled the Company "to assure itself the candidate's antecedents are not undesirable, that he speaks King's English, that he has initiative, some natural power of command and (above all) his share of common sense . . . the truth is that whilst a man does not need to be a Greek scholar to be a District Officer, he does need to be a gentleman, and there is no doubt that the English public schoolboy, with his sense of honour and sense of sportsmanship, has given our nation the prestige that it still enjoys among native races."[25]

Before becoming a District Officer a recruit had to learn certain things, notably the Malay language, Government procedures and official regulations, and, in order to act as a magistrate, the relevant penal codes. But, during training, a prospective D.O. might be faced with demands for knowledge which he did not yet possess. In Sarawak at the end of the last century an administrative recruit who had been less than twelve months at an outstation was temporarily left in charge of it:

> It was a proud moment for a cadet, tempered in my case by the knowledge that I was by no means proficient in the language. I was told to carry on with the Court work. So in the course of duty I took my seat at the magistrate's table. A case was called.

> The disputants did all the talking, I merely listened. I caught a word here and there and made a note of it; it did not help me much; what it was all about I had not the slightest idea. When the parties had talked themselves out I was expected to give judgement. But here I stuck; I had no notion what to do. Then I had a brain wave. I turned to Tuanku Putra to ask his opinion. He gave it, though I was none the wiser. However, I nodded my head in complete agreement and I told him to inform the Court what "we" had decided. The scheme panned out beautifully and I settled all the cases, scarcely opening my mouth.[26]

In North Borneo (and also in Sarawak) before the World War II the District Officer was "so many officials rolled into one that it would be easier to say what he is not than what he is."[27] In both territories, once the administrative organization had been established, the District Officer had four main groups of functions. He had a revenue-collecting function, and a law and order function, which included both police and magisterial aspects. He had an executive function in that he was responsible for supervising the administration of all other Government policies in the district, apart from law and order and revenue collection. Finally, he had the "residual" function of representing Government in all political and social aspects.

The Role of the District Officer

It is not possible to trace in detail the changes in the District Officer's functions which have occurred since.[28] More important than any formal changes is the circumstance that the world in which he operates is now "political". However, even before 1963 when D.O.s became exposed to politics, improved communications and stricter control from the state capital, left him less room for using his discretion than previously. Comparing the period around 1914 with that in the 1930s, one former D.O. said that at the earlier time the "District Officer was very much 'the all powerful'. When the change came many years later many of us felt that life was not worth living."[29] The broad shifts in his formal functions can be indicated in summary form: the law and order and revenue functions have declined in importance; the residual function still exists; the executive function has become much more complex because of an increase in the number of specialist officers with whom the D.O. has to deal; the D.O.s rôle has been altered by the introduction of elected local government authorities; it has also been changed by his having acquired heavy responsibilities for development.

The first three of these shifts are dealt with below. The local government and development aspects will be considered in later sections of this chapter. The D.O.'s job is at least equally demanding, although in different ways, than it was in, say, 1900.[30] His power may be less, but he has heavier responsibilities.

The D.O.'s law and order function has declined because of more settled conditions in each territory and the growth and better training of police forces. However, this aspect of the D.O.'s work still matters if rebellions or riots take place, as in 1962 in the Fifth Division during the Azahari rebellion, or in Sibu or Miri during the visit of the United Nations team in 1963. The magisterial function remains, and before administrative officers can try cases they are required to pass examinations. Even now, land disputes still take up time and attention. Even "in the heart of" relatively sophisticated Penampang (Sabah) the A.D.O., along with a Native Chief and two O.T.s, heard and settled a land dispute between the recently-formed Penampang Service Council and a private individual.[31] But much of the work has been passed on to full-time magistrates. In Sarawak this was achieved by the introduction of a Circuit Magistrate system in the mid-1960s, which took over District Court cases, leaving Native Court cases to D.O.s and other administrative officers. In Sabah there is no corresponding Circuit Magistrate system, but in half-a-dozen main centres there are stipendiary magistrates to provide relief for the D.O. from court work.

In both Sarawak and Sabah local government rates have now largely replaced other forms of taxation collected locally. Responsibility for collecting these has correspondingly passed from D.O.s to the local authorities, although D.O.s on their tours are still expected to exhort people to pay.

The D.O.'s duties as the representative of the Government and promoter of national solidarity remain; indeed they are more important than ever, now that nation-building inside

Malaysia is being attempted. Consequently, when it is Agricultural Week at Kapit Methodist Secondary School, June 1967, it is the District Officer who "graces the function by planting a fruit tree". District Officers are also in demand to preside at Civics Weeks, National Language Weeks, and other manifestations of, and incentives to, national solidarity.

There are also social obligations, which the D.O. must fulfil as the representative of Government. Whether he is a Muslim or not, he must attempt to visit Muslim houses in the area during *Hari Raya Puasa*, at the end of the fasting month. The numerous demands on his time do not absolve him from carrying out his social duties. When he has given a "lecture" on a visit to a longhouse, his work is not over. He is expected to stay and talk, eat and drink, although younger D.O.s usually try to leave before the feasting, if this can be done without giving offence to the more traditional of their hosts.

In his executive rôle the District Officer retains responsibility for certain subjects that have not been assigned to specialist or technical officers at district level. In Sarawak, for instance, he is concerned with probate, prisons, registration of births and deaths, registration for elections, registration for national service, giving advice on passports etc. This range of functions is evidence of the D.O.'s versatility and adaptability, but it also has its drawbacks. The D.O.s attention is distracted from the complex of development functions, which is becoming more and more obviously the core of his job. Nor, in his performance of these miscellaneous functions, can the D.O. be held responsible to the same extent as if he were a professional officer. As the Assistant Commissioner of Prisons, Sarawak, testified plaintively:

> I had to rely solely on my deputy for the information I got some five months or four months later. Now he is not a professional Prison Officer; he is a District Officer. In addition to his other duties he has to take the job of Deputy Prison Officer . . . I relied solely on him in good faith for the information he sent me months later to be correct . . . it is not so easy dealing with a District Officer appointed as deputy—if he were a professional Prison Officer I certainly would take action.[32]

The D.O. still has to deal with chiefs in his "inter-hierarchical" position or rôle,[33] even though the relationship has changed with the times. One Sarawak *Penghulu* showed the effects of "modernization' by asking the D.O. for a helicopter to help him carry out his official duties. The D.O. did not refuse directly, but pointed out that a helicopter would be useless unless the *Penghulu* could supply voluntary labourers for the construction of an impossibly large number of landing areas, which put an end to further discussion on the topic.

However, increasingly the D.O.s executive rôle consists in working with people who are not unequivocally his hierarchical inferiors, who are neither his civil service subordinates nor chiefs or headmen. He is able to make use of the prestige of his office, and is expected to do so, but he cannot get along satisfactorily *only* by using the prestige of his office. The "co-operative" aspect of the present rôle is conveyed by the number of committees he belongs to. In late September, 1966 the D.O. Ranau, Sabah, was Chairman of the following committees: District Rural Development Committee; Land Utilization Committee; Local Education Committee; District Rubber Smallholder Committee; Sabah Credit Corporation Committee; District Tenders Board.[34] A Sarawak D.O. in the late 1960s would find himself Chairman of the District Development Committee, the Sarawak Development Finance Corporation Committee, the District Relief Committee and the Land Selection Committee. He might be on several temporary *Berjaya* ("Success") committees and on other committees composed mainly of voluntary members, such as a Social Welfare Committee. On the average a D.O. spends the equivalent of three or four days a month on committee work.

Professional and Technical Officers

The growth of committees is one reflection of the change in the D.O.'s functions. Another indication is given by the greatly increased number of professional and technical officers in Sarawak and Sabah, with whom D.O.s and other administrative officers have to work. In Sarawak at the end of World War II many of the duties which had been done by D.O.s and Residents were now carried out by technical officers, for example in the fields of conservation, health, medicine and communications.[35] By 1925 there were forty-six European specialist civil servants as opposed to thirty-three general administrative officers, although the proportion of specialists to generalists fell slightly in the early 1930s when the government was in financial difficulties.[36] But by August, 1967 the number of technical officers had risen to 168 as compared with 55 administrative officers. The ratio of specialists to administrators, which in 1925 had been 4 to 3, by 1967 had become 3 to 1.[37] In North Borneo in 1916 there were 51 European technical officials (11 in Railways) and 30 generalists, a ratio of 5–3.[38] But by June, 1968 there were in Sabah 208 technical officers compared with 47 administrators, at Division I level,[39] a ratio of about $4\frac{1}{2}:1\frac{1}{2}$. If federal officers working in the Borneo states, who are nearly all technical officers, are included, the ratio of technical to administrative in each state is about 6:1. The bulk of the technical officials are stationed in the field. In both states the departments which are most strongly represented in the field are; public works, agriculture, medical and police. The D.O.'s problems in dealing with technical officials are described in a later section of this chapter.

District Officers: Travelling and Turnover

Although the D.O. has until now been a generalist *par excellence*, he must operate on the basis of knowledge in depth about one thing, his district. To achieve this, two requirements must be met, one in space and one in time. The D.O. must travel frequently inside his district, and his posting to a district should last a certain minimum time.

Although the average size of a district is less than in India, Pakistan or in many African countries (but greater than in Malaya), travelling is still difficult and time-consuming. And yet it is vitally necessary. It has even been suggested that differences in the amount of travelling by D.O.s and other government officers may have partly accounted for the differing degrees of support given to the Brunei rebellion of 1962 by various groups in the Fifth Division of Sarawak.[40] Communications, of course, are improving in both states. But paper work is also increasing, sometimes without any corresponding increase in administrative staff in the field. Consequently, fewer houses may be visited by D.O.s than were visited several years ago.[41] It has been said that some local D.O.s may be more reluctant to travel than expatriates were, also that when travelling they may visit a disproportionately high percentage of their own ethnic group. Travelling may be curtailed for financial reasons. In one Sarawak district in 1965 extra expenditure had to be incurred in the course of revaluing rateable property, a joint operation between the district office and the local council staff. The transport and travelling vote of the district was therefore overspent, and no routine travelling could be done during the last quarter of the year.[42]

Improved communications may lead to "flying visits" to areas which formerly were so remote that, the D.O., forced to stay there overnight, benefited from hearing about local problems at length. The importance of travelling in Sarawak was underlined by an instruction by the Chief Minister in 1965 that all District Officers, and Sarawak Administrative Officers, should be on tour a minimum of ten days and nights a month.[43]

It is also impossible for a D.O. to get to know his district thoroughly in less than six months. If he spends less than about two years in one post, this six-month "investment period" does not give a satisfactory return. Yet there have been many complaints about too frequent transfers of D.O.s and other administrative staff in Sabah; some D.O.s have even been posted away before they have spent a year in one district.[44] The average length of a Sabah D.O.'s tour of duty in the late 1960s was nearer one year than two years. Rapid turnover of D.O.s and other administrative officers is not new.[45] To be sure, there are special reasons why it has occurred in the last few years, including "Borneanization" of the administrative service, and the need to send many officers on training courses. Nevertheless, tours of duty of less than two years are resented by the inhabitants of a district, are harmful to efficiency, and, if at all possible, ought to be avoided.

The Duties of the Resident

The duties of the Resident corresponded to those of the District Officer but on a larger scale. "The prime duty of the Resident is to preserve order in his district and to punish crimes of violence. But he is responsible also for every detail of administration, including the collection of taxes and customs duties, the settlement of disputes and the hearing of complaints of all kinds, the furnishing of reports to the central government on all matters of moment, the development of trade and the protection of traders . . ."[46] The Residents, according to another authority, "got to know the working of every government department on the one side, every racial group and problem person individually on the other. They could—and incessantly did—settle personal matters for remote *ulu* [backwoods] villages in the same hour as they ruled on a major land settlement plan (within the overall policy)." This was achieved by "an amalgam of breeziness, ragging, bullying, common sense, command of languages and laws, carelessness of forms . . ."[47]

This situation has changed and so has the Resident's rôle. With the improvement of communications responsibility has shifted away from the Resident and to "Headquarters". And "Headquarters" may be one or more of several ministries in Kuching (or Kota Kinabalu), or even in Kuala Lumpur. "Thus medical services, trade and customs, marine and above all police, which used to be intimately tied in at every level of decision with the Resident's will (he virtually ran the police direct, when he wished), operate at his behest only for convenience, by courtesy and when suitable".[48]

The Resident, like the District Officer, remains "the father and mother of his people", that is of those of his people who still need to be taken care of via such a rôle. He is trusted because he stands for "Government" unconfused by politics.[49] He is able to praise and at the same time to prod. While awarding school prizes he can point out that not all *kampongs* have as good school buildings, but that buildings cost money and so rates should be paid promptly. The rôle must be played in a slightly different way than it was when the actor was an expatriate. For all his breeziness, the expatriate gave the impression of aloofness to the local population. His successor must "mix", but not too much. If a Muslim, the Resident must go to the mosque regularly, and must not be known as one who drinks alcohol openly. The Resident's functions have also changed just as the D.O.'s have changed. His job (like the

D.O.'s) has become more impersonal and less rewarding in terms of human contacts. He is chairman of various committees, for example in Sarawak on development, security, government housing and so on. Like the D.O., he also has the task of trying to co-ordinate technical officials. An increasingly time-consuming function is the "ceremonial" one of planning and managing tours for Ministers, both state and federal, and for other V.I.P.s and quasi-V.I.P.s.

The Evolution of Local Government in Sarawak

The territory of both Sarawak and Sabah is now completely covered by a system of local councils which have their own budgets and are financially "responsible". However, the councils are subject to control by their respective state governments and are far from being autonomous.

It has been remarked that initially in Sarawak, before Malaysia, "local government was imposed by the Central Government; people did not want district councils, nor were men willing to serve as councillors".[50] This does not mean that the practice of group discussion at grass-roots level was alien to Sarawak. But the units of local government which were set up outside the towns covered much larger areas than any indigenous groups had covered, and the people inside them did not share any obvious community of interest. The evolution of local government in Sarawak was complicated by World War II and by experimental policies, some of which were altered later.

After the war a considered policy for promoting local government was put forward in the form of a "Note" by the Governor of Sarawak, Sir Charles Noble Arden Clarke.[51] The main emphasis was placed on local government as a means of national integration.

> In Sarawak we are dealing with a plural society, that is, a society comprising a variety of elements which differ in race, language, custom, religion and culture and which live side by side, yet without mingling, in one political unit.
>
> 2. Our objective is to weld these elements into a united body of Sarawak citizens capable of managing in cooperation with each other their own and their country's affairs.

Other considerations were also mentioned. Training in self-government could best be given by the development of local government institutions (as well as by having some Sarawak citizens enter the higher ranks of the civil service). The introduction of local government would also help to bridge a gap between the people's desire to keep their taxes low and their demand for more benefits, for example in the form of schools; it was believed that local government authorities would willingly raise some more money to pay for the improvements that they themselves wished to bring about.

In view of the prominence given to racial integration in the "Note", it is curious that each of the authorities first actually proposed in it was confined to a single ethnic group.[52] But experiments with other types of local authority also took place, including the first racially-mixed local authority in Limbang in 1948. By 1957 the pattern was established of local government areas corresponding to the existing administrative districts, a size which entailed their being multi-racial.[53] The main urban areas were served by the Kuching Municipal Council and the Sibu Urban District Council. Direct elections for all councils were held in 1959 and 1960, with the franchise confined to rate-payers, and again in 1963 with an extended franchise which included all adults with certain residence qualifications.[54] By 1963 the local government system was "highly developed" in three senses; the whole territory of Sarawak was covered by local councils; there were no nominated members on these councils; no officials, such as District Officers, sat on the councils.

In practice the councils vary greatly in their importance. The poorer councils' functions are confined largely to primary education, and, in a lesser degree, to health services. The Estimates for 1968 for the Lubok Antu District Council, for example, showed a total budget of only just over half a million dollars, about 80% of which was allocated to education.[55] On the other hand the Kuching Municipal Council 1970 expenditure amounted to almost five and three-quarter million dollars, of which about two-fifths was allocated to education.[56] The functions of the KMC, as laid down by statute, already broad, can be extended even further with the approval of the Ministry of Local Government. The Council, for example, runs a welfare and health clinic by arrangement with the Federal Government, health being federal and not a state subject.[57]

The Local Government in Sabah: Origins

In Sabah there was a pre-war experiment in local government in which twelve villages[58] were put under the control of a chief who was given some financial control, including the power to collect taxes and licences. But the scheme was never completely financially viable, and what success it had was due largely to the qualifications of the chief, Sedomon, rather than to the co-operative efforts of a local council. After the war a number of sanitary boards (authorized by an ordinance of 1931) and other local bodies were established, but the trend, starting with Kota Belud in 1952, was to create a new type of local authority. By 1960, according to the North Borneo Secretary for Local Government,[59] this new type differed from previous local government bodies in three main ways. Its jurisdiction extended over a wider area, a whole district. The membership of the Council was entirely composed of persons who were not government officials.[60] They had full responsibility, and were themselves "in charge of the spending of the local revenues in the best interests of the people, with some money added from the general revenues of Central (North Borneo) Government". By virtue of a 1953 ordinance, Town Boards were set up in Jesselton and Sandakan in 1954, and in Tawau and Labuan in 1955; each board had full financial responsibility, and a majority of its members was to consist of persons not holding any government office.[61]

Two points might be added about the new district councils. First, because they covered a whole district, they were necessarily multi-racial. Attempts to O.K.K. Sedomon to revive the pre-war Bingkor Native Authority did not receive official support. The policy of the Government, as expressed by the Resident of the Interior, was that if the country was to prosper all races must work together and that a purely native authority would tend to widen the gap between Chinese and Natives. Second, much of the success of the Kota Belud Council was apparently due mainly to the efforts of the D.O., the Council's president, and of O.K.K. Hasbullah bin Haji Mohammed

Arshad, deputy assistant district officer and its vice-president. Even in Kota Belud there was little enthusiasm for local government.[62]

In 1961 a Local Government Ordinance (Sabah No. 11 of 1961) altered the existing law on the powers of the district councils, and also of the Town Boards in Jesselton, Sandakan, Tawau, and Labuan, by providing for powers to levy cesses and make by-laws and for more financial help by the Government. The local bodies were therefore able to extend their activities in building minor roads, improving agriculture, developing rural services and safeguarding public health. In practice, as might be expected, there are wide differences between the activities carried out by various councils depending on population and financial resources. The annual expenditure of the Kota Kinabalu Town Board, for instance, is over thirty times that of the Labuk-Sugut District Council.[63]

There was one important difference between local authorities in Sabah and those in Sarawak. In Sarawak primary education was an important local function; the smaller authorities spent about 80% of their budget on it, getting about three-quarters of this amount back in the form of government grants. In Sabah, however, local authorities were not given the function: it is carried out by a State Board and by Local Education Committees. Because of the financial difficulties of some Sarawak councils, it has been suggested that perhaps Sarawak should have followed the Sabah example and should not have made the local councils responsible for primary education. On the other hand, there were obvious advantages in the Sarawak solution. If local councillors were able to decide where a school would be located, there was more likelihood of good attendance, because local wishes would clearly have been consulted. Also, the education function was a very important one, and it was thought that its allocation to councils would help to arouse interest in local government and attract good-quality local government officials.[64]

The development of the local councils in Sabah has been appreciably slower than in Sarawak. When district council elections were first held in 1962 and 1963 they applied to a total of only fifteen district councils and Town Boards. It was not until July 1968 that the system of district councils covered the whole state (nineteen district councils and four Town Boards). Furthermore, not all the members of the councils are elected; three councils consist entirely of appointed members.[65] Even most of the "elected" councils also have appointed members,[66] usually slightly fewer in number than the elected members.

The deliberate pace of the movement towards local self-government in Sabah is shown by the fact that even in the early 1970s there were still some nominated members on the councils.[67] The appointed members were more "traditional" than the elected ones in so far as they contained a higher proportion of chiefs (O.K.K.s and N.C.s) and headmen.[68] Finally, even on councils which are partly elected, the D.O., or A.D.O., is Vice-Chairman so that, in appearance at least, the councils are less free from government control than their counterparts in Sarawak.[69]

The Working of Local Government, Sarawak and Sabah

The district councils in Sarawak meet about four or six times a year. They have committees, which meet with about the same frequency, usually General Purposes, Finance, and Education, sometimes also Public Health and others. Some council clerks try to restrict the number of meetings, in order to cut down the expense of paying councillors' travelling allowances.[70] In the Kuching Municipal Council and in Sibu the council and its committees usually meet once every month, and the committee structure is much more elaborate. The Sibu Urban District Council had the following committees in mid-1968: Finance and Establishment, with sub-committees on Selection, Tender Board; Low Cost Housing; Public Health and Town Planning with subcommittees on Health Campaign, Land Subdivision; General Purposes, with subcommittees on Swimming Pool, Fire Brigade, Hawkers; Works, with sub-committee on Building Plans, Traffic, Education, with a Library subcommittee.

Sabah local authorities operate along similar lines, but even the four Town Boards do not have as differentiated a committee structure as Sibu or Kuching. The Sandakan Town Board, for example, has only five committees; Finance and

General Purposes, Building Plans and Town Planning, Highways, Public Health, Rating Appeal Tribunal.[71] The district councils have even fewer committees, the minimum being a Finance and General Purposes Committee, and a Health Committee.

Many criticisms have been made of the efficiency of local bodies in Sarawak, some directed mainly at the poor quality of the members. A low opinion of the councillors has been expressed, for example, by several District Officers in their annual reports. It is said that councillors sometimes tend to consider only the interests of their own area as opposed to that of the district as a whole. There is an inclination to discuss in the full council what already has been, or should have been, discussed in committee. According to one council secretary, it is often the small points, for instance the issue of hawkers' licences, that take up most time, while, in Parkinsonian fashion, items involving huge expenditures which are of no personal interest to anyone on the council go through almost automatically. And, even allowing for the fact that being a councillor is not a full-time occupation, councillors are accused of not travelling enough in their area in order to meet the people. Other criticisms are directed against incorrect financial or accounting procedures. One council collected over $200,000 in motor licensing fees which should have been handed over to the state government; in fact the money was not handed over and apparently some of it was spent.[72]

More sinister than criticisms about efficiency are allegations of bribery and corruption on Sarawak councils. The maximum allowance which can be paid to councillors is only $35 per month, plus travel and subsistence allowance when they attend meetings. There are, of course, other rewards, for instance status and the general publicity which is financially useful to councillors who are in business. But there are pressures on councillors, which could lead to financial inducements being offered. For instance, councillors may "stretch" the regulations on what particular types of premises may be put up on particular pieces of land. Their aid may be enlisted to delay action when buildings have been scheduled for demolition. And some councillors are always on the look-out for personal advantage, for instance through obtaining contracts, which may not be awarded to the lowest tender.

Even in councils with able and vigilant officials some "fast ones" get through. Council business is sometimes affected by "politics", although this seldom takes the form, even in SUPP-controlled councils, of "dragging in" irrelevant political issues when local questions are being considered.[73] "Politics" shows itself typically in the actions of persons who believe they have political contacts seeking to bend the normal rules. Thus the SUPP chairman, Ong Kee Hui, when the party gained control of the Kuching Municipal Council, had many requests for hawkers' licences sent to him through his party, which he refused to support. The fact that local councils are *local* is no guarantee against corruption. Indeed the reverse is true; local councils are particularly inclined to be corrupt in the absence of strict controls. If a great deal of money is at stake, say in the allocation of building licences, external control by the Ministry of Local Government may be needed to prevent corruption. Such control is absent as far as the Kuching Municipal Council is concerned; opportunities for making money improperly are fewer on rural district councils than on the KMC. This suggests that it might be advisable for control by D.O.s over local councils to be maintained for some time to come.

In Sabah, local council discussions have been criticized for irrelevancy. Some councils on the West Coast, for instance, have been inclined to debate development questions at length, which, strictly, were outside their scope. They have also been blamed for inactivity. In the words of one Resident, all the councillors do is "sit on their bottoms". There have been few allegations of corruption directed at local authorities in Sabah. This is probably because of the strict control exercised by the D.O. over district councils. In the Town Boards there are pressures on officials, but the safeguards are apparently adequate. Tenders above a certain amount are publicly advertised, and then are decided on by the Ministry of Local Government after advice by the local officers. Also, as is mentioned below, many of the top officials who work for the council are not actually employed by it; they are therefore immune to threats from councillors, because they do not depend on them for the retention of their jobs or for promotion.

Local Government Finance

A major weakness of local authorities in both areas is their poverty and financial dependence on the state government. In Sarawak less than 20% of the current revenue is raised locally; the rest comes from government grants.[74] The district councils in Sabah are similarly dependent, although the Town Boards raise over three-quarters of their revenue locally. The Sarawak Governor's "Note"[75] had hoped that local responsibility would encourage local spending. The previous system by which members of different ethnic groups would be taxed in different ways (e.g. by poll tax or by door tax in longhouses) would be ended. Local rates would apply to all ethnic groups, and would be determined by the local council. Much of the expenditure would be met by government grants, but the amount would depend on the willingness of the councils to levy rates.

The lesson to be conveyed was that government services provided locally had to be paid for, although the state government grants would lessen the impact on the ratepayer. To some extent the changes made along these lines had the desired effects, and demands for local services led councils to spend in order to obtain them. Some of the Sabah district councils, soon after they were set up, raised extra money locally for extending their schools, improving bicycle tracks, or developing communal grazing grounds.[76] However, sometimes in both states councillors were eager to request "aid for better amenities but they seldom or never took the trouble to shoulder some of the responsibility for better services".[77]

The lesson that one could not get something for nothing was apparently contradicted by the provision of benefits through Minor Rural Projects,[78] even though these projects were essential for maintaining national unity and although they were meant to embody the principle of self help. Opposition to extra taxation was expressed not so much by councils refusing to levy increased taxation by raising rates but rather by ratepayers' refusal to pay rates once they had been imposed. All kinds of excuses were given for non-payment: poverty, political instability, the quaint belief that since it was "the Government" that collected rates, one need not pay them if one was not a Government supporter. There were often plausible reasons why rate collection was poor, for example, in Miri in 1963 the harm done by the Azahari rebellion and a serious flood. But to these local reasons the District Officer, in his Annual Report, added "sheer pig-headedness".[79]

In the middle of 1966 the Kuching Rural District Council was the biggest offender in Sarawak; the amount of uncollected rates amounted to nearly half a million dollars, more than one year's rate revenue.[80] Councillors were schizophrenic on the subject of rates; in several council areas the councillors who had themselves voted the rates were among those who were delinquent in their payments.[81] As the Sarawak election of 1969 drew nearer, it became suicidal for politicians to urge the payment of rates. The Minister for Local Government simply avoided any public pronouncement on the subject. The task of urging people to pay rates was left to council officials, District Officers and Sarawak Administrative Officers, and to an official of the Ministry of Local Government sent to tour the state especially for this purpose.

In Sabah at the end of 1965 the local authorities with the highest amounts of rates outstanding were the Jesselton and Tawau Town Boards. Court action was taken against very few defaulters. As in Sarawak, the collection of rates had become a political issue.[82]

One reason for resistance to rates was that the amount to be paid was generally higher than it had been under the poll tax (or in longhouses, door tax) system which they replaced. Another source of opposition arose because in each state "differential" rating was introduced, according to the size or location of the property rated. Some ratepayers did not understand why they should pay more than others just because they had a bigger house. Conversely, the fact that others pay more rates than they do, does not reconcile poorer people to paying rates, although attempts were made, in both Sabah and Sarawak, to reassure them. The Chairman of the Sandakan Town Board tried this type of reasoning on the inhabitants of Kampong Ayer. Tan Tze Chu said that he himself had to pay $32 per month in assessment and he could not understand why the petitioners, who had pleaded poverty as one reason for objecting to their assessment, should grumble when they were only assessed for $10 per month.[83]

In Sarawak it is a little hard to believe that the rural people in Simanggang district were quite as easily persuaded as the D.O. claimed that they were, when he wrote that the "rise in rate assessment wasn't welcomed by the population at the start. Almost everybody had to pay more. However, when explanations were given for the rise and the *Ulu* people were told that five or so dollars per door per year wasn't really much compared to what a Government officer was taxed and had to pay for living in Government quarters, they began to accept the rise as a matter of fact."[84]

To make this issue even more confusing, varying rates may be levied, not because of differences in ability to pay as indicated by different standards of housing etc., but because of differences in the standard of services provided by the local authority. The protesting inhabitants of Kampong Ayer asked for a lower assessment of their poverty, partly because they were poor, but also because they did not enjoy some of the services, such as water supply and through roads, which were being received by others in the Sandakan Town Board Area.[85]

Many local councils would have financial difficulties even if there were no problems about collecting rates. With this additional problem they may be too poor to afford to hire competent staff and so become caught in a vicious circle of poverty and inefficiency.[86]

Local Government Staff

The poverty of most Sarawak local councils is reflected in the numbers and nature of the staff they employ. This generalization does not apply, of course, to the Kuching Municipal Council, nor to the Sibu Urban District Council, the Kuching Rural District Council, or the Miri District Council. The Kuching Municipal Council, for example, had a 1969 establishment of 24 in the Municipal Secretary's Office, 20 under "Treasury", 156 under "Primary Education", 69 under "Public Health", 36 under "Public Works", 3 under "Swimming Pool" and 41 under "Fire Brigade."[87] The Lubok Antu District Council on the other hand, is one of the poorest in Sarawak. Although in 1968 it has 116 staff on its establishment under "Education", it has only 17 Administration, 11

Public Health, and one Public Works.[88] Not even the KMC is completely self-sufficient in technical staff. But it is rich enough to be nearly self-sufficient; where there are gaps, the Council either employs an officer part-time, for instance as a medical consultant, or in a few cases makes use of government officials, for example on traffic, education or town planning. Most councils, however, are almost completely dependent for technical help on officials, whom they do not employ and who are responsible to either the state or the Federal Government.

In Sarawak each local council has a secretary, who is its chief administrator.[89] But, although the council secretaries include some dedicated and hard-working men, the general level of ability is not high. Many have not even completed secondary education, and have come up through the ranks of the state civil service. Until recently the average quality was strengthened by the secondment of younger, more educated, men from the state administrative service, who later went back to occupy important positions in that service. The relatively low esteem in which the post of council secretary is held is shown by the fact that there are only three councils where the secretary post is graded as being in the First Division of the civil service, the Kuching Municipal Council, the Sibu Urban District Council and the Kuching Rural District Council.

In Sabah the local authorities depend heavily on the services of officials who are not employed by them. On the technical side, even the four Town Boards (Kota Kinabalu, Sandakan, Tawau, Labuan) are dependent on the services of such officials as the Divisional Engineer, Town Planning officials of the Lands and Surveys Department, the Government Valuer of the Land and Survey Department, and the Engineer of the Sabah Electricity Board. In the Kota Kinabalu Town Board, for example, the senior Public Works man actually employed by the Board is the *Assistant* Town Engineer, but his activities are directed by the Divisional Engineer, employed by the State Government but working part-time for the Town Board. On the administrative side, the councils have to rely on the help of the D.O., who is Chairman or Vice-Chairman of the Council, and until recently on the A.D.O. who has performed the duties of secretary. However, this situation is changing. The Town Boards in the early 1960s started appointing their own executive officers, the equivalent of council secretary in Sarawak. By 1969 this practice had spread to some district councils. In June, 1969, the executive officers of the Kota Kinabalu and Sandakan Town Boards were both graduates, and the executive officer of the Tawau Town Board was a former D.O. These three were all Division I officers, comparable to a D.O. in rank and pay. However, even if and when the district councils acquire "executive officers", their rank and pay will be lower, in accordance with the smaller range of functions and lack of financial resources of the councils.

In both states, apart from any other factors, the supply of competent council secretaries or executive officers is limited by the general shortage of skilled administrators.

State Government Control of Local Authorities

Inadequate resources and financial dependence on the government are accompanied by close government control. In 1964 the then Minister for Local Government in Sabah described the minister's methods of control. "He tries to interfere as little as possible with the day-to-day working of the Town Boards and District Councils but one of his duties is also to protect the interest of the State and therefore he has to see that the Town Boards and District Councils do not get too enthusiastic and go beyond the legal powers given them by the Local Government Ordinance. In the interests of the public he has also to see that they perform all these functions the law requires them to do." The Boards and Councils, for instance, "cannot enter into a contract of a value exceeding a certain amount without his approval: their Estimates of Revenue and Expenditure for the year have to be approved by the Minister: he has to give approval to any rate that it is intended to levy and the appointment of certain grades of staff has also to be approved by him."[90] Protecting "the interests of the State" may take the form of overruling the policy decisions of a local authority. One instance of this occurred when the Sabah Chinese Chamber of Commerce made representations to the Chief Minister because the Jesselton Town Board had refused to put up a public market at Kampong Ayer. As a result the Minister of Local Government ordered the Board to put up a market.[91]

Government control in Sarawak is of a similar nature, although its extent was somewhat understated when it was described as "*confined* to the field of major policy principles, and the approval of annual revenue and expenditure estimates, by-lays and senior staff appointments".[92]

These descriptions, however, refer to governmental control from Kota Kinabalu or Kuching. They do not convey the full flavour of the control exercised in the field, mainly by D.O.s and Residents. The situation has not greatly changed in Sabah since November 1963 when a resident observed that, although the district councils at Lahad Datu and Semporna were working fairly well, the D.O. was still the mainspring. He added that in the rural context it was very difficult to distinguish between central and local activities in practice.[93] The D.O.'s dominating rôle in Sabah is ensured by his being Council Vice-Chairman, or Chairman in the case of wholly nominated councils. In the Town Boards, however, as opposed to the district councils, his presence is becoming more and more of a formality.

Another way in which central control makes itself felt via officers in the field is through the influence of state government technical officials. Although they may work for councils and boards, they are employed and paid by the state government, and naturally are concerned to enforce its policies. Some of their influence on local authorities is exercised at committee meetings, which they may attend as advisory members. For example, the Divisional Engineer, the Medical Officer, and the District Surveyor are advisory members of the Building Plans and Town Planning Committee of the Sandakan Town Board.[94]

It would be wrong to imagine that the control exercised by the Resident or D.O. in Sabah was always aimed at increasing bureaucratic efficiency. It is sometimes designed to protect the people against an over-zealous council. For example, a council may propose to extend the area from which rates are collected because a few poor people are putting up new houses which are a little more substantial than their previous *atap* (thatch) houses. The Resident, however, taking account of the poverty of these people, may write a minute to the Ministry of Local Government advising against such an extension.

In Sarawak, control by government officers in the field is less obvious. The D.O. is not a member of the local council, nor is he its executive officer, although he may be invited to attend its meetings or its committee's meetings. In practice, however, D.O.s can exercise a strong influence on councils through the council secretaries, as well as in other ways. With very few exceptions they are superior to the council secretaries in ability and education, and are unambiguously higher in status. Their superiority is reinforced by history. At an earlier period of the councils' evolution a D.O. was the chairman, and the administrative officers who were temporarily seconded as council secretaries were junior to a D.O. in status. Nowadays the secretaries and D.O.s work well together, "but on the basis that the D.O. is the boss". The nature of the relationship is such that a secretary may even regard his council as part of the state government rather than as an autonomous body. One secretary, referring in conversation to the information on the council contained in the D.O.'s Annual Report, said that the D.O. asked the council "to send in the material, the same as *other departments* did".[95] However, the relationship has its subtleties. The D.O., generally speaking, does not direct the council or the secretary what to do; it is more a matter of the secretary's checking with the D.O. that a proposed council policy is not out of line with Government policy. The secretary may also "need" the D.O. to strengthen his hand against the council. For instance, if the council refuses to believe the secretary when he objects that a proposed line of action is illegal, he may seek the D.O.'s opinion in writing in order to convince the council. As in Sabah, state technical officers attend committee meetings of local councils in an advisory capacity.

Objections are sometimes voiced against the strictness of the control by Residents and D.O.s in Sarawak. They are partly directed against controls over finance or appointments, but the main thrust has been against the complexity of the channels of communication.

"Council's correspondence first passes through the District

Officer, then through the Resident who either takes up the matter at issue direct with the State Secretary or the Permanent Secretary of Local Government or forwards the correspondence to the Ministry of Local Government. This process is reversed when Government replies.

"In the early days of the Councils when a District Officer was *ex-officio* Chairman of his district council, this procedural practice created little inconvenience as the District Officer in any case works under the direction of the Resident. Ever since elected Chairmanship has been introduced this process becomes lengthened and results in unnecessary slowing down of work and wasteful delays."

The minister, when replying to this complaint, pointed to the fact that most local government revenues come from government grants, and said that it was necessary to rely on Residents and D.O.s to make sure that the grants were spent as intended. For a local authority to short-circuit the channel of communication through Residents and D.O.s "might very often mean added delay whilst any necessary reference was made to Residents".[96] This type of reply, given more than once, hardly seems to meet the main point of the objection—that the "channel" should be reshaped to exclude D.O.s and Residents altogether. Few complaints are heard in Sabah about excessive government control. The D.O.'s rôle has been so dominant that it has been assumed that central control is necessary. Now that more and more councils are hiring their own executive officers, more complaints may be voiced.

So far no council in either state has been taken over and directly administered by the state government on the score of inefficiency or impropriety, as happened to some councils in Malaya. This is an indication of how strict government control of most of the councils already is.

It would be wrong to think that, because central control over local councils is fairly strict, the system must necessarily work with precision. Sometimes the pressures from the state government are just too much for a council which is working under difficult conditions, even when it has help from the D.O. "The Council and the Administration again experienced great difficulties in understanding circulars and practice notes from the Ministry of Local Government which usually come in heaps like books. The time taken to read them all equals the time taken to reference[97] all the properties required. These circulars and practice notes are no doubt good, but when consideration is given to the shortages of staff experienced almost everywhere, inaccuracy and mistakes are inevitable."[98]

In spite of their tribulations, local councils in both states have been successful in several respects. Unlike some of their counterparts in Malaya, Opposition-controlled councils have worked with the state government in reasonable harmony. Even if participation at local council level is not widespread, it does at least exist and probably has surpassed most expectations. Also, in spite of the administrative problems they encountered, elected local councils were a step on the way to directly-elected state legislatures.

Development Organization, Sarawak and Sabah

The formation of Malaysia was accompanied by a heavy concentration on "development' in the Borneo states especially in the rural areas; indeed the prospect of increased development had been one of the attractions which helped to persuade the two territories to join Malaysia. This did not mean that there had been no expenditure on "development" projects before 1963. But there was a jump in the amount of development expenditure, particularly on "agriculture and rural development"[99] from that date onwards, and great emphasis was also placed on the concept, almost the mystique, of development.

The evolution of the development organization, from 1963 onwards, followed the general pattern in existence in the states of Malaya, and it was similarly tied in with the development machinery at federal level.[100] Theoretically, it would have been possible to have instituted a different system in Sarawak and given responsibility for development functions to local government authorities; by Malaysia Day, 16 September, 1963 the whole of Sarawak (but not yet Sabah) was covered by local authorities. But there is no evidence that such an arrangement was ever seriously considered. Apart from a natural desire to follow the prestigious Malayan system, it was quite evident that the local bodies just did not have the resources or the staff to manage development tasks properly.

Some of them were too poor even to take over successfully the maintenance of small stretches of road which had been built for land settlement schemes. They would have been quite incapable of ensuring the inter-departmental co-ordination needed for carrying out development projects. Additionally, according to a former Sarawak Minister who was closely connected with development, there would have been too many particularistic political pressures if development functions had been given to local councils.

In each state the main link between the national and the state development organization is an official known as the State Development Officer (S.D.O.), who is nevertheless a federal government officer, and who until now has been recruited from West Malaysia. He is responsible both to the Chief Minister of the state and also to the (Federal) Minister of National and Rural Development. The S.D.O. has to coordinate the technical officers concerned with development at state level in the fields, for example, of Public Works, Health, Education, Lands and Surveys, Drainage and Irrigation.[101] There is also a system of development committees in each state which is linked to the National Development Planning Committee in Kuala Lumpur.[102]

The committee organization in Sabah corresponds quite closely to its counterparts in the states of Malaya. There are two tiers, at state and district level. The State Development Committee consists of the Chief Minister, five other Cabinet ministers, and five key officials drawn from the departments which are most concerned with implementing development measures.[103] Under it is a small working committee of officials. District Development Committees have the D.O., or the A.D.O., as chairman plus about half a dozen technical officers and three or four local councillors or chiefs. The councillors selected usually include the chairman of the appropriate district council.

The Sarawak pattern is more elaborate. The State Development Planning Committee is larger than its Sabah counterpart, consisting of the Chief Minister (chairman), other ministers and four officials. It also has a Working Sub-committee of fourteen officials.[104] Below this, however, is an additional committee level which does not exist in Sabah or in the states of Malaya. There is a Divisional Development Committee, chaired by the Resident and with an Administrative Officer (Development and Planning) as Deputy Chairman and Secretary. The other members consist of half a dozen technical officers and the Council Negri members in the division.[105] The Committee has a Working Sub-committee consisting of the Resident, the Administrative Officer (Development and Planning), the Divisional Engineer, the Divisional Agricultural Officer, the Divisional Education Officer, and the Superintendent of Lands and Surveys. Finally, the District Development Committee is composed of the D.O. (Chairman and secretary), up to eight technical officers (as and when required), the Chairman of the District Council, the Chairman of the General Purposes Committee of the District Council, and all members of Parliament and Senators in the District.[106] Unlike Sabah, there are no chiefs or *Penghulus* on the committee, unless they happen to be members by having qualified in some other capacity.

The mere listing of the membership of the district development committees in both states indicates the preponderance of the official element over the non-official. In practice there is seldom any voting on the committee, and confrontations of officials on one side and non-officials on the other just do not happen. It is the view of several official members that some of the unofficials do not understand very much of what goes on; they are no doubt participating, but they are participating mainly in their own education. The unofficial representation in Sarawak, as described above, dates only from 1968. Before then the choice of unofficial members was less rigidly provided for, and depended on the approval of the Chairman or Deputy Chairman of the State Development Planning Committee. The 1968 change probably had the effect of raising the quality of the unofficial members on the District Development Committee; the Chairman, and the Chairman of the General Purposes Committee, of a rural District Council might be expected to be more competent than most other members of the councils. The 1968 provisions also provided a solution to the charge that the selection of unofficial members was partly politically motivated.[107] But the actual 1968 provisions were odd in one respect. Council Negri members in the Division were to be members of the Divisional Development Committee, but Members of Parliament and Senators in the District, whose "constituencies" were wider than those of Council Negri members, were to sit on District Development Committees, which covered an area smaller than a Division.[108]

Neither Sarawak nor Sabah has a regular system of *kampong* committees tied in with its development machinery, although this is now the practice in Malaya.[109] In both states the intention is to introduce such committees during the next Five Year Plan. In Sabah these *kampong* committees are seen as a logical complement to the use of Community Development Officers, and in 1969 Tun Mustapha called for a development committee in each *kampong*.[110]

Development Machinery: Articulation, Aggregation, Implementation

The development machinery just described is, so to speak, a two-way street. In one direction grass-roots requests for smaller projects from individuals or groups are fed into the machinery at District Development Committee level via the D.O. or some other member of the committee; sometimes they may be submitted via a local authority councillor, even if he is not a member of the District Development Committee. They may be debated at length at a meeting of a local council, a procedure which was not envisaged when the development machinery was constructed. This practice was widespread in the West Coast Residency of Sabah in 1966. It also occurred quite often in Sarawak, at least until 1968; after that it was less common, possibly because of the introduction of the new system mentioned earlier, by which the Chairman, and the Chairman of the General Purposes Committee, of all councils in the area are members of the District Development Committee.

Local councils may now be inclined to forego time-consuming discussions on development in the belief that the development interests of the area will be adequately taken care of by these two council representatives. The development proposals which are approved at each level are forwarded to the next higher level. The final decision on what is approved for inclusion in the current plan is made in Kuala Lumpur by the Ministry of National and Rural Development, the National Development Planning Committee, and the Cabinet. One apparent source of confusion, which in practice does not cause any serious difficulty, is that, because of the federal-state division of powers, some development items are listed in the federal budget and others in the state budget. The development machinery is not intended to serve just as a channel for the articulation and aggregation of demands. Once development plans have been drawn up and approved, it also has the task of seeing that they are implemented. The initiation and implementation of large development projects is the responsibility of government departments. For some projects a particular department may have a preponderant role, for instance the Public Works Department in making roads. But the responsibility for co-ordinating the work of government departments, other bodies, and, at grass-roots level, individual people, rests with the development committees and the officials who assist them.[111]

Minor Rural Projects

One particular type of development project has acquired an importance far out of proportion to its cost, which constitutes only one or two per cent of the total expenditure on development in the two states. Its raison d'être has been well expressed by a former State Development Officer for Sabah:

> It is a well known fact that most of our development projects costing hundreds and thousands of dollars undertaken by major Government departments will take some time to complete. Some may even take years to complete. So while the major Government departments are undertaking projects costing thousands and millions of dollars which will take time to complete, the Government at the same time is obliged to show to the people some concrete and tangible evidence of its sincerity to carry out our development plan. Realising this, the Government has made a special provision for Miscellaneous Minor Rural Development Schemes which can be utilised to carry out hundreds of minor projects in all parts of the State which can be implemented quickly with a matter of 2 or 3 months only.[112]

Examples of projects included minor water supplies, rural roads and footpaths, bridges, jetties, community halls, recreational facilities, fire extinguishers, and river clearance. A comparison has been drawn with a "cover crop", vegetables grown for subsistence while the main crop, for example rubber, is taking time to show results. The normal channel for the submission of Minor Rural Projects is through District Development Committees.

Occasionally a project has misfired. In one Sarawak project, the whole point was lost, because local wishes had *not* been met. The Kampong Jepak cycle-track "was originally built along the inland virgin swamp from Kuala Bintulu to Sungei Mas. But later the people in the area condemned this planning as they were not consulted and subsequently not prepared to make use of the path unless the area through which the track lies was opened up for them."[113]

Minor Rural Projects have been criticized from several points of view. Expenditure on such minor items may be less productive than expenditure on larger schemes. A more serious defect of Minor Rural Projects is that they may be used for "political" ends.[114] Other criticisms are based on the psychological effects of Minor Rural Projects in encouraging expectations of obtaining something for nothing.

It can be argued, in defence of Minor Rural Projects that in the Borneo territories it was particularly necessary to make an immediate impact with some concrete achievements in the field of development in view of the expectations which had been aroused when Malaysia was formed. The people had to be shown tangible benefits resulting from federation.

The District Officer and Development

In addition to his many other tasks the District Officer also plays a key part in the development process as the Chairman of the District Development Committee and as the person chiefly responsible for the implementation of development projects in the district. If a D.O. knows what he wants clearly enough and is experienced enough, he can promote development proposals of which he himself approves, and in effect veto those which he thinks are obviously silly. To do this, he has to carry the committee with him, and also surmount "political" pressures. Some development requests which are not very reasonable may go forward from the District Development Committee, but the D.O. may ensure that they are placed low in order of priority. There are no express official criteria to guide a D.O. in deciding on, and promoting, project priorities. He may have to strike a balance between equity, which areas have already had projects given them and which have not, and merit, how much good he thinks the various projects will do. If two projects are suggested for the same area he may have to make a value judgement, for instance to give higher priority to a water supply than to a bathing place. According to a former Sarawak D.O., the communal aspect is all-important, much more so than in Malaya, where most rural projects necessarily concern only the Malays. The great majority of the projects which are advocated are communal in their implications. "Every time a councillor advocates a project, it is a *Malay* (or *Chinese* or *Iban* etc.) councillor who is speaking." Development projects must be allocated fairly among communities or there will be dissatisfaction. One of the alleged grievances against the Ningkan Government in 1965 and 1966 was that it was doing too little for the Malays in the development field.

The D.O.'s function of co-ordinating technical officials has become even more important with the current increased emphasis on development. A large part of his task consists in making each technical officer aware of the others' problems and policy, the first step towards co-ordination. There is a tendency for the technical man to concentrate on saying his own piece but not to listen very carefully to what the other technical men are saying. The D.O. has to co-ordinate, through his personality, officers who may be much older and more experienced than himself. If persuasion fails, his only recourse is to send a complaint about the technical officers concerned to the Resident who will approach the Department which employs the technical officer. The D.O. also has to co-ordinate technical officials in their contacts with the public; for instance, he may arrange for agricultural and health officials to pay joint visits to a village.

The Administrative Officer (Development and Planning), Sarawak

Although development is an important aspect of the D.O.'s work, it is only one of many duties. In Sarawak, however, there is an officer at *divisional* level specifically charged with responsibility for development, initially called the Divisional Development Officer. Originally he was part of the Resident's Office responsible to the Resident and, through him to the State Secretary and the Chief Minister. Early in 1967, however, with the creation of the Ministry of Development and Forestry, the D.D.O. became responsible to the State Development Officer and, through him, to the Minister of Development and Forestry (Enche Taib). But when the combined ministry was abolished, the previous lines of responsibility were restored.[115] "This arrangement worked satisfactorily before and is appropriate since the Resident is the Chairman of the Divisional Development Planning Committee."[116] These alterations in the role of the D.D.O. arose because of political changes, not because of difficulties at divisional level. But a further change in 1969 was prompted partly by a dispute in one division about the respective limits of the authority of the Resident and the D.D.O. The D.D.O.'s title was changed to "Administrative Officer (Development and Planning)", to stress that his rôle was subordinate to that of the Resident. At the same time the Resident replaced the D.D.O. as chairman of the Working Subcommittee of the Divisional Development Committee, which had the desirable effect of underlining the Resident's direct responsibility for development.

Like any "technical" officer at regional level the Administrative Officer (Development and Planning) has, in practice, to "be responsible" both to his regional chief, the Resident, and his immediate technical superior, the State Development Officer. However he is an unusual kind of "technical" officer. It is true that he is more specialized than either the Resident or the D.O. But he has the task of co-ordinating officers who are much more specialized than himself and who may outrank him; the Divisional Engineer, the Divisional Agricultural Officer, the Divisional Educational Officer, and the Superintendent of Land and Surveys. One Administrative Officer

(Development and Planning) has described the task of co-ordination as giving him his "greatest headaches", and causing him more trouble even than political pressures.[117] This is so in spite of the fact that two of the other four officials were at school with him and that another was a fellow-student at the University. Arguments often arise over problems of co-ordination, for instance on how to ensure that, in spite of exceptionally bad weather a road is ready in time to serve a land settlement scheme as planned. According to this Administrative Officer (Development and Planning) the problem of co-ordination is much more difficult at divisional level than it is at district level, where it can more often be effected by informal means.[118] The job is even more complex and more "political" than the D.O.'s.

There is no special training or recognized qualification for the job of Administrative Officer (Development and Planning). In late 1967 two of the five D.D.O.s had previously been D.O.s; the other three held other administrative jobs before appointment. One had an economics degree, but said that this training was "useless" for his job. It was the view of the D.D.O.s themselves that the most important qualities required were still in personal relations and, to a lesser extent, knowledge of government procedures. According to one D.D.O. "the best training for a D.D.O. is to have been a D.O.".

Community Development Officers, Sabah

There is no equivalent of the Administrative Officer (Development and Planning) in Sabah, but in 1968 a new type of development officer was created at a lower level to help the Government's drive to encourage Community Development and a spirit of *gotong royong* (self help). Thirty-two Community Development Officers, one to each state constituency, were appointed and put through a training course. They were administered by a new government department, the Community Development Centre, under the Chief Minister, with a former State Development Officer from Malaya as Director. "The Department will work in conjunction with the D.O.s and A.D.O.s but the officers of this Department will be more in contact with the people. As far as I am concerned they are the media of communication between the people and the Government."[119] The Chief Minister contrasted the first stage of the 1966–70 Rural Development Plan, which had aimed at making a co-ordinated effort at governmental level, with the second, Community Development, stage; "the second stage is to incite the people to give their full co-operation to the Government and to concentrate their efforts and their energies for the improvement of their standard of living". He specifically mentioned that community development required all the people to live in a spirit of *gotong royong*.[120]

The idea for this new organization has been ascribed by some to Tun Mustapha, by others to Dato Harris. Ultimately, it apparently derived from the Philippines. There was a valid reason for having a different arrangement from Malaya, where the community development function is carried out by the Adult Education Supervisor in each state constituency; in Sabah some state constituencies did not have an Adult Education Supervisor in their area. The new organization is also justified by the fact that, although D.O.s can tour, they cannot stay in the field long enough to encourage development projects in any given area. The new C.D.O.s would therefore help to sift proposals for development projects put up to district development committees, help to supervise the implementation of approved projects, and act as a medium for getting new ideas put into effect.

The C.D.O.s have a variety of qualifications. Some are well-educated; others are rich, including one who owns timber and "rides about in a big car". The feature they have in common is that all the appointments were "political", made on the basis of political experience (in USNO) on the premise that this experience would enable them to get closer to the people. It might seem surprising that some quite well-qualified persons would be attracted by such a relatively badly-paid job ($150 a month plus travelling expenses). But the job is not only awarded on the basis of past political experience; it may also be an avenue to future political office. Two C.D.O.s were selected as USNO candidates (which meant a virtual certainty of being elected) in the 1969 parliamentary elections and five or six others were placed on the short list of those who were considered for selection as candidates.

Initial reports on the work of the C.D.O.s were quite favourable, but there was some resentment by D.O.s of the ways in which C.D.O.s tried to put up "political" projects, and also of claims by some C.D.O.s that they "outranked" D.O.s because of their political backing. It was even said that a C.D.O. had claimed to be superior because he had "one letter more" than a D.O. A satisfactory relation between D.O. and C.D.O. has yet to be worked out.[121]

Apart from attempting to inculcate new ideas via the C.D.O.s the Community Development Centre has an important training function, and gives short courses, which take the form of lectures, discussions and visits, to *Ketuah Kampong* and Chiefs. The idea behind the courses is apparently that if the chiefs and *Ketuah Kampong* cannot be abolished or "rationalized" except in the long run, they can at least be given some basic training. The Centre also aims at encouraging the formation of effective committees in each *kampong* which will promote development.

Obstacles to Development in Sarawak and Sabah

Development in the Borneo states has met with greater obstacles than development in Malaya. Some of the difficulties arose from deep-seated causes dependent on the nature of development policy and the attitudes of the people. These will be discussed in the last chapter of this book. Other problems arose which were attributable to more obvious factors, and these will be mentioned here.

Development has been impeded in both states by poor communications.

> In places like Tambunan, for example, because of lack of suitable roads it is very, very costly to undertake major projects. The cost of transporting material there is prohibitive. At the same time communications in the widest sense of the word also involve the communication of Government policy to the people. Unless and until the rural people are able to read and write and perhaps have a fair idea of Government machinery, it is most difficult to convey to them the basic idea behind our development plan.[122]

Other obstacles lay in a shortage of skilled labour and even organized unskilled labour, a lack of public works contractors with adequate resources and the preference given to army demands for resources over civilian demands during the Confrontation with Indonesia.

Some early setbacks were probably in the nature of "teething troubles".[123] State ministers were still getting used to their jobs and, although federal-state co-operation on development worked smoothly on the whole, some of the original procedures seem to have been cumbersome.[124] Initially in the Borneo states there was not the same drive for development from the top as there was in Malaya through the agency of Tun Razak. By 1968, however, it was clear that in Sabah Tun Mustapha was showing at state level some of the dynamic characteristics of Tun Razak at federal level. This was brought about by the combination of a strong personality and, after 1967, by the absence of an effective opposition, which enabled him to give more time to development and less to politics.

In August, 1966 some remarks of the federal Finance Minister, Tan Siew Sin, on the underspending of development money in the Borneo states,[125] were given wide publicity. As reported in the Press, the issues were oversimplified, including the allegation that expatriate officers in the two states were partly to blame. In point of fact, underspending arose for several reasons.[126] The release of funds might be delayed because of the need for federal authorities to scrutinize projects or because there was delay in the relevant foreign grants or loans being released.[127] Estimates of expenditure were sometimes deliberate overestimates, designed to ensure an adequate supply of funds in spite of expected delays in the release of funds by the Federal Government. Funds which were available sometimes could not be spent because of the shortages of labour and technicians previously mentioned, or because of delays in acquiring land, carrying out surveys and so on.

The late arrival of funds is no excuse for not trying to plan ahead, but there are limits to what can be done on this score. According to a Sarawak Resident some development funds were released to his Division only on 12 December, 1967, which legally, had to be spent before the end of the year. How could he possibly have managed to use them in the time? Finally, there are considerations which are unpredictable, such as the weather. If the weather is better than average, there may be requests for additional expenditure on road works: if it is worse than average, under-expenditure may be unavoidable.[128]

"Under-spending", then, is illustrative of the difficulties of planning in a developing area where, in addition to the unpredictabilities inherent in all planning, there are also labour shortages, poor communications and an organization for development which has only just been established.

Political Aspects of Development

In this context "political" may have a range of meanings. Development may serve legitimate national political ends, such as increasing the distribution of certain benefits in a planned way, irrespective of adding to the strength of the leaders of the party in power. Alternatively, "political" may mean "party political", of benefit to a particular party. Or it may not even imply advantage to a party, but only to an individual politician. In practice it may be difficult to disentangle these meanings.

A prominent political aspect of development has been the use of Minor Rural Projects for political purposes. Ministers on tour may make political capital out of announcing, with maximum publicity, a grant which benefits the area. The personal, or party, publicity element is sometimes indistinguishable from the clearly legitimate object of keeping the people informed of the progress of development projects in the State.

Such grants are often termed "spot grants". To understand the political aspects of Minor Rural Projects, some clarification of the term is necessary. First, some other types of grant may be announced during ministerial visits, and may therefore also be called "spot grants". An example is the grants to mosques and churches which mainly come out of lotteries (Social Welfare) funds.[129] In Sarawak there is also the Timber Cess Fund, which goes to meet requests for development money which come up via the channel, *Penghulu*, D.O. and Resident.

Second, some grants announced on the spot may not constitute any departure from the development requests which have gone through the development committee system. Priorities may not have been changed from what was requested; the minister is merely taking credit for the allocation. In other cases the priorities may have been changed at a higher level by accepted procedures. In a few instances a minister has announced a grant which was neither contained in the original district committee requests nor approved at higher levels; consequently money may not be available to pay for the grant, and sometimes it fails to be implemented.

"Politics" can enter into Minor Rural Projects in different ways. Irrespective of what areas are selected to benefit from it, the politician who announces a grant gains credit for himself and his party by the mere fact of the announcement. Once or twice in Sarawak two different ministers announced the same project as "news' within a few days of each other. When Dato Ningkan was Chief Minister of Sarawak there was some resentment among politicians in other Alliance parties because he announced so many development grants himself. In the Tawi Sli government there was apparently an agreement to allocate an area to each minister in which he was entitled to announce grants. The area corresponded roughly to his party's main geographical source of support and sometimes to his own area of greatest personal influence. For example, most Pesaka grants were announced either by Tan Sri Jugah, for Third and Fourth Divisions, or by Dato Tawi Sli, for Second Division. As Chief Minister, however, Taw Sli was not tied down to any one area, and he made numerous grants in the First Division, including Kuching. One of the criticisms of Taib, which contributed to his having to leave the Sarawak Cabinet at the end of 1967, was allegedly that he had announced M.R.P.s "outside his area". Development is a federal subject, so in Sarawak, and also Sabah, some announcements of projects were made by the Tengku, Tun Razak, and other federal ministers. In Sarawak these federal ministers included Dato Rahman Ya'akub before he became Chief Minister in 1970 and, after November 1967, Taib. Because these ministers had a Sarawak state rôle as well as a federal rôle, their announcements of projects clearly had implications for internal Sarawak politics.[130] A sample check of newspaper reports of M.R.P. announcements, July 1966 to May 1970, showed that the greatest number of announcements was made by Dato Ling

Beng Siong (SCA), followed by Dato Tawi Sli (Pesaka), Awang Hipni (Bumiputera), Dato Rahman Ya'akub (Bumiputera), Taib (Bumiputera), Dato Teo (SCA) and Tan Sri Jugah (Pesaka).[131]

In Sabah many of the early announcements of Minor Rural Projects were made by Harris, the Finance Minister. Later on, the bulk of the grants were announced by Tun Mustapha as Chief Minister, and he subsequently assumed formal ministerial responsibility for development.

It is not easy to decide which parties benefited most from the distribution of M.R.P.s. The exact area to which a grant has been allocated cannot always be ascertained from a news item which merely indicates the district or the town, for instance "Kuching". There are, of course, reports about particular projects. There is evidence from a reliable source that a former Sarawak Cabinet member obtained electric light, a dispensary, and so on, for "his own" longhouse, while neighbouring longhouses still lacked these amenities. In 1964–5 the Sarawak Government, under the chief ministership of Dato Ningkan, gave far more fire extinguishers to longhouses in the Second Division, where Ningkan's party (SNAP) was relatively strong than to longhouses in the Third Division where it was weaker.[132] But, although Tan Sri Jugah's elemental blast of 7 October, 1967 in Kapit complained of bias against the Ibans in the allocation of projects, there does not appear to have been any pronounced party or ethnic discrimination in Sarawak up to 1970, even from 1966 onwards when SNAP was in opposition. The lack of any marked discrimination against SNAP when it was in opposition may have been due to the importance of the Iban vote and to the disinclination of an Iban government party, Pesaka, to penalize other Ibans. However, there does not seem to have been discrimination, either, against the mainly Chinese areas where SUPP was strong.

Sabah newspaper reports of M.R.P.s indicate that in the four months or so before the 1967 state election more grants were made to constituencies later won by USNO than to those won by UPKO. After the election UPKO members stated that M.R.P.s were being denied to state constituencies which had returned an UPKO member. This was said to be one of the pressures which resulted in the dissolution of the party and in many of its members joining USNO. When Payar Juman defected from UPKO to USNO one of the reasons he gave for his action was that his constituency was being starved of development money.[133] However, even if some seats won by UPKO were deprived of funds for M.R.P.s, not all the UPKO seats were so badly treated. According to the *Sabah Times*, then a pro-UPKO paper, from the end of the 1967 state elections to the dissolution of UPKO at the end of the year there were six M.R.P. grants to UPKO constituencies[134] and only two to USNO constituencies. From 1968 onwards there did not appear to be any obvious political implications in the distribution of M.R.P.s in Sabah. Just before the 1969 parliamentary elections, however, there seemed to be a concentration on the three seats in which the strongest opposition to the Alliance candidates was expected, in Sandakan, Kota Kinabalu, and Tawau, where Chinese Independents were fighting the SCA. After the suspension of the elections this tendency continued and was intensified when the election process was completed in 1970. Shortly before polling took place 35 M.R.P.s were announced, of which 31 were in these three seriously-contested seats, 12 in Sandakan, 12 in Tawau and 7 in Kota Kinabalu.[135]

Because M.R.P.s have political aspects, the development machinery has not produced the same results as it would if there had been less keen political competition. There have been examples of projects being adopted which do not reflect the priorities of the people themselves as articulated and aggregated through the development machinery. This applies to major development projects as well as to M.R.P.s. Statistically, the damage was less than some of the more colourful examples of "political" allocations would suggest. A former State Development Officer in Sarawak estimated that about 90% of total development spending corresponded to "needs", objectively considered. This opinion probably applies to Sabah as well. What was disturbing in Sabah before the 1967 elections was that the changes made for political reasons in the priorities of the District Development Committees were so great that they threatened to destroy the value of the development machinery as a way of expressing the wishes of the people.[136] Since the dissolution of UPKO, however, and the virtual disappearance of an opposition in Sabah, the Government, and in particular the Chief Minister, Tun Mustapha, has been extremely tough in resisting "political" pressures.

Another political aspect of development concerns the presence of members of opposition parties on development committees. This need not create a special problem in the allocation of resources, because of the preponderant rôle played by officials on these committees, and because of the control exercised over committee proposals by committees higher in the hierarchy on which the Opposition is not represented any way. Nevertheless, sometimes Alliance politicians feel that it is wrong that opposition members on development committees should receive "credit" for having initiated development proposals. Actually, Alliance politicians in Sarawak, and Sarawak officials, testified that, before July 1970 when SUPP joined the government, SUPP representatives in development committees in the First Division had been useful and constructive. In 1967 Dato James Wong (SNAP) attacked the removal of some elected representatives from the Divisional Development Committee, Fifth Division.[137] A solution was found by making the automatic choice of certain elected representatives from local councils to serve on development committees which was referred to earlier.

Political Pressures On District Officers

Particularistic political pressures on the D.O. are now strong for a number of reasons; independence was accompanied by the rise of political parties and elections; chiefs have become politicized; the D.O.s themselves are now locally recruited instead of being expatriates and it is therefore harder for them to remain aloof from politics; an increase in the number and nature of governmental functions and in the amount of development money available has provided incentives for greater political activity. The D.O., like other civil servants, has to face adjustments to new conditions. He is now responsible to an elected government, which was not the situation before 1963. Policies formed through the democratic political process are therefore now regarded as legitimate, and he is accountable for carrying them out. It is good that the D.O. should feel pressures which are a reflection of a new emphasis on welfare and of changed values. Politicians are also obvious instruments for helping to promote desired changes. The real problem arises when those wielding political power, or who have political "connections", desire the D.O. to perform actions which deviate from the agreed and established policies arrived at through the process of democracy.

The political impact on the D.O. comes from several directions, but perhaps shows itself most clearly in the field of development projects. His authority is undermined when a minister visits an area and announces a spot grant. It sometimes looks as if the D.O. had not really tried to help the people, otherwise surely the grant would have been confirmed through the District Development Committee of which he is the chairman. It has been known for a D.O. in Sabah to protest against what he regraded as the announcement of an "excessive" number of spot grants in his area, but without effect. Occasionally in the past when a Minister in Sarawak announced a spot grant for which there was no corresponding money available, it was the unfortunate D.O. who had to try and explain what had gone wrong.

The D.O., as chairman of the District Development Committee, can usually block "political" proposals for development if he wants to, but there is no guarantee that they may not be reintroduced at state level via party channels. The D.O. may also be by-passed on such questions as land applications; instead of applications going through the channel, D.O. and Resident, individual Natives may approach ministers through their political contacts. Mavis Puthucheary has referred to the potential conflicts which may arise between politicians and administrators.[138] The former tend to favour projects with an immediate appeal to the electors, such as mosques and roads. The latter are more concerned with long-term, economically-viable projects.

An impassioned attack on political intervention was made by Dato Stephens late in 1967:

> Matters which should rightly be the concern of the Civil Servants are now taken over by politicians. District Officers and Residents

are continually pestered by politicians in their areas, many of whom are known to raise threats in their attempt to get what they want. D.O.s now have to spend a large part of their time talking to small fry politicians, often about unimportant personal requests; if they do not they become the subject of attack; cooked up reports are made about them and they are in for trouble from the top. This sort of thing is helping to slow down all work, and especially development work."[139]

For several years before the 1969/1970 Sarawak elections politics also intruded into the lives of Sarawak D.O.s. They were sometimes asked which party they supported, and found it difficult to explain their neutrality and the justification for being neutral. Sometimes Ibans in the Third Division came to a D.O. and showed their party badges as a sign that they belonged to the "Government" party; if he failed to be impressed, they openly expressed their dissatisfaction.

Political pressures may be present in fields other than development, and may actually operate so as to hinder development. Natives in Sarawak who occupy land illegally and fell timber on it are usually dealt with very leniently, the only penalty exacted being a small fine, because they often have the support of a political party, and sometimes even of the Minister who is responsible for Lands and Forests.

The conflict between politicians and civil servants, as described by Mavis Puthucheary in Malaya, can be resolved at ministerial level "and if the civil servant is found to be in the right, he is decisively supported against the politicians."[140] But it is not easy to generalize about the D.O.–politician relation in Sarawak and Sabah. One view is that the office of D.O. is still held in great respect by politicians, irrespective of the calibre of the man who occupies it. An opposite view of the D.O.s present status is: 'To some of the older people below him he is still a god; to the politicians above him he is nothing". Certainly, it cannot be assumed that the conflict, if one arises, is between bright, educated, young D.O.s and older, less-educated politicians. Some politicians are well-educated; not all D.O.s are well-educated,[141] and some are not young but are men with long service who have been promoted. One important factor is that those D.O.s who are young and educated tend to be jealous of the financial advantages that some politicians enjoy. What is plain is that, even if value-loaded terms, such as "interference", are avoided, a new element has been introduced into the life of the D.O. He may be given orders to do things which may conflict with the law. He cannot remain unambiguously the "father and mother" of the people, if he is also responsible to a government elected by the people through the medium of a political party. He must be sensitive to the importance of the politician and be prepared for political norms which are not expressed in text-books on the working of British government.

The Sabah situation has changed since Dato Stephens made his attack on political pressures on civil servants. In one way civil servants are now more secure than before. They are not faced with the uncertainties arising from a possible change in government, as they were around 1967, or as their counterparts in Sarawak were, 1966–70. And, because the rule of the Government is almost unchallenged, leading politicians are less likely to seek all the political support possible by upholding the claims of minor political figures against civil servants. At the same time, just because the Government is so powerful, civil servants may feel unprotected against it, and D.O.s in the field may see the emergence of politicallly-appointed Community Development Officers as a threat to their authority.

The Future of the District Officer

In countries other than Malaysia it has sometimes been questioned whether District Officers should remain at all. Nationalists raised this question in some African countries when they attained independence. The issue has also been raised in Pakistan.[142] Maybe in the long run there might be "democratized D.O.s", rather like the County Managers in Eire.[143] In that case in Sarawak and Sabah the D.O. might be converted into an employee of local government authorities, supplanting the existing local council secretary or executive officer. But local government authorities, with a few exceptions, are so weak in both states that it is difficult to see anything like this happening soon. And the present lack of administrators is so great that, if D.O.s were given entirely local government functions, there would be a severe shortage of administrators to manage development. It was certainly an exaggeration to say in 1965 of Sarawak that the "District Councils and Divisional Councils [*sic*] were working the District Officers and Residents out of their jobs."[144] However, for the next few years the important question to ask about the D.O. is not: how can he quickly be replaced by, or converted to the service of, local authorities? It is rather: how can he best be harnessed for development work and for the increasingly complex task of co-ordinating technical officers entailed by such work?

The D.O. has many burdens to bear. He has his law and order, magisterial, ceremonial, and national integration functions to perform. In his development work he is subject to the political pressures previously mentioned. When officials in both states were asked about the D.O.'s development rôle, the answers were largely in agreement. Development was recognized to be the most important responsibility of the D.O., and it was calculated that he spent roughly half his time on it. But the weight attached to his development function was not so great as for a D.O. in Malaya.[145] Nor would his development performance be given quite the same degree of consideration as a criterion for his promotion compared with Malaya. The different emphasis on development compared with Malaya reflected Malaya's earlier concern with planned development and the greater exposure of the development effort in Malaya to the impact of Tun Razak's forceful personality.

Although the development function has not yet been accorded quite the same high degree of esteem in the Borneo states as in Malaya, it is nevertheless the most important function now performed by the D.O. Even if local government in Sarawak and Sabah were able to stand on its own feet without the aid of the D.O. some version of the D.O. would still be necessary for development purposes. Once this argument is accepted, the main problem is seen to be; how can the D.O., or his equivalent, be made most efficient for the purposes of development? As regards distribution of functions, two broad approaches could be tried. Some of his non-development functions could be taken from him, or some of his development functions could be removed. The first approach could be followed by relieving the D.O. of more and more of his magisterial functions, some of his administrative work in the office,[146] or by the delegation of some of his functions concerning land.[147] Alternatively, if the second approach were followed, he could be given an assistant specifically charged with development responsibilities.[148] In Sarawak and Sabah the first approach has been taken to the extent that the D.O.'s magisterial duties have been lightened by the appointment of stipendiary magistrates. The second approach has been followed at *divisional* level in Sarawak by the appointment of Administrative Officers (Development and Planning). It could be argued that if these officers did not exist, the D.O. would have more co-ordinating to do at district level. The appointment of Community Development Officers in Sabah also reflects the second approach, although some problems have resulted from the Community Development Officers not being directly responsible to D.O.s.

In any case, whichever approach, or combination of approaches, is adopted, a co-ordinating rôle for development purposes remains necessary, whether the person filling it is known as "District Officer" or as something else. The model of the French prefect could be studied with advantage, especially as his co-ordinating rôle has recently been strengthened.[149]

Although there may not be any dispute about the need for the D.O., or some equivalent, in a development co-ordinating rôle, there is considerable doubt about how to train people for this rôle. The opinion of practically all D.O.s, and of former D.O.s who have now reached higher rank in Sarawak and Sabah, is that D.O.s must be trained mainly on the job. Whether they are degree-holders or whether they have taken only shorter courses, their main training does, and should, take place while serving in subordinate positions in the administrative service which may later qualify them for promotion to D.O. There is a wide gap between this view of training and the approach of some academic writers. One of these believes that the present generalist administrator should be a highly "differentiated" manager. Supreme skill is required for management and this skill should be learned.[150] With a greater emphasis now being placed on training in Malaysia,[151] it may be possible to devise suitable training courses. However, sufficient attention should be paid to the civil service "on the job" view of training to ensure that there is no attempt to give courses emphasizing such topics as economics or road-making. The focus should be on man management and on how to make good use of the services of technical men. The emphasis should be on development, not by seeking to make the administrator an expert on all technical aspects of development, but by training him to act as an agent of change. Modern methods of teaching public administration through case studies and the use of "syndicates"[152] should be employed.

At present there are weaknesses at D.O. level, which are partly the result of the unexpectedly quick end of colonialism in the two states. "The factors that influence the personal standing of the Deputy Commissioner are his age, status, authority, standard of performance, and duration of stay in a district. The Deputy Commissioner has advantages of status, authority and tradition. But the forces now working against him are also formidable, notably, the cleavage between specialists and generalists, his younger age, and his normally short tenure in the district."[153] This statement referring to Bangla Desh is also applicable to Sarawak and Sabah. Because of the shortage of trained administrators, D.O.s are young and inexperienced. In June, 1968 seven out of the eight D.O.s in the area of one Sabah Residency were only Division II civil servants, holding acting rank, with an average age of about twenty-eight. None of the eight was a graduate. The shortage at higher levels has also led to recruitment for these levels from D.O. level and therefore to a rapid turnover of D.O.s.[154]

Immaturity may make a D.O. less effective. A D.O. must be consistent in his dealings with the people and in what he tells them. He must not be impatient, especially with those who do not understand the printed word. He must be mature enough not to be stampeded into writing inaccurate reports just because he thinks that his superiors would be pleased by hearing good news about pet projects. One D.O. reported that the MARA shop in his district was doing so well that an extension would soon be needed, when actually it was doing rather poor business. It was also a sign of immaturity for a D.O. to request police help from his Resident because he "had a dream" that the security situation had deteriorated. And the

D.O. who asked for three days leave in order to climb Mount Kinabalu was too inexperienced to know that (despite the symbolic value of his quest) the Resident's reply would be to ask how many people he would be able to see and help when he was up the mountain.

In order to co-ordinate technical staff, know how to keep afloat in a sea of political pressures, and also, until standards of literacy and sophistication rise, to be able to lead the rural people effectively, D.O.s would have to be older, more experienced and better-trained than they are today. At present, however, training is insufficient—particularly training in terms of local conditions. Many D.O.s are too young to have had experience and do not have a very good general education. Those who are older have the necessary experience, but are unlikely to be well-educated, and may be less receptive to training for development than the younger men.

Sabah Without Residents?

Although the exact nature of the D.O.'s rôle is in dispute, his continued existence in some form is assured; since at least 1966, however, the abolition of Residents has been under consideration in both states, particularly in Sabah. There are two convincing reasons for retaining Residents in Sarawak which do not apply in Sabah. Sarawak (unlike Sabah) has a development committee at divisional level, of which the Resident is chairman. This gives a Resident in Sarawak a more important co-ordinating job than his counterpart in Sabah. Sarawak is also different from Sabah in that it has a more competitive party system than Sabah has had since the end of 1967. There is therefore a need, which does not exist in Sabah, to have an official at Residency level in Sarawak, who can appeal to national solidarity on an "above-party" basis.

It is not clear exactly what reforms might be made in the system of Residents in Sabah. One of the objections appears to be simply to the title, Resident, which is thought to be suggestive of "feudalism". If Residents were abolished, some of their present functions would have to be allocated elsewhere, for instance their magisterial duties and their chairmanship of the divisional security committee, important in some divisions during the confrontations with Indonesia and the Philippines. The "ceremonial" function would also have to be taken care of. Two arguments are often heard against abolition of the Residents, in addition to the obvious one that senior local civil servants would be denied the chance of obtaining high-level jobs previously held by expatriates. One is that it would be too difficult to deal directly with districts from the state capital if there were no Residents. But, poor as communications still are, the number of districts is only sixteen, and these might be reduced somewhat by amalgamation.[155] Also, some critics have cast doubt on whether Residents, in many cases, are really anything more than "post offices" between District Officers and the various agencies in Kota Kinabalu.[156] It has been said, for example, that estimates sent up from the D.O. for checking by the Resident before being passed on to the state capital are in fact not properly checked.

The other argument for retention is that some of the D.O.s in Sabah are so weak that Residents must be kept in order to redress their deficiencies.[157] It is quite true that many D.O.s are inexperienced. However, even assuming that the calibre of Residents is now significantly better than that of the D.O.s whom they are to reinforce, this is only a temporary argument for the retention of Residents.

An alternative to abolition would be to fill the posts with politicians, or ex-politicians, as was strongly urged soon after independence in some countries in Africa. This would be quite feasible in a state like Sabah which has no effective opposition, and the "ceremonial" functions of the Resident could be well discharged well in this way. Simultaneously, administrative and judicial functions could be handed over to a civil servant at Residency level of lower rank than the existing Residents.

Sarawak and Sabah have always been rather small for a two-tier system of Residents and District Officers. Communications have now improved sufficiently to make it likely that the upper tier, but not the lower, will disappear within the next ten years or so in Sabah and possibly also in Sarawak.

The Withering Away of the Chiefs?

The parallel hierarchy of chiefs and headmen is unlikely to

DORSET INSTITUTE OF
HIGHER EDUCATION
LEARNING RESOURCES
CENTRE

survive in the very long run. The headmen will probably outlive the chiefs. It was observed earlier that the chiefs did not have strong indigenous roots, but were largely the creation of the Brookes and the British North Borneo Company. In Sarawak and North Borneo the chiefs were never built up to the same degree as they were in some parts of Africa through being equipped with offices, clerical help, telephones and so on by the colonial power,[158] although in both states at times when competition between political parties has been intense the chiefs assumed great political importance.[159] Nowadays the chiefs have an obvious potential rival in the form of the local councillor.[160] Sometimes where the local councillor and the *Penghulu* belong to opposite parties, they may clash, for instance over development projects; a Sarawak D.O. may have a difficult point of protocol to resolve in deciding which of the two to call on first when he is on tour.

Originally, because of the limited recruitment possibilities for councillors, many chiefs became elected councillors as well. This could greatly increase the chief's effectiveness, especially if he became Council Chairman. For instance, in both Kapit and Kanowit, Third Division of Sarawak, the chairman of the district council elected in 1963 was also a *Penghulu*. In Kapit out of fifteen non-Chinese councillors, one was a *Temenggong*, one was a *Pengarah*, seven were *Penghulus*, and two were *Tuai Rumah*. The double rôle of such persons greatly increases their ability to help people and to push through development projects for their areas. At the same time, however, the political pressures on chiefs, which are present in any case, are greatly intensified if the chief is also a councillor. Some chiefs have refused to stand for council membership because of their fear of such pressures. As education spreads, the supply of potential councillors from other sources may be expected to increase with the consequence that fewer chiefs will become councillors.[161]

In the long run it is possible that chiefs, and maybe headmen, will wither away, apart from their *adat* and Native Court functions. It is significant that chiefs and headmen are not represented as such on district development committees in Sarawak. They are represented on district development committees in Sabah, but not to the same extent as local government councillors. From time to suggestions are made that chiefs should be "professionalized" by being subjected to qualifying educational standards and to examinations, and made into a salaried subordinate layer of the civil service, as *Penghulus* are in Malaya. However, by no means all existing chiefs are capable of being made professional in this way, so, if the change were not to take the form of a rather drastic purge, the period of transition to the new system would be a long one.[162]

Conclusion

In the last dozen years or so there have been radical changes in administration in the field in both Sarawak and Sabah. The old "parallel hierarchies" of chiefs and headmen on the one hand, and D.O.s and Residents on the other, remain. But local councils have been added, and the machinery for development has been built in. Moreover, the whole style of administration has changed with the end of colonial rule and the coming of political parties. In the old days, when there was "an administrative-oriented decision process", the public official was regarded as the sole transmitter and interpreter of public policy. But now, in "the policy-oriented decision process, the civil servant is but one of a variety of public policy interpreters available to the citizen. If responses to a need for government action are not forthcoming from one source, the citizen will turn to another and still another. Alternatively, he may seek out different bodies for action on different types of demands".[163] This generalization was made primarily with reference to Pakistan, but it fits the existing situation in Sarawak and Sabah quite closely. Compared with the old days of the "administration-oriented decision process", the citizen's range of choice has been widened in two ways. The former administrative hierarchy, headmen, chief, D.O., Resident, has now been crowned with Ministers. There has been a tendency for citizens to go direct to Ministers, either because of a belief that this was the "democratic" way or because of a desire to use political pressure to influence a decision.[164] This tendency, unless the citizen is highly influential politically, is liable to lengthen the decision-making process, because the Minister will normally ask the Permanent Secretary of the Department to write to the D.O. to find out the facts, thus losing time instead of gaining it. A former Chief Minister of Sarawak, who had had experience of administration under the Brookes, spoke out against the tendency:

> The Chief Minister said that it was wrong for the people to take small matters to the Resident or to Ministers without first consulting their own community leaders, the Sarawak Administrative Officer or the District Officer.
>
> He advised the people to try and settle their differences amicably among themselves by first seeking advice from *Penghulus, Kapitan Chinas*, or the *Tuai Rumahs* in their respective areas.
>
> If the decisions made by these leaders are not satisfactory, then the people should refer the matter to SAO or to the District Officer and the Resident, according to the proper procedure in the Government Administration and thrash the matter out said Penghulu Tawi Sli.[165]

Early in 1969 Tun Mustapha explained why he would not be available to see people who came to visit him, unless the nature of their business was important enough to warrant it. And later in that year a new procedure was devised to "protect" ministers in general from indiscriminate visits by members of the public.[166]

The creation of local government bodies, opens up another possibility, however; demands may be fed into this new system instead of into the old administrative hierarchy. The range of possibilities has led to some confusion. Even after local bodies were introduced, citizens would approach the D.O. about their rates because they could not believe that anything that had to do with "Government" did not also concern the D.O. Later, when it was understood that local bodies did have to do with rates, the unpopularity of rates was such that citizens tended to *avoid* going to councillors on other subjects because of the unpleasant association. Often the choice of authority to approach is based on a correct knowledge of their division of functions: a chief is asked to settle a minor dispute; a councillor is asked about rates or schools; a development request, for instance for a bridge, is made to a councillor, or the D.O., or in Sabah to the C.D.O. If the citizen is not sure who deals with what, it has been suggested that he may behave as follows; he asks the D.O. for what he thinks he is entitled to as a right, while if he is requesting a favour he seeks out his councillor. Party, ethnic group, or personality may also be important. Where the approach, other things being equal, would be made to the councillor, the chief or the D.O. may be contacted instead, if the councillor belongs to a different party or ethnic group than the citizen, or is personally disliked by him. Distance may be an important factor. A member of a long-house may have to go a shorter distance to speak to the chief than he would have to travel to speak to the councillor. Finally, his choice may be decided by chance; he may talk to the first person in authority whom he happens to see, provided that he is of sufficient importance, whether it is the D.O., the Resident, a councillor, or a member of the legislature.

The "system" may seem more confusing to the tidy-minded observer than it is to the participants. It will be argued later that political development need not automatically be equated with making an immediate clean sweep of apparently anti-quated institutions, such as D.O.s, chiefs and headmen.

7

Strategies, Styles and Resources of Politics

Herbert Spiro believes that political style "describes the types of arguments that are used in connection with the discussion of issues, mainly in the course of deliberating." He distinguishes five types, characterized by the predominance of arguments based on: purposive interests; violence; ideology; law; and immediate goals.[1] The approach used here is somewhat different, although his five types could have been used with modifications.[2] Political style is taken here to refer not only to arguments, but also to behaviour; it is assumed that a "violent" political style would not only use arguments based on violence but would also be expressed in the application of such arguments through violent behaviour.[3] The purpose of this chapter is to generalize on the basis of material presented previously, and to identify patterns which may permit comparison of style in the Borneo states with political style elsewhere.

Starting with a section on "The Rules of Politics" and one on "Symbols" the chapter continues with sections on the use of money in politics and on concepts of power and status, both for Natives and Chinese. This is followed by an analysis of violence and of an unusual combination, found in the Borneo states, of constraints and inducements.

The "Rules" of Politics

It has been said of developed countries, and in particular of the United States, that there are certain accepted "rules of the game" in politics. "For the mass of the population they may be loose and ambiguous, though more precise and articulated at the leadership level. In any case, the 'rules of the game' are interests the serious disturbance of which will result in organized interaction and the assertion of fairly explicit claims for conformity."[4] However, in 1963 the Borneo states had only just ceased to be colonies, and standards of literacy and education were too low for the mass of the population to have any but the haziest notions of what the rules of politics might be. In 1963 there was considerable uncertainty about the rules of politics in the Borneo states. Colonial precedents and the example of Malaya gave some guidance but not enough. Conflicting views existed, for example, on the nature of constitutional change, the rôle of an opposition, the rules regulating the behaviour of parties inside the Alliance and the rules governing competition between parties.

Politicians' knowledge of their constitutional powers was shaky. One Chief Minister hesitated to dismiss a Minister partly because, if he did, he feared that the Minister concerned might sue him. The intricacies of the constitutional issues involved in the federal legislation which replaced Ningkan by Sli in 1966 and later postponed the date of the Sarawak elections were obviously too deep to be understood by the vast majority of the Sarawak electors. In claiming that the Constitution had been violated, SNAP said that it was a sacred document, not to be tampered with and invoked the concept of *adat* (custom) which was well known to the Natives. But even *adat* can change, so SNAP had the task of distinguishing between those ways of changing the Constitution which were proper and acceptable and those which were not. To a large extent the test they applied was whether constitutional changes, and consequential actions of the government, were validated by a court or not. They were partially successful in promoting this interpretation, with the result that the original court decision in favour of Dato Ningkan probably gained some popular support from SNAP.

Another example of uncertainty concerned the position of Tun Mustapha as Head of State in Sabah, which raised bitter controversy among political leaders in the early stages of the Sabah Cabinet crisis of December 1964.[5] Tun Mustapha's conception of his powers was obviously different from the powers actually exercised by his counterparts in the states of Malaya. The eventual arrangement, arrived at after the Sabah elections of 1967, was that Tun Mustapha became Chief

Minister, a procedure which did not follow conventions established in Malaya, where, once a person had become "non-political", he stayed non-political. But politics in the new state of Sabah were so fluid in 1964 that it would have been quite possible for Tun Mustapha to have remained Head of State and exercised very wide powers, provided that the Chief Minister and the Cabinet had agreed.

In both states, also, there was a dispute about exactly what agreement had been arrived at about the balance to be observed between parties or ethnic groups in appointing the Head of State and the Chief Minister.[6]

The concept of an organized responsible Opposition is not automatically acceptable in the Borneo states. Examples have already been given of the deference accorded to "Government" and to officials appointed by the Government, such as District Officers and Chiefs. The Government, or its representatives, is perpetually compared with the father of a family in speeches advocating racial harmony or the practice of *gotong royong*. Such similes, when added to the traditional respect in which Government is held, make it hard for most people to distinguish between the Government and the political party, or parties, constituting the Government of the day. The task of opposition parties is therefore difficult, especially if they are open to the charge that they are Communist-infiltrated. However, perhaps because the SUPP was the first party to be formed in Sarawak, its existence was accepted as natural even before it joined the Government in July 1970. The dangers arising from the association of some of its members with Communism were deplored by the parties, but proposals to curb it took the shape of purging it of extreme elements rather than of prohibiting it.

In Sabah, however, the concept of an Opposition was not so widely accepted. Denying that an Opposition was necessary, one politician said, in 1964, "Sabah is a small country where people are happy, and there is no reason why this should not continue." When Malaysia was formed there was no organized opposition, nor has there been any since December 1967. Some political leaders see no obvious lines of division which could give rise to an opposition party, except ethnic lines which are thought to be undesirable because they might lead to violence.

Such leaders take the view that in the first fifteen or twenty years after the end of colonial rule there is no need for an Opposition: its existence would merely divert energy from the vital tasks of development. A shrewd Sabah politician thought that an authoritarian government was desirable for about the next fifteen years. An Opposition would have its uses, for example in promoting solidarity inside the various factions in the Government, but ideally it should not be strong enough to win more than about 20% of the vote. Among ex-UPKO leaders two are admirers of Plato and have an essentially paternalistic view of Government.

The difference in the Opposition's rôle in the two states is reflected in their respective Public Accounts Committees. Inherited from Britain, this type of Committee is one of the main instruments by which the execution of Government policies may be assessed, and if necessary criticized and brought to the attention of the legislature and the electors. Sarawak followed the British precedent of having an Opposition member, originally Ong Kee Hui, as Chairman of the Committee, which produces informative reports which are available to the public. The Sabah Public Accounts Committee has a Government member as Chairman (like its federal counterpart in Kuala Lumpur). Its reports are issued only to members of the legislature, which defeats the main object of having a Public Accounts Committee, namely wide publicity.

Opposition parties, and particularly the SUPP until it joined the government in July 1970, are not completely certain of the rules under which they operate, or will be allowed to operate. Moderate leaders of the SUPP, for instance, might have wondered how far the amount of Communist infiltration into the SUPP would have to be reduced for the party to have been allowed to form a government on its own if it won a state election. To what extent should SUPP leaders have co-operated with the authorities in dissuading "their own" demonstrators from violence, for example during the U.N. Team's visit to Kuching in 1963? It was also wearing and time-consuming for the SUPP moderate party leaders to have to find out from the police exactly how regulations to control the use of banners and slogans at party functions, for instance at the ninth Anniversary Celebrations in 1968, were going to be applied.[7]

Examples have already been given, in Chapters 3 and 5, of the lack of uniformity in the use of Alliance Party machinery. In both states the rôle of the Alliance Council was unclear and ineffective, and the exact rôle of the state Alliance *vis-à-vis* the federal Alliance was indeterminate. In late 1966 the system of rotating the chairmanship of the Sabah Alliance was not formally altered, it was just not observed; Tun Mustapha simply remained chairman. In Sarawak collective responsibility in the Alliance Cabinet broke down on the issue of the Land Bills in 1965, because the Alliance party mechanisms for reaching agreement were defective. Even in 1968 the comment was heard: "ministers behave as if Cabinet doesn't exist". Formal Alliance machinery was not used in the discussions between parties before a new Sarawak State Government was formed in July 1970. A provision in the Sarawak Alliance Party that members of the Council Negri, and Sarawak members of the federal Parliament, should pay a percentage of their salaries to party funds, was largely ignored by members of one party and not completely observed by members of the others. For the first two years of this scheme, collections were $14,000 in arrears. A similar provision in the Sabah Alliance Party was also not completely observed.

In the conflicts *between* parties the rules were indeed nebulous. The contending Sarawak parties, 1965–6, were nominally all within a single all-embracing party, the Alliance, but each tried to seek the particular battle arena which seemed most propitious for its cause. There were no clearly established rules on whether disputes should be resolved inside the legislature or inside the party machinery.[8] Nor was it clear which conflicts should be settled inside the state and which at federal level. More generally, what, if any, should be the restrictions on the expenditure of money? When does "subsistence" money paid to party "workers" amount to downright bribery? To what extent should ministers use their official cars when campaigning in an election? Is it breaking the rules to deny development money to constituencies which have returned a member who belongs to the losing party? Did the use of tape to record, and use for political purposes, conversations which were intended to be private, break the rules? How would conventional administrative policies have to be adapted if occurrences such as the "lost file"[9] became frequent?

Politicians are, for the most part, cynical about the methods of politicians, including themselves. "People don't believe the truth. You must tell them lies and promise them everything, then they will support you." "At least X is a fighter. If a man stands up and says he is not a murderer he will be believed." There is some acknowledgement that rules exist, although their provisions may not be generally agreed on, or at least that they ought to exist. Such a view seems to be implied in references to "dirty tricks". Politicians are on the look-out for dirty tricks played by others, and are quick to assure others that they themselves are not playing tricks. Usually their existence is deplored, and they are frequently quoted as an explanation for a switch from one party to another less dirty party. But sometimes dirtiness is accepted as inevitable: "I am learning to be dirty in politics." Admiration for clever political moves, even if dirty, can lead to the statement, "There is nothing dirty in politics." It may even produce the classic, "To help to keep politics relatively clean, you have to be dirty sometimes." Finally, there was the candid comment: "sincerity is bad in politics, honesty is worse. I try to be 50 per cent honest and sincere, otherwise I cannot survive. Some others are 75 per cent dishonest, or 100 per cent."[10] Although tricks are expected, and even largely accepted, promises are supposed to be kept, at least in the short run, if only for pragmatic reasons. It is widely believed that a politician who persistently does not keep promises will not be trusted and that his career will ultimately suffer.

It might be supposed that the uncertainty of the rules would make politics dangerous; a politician could not calculate easily when to withdraw from a contest in time before he was decisively and publicly defeated. Moreover, in small communities like Sabah or Sarawak, conflicts cannot be impersonal, because the participants all know each other well. Any form of conflict could be perceived "as an expression of aggressive, personal hostility". The result of this combination might be to intensify the bitterness of politics and so engender violence, however in the Borneo states there has been very little violence. In point of fact, conflict, at least among leaders, is kept within moderate limits. To be sure, in small communities conflicts cannot be impersonal, but the inevitable personal conflicts are moderated by personal ties. Such ties, some possibly dating from school days,[12] cut across party lines. Others are formed when students from Sarawak or Sabah get to know each other well at a University abroad; when they return they form a "network of intellectuals". Blood relationships are supplemented by "fictitious" relationships. Middle-aged politicians may address older politicians or businessmen, sometimes of a different race, as "father". Sometimes an actual ritual of blood-brotherhood[13] is gone through, for instance that undertaken by Tun Mustapha and Dato Stephens. It is significant of the nature of the relationship between these two that social relations between them never entirely broke down during the period of greatest tension between their parties, from April to December 1967. They visited each other's houses during this time, although only at big receptions. They also played golf together twice, although the subject of politics was avoided.

Politicians who are defeated, displaced or disappointed are almost invariably offered compensation.[14] In 1963 Temenggong Sri Jugah did not become Governor of Sarawak as he had hoped, but he was made Minister for Sarawak Affairs. When Dato Stephens dissolved the UPKO he became High Commissioner for Australia. When Harris left Sabah and politics temporarily to study law in London, he went as *Dato* Harris. The first President of the Sarawak Chinese Association had a short tenure in that office, but was made "patron" of the SCA and later became Speaker of the Council Negri. Thus defeat or disappointment is sweetened, and the "difference between having power and not having power" does not become "so absolute as to affect the total well-being of the individual".[15] The rules of the game may not be clearly defined and conflicts may be personal, but most who do not win the top prizes, at least receive consolation prizes; the fight is carried *à l'outrance* only against some of those who are deemed to be subversive.

This interpretation still applies to Sarawak (August 1971), but has fitted Sabah less well since 1969. In that year, during the parliamentary elections, the state government began to be increasingly intolerant of opposition, and several Independent political leaders, including Yap Pak Leong, a member of the Legislative Assembly, were detained.

Personal ties among leaders, therefore, have helped to reduce political conflict and tension. They have made the application of uncertain rules less threatening, and in a sense have constituted a substitute for rules.

Symbols

According to Pye, in transitional societies the "affective or expressive aspect of politics tends to override the problem-solving or public-policy aspect".[16] The emphasis here is perhaps too strong to apply to Sarawak or Sabah, nevertheless symbols are indeed prominent in the politics of the two states. Names are important, symbolically. One of the arguments used against a proposed merger of Bumiputera and Pesaka which failed to go through in 1966, related to the new party's name; Parti Bumiputera, it is said, wanted "Bumiputera" to be part of the name of the combined party, but Pesaka objected, on the score that "Bumiputera" was a Malay word but not an Iban word.

A more protracted dispute about names in Sabah arose from the leading politicians in UNKO preferring the name "Kadazan" to the name "Dusun", although other Dusuns preferred to be called by that name.[17] Even when UNKO and Pasok Momogun merged to form the UPKO, some Pasok members still objected to the word "Kadazan" in the new title, and wanted it to be changed. There was a parallel dispute about the party symbol for UPKO. The former UPKO members, who came mainly from lowland areas, wanted to keep the *kerbau* (water buffalo)[18] as the symbol, while the former Pasok members, who came from interior highland areas where buffaloes were not common, wished to retain the Pasok emblem of a blowpipe and shield.

During the 1967 elections the UPKO and USNO symbols, the *kerbau* and Mount Kinabalu, respectively, were introduced on almost every possible occasion. Ingenuity was used, for example by UPKO supporters working in the broadcasting service trying to compensate for the fact that UPKO politicians had not been allocated any radio election broadcasts. They played over the radio a Kadazan song about the buffalo whenever they got the chance. The hypothesis might be advanced that during the 1967 election the party symbols performed the function of bridging the gap between the traditional and the modern. Familiar symbols such as the *kerbau* and Mount Kinabalu, it could be argued, were used to lead the electors to take an interest in the political issues of the day. Attractive as this hypothesis may seem, it has little truth in it. Electors were addressed by the parties in terms of the symbols, but most of the time the argument stopped there; it was conducted solely in terms of the symbols. The USNO said that the mountain was a holy place where the spirits of the dead dwelt; the spirits would be offended if the electors did not vote for "Kinabalu". The mountain was constant, while the *kerbau* could be led anywhere by the nose. The UPKO retorted by saying that the *kerbau* was a familiar and useful animal. Surely the electors didn't yet want to go to Kinabalu. It was only for dead people; for the present would they not prefer to live?

Such arguments may have helped to drive home the appeal of party symbols as such, but did little to relate them to the problems of Sabah. The other potent symbols which were prominent in the election were essentially appeals to fears or prejudices. Muslims were told that if UPKO won they would be forced to eat pork. Non-Muslims were threatened by the prospect of an ever-increasing expenditure on mosques if USNO controlled the new government. Where "modern" symbols were introduced, they were not understood too well. The story was current that a candidate who talked about "democracy" caused the electors to ask a subsequent speaker, "What is this *lima kerusi*?" (five chairs). In the district council elections of 1962–3 the Alliance parties themselves had shown their innocence of politics by proposing to adopt the clenched fist as the Alliance Party symbol.

After the USNO-SCA victory at the 1967 elections, the Government had the name of the state capital changed from Jesselton to Kota Kinabalu. The change, by discarding a "colonial" name, facilitated the process of nation building.[19] The choice of the new name had a number of implications. The mountain was already a state symbol, for instance it appears on the Sabah crest. It is also, as Tun Mustapha pointed out during the debate in the Legislative Assembly, sacred in the eyes of the Dusuns. However, "at least two or three of Tun Mustapha's enterprises are named 'Kinabalu'. Besides the USNO's mouthpiece is called 'Kinabalu Times' and the symbol of USNO during the General Elections is also 'Kinabalu' ".[20] Indeed the change was widely regarded as a way of paying tribute to Tun Mustapha; "we will be honouring him every time we pronounce or write the new name."[21] When the UPKO dissolved and its leaders joined USNO, the most common symbol used by politicians appeared to be development, which was combined with anti-colonialism by drawing attention to the colonial government's neglect of the rural areas. Subsequently the revival of the Philippine claim to Sabah led to symbols of military preparedness and of the will to resist aggression becoming pre-eminent.

Money and Politics

The chapter on elections described the expenditure of money from the output side. Another output is mentioned below, money spent on attempts to "buy over" individual politicians. The degree of competition between political parties and the high rate of expenditure in both states (at any rate before the dissolution of the UPKO) suggests that they had moved beyond the first, traditional, phase of political expenditure corresponding to a low level of economic, social, and political development, to another phase in which expenditure had increased heavily.[22]

The input of money needs to be examined in some detail. There were four major sources of money available to the parties in Borneo: parties in Malaya; rich local Chinese; rich local Natives; other. The first and last of these four categories may be quickly dealt with. Financial help from affiliated or sympathetic parties in Malaya was particularly conspicuous at election times. The assistance given between elections took the form mainly of visits of organizers and advisers, although the value of these could not, of course, be expressed in money terms. The last category applied substantially only to the SUPP, which raises a high proportion of its revenue through a large number of small donations or by receipts from funfairs. In other parties donations or subscriptions from members were of minor importance.

The other two sources of finance for the Borneo parties, rich local Chinese and rich local Natives, had differing degrees of importance in the two states. In Sarawak the Alliance, and SNAP when it was out of the Alliance, relied heavily on money from Chinese rather than on money from Sarawak Natives, although at the 1970 election the Alliance had some help from Tun Mustapha. The Sabah parties were also financed from Chinese sources,[23] but the two Sabah Native parties, USNO and UPKO (and also Pasok Momogun[24] before it joined UNKO to form UPKO) also had "Native" sources of supply. To understand why this was so, it is necessary to say something about the role of timber in Sabah politics.

Money and Timber in Sabah Politics

In retrospect Dato Stephens described timber as "in a way our biggest political curse".[25] To explain this statement it is necessary to look briefly at timber policy in Sabah.[26] A distinction is made between Reserved Forest (9,900 square miles in extent, mostly on the East Coast), where timber extraction is on a sustained yield basis over an eighty-year cycle, and other areas where timber removal is on a "once-and-for-all basis.

In the Reserved Forest area on Malaysia Day there were twelve concessions agreements for twenty-one year periods, eight to Chinese Companies (in one of which Dato Khoo had shares) and four to European companies. However, shortly before Malaysia was formed special licences for shorter periods had been granted to three companies in which Dato Stephens, Dato Sundang, and Tun Mustapha, respectively, were the principal shareholders.[27] The British intention was apparently to build up Native financial strength in order to lessen the economic gap between Natives and Chinese. The licences were the answer of the last British Governor to the demands of Native leaders who complained that, although the big European companies and the Chinese had been given timber land, Natives had not, because they were thought to be unfitted to manage licences. The solution envisaged was to give the licences to only a few capable top-level Native leaders, but for them to adopt a form of co-operative ownership in order also to benefit the small men.

The licences actually benefited "small men" in varying degrees; Dato Sundang's licence was not shared to any appreciable extent. The British also accepted the fact that much of the profit from the licences would go to the Chinese contractors, who removed and marketed the timber as annual licensees. However, there was an interesting political consequence, not directly planned by the British[28] The Native elite was so small that the three Natives chosen to receive the licences were prominent members of the Executive Council and also the heads, respectively, of the three new Native, or mainly Native, Sabah political parties. Consequently, it looked as if the licences were being granted at least partly in order to finance political parties.

Sabah politicians sometimes acted as if they indeed accepted the view that timber licences were intended to benefit not only those individuals who were in politics, but also the parties to which the individuals belonged. When Dato Yassin, who had been in England, came back to Sabah and joined the Cabinet, he requested that he also, as a prominent member of the former Executive Council, should be given a timber licence. His case was strengthened by the fact that UNKO and Pasok Momogun had amalgamated, with the result that the new party, UPKO, had two licences, while USNO, of which he was a member, had only one. He was therefore given a licence, bringing USNO's total to two. Later a timber licence was given to some prominent SCA members apparently on the understanding that some of the proceeds would be used for financing the party.

The massive injection of timber into politics, and vice versa, had important repercussions. Some money derived from licences was spent politically: at the same time politicians' appetite for timber grew. The areas covered by some licences were enlarged, or new licences were granted to additional politicians. Timber land could be given to politicians in exchange for less valuable rubber land. Two consequences followed. Some politicians came to regard timber as an easy way of making money, and being politicians they were sometimes in a position to acquire more timber. The ethical codes which applied were those of an open, frontier society. When

Dato Stephens was Chief Minister Dato Khoo's concession was increased from three to ten square miles. According to Dato Stephens, "I would have been happier if he was not a Minister of my cabinet at that time, but felt that the fact that he was should not be the reason for his company to be penalized".[29] The availability of money from timber increased the cost of politics and election expenditures. Politicians had both the money and the incentive to raise the stakes of their bidding for votes.[30]

Timber in Sarawak

Timber also played a political rôle in Sarawak. Some of the elite who had acquired timber in colonial times, such as Dato Ling Beng Siew, Dato James Wong, Tan Sri Jugah and Temeggong Oyong, later became prominent in politics. Others who became political leaders subsequently acquired timber. But there were some differences from the Sabah pattern. Before Malaysia no licences for really large timber areas were given to Natives, comparable to those given to Tun Mustapha, Dato Stephens, or Dato Sundang. After Malaysia licences were allocated,[31] although the top politicians were still not quite so aware of the potentialities of timber licences as were there counterparts in Sabah.

It was only in 1968 that a really large-scale concession in Niah provided for the needs of Sarawak politicians, in Party Pesaka, who were short of money, among other things for the forthcoming elections. The area concerned had been "frozen" as part of a general timber freeze by a previous minister, Taib, pending a survey by a United Nations team of experts.[32] However, later, with Taib out of the Cabinet (November, 1967) the deal went through, despite reports that the federal Anti-Corruption Agency might intervene: land, and the disposal of timber standing on land, was unambiguously a state subject. A further difference, compared with Sabah, was that the nature of Chinese involvement in the timber-politics complex was more intricate. Sarawak politics was more fluid and the number of possible governmental coalitions was greater. Chinese businessmen who were timber contractors were correspondingly more flexible in their political affiliations.[33]

As in Sabah, "timber fever" spread from the top down, and ministers became subjected to constant lobbying. *Penghulus* became interested in obtaining rewards for making favourable recommendations that licences should be given to applicants. Most Natives were not concerned with taking up shares in timber companies: they wanted hard cash or a licence which could be quickly converted into cash.

In the late 1960s, with the end of Confrontation and with more settled conditions in Indonesia, there were moves by timber magnates in both Sarawak and Sabah to acquire timber concessions across the Indonesian border in Kalimantan.

Money and Power: Native Politicians and Chiefs

A preliminary approach to money and power might be to consider the hypothesis that for the non-Chinese money was merely a means towards an end, namely power, while, conversely the Chinese valued power only as a means towards the end of increasing their wealth. Such a hypothesis would be based on two premises: that the "traditional" Natives would value power and status more than money, because they had not yet been fully integrated into money economy; that the Chinese, as a minority group in a Southeast Asian context, could not hope for much success in acquiring power but had a wide scope for making money, and would therefore value the latter pursuit to the exclusion of the former.

On this hypothesis, the Native politicians in the two states would resemble the chiefs on the West coast of Malaya around the middle of the nineteenth century.

> Malay chiefs controlled the economy of their districts because they needed the surplus above the producers' needs to sustain themselves and the armed following which was the basis of their power. Moreover they feared to allow anyone else to become rich and thereby have the potentiality of setting up a rivalry in power.
>
> Wealth being merely a means to an end was used to that end, i.e. for political rather than economic purposes. Most of the money which came into the hands of a Malay chief was used for an immediate political purpose, the maximization of his military power and prestige.[34]

The stereotype implied in the above hypothesis would be

misleading in several important respects when applied to Native politicians of the present day in the Borneo states. The suggestion is that a Native in politics originally possesses no wealth, but that he converts status and power into wealth, and then uses the wealth to "generate" more status and power. This view is false for three reasons. First, it should not be assumed that power is exercised only by those Natives who possess inherited status. To be sure, in the politics of the Borneo States, status is of great importance. It is widely deferred to, in the sense that a politician who ranks high in power may nevertheless have to make at least a token acknowledgement of the status of another politician who has less power, but who has also higher inherited status and is older. Status usually coincides rather closely with power. But this does not imply that only those Natives who have inherited status can acquire power, that the circulation of elites is zero or very small. What actually happens is that those who, without having status, acquire power, often quickly add status. The old Malay *Datus* in Sarawak were largely hereditary, thus the conditions for becoming a *Datu* were mainly ascriptive. But nowadays, although some of those who reached high political office, such as Temenggong, Jugah or, briefly, the Datu Bandar, already ranked high in status, others who were not already high in status were appointed (non-hereditary) *Datos* shortly after becoming ministers.

Secondly, there are prominent examples of Natives who had at least some wealth before they were top-rank politicians.[35] This was certainly true of Tan Sri Jugah and Temenggong Oyong[36] and also of Jonathan Bangau and Dato Donald Stephens. Even if a man entering politics did not have a business or a large amount of land, he might have other resources. Dato Ningkan and Thomas Kana, for instance, both had "retirement money" from their service with the Shell Company in Brunei which was substantial by Sarawak standards.

Third, it would be incorrect to suppose that Native politicians were concerned with power and status as ends, while they regarded wealth only as a means. To be sure, the attitudes of some Native politicians indicate, even nowadays, great pride in the number of their followers, expressed, for instance, in the often exaggerated claims they make for the membership of their parties. But it is easy to find Native politicians who are interested in wealth for reasons other than its being a means to obtain power. Politics is one of the most promising avenues to wealth for Natives who have the required political ability but who lack money and status.[37] A Native political leader may spend freely on entertainments at his home, to which hundreds are invited, and which have the effect of strengthening his political standing. But the same man may value wealth because it enables him to buy an expensive wrist-watch, a form of conspicuous consumption which brings no direct political advantage. Other Native politicians are clearly interested in politics.

A comparison of the different varieties of *Datus* and *Datos* is instructive. In imitation of the hereditary Malay *Datus*, the Brookes, and later the British, in Sarawak created life *Datus*, who were paid a salary. With the coming of Malaysia, no more of these were created, but "Datos" were appointed as in the states of Malaya. However, appointment as a *Dato* carried no salary. The assumptions underlying the change may have been that in former days *Datus* needed to be paid so that they could have the wealth necessary to match their status. But from 1963 onwards it was not necessary to make provision, through the payment of a salary, for ensuring that the wealth of *Datos* would match their status. Chinese who were given Datoships were already wealthy; indeed their route to Dato status had been via wealth. Natives who became *Datos*, if they were politicians, would already have had opportunities of converting power into wealth. Whether they were politicians or not, the status conferred by a Datoship would be useful in acquiring wealth.

Obvious signs of the importance attached to status and symbols of status are to be found at lower levels of politics. A good example concerns badges for native chiefs, a subject discussed at Native Chiefs Conferences in Sabah after Malaysia was formed. "All the members were dissatisfied with the design of the new badges for District and Native chiefs. The designs were not the ones accepted in the last meeting. Furthermore, they were too big, inclined 'to turn upside down' when worn, and the quality was poor compared with the previous issue. There should also be a difference between the District Chief and the Native Chief badges".[38]

But status is not the only value which is pursued at local level. The Native Chiefs' Conferences in Sabah in the mid-1960s showed that the chiefs were interested in a variety of items; some of these had status implications or would enable them to do a better job, but many indicated mainly a wish for material improvement. For instance, among their proposals were the following: promotions for Native Chiefs; telephones for Native Chiefs; salaries for *Ketuah Kampong*; attendance or duty allowance for *Ketuah Kampong*; mileage allowance for chiefs' outboard motors; free radio licences for *Ketuah Kampong*. Some of these requests looked at individually appeared justified from the point of view of enabling chiefs and *Ketuah Kampong* to work more efficiently. But the cumulative impression was that the Conference was becoming largely a forum for requesting a wide range of fringe benefits, including timber, which would help to enhance their status, but to a much greater degree would increase their wealth.

> A proposal that a Special Timber Licence be issued to Chiefs and Headmen covering the whole state was considered. The Conference strongly felt and recommended that such licences be issued jointly for Chiefs and Headmen of Sabah in order:
>
> (*a*) To raise the standard of living of the Chiefs and Headmen in equality with other races;
> (*b*) To unite and strengthen closer relations between the Chiefs and Headmen irrespective of race, religion or political differences;
> (*c*) To enable Chiefs and Headmen to assist their ra'ayat; and
> (*d*) To enable Chiefs and Headmen to make funds available for education and welfare assistance for their ra'ayat [people] who are badly in need of help.[39]

The reasons just quoted illustrate the widespread belief that timber could solve all the pressing problems of Sabah: economic disparities between different ethnic groups; ethnic integration at sub-elite level; poverty and low standards of education and welfare. This conviction was shared by many other groups; but, curiously, it was only the chiefs and headmen who thought that chiefs and headmen should be a chosen medium for spreading the benefits of timber. Their proposal was rejected by the Government. There was no evidence that chiefs would be capable of handling the timber industry or that, if they were given licences, the resulting revenue would be of substantial benefit to the Natives generally.

The Chinese, Money and Power

There are obvious reasons why Chinese with money in Sarawak and Sabah should be interested in politics and should support particular political parties. With the example of Indonesia in the Sukarno and immediately post-Sukarno period and of some other nearby countries in mind, they desire security to carry on business, and to have at least the same opportunities and safeguards as the Chinese have in Malaya. They also want to maximize their profits from business, and their contacts with government enable them to do this via, for instance, land or mineral concessions, government contracts, or, most important of all, either actual timber licences, or acting as contractors for timber areas allocated to Natives.

All this may be accepted as correct. But it leaves unanswered a perplexing question; why is it that some rich Chinese support a party through contributions and gain access to its leaders without themselves becoming actively involved in leading it,[40] while others go further and join "the front line" of party leaders? It would be quite possible for all Chinese capitalists to adopt the former course and, by analogy with the "Clandestine Communist Organization", constitute a "Clandestine Capitalist Organization". But this is not the universal rule; there are some instances where a "back mountain"[41] has taken up a position in the front line. Conspicuous examples are: Dato Ling Beng Siew and Dato Ling Beng Siong, Dato James Wong, and, for a time, Dato Wee Hood Teck in Sarawak, Dato Khoo Siak Chiew in Sabah. Even inside a family there may be a different approach. Two of the Ling brothers are in the front line of politics, the other four are not.[42]

In Sabah and Sarawak (as in Malaya) it is quite possible for Chinese to participate in "front line" politics, a situation which is in sharp contrast to most of Southeast Asia, where the Chinese, as "paraiah entrepreneurs",[43] are largely excluded from politics. Before 1963, under British rule, prominent

Chinese, such as Dato Ling Beng Siew, Dato James Wong, and Dato Khoo served in the legislative and executive bodies then in existence. And wealth, once power and official position had been gained, could be the basis for acquiring more wealth.

> As things are at present, economic strength is the path to social power. In other words wealth and political privilege go hand in hand. A financially powerful towkay [businessman] automatically gains a high social position, and social position, together with political privilege, in turn brings increased wealth. The circle is complete.[44]

This comment was written shortly after the end of World War II, when Sarawak was a colony and the highest political positions were not open to Chinese. But the point remains valid; wealth can be converted into more wealth indirectly, via power.

The conversion process does not operate crudely through particular ministries. The key ministry for the conversion of power into money in Sabah, and to a lesser extent in Sarawak, is obviously the one concerned with the allocation of timber licences. But in Sabah this ministry has never been headed by a Chinese, although from 1963 to 1964 the Minister was Richard Yap, then a far from affluent Sino-Kadazan. In Sarawak it was originally under Dato Teo, but since 1965 has been under a Native.[45]

Power does not seem to be dependent on the holding of any particular ministry; it seems rather to consist in membership of the Cabinet or in the inner circles of the ruling party. It was obviously important to Dato Ling Beng Siew to have his brother, Dato Ling Beng Siong in the Sarawak Cabinet, although the latter was successively Minister of State, and Minister for Youth and Culture, jobs which are completely removed from direct contact with any direct conversion process of power into money. Membership of the Cabinet, or the inner circles of the party, guarantees a share in the making of important decisions, and may enable the Cabinet member to alter them to his advantage by putting in a word to the right person at the right time. Furthermore, it is plain to others, including businessmen, that a Cabinet member has a share in the making of these decisions; indeed the importance of a

Cabinet member's power may even be exaggerated by outsiders, to his advantage. Such membership also ensures access to information, which may be a useful prerequisite for acquiring wealth.[46] Finally, quite apart from any direct effects, high status will have a general beneficial effect in making business operations more profitable.

The importance of being in the Cabinet, or having a close and trusted relative in the Cabinet, was illustrated by the insistence with which Dato Ling Beng Siew tried to get his brother, Dato Ling Beng Siong, back into the Cabinet in July 1970, after the SUPP had made it a condition of joining in a governmental coalition that the SCA should be barred from the Cabinet.

A good illustration of the general reinforcement effect of wealth and power is provided by the opening of the new building of the Hock Hua Bank in Sibu in March 1968. The Chairman of the Board of Directors was Dato Ling Beng Siew, and he and his brothers constituted almost half of the bank's directors. In the same issue of the *Sarawak Tribune* announcing the opening, a message was printed from Dato Ling Beng Siong (himself one of the directors) in his capacity as Minister for Youth and Culture, in which he was able to say that he had nothing but praise for the bank's management and its foresight in planning.[47]

In societies like Sarawak and Sabah there may be a special reason why an indirect approach to acquiring more wealth, which takes the form of acquiring more power, may sometimes be attractive. There is an element of insurance in such a choice. Unless a Chinese is actually in the inner councils of the Government, and preferably in the Cabinet, he cannot be sure that he is not being discriminated against by being excluded from possibilities of gain. Chinese in Sarawak and Sabah do not fall into Riggs's category of "paraiah entrepreneurs"; they are not wholly excluded from the elite, nor are they prevented from holding political office. But neither are the completely assimilated in the elite.[48] In Sarawak and Sabah they cannot occupy the highest power positions. To be sure, Peter Lo was Chief Minister of Sabah for over two years, and Dato James Wong and Dato Khoo Siak Chew have been Deputy Chief Minister in Sarawak and Sabah, respectively. Nevertheless, Tun Mustapha through his control of USNO, the largest party, was the dominant figure in Sabah politics while Peter Lo was Chief Minister. Moreover, in the powerful Federal Government it is Malays, not Chinese, who hold the ultimate power. Consequently, for the Chinese in Sarawak and Sabah wealth and power have an odd relation to each other. Perhaps just because Chinese cannot attain the *highest* power, in order to protect their wealth they are constrained to seek the *maximum* amount of power that the system will allow them to acquire. "Some people believe that money could do everything. I can tell you that money cannot do everything.... Undoubtedly the Chinese hold the economic power but economic power is not constant all the time, if you don't advance you will slip back. In order to protect our economic status we must take part in politics ..."[49]

However, the previous discussion has assumed that the desire to obtain wealth is the only reason why the Chinese seek prominent political positions. But this is not necessarily so. Chinese attitudes to politics in the two states may approximate less to pariah entrepreneur behaviour in some other Southeast Asian countries than to behaviour in traditional China, where power was highly esteemed as an end in itself.[50] In some instances it is hard to discern any immediate economic reward from front-line activity in politics. Dato James Wong, for example, has maintained convincingly that while he was Deputy Chief Minister, 1963–June 1966, he actually lost money because the pressure of his official duties prevented him from giving sufficient attention to the management of his business interests. Some Native politicians have expressed the contrary view, that the Chinese are interested only in money, in "grabbing" as much as they can in a short time. Certainly some rich Chinese really believe that "you can buy anything with money". They assume that politics is not very different from any other business, and that, just as the Aurora Hotel can be taken over and made to yield a profit, so the SCA can be made successful by investing money in it. Their image of politics as a business leads them to underrate the political ability of Ong Kee Hui, the SUPP leader, who has had some business difficulties in the last few years.

Other Chinese may not appear to be interested in anything except money, because they are simply incapable of distinguishing what is "economic" from what is "political"; they may just have expansive tendencies in all spheres. Mixed motives may often be discerned. It is true that, if a wealthy Chinese becomes a minister, his ministerial car is a status symbol which will bring a financial return to him in his capacity as a businessman.[51] But status may be relished for its own sake. Dato Ling Beng Siew was presumably not too displeased to hear the Sarawak Government referred to (at the period when he was backing the then Chief Minister, Dato Ningkan) as the "Ling Beng Siew Government". Apparently simple transactions may actually be complex, and show the dangers of "reductionism" when assessing motives. When Dato Ling Beng Siew bought the Aurora Hotel in Kuching in 1968, he probably made a good investment from the strictly economic point of view. But the purchase also had political significance; the hotel was a place where political receptions had been held and where big political deals had been concluded.[52] It thus had a power aspect, which to some extent could be converted to economic gain. But there were also considerations of status; it was Kuching's leading hotel, and after Dato Ling had bought it the block of buildings, of which the hotel was part, was given his father's name, spelled out in neon lights. Moreover, Dato Ling bought the hotel in a competitive situation and so derived satisfaction, presumably, because he had outbid a rival.

The purchase of the Aurora Hotel was perhaps a more complex transaction than some others. The fact remains that "purely economic" or "purely political" motives are probably rare.[53] As far as the SUPP moderate leaders are concerned, motives must be only partly economic, or even "anti-economic"; some of the policies they advocate are actually harmful to their economic interests or those of their class. Idealogy is undoubtedly another motive for seeking political prominence, as are the pleasure of being an arbiter in political disputes, the wish to be popular, the desire to defend Chinese culture, and "anti-Communism".

Another motive may be a sheer compulsion to compete in every possible sphere against a long-standing opponent. Original competition between opponents may have been in order to acquire wealth. But subsequent encounters may be conducted not only with an eye to material gains, but also to get the better of the opponent. The bitterness between pro-SCA and anti-SCA towkays during the 1967 elections in Sabah suggests this kind of motive, and was most clearly discernible in the long-standing rivalry between Kwan Yui Ming and Dato Khoo Siak Choo, based on a struggle for supremacy in business. It accounted for Kwan's support of the Independents and opposition to the SCA in general, and to Dato Khoo in particular.

In Sarawak a rivalry developed between Dato Ling Beng Siew and Dato Wee Hood Teck, described in the next section of this chapter.[54] Another extreme Sarawak antagonism arising from business occurred in 1969; Wong Tuong Kwang, who had at one time been a SNAP supporter, had long been in competition with the Ling brothers, particularly Dato Ling Beng Siew. Both were Foochows and both had timber interests based on Sibu. Dato Ling decided not to stand in the 1969 elections, but gave massive support to one of his brothers who was especially close to him, Dato Ling Beng Siong, who was chosen for the Igan constituency. In order to fight against the brother personally, and thus strike a blow at Ling Bieng Siew, Wong contested the Igan seat himself. To improve his chances by fighting under a party label, he joined the SUPP and managed to be chosen as the candidate—an expensive operation, which swelled SUPP financial resources for the election.[55] Comparable examples may be found in other countries, for example in the "continuing game of one-upmanship" between Aristotle Onassis and Stavros Niarchos in Greece.[56]

Dato Wee Hood Teck and Dato Ling Beng Siew

Dato Wee Hood Teck is an interesting example of a wealthy Chinese, who had held office in many organizations and had many charitable causes, but who originally had not sought political prominence. He had contributed financially to SUPP (Ong Kee Hui was his brother-in-law), but that was the limit of his political activities. However, he was persuaded, mainly by SCA leaders, to take a more active part in politics; he came round to the view that not all wealthy Chinese should be "in the front line" politically, but that some of them should, and that he himself should give a lead. He felt that the SCA was "dead", because the leadership was poor and there were hardly any rank-and-file members; he therefore joined SNAP, and in 1966 became Chairman of its new Kuching branch, which was formed in order to win recruits for the party in the First Division.

There was no obvious financial reason for Dato Wee to become politically active; it was not apparent that he would reap any benefits (for example through government contracts)[57] from doing so which he could not have received just by supporting the party financially. He was interested, however, in objectives which were not purely material, being a supporter of SNAP's multiracialist policy and being desirous of promoting new ideas, for instance on evening vocational training for young people. Dato Wee continued to support SNAP after it left the Alliance in mid-1966. He was a member of the top policy-making body in the party, although if SNAP had become the Government he would not have accepted a cabinet post; he had too many business commitments and there were too many potential conflicts of interest. But his decision to continue to play an active rôle in SNAP and to support it generously financially was weakened by the postponement of elections in Sarawak until after 1968, which increased his outlay on the party. Dato Wee may also have been worried by the fact that some sections of SNAP seemed to be increasingly anti-Malaysia, while he strongly supported Sarawak's continued presence in the federation. By late 1968 the financial drain was considerable, and he left SNAP without, however, joining the Alliance.[58]

Dato Wee's departure from front-line politics in SNAP did not mean that he gave up political interests entirely. To say the least, his resignation from SNAP did not damage his chances of obtaining some federal government contracts for supplies, which he was awarded shortly afterwards. His resignation was also accompanied by his selling some urban land, acquired when Dato Ningkan was Chief Minister, for federal government purposes at a rather good price. A few months later it was known that he had become one of the main contractors for the new timber licence in Niah, from which some Pesaka leaders were the main Native beneficiaries. His, brother, Wee

Boon Ping, who had been treasurer of SNAP, resigned at the same time as Dato Wee, and was also associated with him in the Niah arrangement. However, Dato Wee's new link with Pesaka, to which he had made some contributions even before Niah, was not exclusive. He continued to support financially some persons in SNAP, particularly Dato Ningkan.[59] In the SCA he also supported Dato Teo, who was not associated with the dominant Ling Beng Siew group. Allegedly, he also contributed lesser amounts, directly or indirectly, to individual politicians in the other two parties, particularly to some in SUPP. A similar spread of contributions was made by Wee Boon Ping and Wong Tuong Kwang, although they seem to have concentrated on supporting SUPP.

Such patterns of expenditure may be partly explained along the following lines. To some extent Dato Wee Hood Teck's outlay (and that of the other *towkays* mentioned above) represented a spreading of investment risks.[60] The political situation was so fluid that almost any combination of parties might form the next Government. As far as SNAP was concerned, Dato Wee may have felt a sense of obligation to the leaders, in particular Dato Ningkan, of the party in which he had been an office-holder. Some of the expenditure may not have been entirely voluntary; if one is known to have contributed to several parties, it is difficult to refuse a request from another party, although one may give only a token amount. Dato Wee's pattern of expenditure also reflected opposition to Dato Ling Beng Siew. In the early days of the Alliance Dato Ling had been its chief financial supporter. while Dato Wee had supported SUPP in a modest way. After Dato Wee switched to SNAP Dato Ling withdrew support from the party. So from 1966 to 1968 Dato Ling was supporting SCA, Pesaka and Bumiputera inside the Alliance, while Dato Wee was supporting SNAP outside it. Consequently, to sum up, after Dato Wee left SNAP, he "spread" his contribution among the various parties in the way described above, but with the main emphasis on certain Pesaka leaders, some SNAP leaders and one, anti-Ling group, SCA leader, Dato Teo. Dato Ling continued to support the three parties in the Alliance, the SCA, Bumiputera and Pesaka, but with a declining emphasis on Pesaka, as well as a SNAP dissident, Charles Ingka.

The view is sometimes expressed that Dato Wee is "more generous" in his spending than Dato Ling, meaning that he does not calculate the likely return on each cent invested in politics quite so closely. This would be equivalent to saying that his approach of political spending was "less businesslike" than Dato Ling's. This distinction seems to be borne out by the fact that Dato Wee supported SNAP financially on a generous scale for over two years, 1966–8, without any *immediate* return. If he had continued to support SNAP and SNAP had won the next elections, he would have received a return on what, on a Sarawakian time-scale, was a relatively long-term investment in politics. Equally, the benefits he actually received upon leaving SNAP may be regarded as returns on a long-term political investment.

Personal Political Organizations

Sometimes when a wealthy Chinese joins a party and decides to play a front-line rôle, there is an interesting organizational consequence. Instead of the politician contributing money to the party organization as a whole, to be spent as the party decides, he may choose to keep control over some of the money he spends politically, and in effect to create his own parallel personal political organization. In SNAP the organization in the Fourth and Fifth Divisions is largely Dato James Wong's organization, which he, not the party as a whole, pays for. Dato Ling Beng Siew has also done this to some extent by maintaining staff and offices apart from the official SCA organization. In effect these are examples of "partriarchalism" or "patrimonialism"[61] existing side by side with a bureaucratic organization.

Money and Politics: Conclusion

To summarize the argument on the concern for money and power shown by Chinese and Native politicians, respectively: it would appear that the differences between the two are much less pronounced than the rather simple stereotypes put forward earlier might suggest. Wealthy Chinese may have mixed motives for seeking front-line positions in politics, some of which may not be completely clear even to themselves. One of the most important is undoubtedly to increase their wealth. Those who are anxious to make really big money may choose the "political" route of seeking entry to the inner councils of a party or even to the Cabinet; in such a case political activity is really a form of investment. But, although Chinese politicians can, and do, derive financial benefits from front-line political activity, they may also enjoy power benefits. The proportion of Chinese in the population is higher, and the restraints preventing them from seeking power are weaker, than in other countries in Southeast Asia except Singapore. Nor are Native politicians solely concerned with the pursuit of power or status. Some have been exposed to the "demonstration effect" sufficiently for them to have developed a desire to tread the paths of entrepreneurship, or conspicuous consumption, or both. Through politics, often by means of timber, they have been enabled to follow these paths.

It is commonly assumed in the Borneo states that money is the main motivation of politicians, and that politics is primarily a way of making money. Particular ministers or ex-ministers who are believed not to have made money out of politics are pointed out as exceptions. To some extent such views malign politicians. The extent of their wealth may be exaggerated, and even a minister's official car, which strictly speaking does not "belong" to him, may wrongly be believed to indicate millionaire standing. Also some politicians, including Natives, who made money while they were in office, might have become just as rich without ever taking part in politics or supporting a political party. Tun Mustapha and Jonathan Bangau, for example, are said to have demonstrated great entrepreneurial ability. In a period of rapid economic development they would probably have become wealthy even without becoming politicians.[62]

However, when all qualifications have been duly noted, the broad picture is clear enough; money has been a corrupting influence in both states. Some of the classic factors making for corruption during a time of modernization have been prominent, notably the creation of new sources of wealth and power and the increase of political participation.[63] In Sarawak and Sabah the bureaucracy was largely untouched by corruption.[64] But among politicians and Chinese businessmen the same phenomenon was found as in Africa; corruption threw "a bridge between those who hold political power and those who control wealth . . ."[65] Also the high value which, for whatever reasons, politicians placed on obtaining votes, accustomed electors to seek favours and money. In Sabah particularly, the life and work of politicians were disorganized, and the electors, especially in the rural areas, sometimes tended to become parasites, not development-minded or pre-disposed to *gotong royong,* but just disinclined to work. The USNO-SCA pressure on the UPKO after the 1967 elections and UPKO's subsequent dissolution may be regarded as an inter-party struggle. But from another angle, the consequence of the contest was the formation of a monopsonistic "politicians' alliance" against the electors. Frightened by the magnitude of the "side-payments"[66] they had incurred, the politicians in effect made a pact to cease bidding against each other for support and thus limit their outlays.[67]

Violence

In both Borneo states there were numerous examples of violence before the formation of Malaysia, although between 1945 and 1963 it was on nothing like the same scale as in, say, Burma or the Philippines. Brooke rule in Sarawak had its origin in the existence of violence, which gave James Brooke the chance to show that he could impose order inside a small territory. The extension of Sarawak's boundaries was achieved only with the help of armed force, and there were local Iban "rebellions"[68] right up to the time of the Japanese occupation, which was the occasion for more violence. Existing traditions of violence were not reinforced by protracted conflict with the colonial power in order to achieve independence, as in some other parts of Southeast Asia. But in 1949 some Malays who opposed cession were responsible for the murder of the British Governor, and parts of Sarawak, particularly the Fifth Division, were affected by the Brunei rebellion of 1962. Just before Malaysia was formed the visit of the United Nations

Team to Sarawak was the occasion for riots in Sibu and Miri which were organized by elements in the SUPP. Confrontation with Indonesia threatened the Sarawak border, 1963–6. And up to the present time Communist influence has taken the form, not only of propaganda, organization and penetration, but of intimidation and activities actually causing death or injury. In mid-1970 it was estimated that there were about 500 Communist terrorists on the Sarawak-Indonesian border. In the first half of 1970, 79 had been killed, 56 had been captured and 16 had surrendered.[69]

Ethnic stereotypes in Sarawak would identify the Iban as the most extrovert and traditionally warlike members of the population. Reference has already been made to Dato Ningkan's uninhibited style of politics. Some older Ibans, such as Tan Sri Jugah, show animation in recounting stories of the wartime exploits of Ibans in collecting the heads of collaborators with the Japanese. Human heads still constitute the theme of macabre stories which are current from time to time. Just before Malaysia Day, it was rumoured that for a period of twenty-four hours there would be "no government" and that during this time the stock of old heads in longhouses might be replenished with impunity. In 1967 the story was spread that the Government had told its agents to seek out heads, preferably from children, to bury below newly-built bridges so as to ensure that they would be safe.

In Sarawak since 1963, apart from CCO activities, there have been demonstrations by Ibans in the Third Division against restrictions on felling timber, and in Kuching, in summer 1968, there were demonstrations on behalf of detainees, organized by SUPP, and counter-demonstrations by Parti Bumiputera. Potentially more serious, there were small demonstrations at the time of the Cabinet change in June 1966, which could have led to a serious outbreak of violence. The possibility of Malay violence if Bumiputera was excluded from the State Government to be formed in July 1970 was taken into account by the SUPP leaders when they decided to join the Bumiputera-led Alliance in preference to forming a coalition with SNAP and Pesaka. Actual violence, however, has been almost completely avoided.

Sabah has also had a tradition of violence, on a small scale.

In Tregonning's book on Sabah the title of an entire chapter is "Rebels", but the author points out that the resistance to the establishment of law and order by the British North Borneo Company was "of a minor kind", and that the most prominent rebel, Mat Salleh could boast only "of occasional bands of 200 men or more".[70] Violence continued, however, during and after the war with the Japanese. Smuggling is endemic on the East Coast and is sometimes accompanied by piracy; Semporna was actually sacked by pirates in 1954. Sabah felt the impact of the Brunei rebellion, although to a lesser extent than Sarawak. Confrontation with Indonesia was a threat to Sabah, and the Philippine claim, especially after it was revived in 1968, struck at Sabah's very existence as part of Malaysia.

The account of the Sabah 1967 election given in Chapter 4 indicates the potentialities for violence. These might have grown to unmanageable proportions during 1967 after the UPKO had lost the election and after Enche Payar Juman had defected; the demonstrations after the defection could easily have swelled and have led to communal clashes. Dato Stephens gave fear of racial violence as one reason for dissolving UPKO. Commenting on the dissolution of the UPKO, one of its younger leaders observed:

> At this early stage of political awakening in Sabah ... continued political division between the Natives as characterized by UPKO and USNO will inevitably create "bad blood" between the Kadazans and Muslim Sabah Natives. This means that the Kadazans as a whole shall be regarded as the Opposition sympathizers and are therefore guarded against and even victimized or discriminated against by the ruling party. It is genuinely feared that the only resulting consequence could be hatred and violence the differences between the UPKO and USNO were more on personality conflicts than policies and ideology.
>
> Only about 60 years ago, a party of Bajaus of Kampong Mengkabong (Tuaran) suspected of stealing buffaloes from Penampang was ambushed at Likas by the villagers of Kampong Gunsing, Penampang. One unfortunate Bajau was caught and beheaded by the Kadazan pagan warriors. The headhunting era is still fresh in the minds of elderly Kadazans who refresh their memories by telling glorious stories to the youngsters. The call of the gruesome yet romantic era of the headhunting period[71]

could have easily led the beleaguered Kadazans to desperate moves.

Apart from the CCO activities and the Brunei rebellion, actual violence has been slight.[72] To find an example of a "political" assassination one would have to go back to the murder of the Governor of Sarawak in 1949. However, apart from the actual use of violence, in both states there is a *tradition* of violence which could be invoked in modern times, possibly with serious results. A "traditional political resource" is still current, even if usually employed in the form of a threat. A brief speculation may be permitted on how nowadays the descendants of headhunters find the psychic satisfactions which their ancestors obtained in more violent ways.[73] Sport is an important outlet which was encouraged by the British in the Borneo states:

> Mr. Hose told the tribes of Baram that if they went on fighting each other there would soon be no more Kenyah, Kayan, Iban, Kelabit left in the district. Would they like to see their kinds disappearing? Hose was a good Resident. He told the tribes to come together and arranged for them a regatta. In the regatta they could show their prowess at boating. And he told them that if a boat capsized the others should pick [sic] the unfortunate paddlers instead of leaving them struggling in the water. He said that there should be a feeling of brotherliness among all.[74]

Competitive instincts may be expressed through cock-fighting or in litigation. Perhaps political competition, and in particular election campaigns, are another such outlet. The problem is to devise a *controlled* outlet, and in the Sabah election of 1967 there were times when electioneering nearly got beyond control. The decision to "suspend" the elections already begun in Sarawak and Sabah in 1969 presumably resulted partly from the fear, probably unjustified, that the racial violence which had broken out in West Malaysia might be followed by similar violence in the Borneo states.

Constraint and Inducement: Constrained Beneficiaries

The limited extent of overt violence in Sarawak and Sabah and the undeniable increase in corruption in the two states in recent years, prompt the question whether the latter might not be in some sense a substitute for the former. Scott suggests that, to the extent that corruption allows important interests which are blocked from formal participation to participate informally, it may be regarded as a deterrent to politically motivated violence.[75] This does not quite fit the Sarawak or Sabah cases. Corruption has been confined mainly to: (*a*) politicians; (*b*) Chinese big businessmen; (*c*) small beneficiaries from timber concessions; (*d*) individuals who have been paid for their votes, or in the case of headmen, etc. for the votes of others. However, (*a*) were not blocked from formal participation, and in some cases they participated mainly in order to enjoy the benefits of corruption. The first part of the Scott hypothesis might apply to (*b*), although it has been pointed out in this chapter that Chinese businessmen do enjoy a fair degree of political participation as well as economic participation. It would appear that violence is simply not an available political resource for Chinese businessmen. As regards (*c*) and (*d*), it is doubtful if corruption is a substitute for participation. Those concerned are probably mostly still without a felt need to participate. As with politicians, their participation, to the extent that it exists, has actually been stimulated by the prospect of timber or of payment for votes. Corruption is often an expression of, not a substitute for, their participation.

Too little research has been done on the relation between violence and corruption to permit firm generalizations. In Sarawak and Sabah the two are not mutually exclusive.[76] There are examples of the use of protective force, or constraint, *combined with* persuasion, often with a financial element. Simple offers of money (and their acceptance) are fairly common—for instance, offers to Independents elected to Sarawak district councils in 1963, or to headmen and party workers during the 1967 and 1969 state elections in Sabah and Sarawak, respectively. But in some few instances force, or at least apparent constraint, and some form of persuasion are used jointly on a politician.[77]

The most obvious case is that of Payar Juman, who in late 1967 left the UPKO and joined the Alliance Government as a Minister. Payar benefited from becoming Minister of Welfare, and also, according to one allegation,[78] from being given timber land. However, in addition, after his resignation from UPKO he left Sabah for Kuala Lumpur and stayed there for several weeks. Dato Stephens "regretted Payar's action and was still doubtful in his own mind as to whether Payar had done what he had done without pressure and duress. He said Payar had no friends in Kuala Lumpur and the whole thing looked almost like abduction. Payar had never been afforded the opportunity of talking to his people since he was whisked away to Kuala Lumpur more than a month ago."[79]

A somewhat similar case occurred in Sarawak after the 1963 district elections. An Independent councillor who was elected for the Binatang District Council was favourably inclined towards the Alliance Party. He was a key figure, because otherwise SUPP and the Alliance were equally represented on the Binatang Council, and the control of that council could be crucial in obtaining control of the Third Division Advisory Council and even of the Council Negri. The Independent was therefore offered inducements to ensure his loyalty to the Alliance, but at the same time was taken to a house belonging to a prominent Alliance leader and later on a tour of Malaya, in order to prevent his defection.

Two other examples are less obvious, but an element of protection, if not coercion, could nevertheless be discerned. The members of the Council Negri who signed a petition against Dato Ningkan in June 1966, and then went to Kuala Lumpur and sent a telegram demanding his resignation, were kept incommunicado at certain times, for example in ministers' houses on their return to Kuching from Kuala Lumpur, thus combining persuasion and protection.[80] Finally, SNAP had a special problem about their candidate for the Pelagus by election in 1967. He had previously been Pesaka's choice as a candidate. Consequently, during and immediately after the period when he was being persuaded to stand as a SNAP candidate, he was taken to Kuching for a few days to insulate him from influences which might have interfered with the process of consolidating his loyalty to his new party.

In all four examples the political stakes were high. Payar Juman's defection was needed to break the soldarity of the UPKO; the Binatang Independent's support was needed to assure control of the Binatang District Council and perhaps also the Third Divisional Advisory Council and the Council Negri; unless the 1966 signatories held firm, Dato Ningkan might have won over enough of them to regain a majority in the Council Negri: unless SNAP could win quick by-election victories it could not build up sufficient strength to hope to win at the next state elections.

There are other possible examples of the combination of constraint, or protection, and inducement.[81] But those which have just been described are enough to bring out the point that this combination existed. A possible explanation might be that in the fluid state of politics in Sarawak, and until 1968 in Sabah, it may not always be sufficient just to persuade or induce a man to switch his support to a political party or group. A shift in allegiance may quickly be followed by a reverse shift. On truly important occasions an additional guarantee is needed to ensure that the beneficiary in the transaction will not change his mind, that he will not re-defect. This assurance can be provided by "protection" which will temporarily restrict his movements, so insulating him from the attentions or rival political parties or groups. For a time he is a "constrained beneficiary". This kind of practice resembles a "transitional" compromise between the "traditional" use of force and the "modern" use of money or rational argument. Too blatant a use of violence would be condemned, but persuasion alone or persuasion plus money could not be relied on to attain its object.

8

Political Development in the Borneo States

The term "political development" has been used and abused in many different ways. It has become the fashion to refer to it in any study of a non-Western country, sometimes without defining it precisely. The authors of this book do not believe that political development can be defined in any way which is both simple and useful.[1] But, for purposes of interpretation and comparison, it is proposed to examine the political changes that have taken place in Sarawak and Sabah since 1963 in the light of various defiinitions of development that occur in the relevant literature.[2]

Although there are so many definitions, quasi-definitions, or evasions of definition, in the political development literature, there is some area of common ground. Analytically, it is possible to distinguish three broad approaches. One is to see political development in terms of modernization, meaning borrowing from "the West," or, more recently, Japan. A second approach goes beyond the first in investigating the extent to which patterns of behaviour regarded as "modern" are replacing patterns regarded as "traditional". The standard used here for comparing political behaviour would not be the behaviour prevailing in a Western country; it would be an abstract standard of political development, based, for example, on the degree of structural differentiation and/or cultural secularization.[3] A third approach is concerned with the capability of a government to perform certain functions or cope with certain problems. A variation of the third approach would regard political development in terms of *general* capability and performance, as opposed to capability in respect of particular functions or problems.[4]

These three approaches will be used in turn in considering the nature of political change which has occurred in Sarawak and Sabah. But, although this procedure has been adopted for the sake of simplicity, the goal is not *over*-simplification. In all three approaches conflicts and contradictions may be apparent. The aim is not just to list the changes in Sarawak and Sabah, and tick off, in catalogue fashion, those which are examples of political development. Neither is it to produce a bright new theory of political development, based on the study of under two million living people. It is rather to apply the existing theories and hypotheses in order to throw light on the changes; in turn, this application may suggest some strengths and weaknesses in the theories.

Modernization

In the first approach we are concerned with borrowing from, or imitation of, other cultures, usually "Western" ones. ". . . I mean by modernization a type of emulative acculturation in which cultural practices, institutional forms, and technologies are consciously borrowed or adapted by one society from another".[5] The emphasis in this section is on the activity of borrowing rather than on the reasoning, or rationality, behind it. Imitation may range all the way from adoption of particular habits, such as the cultivation by a Native District Officer of his former British superior's precise movements in filling his pipe, to adopting a different life-style from the traditional, accompanied by a belief in the desirability and possibility of changing the environment, or organizing and directing others in order to change it.[6] Initially, the approach is descriptive, to illustrate how modern influences have impinged on existing structures and cultures. At this stage there are references to what is "modern" and what is "traditional". Later, the rationale behind the borrowing is examined, and it is also argued that in Sarawak and Sabah, as elsewhere, there is no necessary incompatibility between "traditional" and "modern" elements.

Impressions about political modernity may be formed by observing the different profiles of politicians and parties. Even the appearance of a politician may suggest an impression; for instance the *hairstyles* of Tan Sri Jugah and Temenggong Oyong, born in 1903 and 1896 respectively, are suggestive of their *political styles*. Tan Sri Jugah's political appeal is chiefly to the older "long hairs" among the Iban. Such traditional leaders, with no formal education, face severe limitations when engaging in politics where the vast majority of the contestants have better facilities for gaining information; pre-literacy and lack of knowledge of English make for dependence on others in this respect. Tan Sri Jugah has a good business sense, and has shown a capacity for innovation in his agricultural methods, but his style is conditioned by his upbringing and by the traditional offices he has held. He is at his best in a situation which demands action, or in discussion in small groups. He can be tough and decisive, for instance on the removal of Taib from the Sarawak Cabinet in 1967; in other political contexts he may be less effective. More specifically, in the 1965 Sarawak cabinet crisis, Tan Sri Jugah was in some difficulty because of statements prepared for him by others which he could not check.[7] It has also been said that, although he signed a document in 1963 agreeing that the Head of State and the Chief Minister in Sarawak could not both be Ibans, he did not understand its precise nature.

Other politicians have more modern profiles, for example Dato Harris (who has had two periods of office in the Sabah Cabinet), born in 1930, a former civil servant, who was trained in Australia. The most obvious symptom of his modernity was his interest in flying; he held office in the Sabah Flying Club, and, along with other members, distributed leaflets from the air in 1967 urging potential electors to ensure that their names were placed on the electoral register in preparation for the approaching state elections. He drove a Jaguar E-type, reputedly the only one in Sabah. His efforts in organizing SANYA, a youth organization, also suggested modernity. Dato Harris exhibited many modern attitudes as a minister. He was critical of attempts to increase the number of Native Chiefs, even though chiefs had their political uses, and of the wasteful expenditures incurred in electoral campaigning. He would have much preferred that the money had been spent on development. In his tours of the countryside he was not complacent about the progress of development schemes, but openly attacked non-modern attitudes. When on tour he rebuked Natives for drinking too much when they should have been working, and was distressed at seeing vehicles owned by individuals rusting because they were seldom used; he suggested that in future the owners should buy fewer vehicles and pool them.[8]

Other stereotypes are not so obviously either modern or the reverse. When he was appointed Head of State in Sabah in 1963, Tun Mustapha, a Native Chief descended from the Sultans of Sulu, with only one year's formal schooling, might have appeared to be a traditional figure.[9] But with his switch to the position of Chief Minister, via the post of Minister for Sabah Affairs, his Suluk dress with pearl buttons, worn on formal occasions as Head of State, was replaced by Western dress. Tun Mustapha also owns property in England, and makes frequent visits there. He is one of the wealthiest men in Sabah, if not the wealthiest, and his style of entertainment in Sabah is lavish. His political donations have extended beyond Sabah and even beyond Malaysia. There are some signs of modernity in his reorganization of the system of native chiefs. And his "modern" electioneering style at the 1967 elections, when he made trips to his constituency by (Government) helicopter, contrasted with the style of Richard Yap, his opponent, who fought a less-well-financed grass-roots campaign. Certainly Tun Mustapha has important prerequisites for promoting modernity, if convinced that he ought to do so. He has a stern and dominating personality—"there is room for only one mountain in Sabah"—and has insisted on assuming personal control over what he regards as the key institutions in the State, for example the youth movement. When he has definitely made up his mind to do something, he is totally committed to seeing that it is carried out. He also has boundless energy:

> Today I am 50 years old. I have lived for half a century now. It sounds so ancient, so old, but I have never felt that I am more than 30. Often below that. And I challenge any of the young men within that age bracket to challenge me in any matter that requires energy and vitality and, believe me, I can easily win over my opponents without any difficulty.... As many of you know, this is not merely a tall story. This matter had been tested over again and again and as I have said earlier anybody who dares to challenge me can step forward now.[10]

Some of Tun Mustapha's energy has been devoted to the

drive for rural development, and has been compared with Tun Razak's notable efforts in Malaysia.

Dato Ningkan, a former chief Minister of Sarawak, is two years younger than Tun Mustapha. His ebullience, indicated earlier,[11] was based on a high degree of personal and political confidence and courage. According to his critics, his efficiency as a Chief Minister was affected by an inclination towards conspicuous consumption, and there were allegations that, when in office, he neglected "grass roots" politics. He obviously had a quick mind and administrative ability, and showed considerable skill in making good use of advisers. In opposition, when there were fewer demands on his time, Dato Ningkan toured the rural areas more often than before and built up an elaborate party organization which commanded much popular support. The party organization was modelled on his experience in the police and on his reading of books on military strategy, particularly on the campaign in the Western desert in World War II. From these came his use of military terminology and the invention of party code-words, such as "Operation Bulldoze" or "Operation Vampire". Dato Ningkan was clearly fascinated, almost to the point of obsession, by the complexity and elaboration of the party structure he had created. "The party organization is just like a civil service." Combined with this was a belief in certain traditional "charms", which would ensure invulnerability; he attributed his protection from danger when travelling over a road, on which a bomb had been planted, to this source.[12] Dato Ningkan does not rely for protection solely on such devices; he also often carries a loaded pistol.

There is nothing odd in an individual holding beliefs which are traditional at the same time he holds beliefs which are modern. Many well-educated persons in "developed" countries place great reliance in astrology. Dato Ningkan, with a secondary-school education, is well-educated compared with the average politician in Sarawak or Sabah. But one politician who has a University degree is open-minded about the power of traditional methods to ensure invulnerability. Referring to the belief that a prominent traditional method of acquiring it did not work if one went to communion, he remarked, not altogether as a joke, that in that case X, another politician, who had recently been to communion, could not really have achieved invulnerability, although sometimes it seemed as if he had.

Given that a particular politician's belief and attitudes combine the traditional and the modern in certain proportions, he may wish to project a public image in which the emphasis is deliberately modified. A politician who for a time was a cabinet minister in one of the two states was a good example of this. His behaviour was much less modern than might have been expected from the elaborate operations map on the wall of his office, which had no obvious purpose except to indicate an overt concern for modernization and development.

Sometimes a politician may wish to stress the traditional element, because he feels that otherwise his image would be "too modern". A good example is Haji Abdul Taib bin Mahmud, a Melanau (and nephew of Dato Rahman Ya'akub), who was formerly a minister in Sarawak, later an Assistant Federal Minister, then Federal Minister. Taib has a degree from Australia, and has made contributions to the Council Negri debates of which few others would be capable; for instance, in the course of a single speech he alluded to the views of the English legal authority, Dicey and to the constitutional relationship between France and Algeria.[13] He has a flexible mind, which is open to receive information from any quarter, and is quick to see future possibilities, for instance in his long-term plans for the use of Sarawak's timber resources. He appears to be interested in ideas and planning as well as in actual administration. However, he has to behave with circumspection. Non-Muslims tend to see him as a channel of federal influence on Sarawak. Many Chinese regard him as anti-Chinese. Muslims are aware of his western education, his comparative youth (he was born in 1936) and the fact that he is a lawyer. It is to his advantage that his European wife is a Muslim, and that he has a genuine interest in Malay literature and in composing *pantuns.*[14] But it would damage his image among Muslims if, for example, he were to speak Malay with a "western" accent, or if on certain traditional occasions he dressed in too western a fashion. He made a point of not becoming a Haji until 1971; an earlier journey to Mecca might have been considered premature.

There are differences in the styles of parties as well as in the styles of individual politicians. Some of these were described in Chapter 3, for example the varying degrees in which parties are dependent on the branch system. As has been pointed out, much depends on the nature of the support which a particular party has. If, like Pesaka, it is strongly backed by *Penghulus* or chiefs who are capable of influencing most electors, then there is no need to set up an elaborate party organization. If the support of *Penghulus* and chiefs cannot be counted on, then the party must create its own organization, as SUPP and SNAP have done.

There are also different styles of behaviour, as opposed to formal organization, which derive from the nature of the party's support. Pesaka, for instance, is conservative (as its name implies), gentlemanly, authoritarian and paternalistic. When the possibility of television's being introduced into Sarawak was discussed, some of the leaders were opposed, because, quite apart from considerations of cost, they feared that it would damage Native customs, such as traditional dances. The party was also opposed to the indiscriminate encouragement of tourism.[15] Pesaka prefers to put its point of view to the Federal Government quietly and by means of deputations,[16] rather than by public statements which might raise the political temperature, as SNAP sometimes did.

SUPP, an ideological party, some of whose members are Communist-influenced, has a quite different style. Its "activists" are more active than the activists of other parties, and (within the limits allowed by the Government) there is an emphasis on rallies and demonstrations. In Sabah there was no great difference between the style of the USNO and the UPKO. The greatest impact at the 1967 election came from the style of the Chinese Independents who were said by their opponents to have adopted a "PAP-style" or even "Red Guard style" of campaigning, with young people shouting at their rallies and, allegedly, writing slogans on walls.

Sabah election campaigning in 1967 provided interesting juxtapositions of the traditional and the modern. Especially in the rural areas it was useless to try to debate issues which were in any way complex. That is why the campaign tended to be fought mainly on obviously prominent religious and ethnic issues. However, candidates could also make an appeal by their style of campaigning and by selecting the "mix" of the modern and the traditional which they thought would be most effective. As was said of the 1968 elections in New Guinea, many candidates, "in effect, ran two campaigns. On the one hand, they sought support in relatively traditional terms, while, on the other hand, they gave speeches and distributed policy statements in accordance with modern electoral practice."[17] In rural areas polaroid cameras were used to photograph groups of voters, sometimes in front of a party symbol. In remote areas candidates were sometimes asked for medical help, mostly for children, and responded by dispensing aspirin. But there was also reliance on the traditional. Some UPKO candidates received blessings from Kadazan "priestesses"[18] in a traditional ritualistic setting which included eating, drinking and dancing. As a further illustration of the interpenetration of the traditional and the modern, the priestesses' blessings were sometimes tape-recorded by the candidate and played back to the audience. Polaroid cameras and tape-recorders were also used during the Sarawak campaign in 1969.[19]

The above illustrations concern parties and politicians, but it is also possible to give "administrative" examples of a confusion of styles. One of these occurred during a tour of a ward of the Kuching Rural District Council by the Sarawak Minister of Local Government and officials.

> Being aware of the absence of a jetty at Sambir and at Tembirat, the District Officer confidently set out barefooted so as to be able to negotiate the mud flats and slippery trunks that serve as walk-ways. This was thought to be a brilliant idea by the other members of the party and all were rather pleased to be barefooted. However, the local people had prepared a special walk with tree trunks three hundred yards long so that the visitors would not need to take their shoes off. To crown it all, the *kampong* worthies were in their Sunday best leather shoes, lounge suits and tie, and the only people bare-footed were the Minister, the District Officer and the Principal Assistant Secretary![20]

Modern and Traditional Influences

It is possible to speculate about the degree of modernity of

Sarawak or Sabah as compared with elsewhere. Politicians who have operated in Malaya as well as one of the Borneo states say that in the latter a more traditional approach is indicated in political campaigning and that issues have to be put in very simple terms. But there are great differences in the degree of modernity, generally not just politically, inside either of the Borneo states, which parallel internal differences in the statistics on communications, literacy, consumption of electric power and so on. Sabah is not "a unified society or economy, but a complex of scattered elements, partly modern, partly backward, with most somewhere in between".[21] This is not just because urban areas differ from rural areas. Each ethnic group's stereotype implies varying degrees of modernity. Chinese are regarded as more modern than Natives. Inside the category of Natives in Sabah, Penampang Dusuns are thought of as more modern than Rungus; in Sarawak the stereotype of the Iban is a more modern one than that of the "minority races". Sub-categories have sub-stereotypes. Second Division Iban are reputedly more modern than Third Division Iban. There are sub-categories even among the Chinese; when the then Acting Chief Minister of Sarawak, a Muslim, urged the villagers of Kampong Semera to acquire some of the modern virtues of the Chinese he specified the sub-category of the Foochows as particularly worthy of emulation.[22]

In conducting party warfare, in framing policy, and in administration, the relation between modern and traditional influences must be assessed, although it is far from simple. Myrdal believes that modernization ideas are dynamic and interventionist, while traditional valuations are static.[23] But this view is disputed by Ward and Rustow, who attack "the widespread illusion that traditional society is some sort of *tabula rasa*, an inert and plastic mass ready to be activated and shaped by the modernizing impact of the West".[24] In Sarawak and Sabah the inland tribes, because of restricted communications, might be thought to have been the most conservative and traditional. However, this supposition is contradicted by Tom Harrisson, who wrote on Sarawak: "There is archaeological evidence that in the past there were changes of fashion and what one might call consumer unrest. The idea that there has been a rigidly stable, conservative outlook among these hill tribes in Borneo is unfounded even in short terms . . ."[25]

Some traditional beliefs certainly die hard. In one area of North Borneo, although changes in some forms of dress, tools, weapons, and housing began during the early period of the British administration under the North Borneo Company, "the core of belief in religious behavior, omens, luck, sickness, death, social behavior, property, law, and subsistence remained generally unchanged until the decade prior to World War II".[26] Even in the 1950s there was said to be duality of belief among Penampang Dusun Christians, who still attended pagan feasts, hesitated to ignore evil omens and believed in the interpretations of dreams and old superstitions.[27]

Educated Natives may leave outsiders guessing about the depth of their traditional beliefs. An Iban who is academically expert on ritual may comment on the way in which some particular ritual was conducted by saying that the procedure was incorrect in a certain respect, so how could the performers hope that it could be effective? Attachment to tradition is especially strong where religion is involved, for instance, in particular ethnic groups, in relation to rice-growing or the preservation of human heads in longhouses. During British rule when Temenggong Koh was told by an official to remove the heads from his longhouse, "he flatly refused, because he said these 'trophies' were necessary to the proper conduct of his religion. When the official threatened to destroy them, the Temenggong retorted by saying: 'If you do this, I shall go to your fort and throw away all your books and documents.' The 'trophies' stayed".[28]

The persistence of traditional beliefs, even among the educated, is not surprising and could easily be matched by examples taken from Western countries. What is harder to determine is the extent to which certain traditional beliefs should be discouraged. To Western eyes some cases seem to be fairly obvious. Malcolm MacDonald[29] has described how Kayan and Kenyah beliefs about the unclean nature of child delivery, forced pregnant women to give birth under unhygienic conditions which led to high rates of infant and maternal mortality. Similarly, when the Yang di-Pertua Negara of Sabah warned the Native Chiefs Conference to discourage sick people from preferring witchcraft to hospital treatment, the traditions he was attacking could be condemned as harmful to health. However, it may sometimes be dangerous to accept innovations uncritically. At the same Conference the Sabah Head of State also asked the chiefs to try to convince the kampong folk to accept the spraying of DDT in their houses in order to curb the spread of malaria.[30] Recent discoveries of the adverse effects of DDT in the West suggests that resistance to innovation should not invariably be condemned.

At times it may be difficult to tell whether opposition to change arises from tradition and superstition, or whether tradition is invoked mainly in order to strengthen objections which are not traditional. When it was proposed to change the *Tamu* (Market) held every ten days in Inanam (Sabah) to a weekly *Tamu*, it was claimed that the change would be an insult to the "Spirit" to whom a buffalo was slaughtered each *Tamu* day. But much of the opposition to the switch was based on logistical grounds: those attending the *Tamu* from remote *kampongs* had to travel long distance to it, and it would be difficult for them to collect their jungle produce and travel to and from the *Tamu* within one week.[31]

The longhouse, a traditional form of organization among some non-Muslim Natives, particularly in Sarawak, has often been quoted in arguments on modernization. Much of the case against it as being too traditional rests on its association with shifting cultivation, which is no longer appropriate to a greater density of population, and to an increasing demand for goods and services beyond the capacity of a subsistence economy to produce.[32] Shifting cultivation may have other adverse consequences: the illegal occupation of land and the illegal felling of timber which sometimes result; the problem of providing services, such as communications and education, for a scattered and itinerant population. For these reasons the break-up of longhouses which is now occurring represents an abandonment of a traditional form of life unsuited to modern requirements. But it would be incorrect to regard this change as a symptom of growing individualism. To be sure, the longhouse was a community in some respects. There was some "sharing", for example of fruit from trees near the longhouse or of pigs which had been hunted and killed. Optimistically, the SUPP has sometimes pointed to these aspects of longhouse life as evidence of the traditional socialist practices. But actually, even inside the longhouse, individualism is dominant. "Ibans are essentially individualists, and on their own are capable of much initiative, but compressed within the archaic framework of longhouse society their opportunities are blighted."[33]

Individualism was carried to extreme lengths during the rubber boom arising from the Korean war; several separate families in the same longhouse might each have an outboard motor, showing a lack both of a spirit of community and a spirit of economy.

The nature of the cultural changes now occurring in Sarawak and Sabah can be only a matter of speculation. Rather obviously, attitudes to education are changing. Some Natives still need to be officially persuaded to send their children to school, but more and more are becoming aware of the advantages of education.[34] Less obviously, MARA officials report that their efforts to encourage the buying of shares are meeting with success even in rural areas.

In one broad field a little more evidence is available: the relation between effort and reward and those governmental policies affecting this relation. Foster has suggested that in Latin America economic development has been retarded because the peasants "view their social, economic, and natural universes—their total environment—as one in which all of the desired things of life . . . exist in finite quantity and are always in short supply as far as the peasant is concerned". Economically, the peasant view is very near the truth, mainly because of the shortage of land. No obvious relation is apparent to him between work and wealth.[35]

Recently Foster's concept of "limited good" (in more concrete terminology, "constant pie") has been put forward as an explanation of the behaviour of some Malayan civil servants.[36] The concept of limited good does not seem to apply very closely to Sarawak or Sabah. Scott himself refers to the fact that slash and burn agriculture (shifting cultivation) "where there is little population pressure, offers some chance to leave the community and strike out on one's own".[37] There is not the same general shortage of land in Sarawak and Sabah as there is in Latin America.[38] Apart from this, it is probably incorrect to say that in the Borneo states effort is inhibited because the relation between reward and effort is perceived to be discouraging. It might be truer to hypothesize: (*a*) that in some few cases rewards are not known to be possible; (*b*) more frequently, some rewards are believed to be attainable almost independent of effort. The reason for the second belief is that expectations of benefits which would arise almost automatically from joining in Malaysia were stimulated by federal and state politicians, 1961–3. "Many simple people believed that it would be cake for tea every day after Malaysia," as an expatriate Resident phrased it.[39] The expectations were partly fulfilled, but were given additional stimulation by the device of Minor Rural Projects (MRPs).[40] In both states, but in Sabah in particular, these expectations were reinforced when it was seen that politicians and others were receiving timber licences, conferring vast rewards for little or no effort.[41] "I came away (from the Conference of Native Chiefs) with the feeling that several of the East Coast Chiefs thought that timber profits should be a sort of *Merdeka* [Independence] bonus and that Rural Development could equally be financed by some other source."[42]

Another reward, obtainable without much effort, consisted of the money distributed during elections in exchange for casting one's vote in a certain way, described in Chapter 4. These rewards, however, were rather in the nature of windfalls, similar to the unpredictably large crops of illipe nuts[43] which occur from time to time. Elections, however, and political campaigning generally, do provide a corrective to unlimited expectations of benefits. In criticizing each other, parties denounce their opponents' promises as unrealistic, thus contributing to the scepticism and the education of the electorate.

Consequently, there seems to be no simple way of generalizing about how the relation between effort and reward is regarded. It would be correct to assume, however, with Lucian Pye, that politically significant sections of the population do not know what the relation is.[44] They may vacillate between belief in constant pie and belief in pie which drops from the sky, although neither concept provides an accurate guide to the amount of pie they would actually receive for any given effort.

Those government policies in Malaysia which broadly may be described as "economic" are not designed solely to increase output. Indeed a perceptive writer on rural development in Malaya has distinguished between output and cultural goals, and has used these concepts in analysing the Federal Government's programmes.[45] The distinction between the two types is not always easy to make. One could imagine, for example, a situation in which it was desired to improve output, but where the approach chosen was through inducing cultural changes, believed to have no important value consequences or side effects but simply expected to increase output. The choice of trying to induce cultural changes in order to increase output, instead of attempting to increase output more directly, would correspond to a decision to invest in a lengthy and roundabout process of production rather than a shorter one. So, although a cultural goal would be selected, it would be chosen not for any intrinsic value, but because it was judged to be the most appropriate means for achieving an output goal.

To some extent land settlement schemes come into this category.

> The aim of the Land Development Scheme Programme is to help new communities achieve a new way of life by adopting a progressive way of earning a living. The objective is to induce the rural people to change over from shifting cultivation to an intensive and permanent form of agriculture. This will enable them to get a relatively high return from their work.[46]

In this particular quotation the cultural change is closely linked to output, the return from work. But, as indicated in the first sentence of the above quotation, land settlement is also meant to promote certain cultural values which are believed to be desirable in themselves, not just as a means to achieve higher output. Several close observers of land settlement schemes believe that economically their output would be greater if they were managed as estates instead of separate allocations of land being made to individual settlers and their families. But much of the appeal of land settlement schemes lies precisely in the prospect that the settler will receive "his own" land; moreover any estate managed by the government would bear too close a resemblance, at least superficially, to "socialism".[47]

Cultural goals are evident in *gotong royong* projects, that is projects where materials and tools are provided by the government but the villagers are expected to provide the labour. From one angle the projects are meant to be carried out through mutual assistance (*gotong royong*), from another they are meant to foster self-reliance rather than reliance on the government. Politicians, Residents, D.O.s and chiefs have all tried to stimulate the villagers to *gotong royong* efforts. Yet there is general agreement that, maybe because of a later start, so far *gotong royong* has been less effective in altering attitudes than in Malaya. Many projects have been successfully carried out, from the point of view of output.[48] But culturally the programme has had its difficulties. In some instances the villagers want cash, not projects; the subsistence money they receive during the project may be more important to them than the project itself. Alternatively, they may not care very much for the actual bridge, water supply, or road which the project will provide, but may merely want to keep up with the Joneses, in the shape of some neighbouring *kampong* which has just acquired a similar amenity. Lack of interest in the end-product of projects is sometimes shown by failure to maintain roads, once they have been built, or to prevent electric generators from deteriorating, once they have been installed.

While there may be a good deal of resistance to new ideas in Sarawak and Sabah on the part of most of the population, there is considerable receptivity to ideas among the elites. In particular, any political move or strategy which has achieved even moderate success is certain to be claimed by more "fathers" than could possibly have been instrumental in conceiving it. In Sabah many innovations have been attributed to Tun Mustapha, among them the inauguration of the Sabah Foundation, the creation of Community Development Officers, and the setting up of an organization to help members of the public who need help in dealing with the government.[49]

Some political and administrative innovations were adopted as part and parcel of the formation of Malaysia. An important example was the adaptation of the existing machinery for development in the two states to conform in broad outline to that in existence in Malaya. But there was not attempted conformity in every detail. In Malaya District Officers held "morning prayers", a meeting of senior officers at district level who were concerned with development, every week. In Sarawak and Sabah, however, it was found that such frequent meetings were not necessary; they would not have contributed substantially to the main object for having them so often in Malaya, cutting down correspondence among officials. Also, when Community Development Officers were introduced in Sabah, an intelligent variation was made in the system in use in Malaya in order to suit local conditions.[50] The Alliance party structure was also introduced in both states from Malaya, although it was not possible to follow the pattern exactly.[51]

Reactions to practices and ideas derived from Britain were ambivalent.

> One of the major elements of instability in many post-inheritance situations is the fact that values, norms, collectivities and roles are as a rule strongly dissociational from the . . . former colonial power . . . while goals tend to be far less dissociational in view of the common world-wide 'culture' of, or commitment to, economic development and national independence.[52]

In Sabah and Sarawak the values, etc. were not strongly dissociational, but, as a matter of convenience, reference might sometimes be made to colonialism in order to underpin an argument about values. On one occasion it was said that the British had given the people of Sabah a fairly efficient colonial administrative system and that the inheritance of the colonial administration had provided them with continuity of experience during the crucial years of the post-independence era. Another time, however, the rural leaders were advised to forget old ideas inherited from the old colonial days and co-operate with the Government in achieving greater progress for their own benefit.[53]

Sometimes opposition to a procedure which has modern features takes the form of stigmatizing it as "colonial". Some of the examinations in the Sarawak civil service during British rule were attacked on this ground by the young men who had to sit them. But after the British left and these young men became the administrative elite they had no desire to relax the requirement, which they now regarded as objectively justified. The "anti-colonialist" argument was reduced to its most absurd form when it was claimed that the Sabah government was adopting "colonial" policy on transport, because when bus companies were formed the Government was forcing them to run on approved schedules.[54]

In some instances one suspects that "modern" ideas are being supported for much the same reasons as the *kampong* dwellers welcomed *gotong royong* projects—to keep up with the Joneses. Tun Mustapha's decision to bring television to Sabah quickly was made for sound reasons, particularly the desire to further a Malaysian national consciousness.[55] But some of the support for television in Sabah, and also for the government's acquiring more helicopters, may have been for symbolic reasons, to "raise the development status of this country".[56] There have been other, unrealistic, attempts at modernity in the entrepreneurial sphere, such as co-operative ventures in providing bus services in isolated parts of Sabah, where they could not possibly be run at a profit.

It is one thing for the elite to accept an idea, in the sense of making a decision to innovate. It is quite another thing to implement innovation, to make the modernization process work. The increasingly important "development" function of the District Officer, described in Chapter 6, is largely a question of promoting modernization in a number of different ways in a number of different places. Other officials, notably the Administrative Officers (Development and Planning) in Sarawak and the Community Development Officers in Sabah, have a similar modernization function. So do the chiefs and, in rural areas, headmasters of schools. Ministers on tour also attempt to encourage modernization by exhorting, persuading and upbraiding those engaged in development, with varying degrees of success. Some ministers have worked hard in trying to explain in very simple terms why development schemes should be pursued with more vigour. One Sarawak minister, visiting a rubber planting scheme where the government subsidy was being withheld because of insufficient progress, compared the "waste" of the subsidy to deliberately burning a pile of banknotes.

Sometimes ministers fail to overcome resistance to change. Two instances were quoted in the Council Negri in 1968.[57] In one of these some local people refused to give up their land (although offered compensation) for a drainage scheme in the Nonok Peninsula. In the other, Japanese experts, investigating sites for a pilot scheme for *padi* planting, found, in the Chief Minister's constituency, some suitable land which could be irrigated all the year round by natural gravity from water stored on hill slopes. But a small number of families with inferior land on the slopes refused to give it up, although they were offered better land in compensation.

For a person to be an effective promoter of modernization he need not himself be "modern" in all, or even the most obvious, respects. A distinction may be drawn "between *being modern*, i.e. highly educated and aware of Western values, and *acting to modernize*, or perhaps simply to change one's society".[58] There are probably limits to this generalization; it is possible to think of *Temenggongs* or *Pengarahs* in Sarawak who were themselves so unmodern that it would be inconceivable that they could successfully act to modernize. But Tun Mustapha is a good example of a man in whom traditional characteristics are strong in comparison with modern characteristics,[59] who nevertheless has shown receptivity to ideas combined with ruthless drive for their implementation.

So far "modernization" has been considered in the sense of borrowing from, or imitating, the West. It is now convenient to look at certain definitions, or criteria, of political development, which ostensibly are based, not on correspondence with Western practices but with reference to absolute standards. The three selected are based on: the degree of differentiation of political rôles and structures; the degree of secularization or rationality in the political culture; the degree of achievement orientation, as opposed to ascription orientation in political recruitment.[60]

Differentiation

"Differentiation" refers to "the process whereby rôles change and become more specialized or more autonomous or whereby new types of rôles are established or new structures and subsystems emerge or are created". In this respect there is no hard and fast dividing line between traditional and modern societies. However, the degree of "multifunctionality" is more marked in the former than in the latter; structures in the former are less functionally distinct, in the sense that they are more likely to perform more than one function.[61] Different authors use the concept of differentiation in various ways. It is usually only one part of a complex theory of political development. No matter how it is used, two obstacles seem to be insuperable. An organization's functions "can be defined in an almost infinite number of ways".[62] And there is no guidance, except with the help of other criteria, on the lengths to which differentiation should be carried; for instance, in any given case there may be a danger that the degree of differentiation will outrun the possibilities of co-ordination.[63]

In some respects the Borneo states are clearly less differentiated than Malaya. Associations and interest groups, for example, are much less elaborate.[64] In the civil service in Sabah not long after 1963 the rôle of permanent secretary did not appear to be very functionally specific. The Permanent Secretary was in charge of a department and acted as adviser to the minister, as one might expect, but also seemed to be sometimes a kind of personal assistant, whom the minister would ask to phone for a taxi. At that time some Sabah permanent secretaries were not functionally specific, because they were functionally not very competent. A minister who wanted an important memorandum drafted might allocate the task, not to the "obvious" permanent secretary from a functional point of view, but to a bright young administrator who had recently graduated abroad. From one aspect Tun Mustapha's wish to remain politically "active" while he was Head of State in Sabah was an example of a lack of differentiation of functions; from another angle it reflected uncertainty about what the appropriate "rules" were.

In some ways the development machinery in Sarawak and Sabah was less differentiated than that in Malaya. The various agencies of the Federal Government, such as MARA, began operations in Malaya and only later extended their activities to the Borneo states. Also, the system of *kampong* committees which existed in Malaya for development purposes had not been fully extended to Sarawak and Sabah by 1970. It is more difficult to assess the degrees of rôle-differentiation of the officials engaged in promoting development "in the field". Formally, Sabah might appear to be more differentiated than Malaya because it possessed Community Development Officers and Malaya did not. So might Sarawak seem to be more differentiated than Malaya because it, but not Malaya, possessed Administrative Officers (Development and Planning).[65] Some confusion arises when the rôles of District Officers and Residents are compared with the rôles of specialist officers in the field. Although the D.O.s and Residents are "generalists", it would perhaps be misleading to say that they were not functionally specific for this reason. Surely in some contexts there must be functionally specific rôles which require generalist qualities?[66] On the other hand, it could be claimed that the generalist administrator is *not* functionally differentiated unless he is "a highly differentiated manager. Supreme skill is required for management and this should be learned".[67]

If the D.O.'s rôle is defined mainly in terms of development, it would follow that, because of the greater emphasis placed on the D.O.'s development activities in Malaya compared with the Borneo states,[68] D.O.s in West Malaysia were more functionally specific than in East Malaysia. The office of Resident presents a trap if the concept of differentiation is applied in an unsophisticated fashion. If Residents have any function, then Sarawak and Sabah could be said to be more differentiated than Malaya, which does not have Residents. But it may be doubted whether Residents have in fact any useful function, at least in Sabah,[69] so the conclusion may not follow.

An interesting example of differentiation is illustrated by the composition of the cabinets of Sarawak and Sabah. To be sure, cabinets in Western countries are differentiated in the sense that some members are chosen because they are thought to be particularly competent in one aspect of a minister's work, other members for their competence in a different sphere. But in these countries, and it would seem also in Malaya, the variations in competence of different ministers in the different spheres are not very pronounced. In the Borneo states' cabinets, however, 1963–9, a high degree of differentiation can be seen. The distinction between ministers goes further than that between instrumental and expressive leadership.[70]

There were at least four categories of ministers; some might be placed in more than one category, but others would qualify for only one, usually the fourth. The first category included ministers who were "expressive" leaders, who had aroused the wide enthusiasm of followers even across ethnic boundaries. Tun Mustapha and Dato Stephens were in this class. Second, there were "working ministers", those who could do their departmental business competently, perform well in the state legislature, and discuss issues intelligently in the cabinet. The shortage of educated persons in politics in both states is shown by the fact that initially a large proportion, though not all, of these "working ministers" in each state were nominated, not elected, members; Peter Lo and Thomas Jayasuria in Sabah, Dato Teo and Taib in Sarawak.

Third, there was another type of working minister, not so articulate or skilled in paper work, who nevertheless effectively filled the rôle of a touring minister in the field, meeting and talking to the people; in Sarawak Awang Hipni was an example.

The fourth category consisted of "representational ministers", whose function was simply to *be* in the cabinet as the representative of a particular ethnic group. Members of such a group were made happier, were more ready to accept the legitimacy of the government, and were more likely to vote for a government party, just because they were "represented" in the cabinet. Payar Juman, after his defection from UPKO in 1967, was appointed minister, not for any personal qualifications, but partly for reasons of political advantage, partly in order to represent the then unrepresented Kadazans in the cabinet. Similarly, the appointment of Penghulu Abok anak Jalin as a minister in July 1970 was in order to represent the Iban in the Cabinet. Penghulu Abok's qualifications were twofold; he was an Iban and he was available.

In Chapter 6 it was seen that there was some apparent confusion of functions, and so a lack of differentiation, between local authority councillors and chiefs. There would seem to be two logical reactions to this situation. It could be argued that the functions were indeed so similar that one of the two structures, presumably the chiefs, should be abolished. Or it could be concluded that, on some definition of function, the functions were in fact sufficiently distinct to justify the existence of both. This second view is supported later in this chapter.

The concept of complexity[71] is closely related to that of

differentiation. Just as there is a possibility that differentiation may be carried too far, so there is also the possibility that procedures may be over-elaborate. Benefits in terms of accuracy or equity may obscure the heavy costs of complexity in a developing country. Some field officials in Sarawak believe that the system of calculating grants to local councils, started in 1967[72] and the complicated procedures for differential rating of property, undertaken a year or two earlier, were both examples of over-complexity.

Rationality

"An action is rational to the extent that it is 'correctly' designed to maximize goal achievement, given the goal in question and the real world as it exists".[73] Rationality is equivalent to Almond and Powell's initial account of "secularization".[74]

In Sabah and Sarawak politics a considerable degree of rationality can be observed, given that actions are subject to the uncertainties existing in a period of rapid social, economic, and political change. In each state there is a "rational" (in the Weberian sense), and on the whole competent, bureaucracy,[75] and in each an economic plan has been framed and is being carried out in a mainly rational way. Governmental actions in the Borneo states are sometimes performed, not just according to the existing rules, but with an intelligent eye to the relevance of rules to goals. The practice of "morning prayers" in the rural development process[76] was found to be rational in Malaya, but it would have been irrational to follow it blindly in the Borneo states under different conditions, so rationally, it was not enforced. Similarly, state schemes for land settlement which worked quite effectively were not replaced by Federal Land Development Authority schemes just because the latter had been successful in Malaya.

In some instances local councils may not follow the rules. Pressures from constituents, for example, may lead them to divert for the construction of new roads money which legally was intended to be spent on the maintenance of existing roads. The rationality, as opposed to the legality, of such a switch could be determined only by cost-benefit analysis which in fact is not carried out.

Unwillingness to follow formal procedures slavishly when they do not maximize goal achievement undoubtedly constitutes rational action.[77] But it has been remarked that in newly-independent countries some local administrators may not be sufficiently goal-oriented to break or bend the rules when it is necessary. The rules serve to protect them in a world of changing values where they are subject to pressures by politicians.[78] In Sarawak and Sabah some officials recognize that it is important to find loopholes in the rules, as the British did, in appropriate cases. Tempering the rules with informality may amount to little more than showing consideration for the public. If a man who wishes to see the D.O. has travelled a long way, he may not be made to wait his turn; the D.O. may see him before the "town" people who live in the immediate area. Informal changes may also be made in the distribution of benefits. A fisherman whose cottage has been damaged by the sea may not qualify officially for relief, but a sympathetic official could find ways and means to provide him with free materials for the repair. Sometimes, however, the checks on official misbehaviour may discourage rational, informal behaviour. Most expatriate officials who were short of funds for essential travelling in the field would contrive to find the money somehow. They would not be deterred by the thought that the Public Accounts Committee might investigate the matter, if it did, they would trust to their ingenuity to think up a cover story. Their local replacements, liable to pressures from politicians, might be more apprehensive that the Public Accounts Committee would catch them out, even if convinced that their actions, though not strictly legal, had been rational.

Generally, the concept of rationality, or secularization, can apply only if it is clear what the goals in question actually are. Obviously, if there is disagreement about them, there will also be disagreement about the rationality of actions taken in order to attain them. Some officials in the development machinery in Kuala Lumpur, for example, feel that the goals envisaged in the Malaysian economic plans are framed in rather strict economic terms and ignore some social aspects. Economic calculations about resettlement may be made which do not take full account of popular wishes, which may for instance underrate the reluctance of fishermen to settle inland.

A particularly confusing aspect of goals concerns religion. Is it irrational, for example, to spend substantial sums on building mosques or other religious constructions? It would seem that religious preferences must be accepted as goals, at least in the short run. In view of the religious goals of the Muslim part of the population of the Borneo states, it must be taken as given that the economic gains to them of rearing pigs should be foregone.[79] Western criticisms of the adverse effects of religious, or superstitious, observances are sometimes met by unanswerable criticism of their own practices. When the then British Governor of Sarawak condemned the Kayan practice of staying indoors upon the appearance of certain omens with consequent neglect of their crops, Penghulu Puso answered him by pointing out that Christianity had a similar taboo, because it insisted that every seventh day should be a day of rest.[80]

The problem is perhaps greatest where religion is apparently inseparable from traditional agricultural practices. In such circumstances advocates of change are faced by a formidable combination of inertia and religion. Just before Malaysia a government official tried to persuade some Iban to change their system of farming. But for them this represented a "fundamental change from their traditional religion and code rooted in shifting agriculture and a subsistence economy to settled agriculture, cash and alien values. A Lemanak headman, in reply to my (frivolous) enquiry whether he would work for 10 cents a day, said: 'Certainly not.' 'Then why,' I said, 'do you farm for an income which is even less?' 'It is our religion and the custom of our people,' he replied."[81] However, it will be remembered that the objections to changes in the timing of the Inanam *Tamu*, or market, were based partly on religious grounds but also on considerations of convenience. Willingness to argue in terms of convenience may suggest that insistence on certain religious practices may not be as inflexible as it used to be. Nevertheless, the fact remains that many actions which appear to the outsider as irrational can be justified by reference to goals which are claimed to be religious.

If the outside observer rejects these, or some of these, he can properly be asked what his alternative criteria are.

Goals in developing countries may differ from those in developed countries in respect of the time dimension. Developing societies are more accustomed to work according to the rhythm, of the seasons than by "clock time".[82] There is also an emphasis on seeking short-term benefits rather than long-term ones. In the Borneo states, and especially in Sabah, the supreme example of such an orientation was the scramble for timber profits. The short-term emphasis was discernible from the bottom to the top, from the small man who wanted to become a member of a Native co-operative to members of a government who benefited from licences which they themselves allocated. In such an atmosphere the needs of conservation and long-term planning were bound to be neglected.

The emphasis on the short term rather than the long term is more marked among Natives than among Chinese. It is the Natives who are least knowledgeable about the relation of reward to effort and the possibility of substantial pay-offs which can be realized only over time. When the Sabah state government answers the pleas of native fishermen to equip them with nets or outboard motors, sometimes the equipment is immediately sold. Natives, having acquired transport licences intended to promote their participation in the transport business, sometimes turn the business over to Chinese to run in exchange for a money payment. Ministers have warned against such an abuse of native privileges. "Let us not resort to an easy way but to an unprofitable proposition in the long run. Let us look forward and think of the future generation coming after us."[83] But the temptations to follow an "easy way" are great.

It has been maintained, with reference to Malaya, that, given the uncertainties which exist in transitional societies, a short-run orientation may be rational.[84] This evaluation probably applied to politicians in the Borneo states. For the first few years after Malaysia, the "rules of the game" were not very clear, and politicians knew that their rivals were capable of "tricks".[85] There were therefore many unpredictable factors which might prevent the achievement of a long-term goal, if it were selected. Short-term goals had fewer chances of being frustrated. Politicians were playing for a few rather big prizes, such as political office, timber concessions, or benefits from government contracts.

The situation is now different, however. In Sabah from 1968 onwards Tun Mustapha had practically eliminated effective opposition inside the state, and was able to take a genuinely long-term view of the state's future. This is not to say that his personal idiosyncrasies played no part in government, but merely that some obstacles to rational government had been removed. There seemed to be a distinct possibility that the new Sarawak government under Dato Rahman Ya'akub which assumed office in July 1970 would adopt longer perspectives than its predecessors. Parti Bumiputera's timber policy, for example, pursued by Taib when he was Minister of Development and Forestry, was a long-term one based on the premise that the number of licences given out should be restricted until a proper survey of resources had been made by a United Nations team.[86]

At a lower level the "prizes" are more numerous and more modest, and the uncertainties are fewer. The general short-term orientation of Natives is not mostly the result of uncertainties which may affect the achievement of long-term goals more than short-term, thus making it more rational to seek to achieve the latter. It is rather the consequence of a lack of economic sophistication and of ignorance about the relation between present effort and future reward. Politically, the Natives' short-term orientation has made them susceptible to handouts or bribery and insufficiently interested in what the parties' policies are.

Although swayed by the claims of individual politicians, governments in Sarawak and Sabah have tried to work for the attainment of future, as well as immediate, benefits. They have been subject to the pressures for early rewards, especially in the form of timber, stimulated during the formation of Malaysia and in election campaigns. Governments in the two states, along with the Federal Government, have therefore had to operate on two different time scales. They have tried to produce some immediately-identifiable quick benefits, notably in the shape of Minor Rural Projects, in order to meet the wishes of the people, most of whose time orientations are short-range.

Simultaneously, they have been putting plans into effect which are so long-term that the people themselves, if given a direct choice, would almost certainly have preferred shorter-range goals.

Bargaining

One component of the secularization (rationality) process, according to Almond and Powell, is the emergence of a pragmatic, empirical orientation, expressed in the conduct of politics through bargaining.[87] Bargaining has been described as a form of reciprocal control among leaders when certain conditions are met, and is inversely related to the amount of hierarchy and to the extent of initial disagreement. Leaders bargain because they disagree and expect that the further agreement is possible and may be profitable.[88] Some examples of this type of bargaining occurred between political parties in Sarawak or Sabah; others related to bargaining on a state-federal level. The two Sabah cabinet crises in 1964 and the Sarawak crises of 1965 and 1966 were good examples.[89] So was the bargaining process in 1963 when the Federal Government refused to accept Temenggong Jugah as Chief Minister of Sarawak, but the compromise was eventually reached of appointing him as Minister for Sarawak Affairs. Some of the bargaining in the early 1960s was confused, because the "rules" of politics in the Borneo states were not yet clear. What rights were to be allowed to an Opposition? How much money should be spent at elections? To what extent would federal influence be used to settle disputes which otherwise might have been left for settlement by the parties in Sabah or Sarawak?[90]

The allocation of seats among Alliance parties in Sabah, 1967, and Alliance parties in Sarawak, 1968–70, is a good example of the breakdown of bargaining. According to Thompson and Tuden,[91] bargaining is a means of decision making when there are differences in preferences but agreement on facts and consequences. But in neither case could the various Alliance parties agree on the facts, that is, on how the voters would vote in particular seats if more than one of the Alliance parties put up a candidate.[92]

Bargaining is a useful category for the analysis of the

political process in Sabah and Sarawak. But the fact that bargaining exists does not in itself tell us anything about the degree of traditionalism or modernity of politics in the two seats. According to Binder, bargaining may be a characteristic either of traditional or "conventional" (that is, Western-type constitutional democratic) political systems.[93] It might be thought that in a purely traditional society ascriptive criteria would so predominate that there would be no room for bargaining; persons of higher status would simply issue orders to persons of lower status. A moment's reflection, however, is sufficient to see that in such societies *effective*, as opposed to *formal*, control by persons in authority is weak, and that in the process of carrying out, or not carrying out, orders bargaining will occur.[94]

Achievement and Ascription

In political recruitment in the Borneo states there are many examples of ascriptive, or particularistic, criteria, as opposed to achievement, or universalistic, criteria.[94a] The most obvious examples of this have been in the civil service. To some extent they follow from the ethnic breakdown in the two states and from the fact that until now the Chinese have been so much better educated that the use of purely achievement criteria would lead to their occupying the overwhelming majority of high civil service posts. The Chinese are therefore under-represented according to purely achievement criteria. They are similarly numerically under-represented in other situations where it is felt that Natives need more help than Chinese in order to attain the existing achievement levels of the Chinese, for instance in the allocation of scholarships.[95] It could be said that in such instances the requirements of achievement criteria had been overridden by the needs of nation-building, although the reactions of those Chinese whose achievement is not recognized or rewarded also needs to be taken into account.[96]

If the under-representation of Chinese in the top ranks of the civil service (according to achievement criteria) is taken as given, within that framework there are signs of differentiation of function in each state between Chinese and Natives. There is a tendency to concentrate Chinese in the state capital at permanent secretary level and to favour a high proportion of Natives in the field as Residents and District Officers. The assumption behind this is that Chinese are better at paper work, while the Natives are better equipped to deal with *adat* questions, more likely to be encountered in the field where the proportion of Natives to Chinese is relatively high,

The use of ascriptive criteria in making civil service appointments, postings and promotions is not confined just to the simple choice between Chinese and Natives. Within the "Native" category ethnic considerations are sometimes prominent, and questions of "racial balance" are seen in terms of advantages or disadvantages to particular groups of Natives.[97] In Sabah there have been accusations that sometimes appointments of Natives in the civil service have been influenced by ethnic preferences of politicians. And in both states a few instances have occurred where the treatment of a civil servant has been based not on his ability or achievement but on the belief that he had been partisan from a party political point of view.

Capability and Capabilities: General Capability

Another approach to political development is through the notion of capability. It may consider the general capability of a government; alternatively or additionally it tries to assess its capability to cope with certain problems or perform certain functions. These two varieties of the approach will be considered in turn.

The idea of general capability is attractive but elusive. In contrast to specified, particular capabilities, it cannot be easily related to performance. It is possible to think of many factors to consider when making a rough judgement on the general capability of a system. Some can be expressed in statistical form, such as manpower resources, economic growth, percentages of the population at school, enrolled in higher education, government expenditures as a percentage of Gross National Product, and so on.[98] It is also relevant to take into account the support performance aspects of capability, not revealed in the statistics usually available; how much tax evasion there is; whether troops stand under fire.[99] The concept of capacity to organize also appears to be closely related to general capability. Such capacity, says Weiner, is a general quality of societies.[100]

Whether or not the relation is as close as Weiner suggests, clearly capability is affected by the degree to which parties and the civil service are well-organized. Almond and Powell relate capability to versatility. Capability must be truly general in the sense of being versatile and convertible. If new challenges arise, the system must be able to redeploy its resources smoothly in order to meet them successfully.[101] Versatility, or adaptability, is also a key concept in Huntington's thesis that political development may be usefully defined as the institutionalization of political organizations and procedures.[102] Not only is adaptability given first place in this list; it is also treated at more length in the article than the other features, and assumes even greater prominence in a later paper by Huntington.[103]

It should be added that capability in itself may not be sufficient to ensure political development, unless there is also the *will* to use it. This point is made explicitly by Halpern and implicitly by Huntington.[104]

When all this has been said, it is extraordinarily difficult to apply the concept of general capability to Sarawak or Sabah. One reason is that it is obviously impossible to make judgements about their general capability without reference to the Central Government and to West Malaysia. This is necessarily so, because Malaysia is a federation, and because of the links between the Alliance Party in the states and at the centre. Economic growth and government expenditures in the Borneo states are determined to a large extent by Central Government decisions on taxation and expenditure. Support performance is dependent on popular attitudes towards government,[105] and these in turn may be affected by policies of the Central Government. If the Central Government were to be seen as defending one of the states from a territorial claim from outside, favourable attitudes to government in general, and support performance, might increase. If the Central Government were to be regarded as postponing state elections unnecessarily, they might decrease. Capability in the sense of having sufficient versatility to meet a new challenge is very much a federal government matter. One of the most likely forms of a new, or increasingly serious, challenge might be a military threat from a neighbouring state or from internal subversion, which would test not just Sarawak or Sabah's capability but Malaysia's. So the reactions of the Borneo states to confrontation, the activities of the CCO, or the Philippine claim to Sabah, cannot properly be evaluated apart from the reactions of Malaysia as a whole.

Capacity to organize and the degree of institutionalization may also be influenced in the long run by Central Government policies. Also, if we wish to know whether or not the will exists to exercise whatever capabilities there are, we must look at the federal, as well as the state, level; it is important that at Sabah state level Tun Mustapha embodies the will to carry out rural development, but it is also important that Tun Razak embodies such a will nationally.

In spite of such difficulties the general capability approach permits a few impressionistic judgements to be made on the Borneo states. General capability must bear some relation to indices, such as those listed in Chapter 1 on communications, education, consumption of electric power, and so on. There is information on support performance in the two states, as shown by attitudes to government, as well as by more objective indices such as the degree of willingness to pay rates. It is obvious, for example, that, until July 1970 at least, in Sarawak support performance among large sections of the Sarawak Chinese was low. The degree of organization of the civil service and the parties in each state can also be estimated, and comparisons made with elsewhere, including the states of Malaya. However, this exercise is not very enlightening. The limits of the general capability approach become obvious when attempts are made to apply it in detailed fashion to specific countries or systems. The limits do not derive solely from the fact that Sarawak and Sabah are subsystems of the Malaysian system. The main problem is that measurement and precision are possible only in respect of those factors which are indeed associated with *political* capability, but which are *least closely* associated with it. Educational and communications statistics may be reasonably accurate, but certain levels of performance in such spheres appear to be only necessary, not sufficient, conditions, for *political* capability.

The other factors associated with *political* capability, support performance, organizational capacity, adaptability, are much harder to estimate except impressionistically. Moreover, different systems are subjected to threats and challenges of differing degrees of intensity, and may also receive differing amounts of assistance from external sources in trying to meet them.[106] This makes it difficult to compare their capabilities in terms of these characteristics.

Capability or Performance in Meeting Particular Problems: State Building and Nation Building

In assessing the capability of a government to cope with certain problems, it is convenient to adapt categories used by Almond and Powell, who link development to the degree of success which a political system has in meeting four problems; state building, nation building, participation, and distribution.[107] When they refer to capabilities, they use six headings; extractive, regulative, distributive, symbolic, responsive, domestic and international, capabilities.[108] However, it has been pointed out that these six capabilities are analogous to infrastructure, but that, in so far as Almond and Powell treat them in functional terms, there is no way of determining for any particular régime to what extent a capability is, or must be, fulfilled.[109] Also, in dealing with resources, Almond and Powell "... concentrate on capacity or potential rather than on the specific levels of resources, available or required, or on how those 'slender' resources can be used most effectively."[110] There seems to be a gain in realism, therefore, in focusing, not on what Almond and Powell call system capabilities, but on the specific performance capabilities of a system or régime in meeting Almond and Powell's four problems.[111] It is in this sense that the term, particular capabilities, is used in the discussion which follows.

In both Borneo states it would be possible to trace historically the process of state building, of increasing penetration into the lives of the people by the apparatus government. In Sarawak attempts to bring outlying areas under control led to an expansion of bureaucracy and to an increase in the number of State Orders, which placed a considerable strain on the system of personal rule by the Brookes.[112] The degree of success in state building obviously depends very much on the efficiency of the civil service. Quantitative comparisons are difficult here, although most Malayan civil servants with experience of Sarawak or Sabah believe that procedures there are generally slower and less efficient than in Malaya. Partly this may result from communications difficulties, from dealing with a more scattered population, which is less literate and less accustomed to contacts with government than in Malaya. But there are also deficiencies in the quality of the civil service in both states. In the Borneo states the relatively short period for handing over from expatriates to local administrators led to short-run dependence either on the older civil servants who were under-educated and under-trained, or on younger ones with better education and training but with little experience. There were few men available to fill Permanent Secretary or Resident posts who combined experience with education and training. In Sabah, particularly, there was a severe shortage of men adequate to fill such posts. Efficiency was also reduced in some instances by rapid turnover. However, these problems should become less serious as time goes on.

The degree of success in state-building may be judged in another way. To what extent is the government considered to be a legitimate authoritative decision-making body? Is there an attitude of respect for the political system or, more specifically, is there a set of values supporting obedience to law?[113] There is no way, unfortunately, that this question can be answered by quoting from survey data as can be done for some countries.[114] There are some data on actual violence, which were cited earlier.[115] There are also instances of disobedience to the law. In both states there is some resistance to the taking of censuses and to health checks on humans and animals. In Sarawak there is endemic illegal tree-felling by Ibans, and in both territories there is persistent non-compliance with the law in the form of failure to pay rates.[116]

State-building, of course, breaks down if there are widespread doubts about the legitimacy of the government, doubts which are felt by a larger proportion of the population than those engaged in the various "rebellions" just mentioned. When the Brookes ceded Sarawak to Britain in 1946 there was a danger of such a breakdown among wide sections of the Malay population, as shown by the resignation of several hundred Malay civil servants. A potentially serious situation occurred in 1966 following the confusing rapid succession of governments and the resultant doubt about which was the "legal" government. Dato Tawi Sli was in the predicament of having to try to "prove" he was Chief Minister in order to refute rumours. "If I were not so, how could I command the services of Departments like Information and Broadcasting? If I am not Chief Minister, I would not have been provided with military and police escorts during my visits to outstations."[117]

Neither of these examples, however, is as serious as the lack of legitimacy of the state (and the Malaysian) government in the eyes of disaffected Sarawak Chinese. The terrorists on the Sarawak-Indonesian border and elsewhere in Sarawak are only the tip of the iceberg. The lack of trust of Chinese in general in Sarawak was shown just before Malaysia by a government order calling in all guns and ammunition from non-Natives (that is, Chinese).[118] Until Sarawak's distribution capability, referred to later in this chapter, has been exercised to benefit the Chinese more, the government will lack legitimacy for many Chinese. One of the tests of SUPP participation in the Government from July, 1970 on is whether it will win sufficient rewards for the Chinese to make more of them accord legitimacy to the state.

With these exceptions attitudes to government are generally favourable, partly because in both states for many years the Government and its officers in the field have not been looked upon as oppressive. Nowadays the government officer "still enjoys an access to the people and their problems which is conspicuously lacking in many other parts of Asia."[119] Attitudes to government are also favourable because of a growing awareness of the government as a source of benefits.[120] Additionally there are still sections of the population, especially in remoter areas, where obedience to government is based on little more than habitual, unthinking compliance.

The problem, or challenge, of nation-building has already been discussed in Chapter 2. The account may have given the impression that nation-building in Sarawak and Sabah was proceeding very slowly and ineffectually while in other developing countries it was having much greater success. However, this is not so; comparatively, Malaysia is not meeting this problem in Sarawak and Sabah less competently than are many other new states. It is becoming evident that in many new states nation-building will be a slow process, and can proceed successfully only when substantial progress has been made in state-building.

Participation

The participation problem, or challenge, as seen by Almond and Powell,[121] commonly has to do with "demands for a share in the decision making of the political system" by various groups and strata. The concept of a "share" in decision-making is ambiguous. Certainly, politicians from the two states have engaged both in political participation and also in decision-making, whether in the Federal Parliament, the state legislature, local councils, or the political party machinery. Their importance in the decision-making process depends on a number of factors, such as the governmental level at which they are operating and whether or not their party is in power. But there can also be political participation which is not strictly *participation in* the decision-making process, although it may *influence* that process. Persons or groups articulating demands are "participating" in the sense that they are taking part in the political process. But they are not engaging in decision-making. They are rather testing the system's responsive capability; they are asking for favourable decisions to be made by others about their demands. This kind of activity, interest articulation, will be discussed in the following section of distribution capability.

The most obvious criteria of political participation in a broad sense consist of voting, and of activity in political parties and in interest groups which make frequent political demands. When elections have been held in the two states the percentage of registered electors voting has been quite high; in the contested seats in the 1963 Sarawak local council elections and in the 1962–3 Sabah local council elections approximately 73% and 79%, respectively, of the electors cast valid votes. In the Sabah state elections of 1967 the percentage of valid votes was about 88% of the electorate; for the Sarawak state and parliamentary elections, 1970, it was about 74%. These figures compare favourably with Malaya, and with many "developed" democracies.

It should be pointed out, however, that there have been limitations on the electoral process in both states. A few of the district councils in Sabah consist wholly of non-elected members, and most councils have some non-elected members. In Sarawak direct elections to the state legislature were not held until seven years after Malaysia was formed. Moreover, much of the electoral and party activity described in Chapter 4 hardly lives up to the high expectations evoked by the term "political participation". Some of the activity was directed to obtaining particularistic material improvements. Some had the object of securing a money payment or of joining in a *kerbau* feast. The main exception to this generalization was the SUPP, among whose Chinese members ideology and grievances about government policy towards sections of the Chinese population led to wider and deeper political participation. Otherwise, party leaders have had to keep two main considerations in mind in retaining and extending their following: to provide immediate material benefits, or the hope of immediate material benefits; to represent symbolically the interests of the main ethnic group(s) constituting their party's followers. Beyond that the leaders, especially in Sabah, have been relatively free of control by the rank and file. The lack of general interest in organized participation as such is reflected in the relative scarcity and weakness of interest groups.[122] It may be hypothesized, in the absence of data derived from surveys, that in both Sarawak and Sabah orientations towards inputs and towards the self as an active participant are minimal; the states are not, in Almond and Verba's term, "participant political cultures".[123]

Distribution

Basically distributive capability depends on the resources available and on the ability of the government to share out, and in the long run increase, these resources. For this a competent infrastructure is necessary, as for state building. The first requisite is a good civil service. In addition, there should be arrangements for decision-making which make for consistency and rule out particularism and corruption as far as possible. From previous chapters it is clear that these criteria have not always been met and there has been considerable vacillation and particularism in land and timber policy, for example.

At first sight the figures for Gross National Product Per Head, given for Sarawak and Sabah in Chapter 1, might suggest that there was no acute distribution problem in the two states. However, the figures quoted there were averages, and there are great, although unquantified, differences in the incomes of various sections of the population. Especially in Sarawak, where there are more rubber smallholders, prosperity has fluctuated with the price of rubber, and from 1965 to 1968 this was falling. Moreover, success in solving the distribution problem cannot be estimated just by looking at how much has been given to whom. It should be measured rather by comparing what is distributed with the *demands* for distribution. In both states there is now an orientation towards outputs; there are "expectations that the activities of the government will produce changes in society or in the lives of its members".[125] This was not always so. In 1959 the Governor of North Borneo told the Legislative Council: "In 1954 I was depressed to find that nobody seemed to want anything: today everybody wants something. They cannot all have it, certainly not all at once, but I am delighted that they should clamour for it".[126] Obviously, the growth of expectations varies in different areas, depending on their remoteness and on how hierarchical and authoritarian their traditional form of government is.

In Sarawak among the remoter, upriver Ibans increasingly "the question is no longer how to avoid central authority; rather, it is how to obtain a greater share of the resources which only authority can command".[127] One of the most spectacular changes in expectations over the last few years has occurred among the Kenyahs in Sarawak. Even after Malaysia was formed they were said to be completely dominated by their traditional leaders, prepared to support any government so long as it was the government, and to be making no demands on their representatives in the Council Negri to do anything for them. Within the last year or two this has altered. Children who have received some secondary education return from school, question established practices, and there are signs that constituents now expect something from government through their representatives. At the 1970 elections SNAP received more votes in Kenyah areas than Pesaka, although the Kenyah Temenggong, Dato Temenggong Oyong Lawai Jau, is a Pesaka leader. SUPP also polled well in Kenyah areas.

Some of the rise in demands for distribution benefits was caused by the expectations aroused when Malaysia was being formed. Those who suffered from the increased cost of living in Sabah which occurred after 1963 were particularly bitter about having apparently lost, not benefited, from Malaysia.

The machinery through which interests are articulated was described earlier.[128] There is no doubt about the existence of channels for articulation. Indeed it was remarked there that confusion might arise from embarrassment of choice; should the would-be articulator choose his *Penghulu* or chief, the D.O., his councillor, or his state representative as a channel for articulating his demands? Problems arise, however, because the expectations of output benefits which have been stimulated relate mostly to the short term. Consequently the demands on politicians, or on semi-politicized persons such as chiefs or *Penghulus*, are frequently for timber licences or for money. The greatest concentration of such demands occurs in the state capitals, when politicians are visited by individuals or by delegations. Dato Stephens has said that when he was Chief Minister the great majority of those who came to see him were interested mainly in getting timbered land.[129] Some other Sabah ministers, regarded as especially sympathetic to people with demands, had numerous visitors who, whether their particular demands were met or not, always asked for money to pay their fare home. These pressures on ministers eventually led to measures described later in this chapter.

Government also provides long-term benefits, for example in the form of land settlement and education. There is indeed a demand for such benefits among some sections of the population. But for other sections the Government first has to provide benefits and then persuade some potential users to accept them; to give up shifting cultivation in exchange for land on a settlement scheme, or to send children to school regularly. An important future distribution problem will be to provide an adequate supply of jobs. A few years ago it was true that "unemployment, that is to say not having a job despite efforts to find one, hardly exists . . .", although it was added that young people leaving school after six or nine years' education had some difficulty in finding work.[130] In Sarawak, where employment opportunities are less numerous than Sabah, it was estimated that in 1963 only about 5% of those completing their primary schooling were unoccupied.[131] However, in 1967 Enche Taib foresaw that in the 1970s there would be a surplus of adolescents with only primary education on the job market.[132] Until recently Sabah actually had a shortage of labour, and encouraged immigration to fill certain types of job.[133] But both states may have problems in the future: industry is unlikely to expand very much, and agricultural production for export is not likely to give much additional employment. One aspect of the problem is the unwillingness of those who leave school to look for agricultural, instead of clerical, jobs.[134] Both state governments are aware of the need to provide suitable education for future school leavers who enter agriculture,[135] but the attraction of the towns for young people is strong.

In Sarawak complaints about the small scale of long-term benefits distributed by the government come mostly from the Chinese. It is they who suffer most from a shortage of land (Chapter 5). They have good opportunities for education, but memories of "state intervention" in changing the system are still quite recent, and they have seen other ethnic groups make comparatively greater educational advances in the last decade. They have also suffered most so far from the shortage of jobs for school-leavers who prefer, or who are forced to seek, jobs in the towns rather than in the country. All these reasons contribute to dissatisfaction with the government and until July 1970 with the only Chinese party in the government. The Chinese in Sabah have been less openly restive. But the support Chinese Independents received at the 1967 State election indicated considerable dissatisfaction.

"Distribution" may refer not just to goods, or even to opportunities such as education, but also to intangibles, not measurable in money terms. It is necessary sometimes to reassure those who articulate demands for honour or status but who have not yet been satisfied. In 1967, Tun Mustapha congratulated those who had been awarded state honours on the occasion of the Head of State's birthday, " . . . and appealed to those who did not receive the award to be patient and not to be disappointed. He asked them to intensify their efforts and contributions in social welfare and politics so that their turn will eventually come."[136] Another "intangible" type of expenditure is on celebrations and ceremonial visits. The *Yang di-Pertuan Agong's*[137] visit to Sabah in 1968 cost directly over one million dollars. However, not all the benefits consisted in the enjoyment and spectacles provided by the visit. It also made a contribution to the objective of nation-building.

Change: Conflicts and Contradictions, Apparent and Real

So far three approaches to modernization or development have been considered. But there has been no discussion of possible incompatibilities or contradictions within each approach. For instance, in the first approach, on modernization, may it not be anomalous that "traditional" and "modern" structures, such as chiefs and local councillors, should continue to exist side by side? This question has recently been examined by Whitaker, who has pointed to the error in reifying two analytical categories, "traditional society" and "modern society", so that it would seem that a developing society was faced with the choice of either totally accepting or totally rejecting modernity.[138] According to Whitaker, belief in the mutual exclusivity of "modern" and "traditional" patterns is encouraged by acceptance of the assumption that the process of socio-political change is necessarily "eurhythmic". Such an assumption takes the form that: (1) significant change in one sphere of activity, for instance the economy, would occasion corresponding and supportive change in another sphere, for instance the polity or the culture; (2) within a given sphere of social activity, significant change in any one aspect of the activity, for instance, normative, psychological, institutional, structural, promotes consistent change in all or most other aspects.[139]

Believers in the eurhythmic thesis, having grasped the truth that changes in one sphere do often lead to changes in other spheres, have been led to postulate a tidiness and consistency, once change has started, which does not actually occur anywhere. "Modernity is thus not all of a piece. The American experience demonstrates conclusively that some institutions and some aspects of a society may become highly modern while other institutions and other aspects retain much of their traditional form and substance. Indeed this may be a natural state of affairs. In any system some sort of equilibrium or balance must be maintained between change and continuity. Change in some spheres renders unnecessary or impossible change in others."[140] This generalization not only accepts the juxtaposition of modern and traditional structures. It also assigns a positive value to the persistence of the traditional. A corresponding generalization would apply to cultural beliefs as well as to institutions; traditional beliefs may co-exist side by side with modern beliefs.

In both Sarawak and Sabah the traditional has survived along with the modern. In Sarawak this was largely the consequence of Brooke policy which on the whole was continued by the British. This policy was stated very clearly by the second Rajah, Charles Brooke, who contrasted two widely different principles of government, the Native and the European. The first looked to tradition and was averse to even slight changes. The second held to a strict standard of Western civilization, and judged harshly whatever fell short of the standard.

> In accordance with these two principles, there are two ways in which a government can act. The first is to start from things as we find them, putting its veto on what is dangerous or unjust, and supporting what is fair and equitable in the usages of the natives, and letting system and legislation wait upon occasion. When new wants are felt it examines and provides for them by measures rather made on the spot than imported from abroad; and, to ensure that these shall not be contrary to native customs, the consent of the people is gained for them before they are put in force.

> The other plan is to make here and there a clean sweep and introduce something that Europeans like better in the gap. A criminal code of the latest type, polished and revised by the wise men at home, or a system of taxation and policy introduced boldly from the West is imposed, with a full assurance of its intrinsic excellence, but with too little thought of how far it is likely to suit the circumstances it has to meet.[141]

In North Borneo the Chartered Company was perhaps not so protective of native customs as the Brookes in Sarawak, but it was acutely conscious of the need to pay due regard to them.[142]

In such references allowance has to be made for the "colonial" context and assumptions. It may be argued that the Brookes were not just protective of native customs but were *over*-protective. However, they had seen the important point; changes and reforms did not need to take the form of all or nothing. If attempts were made to introduce across-the-board changes, severe social dislocation might follow.

At the present time there is a mixture of traditional and modern rôles and structures in Sarawak and Sabah. There are also some "fake-traditional" roles (akin to neo-Gothic architecture) such as *Temenggongs*. There appears to be considerable overlapping and lack of differentiation. Councillors and chiefs (or *Penghulus*) overlap to some extent; some individuals are both councillors and chiefs simultaneously, and some of the functions are similar.[143] Also, D.O.s and Residents, who are non-modern, not in the sense that they are traditional but in the sense that they are "colonial", have sometimes been regarded as unnecessary. As Whitaker found in Northern Nigeria, some elements of traditional institutions have proved to be functional for the maintenance of modern patterns.[144] In both Sarawak and Sabah parties mobilized the mass electorate partly through traditional channels. Equally, sometimes modern institutions were functional in maintaining traditional patterns in the Borneo states. Chiefs were supported by obtaining enterpreneurial positions through their political connections, and the power and prestige of their children was often reinforced by a Western-type education.

Looking ahead it is possible to foresee an increasing differentiation of functions. If local councils become better established, they may need less supervision by the D.O., and councillors may take over more completely some of the functions which they now share with chiefs and *Penghulus*. Chiefs at the higher levels may wither away, but at the lower levels may continue as interpreters of *adat* and as organizers of community activities. Their functions will become increasingly honorific and, in Bagehot's sense, dignified. D.O.s, increasingly relieved of their supervisory functions over local government and with more and more of their judicial work taken over by stipendiary magistrates, may come to concentrate on the task of co-ordinating development. Residents will probably disappear. But in the meantime adverse consequences from overlapping are not serious. Any confusion which may result is more than compensated for by older, more traditional people being provided with a channel for interest articulation. Such people might not be willing to make use of more modern channels, such as councillors or members of the legislature. Pye has said that non-Western societies need political "brokers", who can perform a rôle similar to that played by the local party leaders who introduced the various immigrant communities into American public life.[145] In effect the chiefs perform such a rôle. They introduce older, traditional people in the more remote areas into political life in Sarawak and Sabah just as the local political leaders mentioned by Pye performed this function for the American immigrants.

Culturally, as well as structurally, there is a mixture of the traditional and the modern, and this mixture can exist in a single individual, as can be seen in the profiles of politicians.[146] There is no possibility, even if it were held to be desirable, that native customs could suddenly be abandoned. This was recognized by Tun Mustapha when he urged that Native Laws and Customs should be revised. "... I would like, short of discarding them, our Native Laws and Customs to be modified and adapted to suit the conditions of modern life."[147] In the time of British rule Malcolm MacDonald advocated a similar policy to *Penghulus* who had (implicitly) a eurhythmic theory of change:

> "You urge," Jugah said to me, "that we should keep our native style of dress, yet the Government wishes us to progress. You

> plead with us to maintain many ancient Iban customs, but the Government insists that we adopt new ways of doing things. The Government itself is making big changes in the methods of administering our affairs." He suggested that a conflict existed between these two policies.
>
> I answered that there was no contradiction. In some matters a change, a development from ancient Iban habits was desirable, for the old methods were out of date and prevented his people from making adaptations which would enable them to survive in the modern world. But in other matters traditional customs were good and should be preserved as an essential part of Iban racial character. So there should be modifications in some features of native life and no modifications in others.[148]

Penghulus Jugah and Sibat raised a further, awkward, question when they said that it was difficult to distinguish where there should be changes and where there should not be changes.[149] But the actual point at issue is quite plain. Traditional elements cannot be summarily dismissed in favour of modern elements. Whatever governmental policies are pursued some of the former will remain. The task of government is to try to manoeuvre traditional elements, as far as this is possible, so as to promote its policies, regardless of what labels are given to the structures and culture which emerge.

The two other approaches to development discussed above were: those based on the criteria of rationality (secularization), differentiation, and achievement; those based on the idea of capability. Inside the first of these two, it does not seem that insoluble conflict could occur among the criteria. Rationality, on the definition given,[150] would appear to override either the differentiation or achievement criteria, or would seem to provide the solution where these other two criteria were in conflict. It should be remembered, however, that rationality was defined with reference to goal-achievement, and it has to be assumed that goals, and relative priorities among goals, are known.

However, where particular capabilities, or the capacities to deal with certain problems, are concerned there are distinct possibilities of conflict. The capabilities are interrelated. "What may appear as an unmanageable lack of social cohesion in the face of a more efficient government machine might be quite manageable; conversely administrative feebleness may raise political storms that would otherwise never occur".[151] Sometimes the relation among capabilities may be supportive. Effectiveness through the distribution capability may foster legitimacy and thus assist in state building and even in nation building.[152] Perhaps if land reform had been carried out in Sarawak in 1965 the regime might have become more legitimate in the eyes of the Chinese, and support for subversion might have declined. Less spectacularly, the population may be reconciled to some of the less attractive aspects of state building, such as tax collection (the extractive capability), if it is convinced that this is making possible distributive benefits, such as new schools. But too often it is assumed that capabilities cannot conflict. Most of the wiser writers on political development are aware of the possibility of conflict, although perhaps they do not always make due allowance for its effect on their own theories.[153]

Some conflicts among capabilities may simply arise from not being able to afford expenditures in several directions simultaneously with limited resources. But other conflicts arise not so much from cost considerations as from alternative, largely incompatible, goals. Two examples may be given concerning chiefs and Community Development Officers. In each case the conflict, broadly speaking, was between participation and distribution, although, more immediately it could be described in terms of participation versus achievement. In both Sarawak and Sabah the chiefs and *Penghulus*, etc., occupy a twilight zone; they are neither full-time government servants recruited on merit according to certain objective criteria, nor are they full-time politicians.[154] In principle, it would be possible to move either in the direction of more participation, by having them become more responsive to the people, or of more emphasis on achievement, by making them civil servants. Actually, Sarawak has moved more in the former direction than Sabah by having *Penghulus* etc., elected in some, but not all, cases.[155] Whatever the precise arrangements in existence in each state, the two requirements, participation and achievement, will often be in conflict. More of the one will tend to be associated with less of the other.

Rather similarly, when Sabah introduced Community Development Officers,[156] the deliberate choice was made of sacrificing achievement criteria, in the form of objective merit qualifications for recruitment, in favour of participation, in the sense of choosing men with political interests, likely to work closely with the people and encourage their participation, and in some instances to use this experience as a step on the way to their further political career.

It would seem that too much preoccupation with the possible dangers of the persistence of some traditional elements in the midst of modernity has tended to distract attention from a more important type of conflict. Policies designed to solve particular problems, or achieve certain goals, may make more difficult the solution of other problems, or goals. This is the reason why there can be no simple, unequivocal definition of political development.[157] The weights placed on competing or conflicting goals vary according to the observer.

Mobilization and Stability

An illustration of possible conflict between goals is provided by the relation between social mobilization and political stability. An increase in social mobilization might promote the desirable end of increased political participation. But it might also tend to lead to political instability, and therefore obstruct the attainment of other desirable political ends, notably state-building, unless certain rather tough conditions are met. It is one of Huntington's central theses that social and economic change—urbanization, increases in literacy and education, industrialization, mass media expansion—"extend political consciousness, multiply political demands, broaden political participation. These changes undermine traditional sources of political authority and traditional political institutions; they enormously complicate the problems of creating new bases of political effectiveness. The rates of social mobilization and the expansion of political participation are high; the rates of political organization and institutionalization are low. The result is political instability and disorder".[158] Huntington expresses the problem via a series of relationships,[159] which may be summarized as follows. Political stability will be adversely affected by social mobilization, unless the latter is accompanied by economic development.[160] To the extent that economic development does not provide sufficient opportunities and benefits, political participation will increase in order to express demands for them. In so far as political participation occurs unaccompanied by political institutionalization, the consequence will be political instability.

Turning to the Borneo states, these relationships, social mobilization, economic development, political participation, and political institutionalization, will be considered in sucession. As measured by most indices,[161] social mobilization in the Borneo states seems to have occurred relatively slowly. It was remarked a few years ago that in Malaya a rise in national income had not been matched by an equivalent increase in many of the amenities of life found in "other industrial revolution societies", as shown, for instance, by indices for literacy, physicians, radios, and urbanization.[162] This conclusion also applies to Sarawak and Sabah in the late 1960s and early 1970s. The Borneo states are obviously nearer to the "premobilized" group of transitional societies, which includes Nigeria and Ghana, than to the "mobilized" group, which includes Mexico and Spain.[163] There are only two respects in which, from the data available (mostly set out in Chapter 1, pp. 10–14, social mobilization seems to be occurring rapidly in the two states. One is the steep rise in the number of radio licences issued in Sabah, although these figures give only an imperfect indication of the increase in the radio audience. The other is the high rate of increase of school pupils in the population aged five to nineteen. The rate of increase was higher, 1963–9, for Sabah than for Sarawak, and in both states it was higher for secondary than for primary school pupils. In Sabah the absolute numbers of secondary school pupils rose by over three and a half times during the period.[164]

In some ways social mobilization in the Borneo states has been controlled or muted. The impact of the mass media has sometimes been lessened by controls, whether external or internal. The most obvious example was the compulsory closing down of some Sarawak Chinese newspapers in 1962 on the ground that they were subversive. Less obviously, there was an almost complete absence in the Sabah press of references to the Chinese Independent candidates during the parliamentary elections of 1969–70. On social mobilization, generally, another observation of Huntington's applies. He remarks that the more highly stratified a society is and the more complicated its social structure, the more gradual is the process of mobilization.[165] Undoubtedly the ethnic divisions in Sarawak and Sabah have had the effect of slowing down mobilization. However, another aspect of social mobilization is unpromising for stability. It is the Chinese who have been most exposed to social mobilization in the form of urbanization, literacy, and so on. But in Sarawak in particular, they are also the least assimilated members of the population from the perspective of nation building. The combination of the two factors would seem to constitute a threat to stability.

The record of both states in economic development has been good, indeed Sabah's has been outstanding. However, to recapitulate three of the points made earlier about distributive capability: although there has been economic progress, it may not match the expectations aroused by promises made during the formation of Malaysia and subsequently by political parties; in a few years' time there will be more educated people looking for jobs than there will be jobs available; many Sarawak Chinese are profoundly dissatisfied with their economic rewards and with the indefinite postponement of reform of the law on owning land.

Political participation in Sarawak and Sabah does not fit the Huntington thesis quite so closely. In the Borneo territories political participation was not the consequence of frustration at the slow provision of economic benefits. The history of the SUPP constitutes the only substantial exception to this generalization. District council elections were held in Sarawak before the formation of Malaysia was proposed, but outside the towns there was little popular demand for them. In North Borneo, where such elections were held for the first time only in 1962, the popular demand was even less. The opportunity for participation in the form of voting came, not as a way of meeting grass-roots demands for participation, but by the decision of the colonial government with the support of some of the local elite.[166] Even after 1963, participation, to the extent that it occurred, was more the product of personal or ethnic loyalty or of the prospect of quick financial gain than of long-term economic frustration.

By 1970 political participation, in the form of opportunities for voting was still rather limited. The Sabah State legislature had its first direct election only in 1967; the corresponding first direct election in Sarawak was completed only in July 1970. At district level in 1970 some of the members of Sabah local councils were still appointed, not elected. There is another cardinal sense in which political participation in the two states is modified. Just as mobilization may be slowed down by complexity of structure, so may the impact of participation be blunted by complexity of the means by which it is expressed. In both states channels of participation are obviously separated by the division of government responsibilities among three types of elected (or in the case of Sabah mainly-elected) body; federal, state, and local. In addition, however, participation, in the sense of the articulation of demands, is not confined to the channels between electors and interest groups, on the one hand, and these elected bodies, on the other. The "traditional" mechanism of the chiefs and the "colonial" mechanism of D.O.s and Residents provide other channels for the articulation of demands. So does the development committee machinery, which quite deliberately, was kept separate from the local authority structure.

From the governmental point of view the complexity of the mechanisms raises problems of aggregating satisfactorily the demands articulated in so many different ways. Also, if complexity were to increase beyond a certain point, there could be a danger that government might become more remote from the people and so less responsible; from the elector's point of view, the complexity might be a source of confusion.[167] But, if the broad lines of Huntington's argument are accepted it may follow that the complexity of the mechanisms may be eufunctional, in so far as it reduces the pressure of demands on structures which are not yet strongly institutionalized, and thus helps them to withstand forces making for political instability.[168]

It would seem that in both states politicians were desirous of reducing political pressures on themselves. Responsible government and elections in which parties had bid for support, raised expectations of benefits and stimulated pressures for direct access to ministers. This was the background to Penghulu Tawi

Sli's advice, given soon after he became Chief Minister, that people should take "small matters" to their own *Penghulus*, or the equivalent, instead of directly to ministers.[169]

In Sabah the pressures for access were even greater. Some "soft-hearted" ministers were besieged in their offices or even in their houses. Approached in this way, they were led to make numerous exemptions to their own departmental policies. One minister was constantly subjected to petitioners who came to his office and threatened to spend the night there unless they were given money to cover their travel expenses home. He met the problem originally by bringing only a limited amount of money to the office each day, later by visiting the office less frequently. After the dissolution of the UPKO at the end of 1967 and the consequent decline of political competition in Sabah, the pressures eased somewhat, but remained sufficiently strong for the government to take measures to contain them. Tun Mustapha, the Chief Minister, introduced a strict policy of limiting access to himself;[170] such pressures were exceptionally strong, because it was obvious that political decision-making in Sabah had become substantially concentrated in his own hands, as described later in this chapter. In late 1969 provision was made for relieving pressures on ministers generally. A new government body was to be created in the Chief Minister's department with the experienced former Resident, West Coast, as Director.[171] The intention was that a member of the public with grievances or complaints against government departments would be required first to approach this body, which would then refer the complainant to the appropriate government department; only very rarely would he be given access to a minister.

Huntington, it will be recalled, maintained that political participation not tempered by political institutionalization would lead to political instability. Sabah is adequately institutionalized administratively, and also possesses a vital feature making for stability, a dominant political party.[172] The USNO has no rival, the other main component of the Alliance, the SCA, being totally dependent on it politically. The dangers to stability which Huntington predicts will arise from participation without an adequate degree of institutionalization, do not actually result from participation as such. They are the consequence of *competitive* participation. In Sabah, even after competitive participation *between* parties largely disappeared from the end of 1967 onwards, except from the loosely-organized Chinese Independents, participation *inside* USNO (and inside the SCA and the small Sabah Indian Congress) continued.

One form which participation assumed was rallies opposing the Philippine claim to Sabah, which promoted nation-building, at the same time giving a "subjective" sense of participation. "The one-party government is therefore typically a device for facilitating mass mobilization while preventing . . . mass 'participation'. To put it another way, the regime may be concerned with developing a subjective sense of participation while actually preventing the population from affecting public policy, administration, or the selection of those who will in fact govern."[173] This description is perhaps rather extreme to apply closely to Sabah, but it is suggestive of its style of non-competitive participation. Competition within the political elite has certainly been minimized,[174] which was possible without severe repression only because the elite was small and the resources available to satisfy it, largely deriving from timber, were relatively large.[175]

However, although participation in Sabah has been substantially controlled and directed through a strong party, the USNO, it would not be entirely correct to say that this was a good example of the Huntington thesis on institutionalization. The strength of the USNO lies mostly in the strength of its leader, Tun Mustapha, who has asserted his control over decision-making as against both the cabinet and the civil service. His pre-eminence in the party reduces the importance of the Cabinet; as a source of advice (although not of decision-making which resides in Tun Mustapha) the Cabinet's expected functions are partly performed by a small group of advisers, most of whom are civil servants.[176]

Tun Mustapha's pre-eminence is too pronounced to require proof by quantification. However, it is instructive to refer to a 1968 document listing the responsibilities of Cabinet members for various categories of "Government Business". Tun Mustapha was listed as responsible for 22 categories. The other ministers were listed as responsible for 5, 15, 14, 6, 11, 12, 3, and 4 categories, respectively. The "responsibilities" were not of equal weight; some ministers with a smaller number of responsibilities were carrying a much heavier load than others with a larger number of responsibilities. But what is remarkable is that the Chief Minister, whose main function in most governmental system is mainly a co-ordinating one, should have so many specified functions, some of them (such as the Public Service, Natural Resources, Development Planning and Budget, and Rural Development) of prime importance. Moreover, he was allocated any residual functions not specifically assigned to other ministers. Tun Mustapha's assertion of his authority *vis-à-vis* the civil service was demonstrated by a substantial transfer of legal powers from his permanent secretary to himself in 1968.[177] In general Tun Mustapha has been increasingly impatient with bureaucrats who have tried to invoke existing rules, procedures and possible legal difficulties as a means of indirectly opposing his wishes.[178]

By 1968 it was rare to find mentions of Tun Mustapha in the Sabah press in which he was not referred to as "able", "dedicated", or "dynamic". There was also an increasing tendency for "his" speeches (especially during his frequent absences from Sabah) actually to be delivered by another politician but still to be attributed to him.[179] In many respects Tun Mustapha's style of "personal rule" resembles Guenther Roth's description of such rule in new states, particularly in the juxtaposition of personal loyalties and material rewards with reform-mindedness and in the social, cultural, and political heterogeneity of the setting.[180] It seems, therefore, scarcely appropriate to view the USNO (or the Sabah Alliance Party) as an example of institutionalization acting as a check on participation. The USNO has no particular ideology, no coherent set of political values. It employs paid full-time field officers and has a strong youth section. But it does not yet appear to be distinguished by "organizational complexity and depth".[181] It is not obvious that the party would continue to play its present dominating rôle once Tun Mustapha had retired from it. It is more plausible to view the USNO as a dominant party which has successfully controlled political participation largely through the outstanding strength of character of Tun Mustapha, aided by the impulse given to solidarity by the intermittent Philippine territorial claim.

Although there is little evidence of *party* institutionalization, nevertheless institutionalization is taking place. It is to be found in those associations or interest groups which are at least government-encouraged, if not government-supported, and which draw their top officials from governmental figures. The most important of these cover the sectors of Language (*Badan Bahasa*), Religion (USIA), and Youth (SANYA).[182] Speculations on Sabah's future after Tun Mustapha leaves the political scene should be based, not so much on the non-institutionalized nature of the USNO, but rather on the existence of institutionalized interest groups such as those just mentioned.

In Sarawak the framework of government, established by the Brookes and the British and continued after 1963, provided institutionalization, but only at levels below the political level. There are several political parties, none of which has a clear electoral majority, and at least until 1970 many of the supporters of one of the prominent parties, the SUPP, were virtually divorced from the political system. Stability was imperilled by the tensions between the claims of loyalty to Malaysia and of "Sarawak nationalism". So although the administrative framework is of high quality, almost certainly higher than in Sabah, the degree of political institutionalization has been low. One of the obvious objectives of the new government, formed in July 1970, will be to try to increase political institutionalization.[183]

To summarize: in both states pressures arising from social mobilization will undoubtedly make themselves felt in the future; in both, especially in Sabah, to some extent they are being alleviated by economic development; in both there are mechanisms which have acted as a check on participation, notably in Sabah the force of Tun Mustapha's personality; in neither has there been any high degree of institutionalization at a political party as opposed to an administrative, level.

Conclusion

The approach of this chapter has been to look at the politics of Sarawak and Sabah in terms of some of the concepts found in such writers as Huntington and Almond and Powell. However, it is not proposed to label or categorize the two states as belonging to such and such a stage of political development. The concept of political development is an ethereal one, depending either on vague definitions which are hard to apply, or on more easily identifiable criteria, which nevertheless need to be assigned different weights and which often conflict. From the information given here the reader is invited to apply his own concepts of political development. As far as political stability, or order, is concerned, a more definite conclusion may be stated. Although demands which might threaten political order were encouraged by too high expectations from the formation of Malaysia and by prospective benefits from timber, there were also checks, described above, which helped to slow down mobilization. The problem of political, as opposed to administrative, institutionalization remains. Before 1970 political institutionalization in Sarawak was hampered by disputes about which government was legitimate; in Sabah Tun Mustapha's rule has been a substitute for, but also an impediment to, political institutionalization.

The aim of the book was to present an extended case study of the political consequences of the formation of Malaysia for the Borneo states. Malaya, already with many political problems and highly dependent on the outside world economically and for defence, assumed new responsibilities in 1963 at very short notice. To a large extent since then the Malaysian government has been preoccupied with pressing and obvious problems in Malaya. It has made generous provision for developing the Borneo states economically, but has not been able to devote the attention to the political problems of Sarawak and Sabah which their inhabitants think they deserve. In particular, one consequence of the May 1969 riots in Malaya was that the Sarawak state elections, already overdue, were suspended for more than a year.

Nevertheless, in spite of the strong impact of the Federal Government on the Borneo states, it is clear that the federal-state relationship is substantially different from that of the Malayan states to the Federal Government. Sabah has asserted substantial autonomy in the person of Tun Mustapha, who, while fully loyal to Malaysia and to cultural methods of nation-building, has staked out a strong bargaining position *vis-à-vis* the Federal Government. Relief at having a "strong man" in control, well-equipped to deal with internal dissension or the Philippine threat, has no doubt persuaded the Federal Government to be more accommodating than they would otherwise have been. Before July 1970 Sarawak had not succeeded in acquiring much autonomy. Indeed, one consequence of the Emergency declared in May 1969 was that, parallel to the Sarawak Cabinet, a State Operations Council was set up, headed not by the Chief Minister[184] but by the Federal Secretary in Sarawak.

With the new government, headed by Dato Rahman Ya'akub, which took office in July 1970, there was a distinct change in the situation. The new Chief Minister was appointed Chairman of the State Operations Council, and it seemed that both while that Council lasted and after its abolition, when there was a return to parliamentary rule (1971), relations between the State and Federal Governments would be smoother than before. Dato Rahman Ya'akub, with his strong UMNO links, would be in a good position to extract the maximum amount of federal help in building up the economy of Sarawak inside Malaysia. His main problems would be internal: how to make his coalition with SUPP last in the face of possible dissatisfaction and disaffection among the party's more extreme Chinese members, how to reconcile the Iban parties, SNAP and Pesaka, to losing the Chief Ministership and the political predominance to which they had assumed they were entitled by reason of their numbers. In both states "autonomy" in certain spheres is possible only when the Federal Government is assured that the state governments are basically in sympathy with its approach to nation-building.

For some time to come, therefore, although undeniably part of the Malaysian political system, Sarawak and Sabah will warrant attention as subsystems with distinctive and interesting characteristics.

Appendix: Data on Political Elites

This appendix aims at providing basic biographical information about the emerging political elites in Sarawak and Sabah. For convenience, these elites have been defined as the candidates (1967 or 1969–70) and committee members of the various parties. It is hoped that, taken together, the tables which follow will provide a better understanding of the profile of each political party, and highlight the similarities and dissimilarities which exist among the parties in their selection of leaders. More generally, the tables should also give some useful indicators about the kinds of persons who have been entering the front line of politics during the early stages of representative Government in the two states.

The data contained in these tables were obtained primarily from the following sources: personal interviews with party officials, candidates and other knowledgeable persons; party records; newspapers; and Information Department hand-outs. Unfortunately, it was not possible to obtain full information on all the persons involved, and in some cases nothing was known about certain individuals who themselves could not be contacted. In order to minimize the likelihood of errors, every effort was made to cross-check the information obtained from one source by referring to another.

Extensive information on Sarawak elites is given in Michael B. Leigh's thesis, which extends back in time to before the formation of Malaysia, not only for the Council Negri but also for District Councils. Leigh makes the important general point that Bumiputera, SCA and Pesaka are led by those who have historically held a privileged position in their own communities; SUPP and SNAP did not have such leaders, and had to create their own local bases.

For Sabah, there is no table which gives the previous party affiliations of the elites covered. This is because only a very small number have moved from one party to another, and also because insufficient information was available about which of the antecedent organizations of UPKO and the SCA their elites had originally belonged to.

TABLE A.1

State Candidates (1967) and Executive Committee Members (for years indicated) of Political Parties in Sabah, by Ethnic Groups

	Party					
	UPKO		USNO		SCA	
Ethnic group	Cands	Ex. Co. (1968)	Cands	Ex. Co. (1967)	Cands	Ex. Co. (1969)
Kadazan	11	25	6	5	—	—
Chinese	—	—	—	—	6[c]	35[d]
Sino-Kadazan	6	11	2	—	—	—
Other mixed Kadazan	2	3	1	2	—	—
Bajau	1	2	4	1	—	—
Murut	2	8	1	1	—	—
Suluk	—	—	3	5	—	—
Orang Sungei	—	—	2	3	—	—
Brunei	—	2	2	1	—	—
Malay	—	—	1	1	—	—
Other indigenous	1	1	2	1	—	—
Other mixed indig.[a]	—	—	—	1	—	—
Other part indig.[b]	1	1	1	2	—	—
Other non-indig.	—	—	—	1	—	—
No information	—	3	—	—	—	—
Total	24	56	25	24	6	35

(*a*) i.e of mixed indigenous parentage.
(*b*) i.e. of mixed indigenous–non-indigenous parentage.
(*c*) 5 Hakka; 1 Teochew.
(*d*) Includes 18 Hakka; 5 Teochew; 3 Cantonese; 6 Hokkien; 1 Hainanese; and 1 Szechuan.

TABLE A.2

State and Parliamentary Candidates (1969/70) and Executive Committee Members (for years indicated) of Political Parties in Sarawak, by Ethnic Groups

Ethnic group	Party									
	SNAP		SUPP		Pesaka		Bumiputera		SCA	
	Cands	Ex. Co. (1967/68)	Cands	Ex. Co. (1968/70)	Cands	Ex. Co. (1968)	Cands	Ex. Co. (1969)	Cands	Ex. Co. (1969/70)
Iban	33	24	13	14	31	12	—	—	—	21[h]
Chinese	16	11	25	32	—	—	1	2	13[g]	—
Malay	9	6	4	5	6	1	22	25	—	—
Land Dayak	4	5	4	6	4	1	4	2	—	—
Melanau	—	1	—	2	3	3	4	4	—	—
Other Indigenous	2	2	3	2	5	2	1	1	—	—
Others	2	2	2	2	1	—	—	1	—	—
Not available	2	—	3	—	—	—	—	1	—	—
Total	68[a]	51	54[b]	63[c]	50[d]	19	32[e]	36	13[f]	21

(*a*) Includes two candidates who contested both the State and Parliamentary elections (This applies to all the following tables on Sarawak).
(*b*) Includes five candidates who contested both the State and Parliamentary elections (This applies to all the following tables on Sarawak).
(*c*) Includes members of the Central Executive Committee and the Working Committee (This applies to all the following tables on Sarawak).
(*d*) Includes one candidate who contested both the State and Parliamentary elections (This applies to all the following tables on Sarawak).
(*e*) Includes one candidate who contested both the State and Parliamentary elections (This applies to all the following tables on Sarawak).
(*f*) Includes one candidate who contested both the State and Parliamentary elections (This applies to all the following tables on Sarawak).
(*g*) Foochow—7; Hakka—3; Cantonese—1; Hainanese—1; Teochew—1.
(*h*) Foochow—8; Hakka—3; Cantonese—1; Hainanese—1; Teochew—4; Hokkien—4.

TABLE A.3

State Candidates (1967) and Executive Committee Members (for years indicated) of Political Parties in Sabah, by Religious Groups

Religious group	UPKO Cands	UPKO Ex. Co. (1968)	USNO Cands	USNO Ex. Co. (1967)	SCA Cands	SCA Ex. Co. (1969)
Muslims	5	13	20	21	—	—
Christians	16[c]	25[d]	2[e]	—	5[f]	12[g]
Buddhists	—	—	—	—	—	6
Confucians	1	1	—	—	—	—
Pagans[a]	1	11	3	3	—	—
Nil[b]	—	1	—	—	1	—
No information	1	5	—	—	—	17
Total	24	56	25	24	6	35

(*a*) All those falling into this category come from the non-Muslim indigenous groups.
(*b*) Those falling into this category are Chinese who have no formal religious affiliations but who sometimes follow traditional practices and ceremonies.
(*c*) Includes 10 Catholics, 2 Anglicans, 2 Evangelists and one Seventh Day Adventist.
(*d*) 22 Catholics, 1 Anglican, 1 Evangelist and 1 Seventh Day Adventist.
(*e*) Includes 1 Catholic.
(*f*) 2 Catholics, 2 Anglicans and 1 Lutheran.
(*g*) 3 Catholics, 4 Anglicans and 5 Lutherans.

TABLE A.4

State and Parliamentary Candidates (1969/70) and Executive Committee Members (for years indicated) of Political Parties in Sarawak, by Religious Groups

Religious group	Party									
	SNAP		SUPP		Pesaka		Bumiputera		SCA	
	Cands	Ex. Co. (1967/68)	Cands	Ex. Co. (1968/70)	Cands	Ex. Co. (1968)	Cands	Ex. Co. (1969)	Cands	Ex. Co. (1969/70)
Muslims	9	7	7	7	6	1	25	30	—	—
Christians	40[c]	29[d]	13[e]	11[e]	32[f]	15[g]	4[e]	4[e]	10[h]	14[i]
Buddhists	—	—	3	—	—	—	1	1	3	4
Confucians	2	4	—	—	—	—	—	—	—	—
Pagans[a]	11	4	11	14	10	—	—	—	—	—
Nil[b]	5	—	10	22	—	—	—	—	—	3
No information	1	7	10	9	2	3	2	1	—	—
Total	68	51	54	63	50	19	32	36	13	21

(*a*) All those falling into this category come from the non-Muslim indigenous groups.
(*b*) All these are Chinese who have no formal religions affiliations but who sometimes follow traditional practices and ceremonies.
(*c*) Includes 11 Catholics, 21 Anglicans and 5 Methodists.
(*d*) Includes 8 Catholics, 16 Anglicans and 2 Methodists.
(*e*) No breakdown was available by denominations.
(*f*) Includes 15 Catholics, 11 Anglicans and 4 Methodists.
(*g*) Includes 5 Catholics.
(*h*) Includes 7 Methodists.
(*i*) Includes 7 Methodists.

TABLE A.5

State Candidates (1967) and Executive Committee Members (for years indicated) of Political Parties in Sabah, by Age Groups

	Party					
	UPKO		USNO		SCA	
Age group	Cands	Ex. Co. (1968)	Cands	Ex. Co. (1967)	Cands	Ex. Co. (1969)
20–29	7	5	5	1	—	—
30–39	8	9	9	10	—	3
40–49	7	20	8	10	3	17
50–59	2	11	2	2	3	15
60+	—	3	1	—	—	—
No information	—	8	—	1	—	—
Total	24	56	25	24	6	35

TABLE A.6

State and Parliamentary Candidates (1969/70) and Executive Committee Members (for years indicated) of Political Parties in Sarawak, by Age Groups

	Party									
	SNAP		SUPP		Pesaka		Bumiputera		SCA	
Age group	Cands	Ex. Co. (1967–68)	Cands	Ex. Co. (1968–70)	Cands	Ex. Co. (1968)	Cands	Ex. Co. (1969)	Cands	Ex. Co. (1969–70)
20–29	4	2	2	7	1	—	—	—	1	2
30–39	10	15	14	17	17	5	6	1	7	5
40–49	13	27	20	20	21	8	13	11	3	6
50–59	2	3	13	13	8	2	9	17	—	3
60 +	2	3	2	6	3	4	2	6	2	5
Not available	37	1	3	—	—	—	2	1	—	—
Total	68	51	54	63	50	19	32	36	13	21

DORSET INSTITUTE OF
HIGHER EDUCATION
LEARNING RESOURCES
CENTRE

TABLE A.7

Educational Background of State Candidates (1967) and Executive Committee Members (for years indicated) of Political Parties in Sabah

	Party					
	UPKO		USNO		SCA	
Education level	Cands	Ex. Co. (1968)	Cands	Ex. Co. (1967)	Cands	Ex. Co. (1969)
Primary	9	31	18	16	—	16[a]
Secondary	13	17	6	5	5	16[b]
Post-Secondary	2	2	1	—	1	3
No formal Schooling	—	—	—	—	—	—
No information	—	6	—	3	—	—
Total	24	56	25	24	6	35

(*a*) 12 Chinese-educated, 1 English-educated and 3 Chinese- and English-educated.

(*b*) 8 Chinese-educated, 2 English-educated and 6 Chinese- and English-educated.

TABLE A.8

Educational Background of State and Parliamentary Candidates (1969/70) and Executive Committee Members (for years indicated) of Political Parties in Sarawak

Education level	SNAP Cands	SNAP Ex. Co. (1967–68)	SUPP Cands	SUPP Ex. Co. (1968–70)	Pesaka Cands	Pesaka Ex. Co. (1968)	Bumiputera Cands	Bumiputera Ex. Co. (1969)	SCA Cands	SCA Ex. Co. (1969–70)
Primary	4	12	10	13	10[b]	1	14	16	—	—
Secondary	36	27	23	27	15	11[c]	14	16	11	15[d]
Post-Secondary	3	2	1	1	3	2	2	2	2	6[e]
No formal schooling	2	7	13	13	22	4	—	—	—	—
No information	23[a]	3	7	9	—	1	2	2	—	—
Total	68	51	54	63	50	19	32	36	13	21

(*a*) A good majority of these probably had little or no formal education.
(*b*) Includes three persons who also received further training in the Batu Lintang Teachers' Training College.
(*c*) Includes three persons who also received further training in the Batu Lintang Teachers' Training College.
(*d*) Includes eight from Chinese-medium schools.
(*e*) Includes one from a foreign Chinese-medium University.

TABLE A.9

Occupational Breakdown of State Candidates (1967) and Executive Committee Members (for years indicated) of Political Parties in Sabah

	Party					
	UPKO		USNO		SCA	
Occupation	Cands	Ex. Co. (1968)	Cands	Ex. Co. (1967)	Cands	Ex. Co. (1969)
Wealthy Businessmen	3	7	2[d]	3[g]	5	31
Small Businessmen	2	5	3[e]	2	—	—
Govt. Servants	9	12[a]	6	4	—	—
Teachers	3	5	1	1	1	1
Traditional Elites	3	16[b]	4[f]	3[h]	—	—
Clerks	1	1	3	4	—	1
Business Employees	—	—	2	1	—	—
Farmers	1	2[c]	3	4[i]	—	1
Professionals	1	1	1	—	—	1
Others	—	1	—	2	—	—
No information	1	6	—	—	—	—
Total	24	56	25	24	6	35

(*a*) Includes one traditional elite.
(*b*) Total should be 18. See footnotes (*a*) and (*c*).
(*c*) Includes one traditional elite.
(*d*) Includes one traditional elite.
(*e*) Includes two traditional elites.
(*f*) Total should be seven: see footnotes (*d*) and (*e*).
(*g*) Includes one traditional elite.
(*h*) Total should be 5: see footnotes (*g*) and (*i*).
(*i*) Includes one traditional elite.

TABLE A.10

Occupational Breakdown of State and Parliamentary Candidates (1969/70) and Executive Committee Members (for years indicated) of Political Parties in Sarawak

Occupation	Party									
	SNAP		SUPP		Pesaka		Bumiputera		SCA	
	Cands	Ex. Co. (1967–68)	Cands	Ex. Co. (1968–70)	Cands	Ex. Co. (1968)	Cands	Ex. Co. (1969)	Cands	Ex. Co. (1969–70)
Businessmen	4	11	12	10	4[f]	7[k]	10	13[n]	11	16
Government servants	6	4	—	—	8	3[l]	7	9	1	—
Farmers and Petty traders	6	16[b]	25	29	16[g]	—	7	1	—	—
Teachers	9	1	—	—	10[h]	4	3	3	1	2
Traditional elites	5[a]	2[c]	1[d]	1[e]	4[i]	—[m]	—	—[o]	—	—
Labourers	—	—	2	7	3	—	—	—	—	1
Clerks	4	8	9	13	2[j]	1	—	—	—	1
Professionals	4	1	1	1	—	1	2	2	—	—
Pensioners	6	4	—	—	1	1	—	2	—	1
Others	4	4	1	2	2	2	1	5	—	—
No information	20	—	3	—	—	—	2	1	—	—
Total	68	51	54	63	50	19	32	36	13	21

(*a*) Three of these were *Penghulus* while the other two were *Kapitans China* who were also small businessmen.
(*b*) Three of these were also traditional elites.
(*c*) The total should be 5. See footnote (*b*)
(*d*) *Kapitan China.*
(*e*) *Kapitan China.*
(*f*) One of these was also a traditional elite.
(*g*) Six of these were also traditional elites.
(*h*) One of these was also a traditional elite.
(*i*) The total should be 13. See footnotes (*f*), (*g*), (*h*) and (*j*).
(*j*) One of these was also a traditional elite.
(*k*) Four of these were also traditional elites.
(*l*) One of these was also a traditional eltie.
(*m*) The total should be 5. See footnotes (*k*) and (*l*).
(*n*) Two of these were also traditional elites.
(*o*) The total should be 2. See footnote (*n*).

TABLE A.11

Residential Breakdown of State and Parliamentary Candidates (1967) and Executive Members (for years indicated) of Political Parties in Sabah

	Party						
	UPKO		USNO		SCA		Total
Home town/area	Cands	Ex. Co. (1968)	Cands	Ex. Co. (1967)	Cands	Ex. Co. (1969)	
West Coast Residency							
Kota Kinabalu	—	—	—	2	2	14	18
Penampang	6	10[a]	2	—	—	—	18
Papar	1	4	—	2	—	1	8
Tuaran	2	—	3	1	—	2	8
Kudat	—	1	3	6	1	2	13
Kinarut	1	2	—	—	—	—	3
Kota Belud	1	2	2	2	—	—	7
Ranau	1	3	1	1	—	—	6
Other W.C. Residency	—	3	2	1	—	—	6
Total W.C. Residency	12	25	13	15	3	19	87
Sandakan Residency							
Sandakan	1	2	2	2	2	8	17

Kinabatangan	1	2	1	—	—	—	4
Labuk	2	—	—	—	—	—	2
Sugut	—	—	1	—	—	—	1
Total Sandakan Residency	4	4	4	2	2	8	24
Tawau Residency							
Tawau	—	—	1	—	1	3	5
Lahad Datu	—	1	—	—	—	1	2
Semporna	1	2	1	—	—	—	4
Total Tawau Residency	1	3	2	—	1	4	11
Interior Residency							
Tenom	1	4	1	1	—	—	7
Sipitang	1	1	1	2	—	—	5
Beaufort	1	1	2	1	—	1	6
Labuan	—	1	1	1	—	1	4
Keningau	2	7	—	1	—	1	11
Kuala Penyu	1	3	—	—	—	—	4
Tambunan	1	2	—	—	—	—	3
Other Interior Residency	—	2	1	—	—	—	3
Total Interior Residency	7	21	6	6	—	3	43
Not available	—	3	—	1	—	1	5
Total	24	56	25	24	6	35	170

(*a*) There were three others who, although they were not originally from Penampang, had lived there for some time.

TABLE A.12

Residential Breakdown of State and Parliamentary Candidates (1969/70) and Executive Committee Members (for years indicated) of Political Parties in Sarawak

Home town/area	SNAP Cands	SNAP Ex. Co. (1967–68)	SUPP Cands	SUPP Ex. Co. (1968–70)	Pesaka Cands	Pesaka Ex. Co. (1968)	Bumiputera Cands	Bumiputera Ex. Co. (1969)	SCA Cands	SCA Ex. Co. (1969–70)	Total
1st Division											
Kuching	3	5	7	16	3	—	9	19	4	5	71
Bau	—	1	2	1	2	1	2	1	—	—	10
Serian	2	3	1	1	—	—	—	1	—	1	9
Lundu	1	2	1	—	1	—	1	1	—	1	8
Other 1st Division	1	3	4	6	—	—	4	3	—	—	21
Total 1st Division	7	14	15	24	6	1	16	25	4	7	119
2nd Division											
Seratok	3	3	1	2	1	1	—	—	—	—	11
Simanggang	3	5	1	1	3	1	3	1	—	—	18
Betong	2	3	—	—	2	—	—	—	—	—	7
Lubok Antu	—	1	1	1	2	—	—	—	—	—	5
Other 2nd Division	1	—	1	1	4	1	2	—	—	—	10
Total 2nd Division	9	12	4	5	12	3	5	1	—	—	51

3rd Division											
Sibu	8	4	5	6	4	5	—	3	5	—	40
Kapit	3	1	2	2	4	2	—	—	—	4	18
Kanowit	2	1	3	2	3	2	—	—	—	—	13
Sarikei	2	1	3	2	1	—	—	—	1	2	12
Julau	2	—	—	—	2	1	—	—	—	—	5
Binatang	2	1	2	1	1	—	—	—	1	1	9
Song	2	—	1	1	2	—	—	—	—	—	6
Mukah	1	4	1	3	1	—	3	2	—	—	15
Other 3rd Division	4	—	3	2	5	1	1	1	—	—	17
Total 3rd Division	26	12	20	19	23	11	4	6	7	7	135
4th Division											
Miri	2	1	1	1	1	—	—	1	1	5	13
Bintulu	2	2	4	2	3	2	2	—	1	—	18
Baram	2	3	1	1	3	1	—	—	—	—	11
Other 4th Division	—	—	2	—	—	—	—	—	—	—	2
Total 4th Division	6	6	8	4	7	3	2	1	2	5	44
5th Division											
Limbang	1	4	—	1	—	—	1	1	—	—	8
Lawas	—	3	—	—	1	—	2	1	—	—	7
Total 5th Division	1	7	—	1	1	—	3	2	—	—	15
Not available	19	—	7	10	1	1	2	1	—	2	43
Total	68	51	54	63	50	19	32	36	13	21	408

TABLE A.13

Previous Party Affiliations of State and Parliamentary Candidates (1969/70) and Executive Committee Members (for years indicated) of Political Parties in Sarawak

Previous party	Present party: SNAP Cands	SNAP Ex. Co. (1967–68)	SUPP Cands	SUPP Ex. Co. (1967–70)	Pesaka Cands	Pesaka Ex. Co. (1968)	Bumiputera[c] Cands	Bumiputera[c] Ex. Co. (1969)	SCA Cands	SCA Ex. Co. (1969–70)
SNAP	—	—	—	—	5	2	2	—	—	—
SUPP	1	4	—	—	5	1	—	—	2	2
Pesaka	2	2	1	1	—	—	—	—	—	—
Bumiputera	—	—	—	—	1	—	—	—	—	—
SCA	—	—	—	—	—	—	—	—	—	—
PANAS	2	2	6	2	5	2	17	16	—	1
BARJASA	2	5	—	—	5	—	13	19	—	—
MACHINDA[a]	—	1	2	—	—	—	—	—	—	—
TUPP[a]	—	—	—	—	1	2	—	—	—	—
Nil	41	36	48	61	29	12	—	—	11	18
No information	20	2	—	—	—	—	2	1	—	—
Total	68	52[b]	57[b]	64[b]	51[b]	19	34[b]	36	13	21

(*a*) Parties formed after the 1963 district council elections but dissolved before the 1969–70 state elections.
(*b*) The totals exceed the actual numbers of Candidates or Executive Committee members for the party indicated, because one or more persons in the total switched parties previously, before the switch indicated here.
(*c*) Note that Bumiputera was formed through the merger of PANAS and BARJASA.

Notes

Chapter 1

1. One special type of settlement was intended for those, in both states, who had to leave their previous areas because of the threat from Indonesia during Confrontation. Not to be confused with other types of resettlement was a type of resettlement of Sarawak Chinese, enforced after some Communist-inspired activity in 1965. The Chinese settlements, like the "new villages" set up during the fighting with the Communist rebels in Malaya 1948–60, were intended to isolate Communist terrorists from contact with possible helpers.
2. The above statistics are taken mostly from annual issues of: *Malaysia Official Year Book* (Kuala Lumpur); *Annual Bulletin of Statistics, Malaysia* (Kuala Lumpur); *Sarawak Annual Bulletin of Statistics* (Kuching); *Annual Bulletin of Statistics, Sabah* (Kota Kinabalu).
3. See Chapter 6. In 1963, although most of the population of Malaya lived inside the area of elected local government authorities, some parts of the country did not possess such authorities. In 1965 and 1966 some important local authorities in Malaya had their functions taken over by the appropriate state government.

Chapter 2

1. See particularly: Philip E. Jacob and James V. Toscano (eds.), *The Integration of Political Communities* (Philadelphia, 1964); Amitai Etzioni, *Political Unification; a Comparative Study of Leaders and Forces* (New York, 1965); Karl W. Deutsch and William J. Foltz (eds.), *Nation-Building* (New York, 1966).
2. Gabriel A. Almond and G. Bingham Powell, Jr., *Comparative Politics; a Developmental Approach* (Boston, 1966), p. 36.
3. T. H. Silcock, *The Commonwealth Economy in Southeast Asia*, (Durham, N.C., 1959), p. 73. For British policy on relations and co-operation among the territories, 1945–61, see B. Simandjuntak, *Malayan Federalism*, 1945–63 (Kuala Lumpur, 1969), pp. 118–24.
4. Newly-independent Malaya was constitutionally a federation; however, the choice of a federal structure was dictated largely by the existence of Malay Rulers at the head of nine of the eleven states. In practice the powers of the states were weak compared

with those of the Federal Government, and were confined mainly to land (R. S. Milne, *Government and Politics in Malaysia* (Boston, 1967), Chapter 5).

Broadly speaking, the ethnic differences and disputes which troubled Malaya did not coincide with state boundaries, and so did not take the form of a struggle between the states and the Federal Government. But Sarawak and Sabah had greater constitutional powers than the states of Malaya, and some contentious issues assumed both ethnic and "states' rights" aspects.

5. Signed on 19 December, 1961. For the text, see *North Borneo Government Gazette*, Vol. XVII, No. 7 (1 February, 1962), cols. 54–60.
6. See *Report of the Commission of Enquiry, North Borneo and Sarawak* (Kuala Lumpur: Government Press, 1962), subsequently referred to as "the Cobbold Report"; *Malaysia Report of the Inter-Governmental Committee* (Kuala Lumpur: Government Press, 1963). The Cobbold Report reproduces, as Appendix F, the memorandum produced by the Malaysia Solidarity Consultative Committee. On the process generally see R. S. Milne, *op. cit.*, pp. 60–73. In the following account the negotiations with Singapore and Brunei are ignored. On Singapore's entry into Malaysia see Milton E. Osborne, *Singapore and Malaysia* (Ithaca, N.Y., 1964).
7. *Straits Times*, 28 August, 1962.
8. *Ibid.*, 9 September, 1960.
9. Interview, Singapore, 18 October, 1964. For a list of parties and prominent political leaders in Sarawak and Sabah, see Appendix at end of Chapter 3.
10. Among some groups in the Fifth Division of Sarawak, especially the Kedayans, there was considerable support for incorporation in Brunei, as the sympathy in this area for the Azahari rebellion indicated.
11. *Sarawak By the Week*, 26/61, 25 June–1 July, 1961, p. 3, quoting *The Times* (London). It was reported that the two Governors would have preferred the three Borneo territories to get closer together before joining a Malaysian Federation (*Sarawak By The Week, op. cit.*, p. 1). One of the Governors said that the speech of Tengku's on 26 May, 1961 came as a complete surprise to him and that he did not believe the Tengku would pursue the matter.
12. *Straits Times*, 24 October, 1961.
13. *Council Negri Debates, Third Meeting of the Fourth Session* (26 September, 1962), cols. 26–7.
14. Dato Stephens, interview, Kota Kinabalu, 18 June, 1968.
15. *Council Negri Debates, First Meeting of the Sixth Session* (4 September, 1963), cols. 47–8 (Taib bin Mahmud, Minister for Communications and Works).

16. Tun Razak, *Straits Times*, 21 August, 1962. The states already had development plans of their own, but on a smaller scale.
17. Notably, for Sabah, health until the end of 1970. Education was delegated to Sarawak, although not by the Constitution because the Sarawak local government authorities were already performing this function; they continued to perform it until the state government took it over in 1972.
18. By 1968 the value of this grant had reached $18 million. Sarawak had, in effect, two corresponding grants. One was fixed at $5.8m for each of the five years, 1964–8. The other, sometimes known as an "escalating grant", was fixed in advance for each of the five years, each year's figure being higher than the previous year. Actually, after the initial five years the escalating grant was cut, and in October 1969 it was announced that the $5.8m grant was abolished. There was no time limit set for the operation of the Sabah grant, although the Federal Government made an unsuccessful attempt to renegotiate the terms (p. 421, Fn. 145 below).
19. J. P. Ongkili, *The Borneo Response to Malaysia, 1961–1963*, Singapore, 1967), pp. 58–9, quoting the Tengku (*Straits Times*, 15 August, 1967).
20. *Dewan Ra'ayat Debates*, III, No. 16 (16 October, 1961), col. 1606.
21. *Sarawak Gazette*, Vol. LXXXIX, No. 1262 (30 April, 1963), p. 81.
22. *Council Negri Debates, Third Meeting of the Fourth Session* (26 September, 1962), col. 50.
23. Tengku Abdul Rahman, *Dewan Ra'ayat Debates*, III, No. 16 (16 October, 1961), col. 1608.
24. Etzioni, *op. cit.*, pp. 77–9.
25. *Ibid.*, p. 315.
26. William H. Riker, *Federalism, Origin, Operation, Significance* (Boston, 1964), p. 12.
27. *Ibid.*, p. 31. Cf. A. H. Birch, "Approaches to the Study of Federalism", *Political Studies*, Vol. XIV, No. 1 (1966), pp. 29–32.
28. Thomas M. Franck, "Why Federations Fail" in Thomas M. Franck (ed.), *Why Federations Fail* (New York, 1968), p. 177.
29. *Ibid.*, p. 172.
30. And could have led to a union of British territories in the area in 1945 (p. 18, above).
31. Herbert J. Spiro, "The Federation of Rhodesia and Nyasaland", in Franck (ed.), *op. cit.*, p. 86.
32. F. G. Carnell, "Political Implications of Federalism in New States" in U.K. Hicks *et al.*, *Federalism and Economic Growth on Underdeveloped Countries* (London, 1961), p. 59.
33. Tengku Abdul Rahman, *Dewan Ra'ayat Debates*, IV, No. 3 (28 April, 1962), cols. 451–2.

34. K. J. Ratnam, *Communalism and the Political Process in Malaya* (Kuala Lumpur, 1965).
35. The informal arrangement between Malay and Chinese elites before Independence, in which, broadly speaking, the former were to be politically, the latter economically, dominant.
36. R. S. Milne, "Political Modernisation in Malaysia", *Journal of Commonwealth Political Studies*, Vol. VII, No. 1 (1969), p. 16.
37. Cf. Gordon P. Means, *Malaysian Politics* (London, 1970), pp. 299–300.
38. Nation-building "refers to the process whereby people transfer their commitment and loyalty from smaller tribes, villages, or petty principalities to the larger central political system" (Almond and Powell, *op. cit.*, p. 36), with the proviso that the transfer is not total; local and national loyalties may exist simultaneously. The term, integration (see the references in footnote 1 of this chapter), has been usually avoided here because of its ambiguity.
39. An example may be taken from the first category discussed below, ministerial contacts. Some state ministers resented the fact that federal ministers expected an elaborate welcome when visiting the Borneo states, while they themselves were not welcomed on the same scale when they visited Malaya. Such an attitude may have been unrealistic in view of the obviously higher status of federal ministers. Nevertheless, the resentment was felt (Cf. Philip E. Jacob and Henry Teune, "The Integrative Process" in Jacob and Toscano (eds.), *op. cit.*, pp. 27–8). This was one reason for not attempting to quantify interactions, or increases in interactions, arising from the formation of Malaysia. A second reason was the absence of some necessary data (but see p. 420, Fn. 136, below).
40. The Federal Cabinet has included other members from the Borneo states: the Datu Bandar; Enche Peter Lo; Dato Ong Kee Hui (from December 1970); Enche Abdul Taib (from December 1971).
41. *Straits Times*, 9 August, 1966 (Tun Ismail). For a brief period Trengganu had not been under an Alliance Government (R. S. Milne, *op cit.*, pp. 73–82). Cf. Riker, *op. cit.*, p. 129; "The federal relationship is centralised according to the degree to which the parties organised to operate the central government control the parties organised to operate the constituent governments".
42. An explanation of abbreviations of party names is given in the Appendix at the end of Ch. 3.
43. *Vanguard*, 10 July, 1970.
44. *Sabah Times*, 2 April, 1968.
45. *Legislative Assembly Debates*, Vol. III, No. 8 (22 December, 1967), cols. 301–2 (Tun Mustapha). See also pp. 48–49, below.
46. The terms of reference were "1. To establish and maintain close and cordial relationship, co-operation and understanding between the federal state governments themselves on matters pertaining to

administration, legislation and implementation of Federal and State policies; and 2. To establish, consider, and deal with any problem relating to administration, legislation and Federal and State policies with a view to recommending common methods and practices" (*Sabah Times*, 23 September, 1967). See also *ibid.*, 18 November, 1966.

47. Approximate because from names in the Staff Lists it is not always possible to tell who is an expatriate.
48. The Sarawak Government claimed that expatriates were removed from key jobs more rapidly in Sarawak than they had been in Malaya (*Borneanization Progress Report, March, 1966* (Sarawak Government, unpublished); *Vanguard*, 5 July, 1967 (Dato Ningkan)). However, as stated below, expatriates in the secretariat were replaced more slowly than in Sabah.
49. *Cobbold Report*, Appendix "B", Table 6, p. 104. The supply of graduates also had to meet the demand for educated politicians.
50. *Malaysia Report of the Inter-Governmental Committee 1962*, *op. cit.*, Annex B.
51. *Straits Times*, 15 August, 1960.
52. In both states there were provisions regarding positions in the public service for Natives (*Federal Constitution*, Article 161A; *Sarawak Constitution*, Article 39; *Sabah Constitution*, Article 41). There were complementary provisions on scholarships and training privileges. The Natives in the Borneo states still did not have the same privileges as the Malays in Malaya, e.g. as regards reserved places for scholarships and entry to institutions of higher learning, but they were given these by the Federal constitutional amendments made in March, 1971 (*Straits Times*, 2 March, 1971).
53. It was no doubt for this reason that in the mid-1960s the Sarawak Dayak Association wanted a quota to be laid down and imposed by the establishment office for public service jobs, not just for Natives but for particular ethnic groups of Natives.
54. See pp. 172, 233.
55. *Straits Times*, 22 November, 1962.
56. *Ibid.*, 19 August, 1964.
57. *Borneo Bulletin*, 12 September, 1964.
58. *Straits Times*, 24 February, 1966.
59. *Ibid.*, 9 October, 1964 (Rahman Ya'akub).
60. *Ibid.*, 25 June, 1964 (Tuan Syed Nasir, Director of the Language and Literature Agency).
61. *Ibid.*, 7 April, 1964.
62. See Ch. 5. Some of the expatriates' difficulties arose because in both states the first Chief Minister was a non-Muslim Native. When he came under attack from Kuala Lumpur the expatriates who served him were also bound to come under fire. It has also been alleged that expatriates in Sabah were hostile to politicians as such. "Interviewing in North Borneo after the Federation of

Malaysia was mooted, I found the expatriate civil servants extremely hostile to emerging political developments. Their most common reaction was to note that until a few months previously, North Borneo had been a paradise undisturbed by any hint of political activity" (Gayl D. Ness, *Bureaucracy and Rural Development in Malaysia* (Berkeley and Los Angeles, 1967), p. 174, fn. 21). One expatriate's comment on the above was; "they may have grumbled about politicians but they did everything they could to make the system work". Another (Sarawak) expatriate remarked that, while some of his fellow-expatriates were lukewarm about the introduction of politics, others welcomed it. Expatriates did not behave as a monolithic group any more than politicians or local civil servants; they had their own cliques and personal feuds.

63. *Inter-Governmental Committee Report*, Annex B, paras, 5–13 and 30. See also *Council Negri Debates*, *First Meeting of the Sixth Session* (5 September, 1963), cols. 71–2 (the Chief Secretary).
64. *Straits Times*, 7 July, 1966; *Utusan Melayu*, 7 March, 1966; *Staff Lists* for Sarawak and Sabah, 1968. To complicate the issue there were also some expatriates in federal posts, e.g. in the police.
65. Cf. Peter Mojuntin's complaint that the four top posts in the board were not held by Sabahans (*Sabah Times*, 27 September, 1967).
66. There was more local criticism of the holders of these two posts in Sabah than in Sarawak.
67. Originally there was a single Federal Secretary for the two states, stationed in Kuching, with a deputy in Jesselton. Later, a Federal Secretary was appointed for each of the two states. The Sarawak Coalition Government of 1971 tactfully changed the title to Secretary-General, Ministry for Sarawak Affairs.
68. Tengku Abdul Rahman, *Sabah Times*, 21 January, 1967
69. Abu Hassan bin Abdullah, *Vanguard*, 4 November, 1966.
70. Peter Mojuntin, *Sabah Times*, 11 July, 1967.
71. Dato Donald Stephens, *ibid.*, 13 March, 1965.
72. *Vanguard*, 15 November, 1969. The Federal Secretary's spirited reply appeared in *Sunday Tribune*, 16 November, 1969.
73. Cf. W. H. Morris-Jones, *The Government and Politics of India* (New York, 1964), p. 111.
74. In Malaya rotation of administrators at senior level in the states is ensured by a system in which such posts are filled by officers seconded from the Federal Government (Milne, *op. cit.*, p. 152).
75. One Sarawak State Development Officer was promoted from that post to the job of Federal Secretary. One State Development Officer in Sabah became Federal Secretary there, but only after an intervening posting to West Malaysia. Another Sabah State Development Officer, after a brief spell as Acting Federal Secretary, was appointed to an influential position as "Technical Adviser" in the Chief Minister's Department; in 1969 he was on Malayan Scale E at a salary of $33,750 p.a., over $9,000 p.a.

more than the salary of the Permanent Secretary to the Chief Minister. He later became Federal Secretary.

76. For a description of its operations, see: *Sabah Times*, 16 May, 1967; *Sabah's Revolution for Progress* (Kota Kinabalu, 1971), pp. 225–8.
77. Gayl D. Ness, *Bureaucracy and Rural Development in Malaysia, op. cit*,. pp. 136–9.
78. *Kinabalu Sabah Times*, 2 September, 1969; *Sarawak Tribune*, 19 February, 1970.
79. *Sabah Times*, 12 February, 1968; *Vanguard*, 23 April, 1970.
80. See p. 42.
81. See pp. 280–281, 288–292.
82. However, in the Borneo states it has occasionally made loans to Chinese in rural areas where there would be indirect benefits "to the people as a whole".
83. In fact various provisions were made to soften the impact of the change. Cf. Margaret Roff, "The Politics of Language in Malaya", *Asian Survey*, Vol. 7, No. 5 (1967).
84. *Constitution of Malaysia*, Article 161.
85. Originally referred to in Malay as "Bahasa Kebangsaan", later as "Bahasa Malaysia".
86. See Michael Buma, "Language Problems in Sarawak", *The Sarawak Gazette*, Vol. XCII, no. 1299 (31 May, 1966), pp. 151–2. This issue contains other useful articles on language. On the use of Malay in the Chamber of Commerce and the courts under the Brookes, see *State Orders* (*Green Book 1933*) *Issued by His Highness the Rajah of Sarawak or with his Sanction* (Kuching, 1933), pp. 14 (10 February, 1873) and 19 (1 June, 1870).
87. *Sarawak Annual Bulletin of Statistics, 1969* (Kuching, 1966), Table 17.6, p. 111. Schools broadcasts, not divided into languages in the table, are excluded. Further increases in the Malay content were announced later, e.g. in news bulletins (*Sarawak Tribune*, 28 January, 1970).
88. *Sabah Since Malaysia* (Kota Kinabula, 1967), p. 101. In both states newspapers were predominantly in English or Chinese.
89. See, e.g., the resolution passed at a meeting of the Kuching Chinese General Chamber of Commerce, the Boards of Management of Chinese Secondary and Primary Schools, and representatives of all registered Chinese societies in Kuching (*Sunday Tribune*, 22 May, 1966). Similar resolutions were passed at meetings of Chinese organizations in Sibu and Miri.
90. See correspondence from the Office of Broadcasting and Information, Jesselton to the Secretariat, 31 July, 1963. Cf. Margaret Roff, "The Rise and Demise of Kadazan Nationalism", *Journal of Southeast Asian History*, Vol. X, No. 2 (1969), pp. 328 and 331.
91. *North Borneo News*, 10 November, 1962 (Peter Mojuntin).

92. *Straits Times*, 16 July, 1964.
93. *Sarawak Tribune*, 6 February, 1969.
94. In 1960 there were approximately 48,000 persons literate in English in Sarawak and only 34,000 literate in Malay. In North Borneo, with only about two-thirds of the Sarawak population, there were approximately 23,000 persons literate in English and 29,000 literate in Malay. Moreover, although for the previous ten or a dozen years the percentage *increase* in literacy was higher for English than for Malay in each territory, Sarawak had a higher rate of increase in literacy in English than Sabah, while Sabah had a higher rate of increase of literacy in Malay than Sarawak (L. W. Jones, *The Population of Borneo* (London, 1966), Table 64, p. 131).
95. *Vanguard*, 1 July, 1966.
96. In his letter to Ningkan, 26 March, 1966.
97. *Borneo Bulletin*, 7 May, 1966. Cf. the Tengku (*Sarawak Tribune*, 6 March, 1970).
98. *Sarawak By the Week*, 33/66, 7–13 August, 1966, p. 2.
99. E.g. *Kinabalu Sabah Times,* 8 May, 6 August, 9 September, 15 September, 1969.
100. *Ibid.*, 5 September, 1969.
101. *Ibid.*, 4 September, 1969.
102. *Ibid.*, 15 March, 1970.
103. *Malaysia Report of the Inter-Governmental Committee 1962, op. cit.*, para 17.
104. *State of Sabah, The Annual Summary Report of the Department of Education, 1963* (Jesselton, 1964), p. 6.
105. *Malaysia: Sarawak Education Annual Summary for 1964* (Kuching, 1966), p. 1.
106. Some schools refused to accept aid on this condition. See: *A Guide to Education Department Annual Summary for 1964.* (Kuching, 1966), p. 107, below.
107. *Sarawak Tribune*, 19 February, 1965 (Dato Ningkan).
108. *Straits Times*, 22 July, 1964.
109. *Sarawak Tribune*, 17 December, 1964.
110. *Daily Express*, 4 August, 1965.
111. *Sarawak By the Week*, 33/66, 7–13 August, 1966, p. 2.
112. *Vanguard*, 14 April, 1969.
113. In National English Primary Schools (*Straits Times*, 11 July, 1969).
114. *Kinabalu Sabah Times*, 23 December, 1969. Between 1976 and 1980 *Bahasa Malaysia* would become the medium, by stages, in all secondary schools (*ibid.*, 5 August, 1970).
115. Cf. his remark, while visiting Sarawak as federal Education Minister that Sarawak must make a serious effort to study the National Language, and that, while Sabah and West Malaysia were following the national system of education, Sarawak still followed the old British system (*Sarawak Tribune*, 18 March,

1970). It might be expected that the SUPP, in exchange for joining the new government under Dato Rahman Ya'akub, would require some concessions in Chinese education. However, the changes announced in West Malaysia in July 1969 by Rahman Ya'akub, affected English primary schools and not Chinese primary schools, so there was no direct conflict between him and the SUPP on this point.

116. *Sabah Times*, 7 March, 1967.
117. See pp. 97 and 98.
118. *Sabah Legislative Assembly Debates*, Vol. III, No. 8 (22 December, 1967), cols. 393–5 (Tun Mustapha). On the Sabah Foundation's endowment with forest reserve timber, 1970, see p. 467, Fn. 30, below.
119. *Sabah Times*, 13 January, 1969 (Tun Mustapha). The larger number of places in the Malay medium reflects both the desire to accelerate the use of the National Language and also the fact that in 1968 there was only one secondary school in Sabah in which Malay was the medium of instruction.
120. *Sabah Since Malaysia*, 1963–1968 (Kuala Lumpur, 1969), p. 41.
121. *Malaysia Report of the Inter-Governmental Committee 1962, op. cit.*, para. 24 (10) and (11). Contrary to a popular belief, however, the Federal Government did not make any definite commitment about what its share of this expenditure would be.
122. Henry Teune, "The Learning of Integrative Habits" in Philip E. Jacob and James V. Toscano (eds.), *op. cit.*, pp. 273–4. Note, however, that in the long run commitment to the political system *per se* is a commitment to it over and above its actual performance (Sidney Verba, "Comparative Political Culture" in Lucian W. Pye and Sidney Verba (eds.), *Political Culture and Political Development* (Princeton, 1965), p. 529).
123. See pp. 287–288.
124. A Tun Razak estimate, excluding defence but including capital expenditure, was that there was a transfer from the Central Government to Sabah of about $39 million each year, 1964–6. He also estimated that $95 per head was spent each year in Sabah, 1964–6, on non-security capital expenditure, compared with $66 per head in West Malaysia (*Kinabalu Sunday Times*, 23 July, 1967).
125. *Sabah's Economic Progress* (address by the Hon. Enche Haris b. Mohd. Salleh) (Jesselton; Federal Department of Information, 1965), p. 32.
126. *Sabah Budget, 1969* (text of a speech by Hon. Enche Salleh Sulong) (Kota Kinabalu; Federal Department of Information, 1968), p. 13. The 1969 estimates for recurrent expenditure also included $7.6 million for local security measures normally a federal responsibility (*ibid.*, p. 15).
127. *Council Negri Debates, First Meeting of the Fifth Session* (13 December, 1966), col. 39 (Penghulu Tawi Sli).

128. *Ibid., Third Meeting of the Sixth Session* (16 December, 1968), col. 322 (Tawi Sli).
129. See pp. 282, 288–292.
130. *Sabah Times*, 21 January, 1967.
131. *Sarawak Tribune*, 14 August, 1965.
132. *Vanguard*, 30 May, 1967. In one respect Sarawak's economic performance did improve during the 1960's. In 1968 and 1969 it had a trade surplus as compared with a deficit in previous years. In the early 1970s there was a phenomenal rise in its production and its exports.
133. *Report on the Economic Aspects of Malaysia, by a Mission of the International Bank for Reconstruction and Development* (Kuala Lumpur: Government Press, 1963).
134. *Daily Express*, 11 March, 1966 (Peter Lo).
135. *Sarawak Annual Bulletin of Statistics, 1969* (Kuching, 1969), Tables 15.3 and 15.4, pp. 71 and 72.
136. *Annual Bulletin of Statistics, Sabah, 1968* (Kota Kinabalu, 1969), Table 14.6, p. 118. In the corresponding table for exports, West Malaysia is not listed separately (Table 14.9, p. 121).

     There is a shortage of data on transactions between Malaya and the Borneo states which would illustrate changes after the formation of Malaysia. For example, most figures on mail flows in the annual statistical bulletins of the two states do not distinguish between transactions with Malaya and those with the rest of the world. However, data on C.O.D. (cash on delivery) parcels received in Sarawak are an exception, values being given for the United Kingdom and for Malaya. The average value for 1964–6, compared with the average for 1960–2, showed a 9% increase for C.O.D. parcels from the U.K., but a 59% increase for such parcels from Malaya (*Sarawak Annual Bulletin of Statistics, 1968* (Kuching, 1968), Table 17.2, p. 107).
137. *Sandakan Jih Pao*, 11 November, 1965. Numerous other complaints were made in the Sabah Chinese newspapers at this period, reflecting dissatisfaction not only from consumers but also from associations. Among the latter the Jesselton Chinese Chamber of Commerce complained about the effects on development of a proposed new tariff on imported cement (*Overseas Chinese Daily News*, 27 January, 1966).
138. *Sabah Times*, 10 January, 1967. Other estimates ranged as high as 30 or 40%. Comparable complaints of the effect of new duties on the cost of living were still being made in 1969 (*Kinabalu Sabah Times*, 19 and 25 September, 1969 (editorials)).
139. *Address by Tun Mustapha at USNO General Assembly, 8 March, 1969* (Kota Kinabalu, 1969), p. 22.
140. There are no official figures available for Sarawak cost of living changes over a period. However, the federal Finance Minister maintained that retail prices, excluding rent, were only 11% higher in Kuching than in Kuala Lumpur, while in Jesselton

they were 20% higher (*Vanguard*, 22 January, 1967). It was also relevant that freight charges from Malaya to Sarawak were lower than those to Sabah.

141. *Api Siang Pao*, 22 August, 1968.
142. *Vanguard*, 24 April, 1969. Agricultural exports from the Borneo territories faced similar problems. Dato James Wong pointed out that an investor in an oil palm estate would choose West Malaysia rather than Sarawak because of less expensive labour and better communications (*Council Negri Debates, First Meeting of the Seventh Session* (14 December, 1968), cols. 199–200)).
143. *Tax Changes within Malaysia* (Kuala Lumpur: Government Printer, 1964), p. 1.
144. *Sabah Times*, 11 August, 1967.
145. *Ibid.*, 26 January, 1967. The imposition of the tax was in reality an attempt by the Federal Government to revise its financial arrangements with Sabah, which it now thought were unrealistic (see p. 413, Fn. 18).
146. This aspect of the proposal was intended to penalize the "Ali Baba" form of business, i.e. the alienation of timber licences to Chinese by Natives. The Chief Minister believed that it was somewhat late in the day to discourage Ali Babas, and that Natives could never run the timber business unaided at this stage (*ibid.*).
147. *Borneo Times*, 3 February, 1967. In 1969 it was announced that a new excess profits tax on logging operations would replace the disallowance, for federal tax purposes, of half the royalties paid to state governments for extracting timber (*Sabah Times*, 10 January, 1969).
148. They were abolished in Sabah from 1968 onwards. The Federal Government had stated that it did not object to these fees being reduced to the level prevalent in West Malaysia, provided that the relevant state government, which received the revenue, was prepared to forego it (*ibid.*, 23 August, 1967).
149. *Straits Times*, 29 May, 1963.
150. Etzioni, *op. cit.*, p. 59.
151. *Vanguard*, 9 September, 1967.
152. See p. 22, above.
153. *Daily Express*, 21 August, 1965.
154. Obviously there is an overlap between the two categories, "finance" and "constitutional". For instance the dispute between the Federal Government and the Sarawak government about mineral rights outside the three-mile limit obviously falls into both categories. The Federal Government extended the Continental Shelf Act and the Petroleum Act, both of 1966, to Sarawak and Sabah over the protests of the Sarawak Government which was unwilling to lose the possibly large revenues involved (*Sarawak Tribune*, 15 November, 1969).
155. See: Chapter 5, p. 225; *Reasons for Central Government Action*

(Kuala Lumpur; Tun Razak Statement, 15 September, 1966), reproduced by Information Department, 1966).

156. *Council Negri Debates, Third Meeting of the Sixth Session* (27 September, 1968), cols. 186–210.

157. *Monitoring Report on Chinese Newspapers published in Kuching*, 18 and 19 May, 1969 (prepared by Malaysian Information Services, Sarawak) (radio broadcast by the Tengku). Less than two months before, Tun Razak had said that he was happy with the security situation in Sarawak (*ibid*., 28 March, 1969). In Sabah there were no state elections, so only the small number of elections in contested seats for the Federal Parliament was postponed.

158. *Vanguard*, 16 May, 1969.

159. *Sarawak Tribune*, 29 May, 1969.

160. See pp. 306–307.

161. Means, *op. cit*., p. 373.

162. *Sabah Times*, 9 August, 1967 and 27 February, 1968; *Sabah Legislative Assembly Debates*, Vol. III No. 5 (21 December, 1967), cols 13–14 (*Written Answers to Questions*, Payar Juman).

163. *Sabah Times*, 23 June, 1966 (Enche Peter Mojuntin).

164. *Ibid*., *passim*, June–September, 1967. The June 29 and 30 issues list the Twenty Points and claim to show how some of them (in particular on immigration from Malaya to Sabah) were being broken. The opposing USNO case is given in the *Kinabalu Times* over the same period. Opponents of the UPKO were quick to remark that the Twenty Points had been soft-pedalled by the UPKO while it was still hoping for Cabinet seats immediately after the 1967 state election.

165. *Vanguard*, 25 April, 1968.

166. Maurice Freedman, "The Growth of a Plural Society in Malaya", *Pacific Affairs*, Vol. 33, No. 2 (1960), p. 167. Cf. David E. Apter on "racial groups" and "racial communities", "Introduction" to part IX in H. Eckstein and D. E. Apter (eds.), *Comparative Politics, a Reader* (New York, 1963), p. 653.

167. R. M. Pringle, *The Ibans of Sarawak under Brooke Rule 1841–1941*, (Ithaca, Cornell Ph.D. thesis, 1967), pp. 560–1.

168. See pp. 98–99.

169. See pp. 5, 89.

170. Ongkili, *op. cit*., pp. 16–17.

171. See the report of a social survey carried out by the Lands and Survey Department on the behaviour patterns of secondary school students in Sabah, quoted by *Sabah Times*, 17 May, 1968.

172. Robert Blake, *Disraeli* (London, 1966), pp. 376–7.

173. See pp. 261–262.

174. *First Legislative Assembly, State of Sabah, First Session, Order Paper, Monday 2 November, 1964, Notice of Motion, Philippines Claim to Sabah*. Tun Mustapha, however, did not believe in leaving "i's" undotted of "t's" uncrossed. In discussing Common-

wealth agreements on defence of the country he added, "Whenever I mention the word country I mean Malaysia" (*Address by Tun Mustapha at USNO General Assembly, Kota Kinabalu, 8 March, 1969*, p. 3).

175. Cf.: Karl Deutsch and William J. Foltz (eds.), *op. cit.*, p. 105; I. Wallerstein, "Ethnicity and National Integration in West Africa", *Cahiers d'Etudes Africaines*, Vol. I, No. 3 (1960), pp. 129–39.
176. Etzioni, *op. cit.*, p. 17. He defines "integration" on p. 4.
177. Tajang Laing, Minister of State (a Kenyah), *Straits Times*, 27 March, 1966.
178. *Far Eastern Economic Review*, 13 February, 1971 (letter from the Permanent Secretary to the Chief Minister, Sabah). Higher figures have been mentioned since then.
179. Cf. Robert Melson and Howard Wolpe, "Modernization and the Politics of Communalism: a Theoretical Perspective", *American Political Science Review*, Vol. LXIV, No. 4 (1970), p. 1,123 (Proposition 9).
180. *Sabah Times*, 1 July, 1967 ("Our Political Correspondent").
181. *Ibid.*, 11 December, 1967.
182. See p. 213.
183. *Straits Times*, 31 August, 1962.
184. *Ibid.*, 28 January, 1966 (editorial).
185. *Council Negri Debates, Third Meeting of the Seventh Session* (14 December, 1968), col. 216.
186. Businessmen's loyalties may have gained strength from the fact that smuggling profits fell when relations with the Philippines improved. In 1968 it was estimated that, after an anti-smuggling agreement had been concluded with the Philippines the previous year, $30 million had been lost by East Coast traders through curtailment of cigarette exports to the Philippines (*Sabah Times*, 30 July, 1968). The agreement was revoked shortly after this date.
187. *Council Negri Debates, Third Meeting of the Fourth Session* (26 September, 1962), col. 35.
188. *Cobbold Report*, para 237.
189. *Straits Times*, 10 and 14 August, 1965.
190 *Ibid.*, 17 August, 1965; *Sabah Times*, 6 September, 1965; Margaret Roff, "The Rise and Demise of Kadazan Nationalism", *op. cit.*, pp. 340–1.
191. See p. 422, Fn. 164.
192. *Straits Times*, 17 August, 1965.
193. *Sunday Tribune*, 2 November, 1969.
194. *Sarawak Tribune*, 14 January, 1969.
195. Immanuel Wallerstein, *Africa: the Politics of Independence* (New York, 1961), p. 88.
196. *Sarawak Tribune*, 23 August, 1965.
197. *Ibid.*, 21 August, 1965.
198. *Daily Express*, 24 November, 1965.

199. *Sabah Times*, 13 September, 1966.
200. "... once in power, a Party can use its position to strengthen its position enormously; it can grind the Opposition down. But the initial hold on power can only be won or maintained if the Party succeeds in establishing itself as the Party of the Region, the Party of the major tribe, and if it can show reasonable results in terms of economic development and of the standing of the Region in the Federation" (John P. Mackintosh, *Nigerian Government and Politics* (London, 1966), p. 521).
201. *Kinabalu Sabah Times*, 22 September, 1969.
202. *Ibid.*, 16 October, 1968.
203. *Address by Tun Mustapha at USNO General Assembly, Kota Kinabalu, 8 March 1969* (Kota Kinabalu 1969), p. 6.
204. See p. 50, above. Sabah's status was also an important consideration here. By 1966 the Federal Government was convinced that the "growth" grant for Sabah was too generous. It therefore imposed new regulations on timber royalties (p. 54, above), designed to extract extra revenue from Sabah. It also tried to have the growth grant ended; Tun Mustapha however, successfully resisted this. He was willing to spend "Sabah's money" on projects which might have been paid for by federal money, but he was unwilling to have the agreed amount of "Sabah's money" curtailed.
205. See pp. 24–25.
206. A further illustration of Sabah's independent approach, based on financial strength, occurred in 1972 when it was the first state in Malaysia to seek the Federal Government's approval to set up a State Bank.
207. See Etzioni, *op. cit.*, pp. 321–2.
208. *Sarawak Tribune*, 8 July, 1970.
209. *Straits Times*, 28 July, 1970.

Chapter 3

1. In Sabah there were also Indonesians, fairly easily assimilated into the Muslim population, and a smaller number of Filipinos.
2. For party names, see pp. 155–6.
3. In the form of Kadazan and Muslim associations. In this book there are frequent references to interest groups, but no systematic analysis of their political influence has been attempted. Substantially, a comment on Malaya made in 1963, would also apply to Sarawak and Sabah: "the type of activity one generally associates with functionally specific groups in Western democracies is generally lacking in Malaya" (K. J. Ratnam, "Political Parties and Pressure Groups", in Wang Gungwu, ed., *Malaysia, a Survey* (New York, 1964), p. 345). If such groups were placed in categories, certainly functionally specific groups in the Western sense, which were formed without regard to ethnicity, such as

trade unions and manufacturers' associations, would constitute one category. But there would be three other important categories. One would compromise the ethnic or religious associations just referred to, out of which political parties developed. Another would include organizations confined to Chinese, such as clan associations and Chinese Chambers of Commerce. A third would consist of organizations such as the *Badan Bahasa Sabah* and the United Sabah Islamic Association, which might not have formal constitutional links with a state government, but which were working with them towards shared objectives (see pp. 45, 61, above).

4. The term Native has no pejorative implications in the Borneo states. It should also be recalled from Chapter 1 that some of the Native inhabitants of the two states, especially Sarawak, are called "Malays".
5. Sometimes the Native membership reached a high figure, although the party always remained under Chinese leadership (see p. 75, below).
6. The Sarawak Alliance (originally Sarawak United Front) and the Sabah Alliance were both formed late in 1972. For a list of Alliance parties in each state in 1963, see pp. 155–156.
7. See pp. 370–373.
8. See pp. 62–63.
9. A number of a prominent and long-established Chinese family and a former President of the Kuching Municipal Council.
10. It opposed the haste with which Malaysia was being formed and feared the effects on both Chinese and radicals (K. J. Ratnam and R. S. Milne, *The Malayan Parliamentary Election of 1964* (Singapore, 1967), pp. 269–70).
11. See *ibid.*, pp. 281–2.
12. Derived from Tables XI and XIII in *ibid.*, pp. 283–4.
13. Some also hoped, if elected, to switch their allegiance to a party in exchange for money.
14. SUPP membership claims were probably relatively well-founded, compared with other parties. But it should be noted that the total membership claimed by all parties in 1969 exceeded the number of electors registered for the elections by nearly 40,000 (*Introduction to Sarawak's First General Elections, 1969* (Kuching, 1969)).
15. Appendix, *Data on Political Elites*, Table A.2. See also Michael B. Leigh, *The Development of Political Organization and Leadership in Sarawak, East Malaysia* (Ithaca, 1971) (microfilmed), pp. 28 and 114.
16. For example, when the Lundu branch was closed in 1969, the Government argued that many of the registered officials of this branch appeared to have defected to Indonesia because they could not be traced (*Straits Times*, 31 May, 1965).
17. *Ibid.*, 27 April, 1965.
18. Chan was the unofficial leader of the Party's left wing and its only

representative in the party's highest circles. On his release late in 1969 he appealed to SUPP members to support the moderate leaders and to accept their policies.

19. Singapore was then in Malaysia, and the PAP provided much of the impetuous leadership for the Convention.
20. Notably the PAP, which had earlier suppressed the Barisan Sosialis, the most left-wing party organization in Singapore. The SUPP left was scandalized by the fact that the parties closest to it ideologically in Malaya and Singapore, respectively, namely the Socialist Front and the Barisan Sosialis, were not included in the Convention.
21. The President (Ong Kee Hui), Secretary-General (Stephen Yong) the Treasurer (Ho Ho Lim) were the first to walk out and were followed by fourteen others (*Straits Times*, 24 June, 1965).
22. *Ibid*., 13 March, 1964.
23. This included two SUPP leaders who were chairmen of Solidarity Week Committees in the Third and Fourth Divisions (*ibid*., 12 November, 1964).
24. But the moderate leaders have never responded to challenges by other parties and by the Government to state publicly that they were anti-Communist.
25. The left-wing was weakened not only by the detention of its activists but (perhaps even more seriously) by the public statements which some of them made on their release, denouncing the Communists and their cause.
26. In late 1968, for example, the police permit for a fun fair organized by the SUPP in Sibu was withdrawn the day before the event. One of the party's leaders complained in private that it was precisely action of this kind which would strengthen the left-wing and weaken any commitment to democratic competition. Apparently a great deal of preparation had gone into the proposed fair and the sudden withdrawal of the permit had disappointed a large number of people, particularly as there had been no adequate explanation.
27. See p. 329.
28. See pp. 235–239.
29. About 52% of Sarawak's Malay population lives in the First Division.
30. The prospect of joining Malaysia was a very attractive one to the Malays in Sarawak as this would have made them a part of the new nation's politically dominant community.
31. *Straits Times*. 17 April, 1963.
32. *Loc. cit*.
33. *Ibid*., 29 April, 1963.
34. By which the district councils elected divisional councils, which in turn elected the Council Negri. The Council Negri chose the Sarawak members of the Federal Parliament.
35. *Straits Times*, 2 July, 1963.

36. An important official of PANAS, who was apparently away when the agreement with the SUPP was reached, has claimed in private that he was prepared to give the Alliance three First Division seats in the Council Negri, leaving seven for PANAS.
37. *Straits Times*, 25 June, 1963.
38. *Ibid.*, 26 June, 1963.
39. *Ibid.*, 2 July, 1963.
40. *Ibid.*, 12 July, 1963.
41. It was argued that the SUPP had rejected the proposal not so much because it was outraged by the cynicism behind it but because of the fear that collaboration with the Alliance would seriously damage its image in the eyes of its supporters.
42. In May, 1962, for example, the Datu Bandar, in discussing the possibility of an alliance of all pro-Malaysia parties, had stated that his party was then "finalizing" plans to merge with BARJASA.
43. It was hoped that the two parties, having merged, would constitute the "Sarawak UMNO". This plan, however, contained certain problems because many of the members of the two parties were not Malays and membership of UMNO was open only to members of that community.
44. In October 1964 Rahman Ya'akub, BARJASA's leader, after complaining that the attempts to dissolve the two parties and to form an UMNO branch in Sarawak were being "discouraged", expressed the hope that PANAS and BARJASA would 'sink their old differences and come together as a united party in the Sarawak Alliance" (*Straits Times*, 2 October, 1964).
45. Leaders of BARJASA, with their advantage of being in the Alliance and thereby of having closer ties with the UMNO, could have hoped that dissolution would place them in a preeminent position in the Sarawak UMNO while removing the threat of competition from PANAS. PANAS leaders, on the other hand, confident of their greater following and having reasonably cordial relations with UMNO leaders, may have hoped that they would be the ones to inherit dominance in the local UMNO.
46. UMNO initiative was clearly indicated in some of the newspaper reports during this period. In October, 1963, for example, after Ghazali Jawi (the then Minister of Rural Development and a former Secretary-General of UMNO) had visited Sarawak in order to explore the possibility of opening an UMNO branch there, an UMNO official in Kuala Lumpur stated that the leaders of BARJASA and PANAS had expressed their "willingness" to dissolve their parties (*Straits Times*, 17 October, 1963).
47. During interviews, prominent members of the Malay community were frequently given a pro- or anti-cession label.
48. Pro-Indonesian and anti-Chinese sentiments were apparently quite pronounced among its members.

49. Dato Rahman Ya'akub, for example, subsequently played an important role in promoting Islam in Malaysia. As Minister for Education between 1969 and 1970, he also was responsible for implementing a new education policy which required the progressive use of Malay as the chief medium of instruction in Government schools. His vigorous efforts in this regard undoubtedly earned him a good reputation among Malay nationalists.
50. Although the postures adopted by its leaders, and the presence of ex-*Barisan Pemuda* members, gave BARJASA a distinctly Malay-Muslim image, it did not at any point entirely restrict its membership to Malays and Muslims. Some non-Muslim Natives, and even a handful of Chinese, were among the founding members and some of these remained in the party even after its Malay-Muslim identity became pronounced.
51. During this period BARJASA also appeared to have more success in recruiting younger, better educated Malays into the party.
52. Most notably during the Alliance crises of 1964 and 1965, which are discussed in Chapter 5.
53. Indeed, this was one of the factors which made merger possible.
54. Ainnie bin Dhoby had earlier been the Assistant Secretary of *Barisan Pemuda Sarawak*, and in this capacity had earned a reputation as one of the promising young leaders of the Malay community.
55. The SUPP also had a number of Malay members, but did not have any prominent leaders from that community.
56. In other words, although Bumiputera may not have had any doubts about its following among the Malays, it was afraid that the advantage it could derive from this (especially in achieving its second objective of pre-eminence within the Alliance) would be undermined if this could not be converted into a sufficiently large number of seats in Council Negri.
57. Especially if one or more of the other parties had also decided to field prominent Malay candidates and thereby threatened to split the Malay vote.
58. Bumiputera may, of course, have been right in believing that conflict with Pesaka was inevitable and that it was necessary to prepare for this well in advance.
59. *Vanguard*, 1 November, 1968.
60. *Ibid*., 3 November, 1968.
61. *Sarawak Vanguard* (Chinese), 5 November, 1968.
62. *Sarawak Tribune*, 1 May, 1969.
63. *Vanguard*, 3 May, 1969. There were also reasons for believing that even Bumiputera had not been formally consulted on the matter. However, this was not of much consequence because of Rahman Ya'akub's position in the party.
64. Pesaka's Malay leaders, however, along with their counterparts in SNAP, were undoubtedly more perturbed because this was likely

to have a direct bearing on their own chances as candidates in Malay-majority constituencies.

65. But this was not by any means taken for granted, either by Pesaka or by any of the other parties. There were some hopes that the Malays in Sarawak were themselves concerned about their local Sarawakian identity and did not favour increased federal control. Reference was often made to the alleged unwillingness of the Malays to isolate themselves in this manner because they could be swamped by the Ibans and suffer in the end.
66 As Minister for Education he had earned the admiration of the particularly in Malaya) for his dedication and resourcefulness in implementing Malay as the sole official language of the country and in restructuring the educational system so as to give Malay greater prominence. As a Federal Minister he had also achieved prominence through his activities in promoting Islam.
67. Bumiputera also benefited from the fact that whenever the Tengku or Tun Razak visited Sarawak they showed special concern for that party and for the Malay community.
68. It was widely believed that Bumiputera received assistance from the Alliance in West Malaysia, although only for election purposes and not for day-to-day expenses. There were also persistent rumours, especially after the election, that some assistance had also come from Datu Mustapha, the Chief Minister of Sabah.
69. Education, it must be remembered is a federal subject. As all adult education is conducted in Malay, those chosen to be teachers were almost invariably Malays. See pp. 48, 133, 198.
70. See Appendix, *Data on Political Elites*, Table A.2.
71. These were BARJASA (Malay/Muslim), the SCA (Chinese) and Pesaka (Iban).
72. See Appendix, *Data on Political Elites*, Table A.12.
73. See Chapter 5.
74. In the event, Dato Wee Hood Teck's contribution proved invaluable and enabled the party to have an edge over its rivals by having a vast (and expensive) organization during a very critical period. It was widely believed that Dato Wee personally met the salaries of a good majority of paid officials between 1966 and 1968. He was also known to have made other *ad hoc* contributions to the party before as well as during this period. When in 1968 Dato Wee left SNAP, the party lost this important source of income, but increased support from some of its other backers helped to offset some of the consequences. Dato Wee was believed to have continued to support some of SNAP's key candidates (along with candidates from other parties) on a selective personal basis. See Chapter 7 for a fuller discussion of Dato Wee's involvement in politics.
75. Even the office-bearers, who constitute the Working Committee,

are too numerous to function effectively as there are eighteen of them, from different parts of the state.

76. Following Dato Wee's resignation from the party, some field officers had to be "laid off" because of the sudden shortage of funds. However, as the elections approached in 1969 there was a definite increase in the number of field officers, but the members were once again reduced following the suspension of the elections and the termination (by law) of active campaigning. Naturally, there has been very little need for field officers since the completion of the election in 1970.
77. As in the case of Dato Abang Othman and Dato Dunstan Endawie, who were given nominal appointments as field officers so that they could be paid the salary which they had earned as Ministers prior to the fall of the Ningkan Government. It may have been felt that in the absence of such compensation, financial considerations may have weakened their resolve to stay with the party during its period in the opposition. This consideration, however, could not have applied equally in the case of Dato Ningkan who also drew a monthly "ministerial" salary from the party: even without this salary Ningkan would have been able to live in some comfort because by this time he was already a man of reasonable private means. Othman and Endawie, on the other hand, would not have had much to fall back on and the decision to stick with Ningkan would have been much more difficult if, by giving up their ministerial positions, they also had to give up the only means of getting anything like their ministerial salaries.
78. For example, as stated in the party constitution.
79. Cf: Richard Sandbrook, "Patrons, Clients, and Factions: New Dimensions of Conflict Analysis in Africa", *Canadian Journal of Political Science*, Vol. V, No. 1 (1972), pp. 104–19; John Duncan Powell, "Peasant Society and Clientelist Politics", *American Political Science Review*, Vol. LXIV, No. 2 (1970), pp. 411–25.
80. Of whom there were nine in August 1967.
81. This point was also made about the leaders of the party. It was argued that Pesaka's leaders, being older, were not capable of standing the pace of campaigning in a state where communications were poor and where one often had to spend several days away from home every month in order to establish meaningful contact with the electorate. Youth and sheer stamina, it was believed, were important ingredients of success in Sarawak politics. Data on candidates are incomplete, but SNAP's Executive Committee members were younger than Pesaka's (Appendix, *Data on Political Elites*, Table A.6). See Leigh, *op. cit.*, pp. 294, 298.
82. See pp. 245–246.
83. See pp. 62–63, 105–106.
84. See Chapter 5, pp. 214–222.

85. Preservation of state autonomy as guaranteed by the Constitution was the party's official interpretation of its slogan.
86. He was in fact convincingly defeated by Ningkan.
87. According to some, they were urged to form the new party by an expatriate District Officer in the Third Division who had convinced them that Iban interests would otherwise suffer.
88. In joining PANAS earlier, Temenggong Jugah had apparently been convinced that the Ibans, because of their size, could not be dominated within that party. But PANAS's increasingly Malay character had apparently helped to revive within him old Iban resentment of Malay domination and he had therefore begun to see the need for a separate Iban party.
89. Article 3 of Pesaka's constitution, for example, states that one of the party's objects is to "safeguard and guarantee the rights and survival of the indigenous races of Sarawak". Another object, however, is "to foster and promote goodwill and harmony among all races in Sarawak".
90. Although SNAP opened its doors to Chinese, it shared Pesaka's fear of Communist subversion, which was always associated with the Chinese.
91. J. A. McDougall, *Shared Burdens: A Study of Communal Discrimination by the Political Parties of Malaysia and Singapore* (a thesis submitted for the degree of Ph.D. at Harvard University in April 1968), p. 92.
92. Although Bumiputera was not formed until early 1967, the likelihood of a BARJASA-PANAS merger, with support from Kuala Lumpur, had become quite evident by the time of Pesaka's decision to admit Malays.
93. Anticipation of support from the Central Government, it was believed, was the one factor that could most encourage the Malays to contemplate the possibility of a dominant status while being significantly outnumbered by the Ibans. If they were divided, they were less likely to harbour such ambitions.
94. Pesaka, of course, had an easy answer to this because there were also some prominent Malays in SNAP.
95. *The Chinese Daily News*, 7 February, 1969.
96. The best example, of course, was Dato Ling Beng Siew, the President of the SCA, who had to carry the main burden of financing his own party.
97. Given the intense rivalry between Pesaka and Bumiputera, even a policy of making identical donations to the two parties was not likely to solve the problem because each of them expected its financiers to strengthen its position *vis-à-vis* the others. See also Ch. 7.
98. Dato Rahman Ya'akub, who was Minister for Lands and Mines between 1965 and 1969 and Minister for Education between 1969 and 1970, and Inche Taib bin Mahmud, who was made Assistant Minister for Commerce and Industry, in 1966, after

his position in the State Government had become untenable as a result of conflict with Pesaka leaders, and who became a Minister in 1971. True, Temenggong Jugah was also a Minister in the Central Government, but his appointment (to the sinecure post of Minister for Sarawak Affairs) was primarily a compensation for his failure (partly as a result of Central Government intervention) to obtain appointment as Sarawak's Head of State in 1963.

99. There was no serious challenge to Jugah's leadership of the party, and the rivalry was over who would be the next Chief Minister. Jugah was himself not a candidate for the state election and the fact that Tawi Sli (who had replaced Ningkan as Chief Minister and who had himself earlier been in SNAP) was generally regarded only as a temporary, non-controversial stand-in, had left the succession issue wide open. It was generally accepted that Tawi Sli woud not continue as Chief Minister, but there was never at any time any agreement within the party as to who would succeed him.

100. *Vanguard*, 1 May, 1969. However by this time Pesaka leaders were believed to have received finances, which could be used for the election campaign, from the Niah timber arrangement (see p. 317 below).

101. For the main points raised by the Chinese when the terms of Malaysia were discussed, see *Report on the Commission of Enquiry, North Borneo and Sarawak* (Kuala Lumpur, 1962), paras. 72–77. Chinese wishes on citizenship was largely met; most Chinese were able to qualify as citizens under one heading or another. Chinese views on language were partly met by the retention of English as an official language for at least ten years, but the Chinese language was denied an official status. In opposition to prevailing Chinese wishes, the new Malaysian Constitution included some formal provisions (Article 161A) for privileges for Natives (i.e. non-Chinese).

102. See pp. 322–332.

103. See *Sarawak Tribune*, 27 April, 1963.

104. See Ratnam and Milne, *op. cit.*, pp. 282–7; R. O. Tilman "Elections in Sarawak" *Asian Survey*, Vol. III, No. 10 (1963); *United Nations Malaysia Mission Report* (Kuala Lumpur, 1963), para. 112. See also Appendix.

105. See pp. 215–6, below.

106. See Chapter 7.

107. *Constitution of the Sarawak Chinese Association* (amended 31 May, 1966).

108. D. McLellan, *Report on Secondary Education* (Kuching, 1959); *Borneo Bulletin*, 12 August, 1961; *Sarawak Annual Report*, 1962 (Kuching, 1963), p. 150.

109. The comparison with Malaya is slightly misleading because the Chinese there, while not constituting the largest single group, in

fact form a higher percentage of the population than they do in Sarawak. After the 1969 election the MCA's weakness (electorally as well as within the Alliance) in some ways became comparable to that of the Sarawak Chinese Association, and its position in the Government remained ambiguous for some time. But the MCA has succeeded in partially re-establishing itself because of an important advantage which it enjoys over the SCA —it has many more opponents, who compete against each other for the leadership of the Chinese community, and for this reason no clear alternative to it has emerged. In Sarawak, on the other hand, there has been far less dissipation of the anti-SCA Chinese vote, and it has been difficult to question the SUPP's claim to be the only credible representative of Chinese opinion.

For a detailed analysis of the results of the 1969 election in Malaya, see K. J. Ratnam and R. S. Milne, "The 1969 Parliamentary Election in West Malaysia", *Pacific Affairs*, Vol. XLIII, No. 2 (1970), pp. 203–26.

110. Against most expectations, the party won three out of the eleven state seats which it contested in the election which was concluded in April 1970. But in two of these seats Chinese voters were in the minority, and in all three the SCA's candidates were able to win only because of the support given to them by Native voters, especially Malays who were encouraged by Bumiputera to support SCA candidates.

111. This problem of having to shift its support from one party to another has been another unique feature of the SCA. The MCA, for example, has had no alternative but to support UMNO. Even in the case of the Sabah Chinese Association the problem has been somewhat different because it had only two parties to choose from, and the decision to favour USNO was made easy by UPKO's efforts to compete for Chinese electoral support. See pp. 128, 133–134, 140.

112. See pp. 182–183, 193–194.

113. In fact, not many thought that there was a likelihood of the Alliance as a whole getting a majority in the new Council Negri.

114. Dato Ling, for example, seemed reluctant even to use the MCA on an intermediary in this regard, and appeared to prefer establishing his own direct links with national Malay leaders. He seemed to regard his party not as a subsidiary of the MCA at the national level but rather as an equivalent of it.

115. In the words of one of the advocates of the new party the SCA's problem was that it had "big stones" but no "little stones" without which the party could not properly be built.

116. Paid workers, for example, were often not employed by the party but were on the payroll of Dato Ling and a few others.

117. Numbering about thirty, this group was made up mainly of professionals although there were also some businessmen. Some had university degrees and most were under forty years of age.

118. They apparently also received encouragement from some Bumiputera leaders.
119. The term invariably used by respondents during interviews.
120. But Dato Ling was careful to ensure that in giving these positions he was not in any way weakening his own position in the party. Note that after the 1970 elections Bumiputera found an alternative to the SCA leadership in the form of the moderate SUPP leadership.
121. See p. 226.
122. See p. 236.
123. A Congress of these Associations was held in March 1961, only a few months before the creation of UNKO.
124. Earlier known as the *North Borneo News and Sabah Times.*
125. Any attempt by them to gain control of the government would have led to a coalescing of the indigenous groups which would have left them hopelessly outnumbered. Also, the Chinese did not constitute a majority in many constituencies, because they were heavily concentrated in the urban and semi-urban areas.
126. The other major parties would then have been Bajau and Chinese, with minor parties representing the Muruts, Bruneis and other smaller groups. This would have augmented the advantage which UNKO already had on demographic grounds.
127. See pp. 406–407, Table A.11.
128. See pp. 19–24, 124.
129. McDougall, *op. cit.*, p. 124.
130. *Ibid.*, pp. 124–5.
131. *Ibid.*, p. 124.
132. The Sabah Alliance was also formed in October 1962, comprising UNKO, USNO, BUNAP and the politically insignificant Sabah Indian Congress.
133. Had the change in fact taken place it could have led to some confusion because Mount Kinabalu was the symbol of USNO, UPKO's rival in the struggle for political dominance in the state.
134. See pp. 312–313.
135. It was in fact rumoured on one occasion that subtle attempts had been made to replace him as Deputy Chief Minister on grounds of health when he was away for medical treatment.
136. Sundang was one of the three Native leaders who had originally been given a special timber licence. This had made him a man of very considerable means. See pp. 315–316.
137. Although Donald Stephens personally bore the major burden of financing the party, he did receive some assistance from others, including well-wishers who were not members.
138. Which they had possessed as the leaders of the first party to be formed in the state, but which they had lost because the next party to be formed, USNO, catered to a wider audience.
139. The SCA was preceded by other antecedent bodies, such as BUNAP; but this will be discussed later.

140. See pp. 128, 133–134, 140.
141. E.g. *Pesatvan Islam Sabah* (Sabah Islamic Association). Cf. McDougall, *op. cit.*, p. 120.
142. See Appendix, *Data on Political Elites*, Table A.3.
143. See p. 396, Table A.1.
144. Like Said Keruak, who was in fact part-Malay.
145. SNAP's policies were more consistent and less confusing to its supporters than UPKO's. For a comparison of the parties' actions during cabinet crises see Chapter 5.
146. In other words, they were convinced that in the absence of federal (and, more particularly, UMNO) intervention, they would have no difficulty in establishing their political dominance in their own states.
146a. This, however, does not mean that USNO did not employ any field officers who were paid out of party funds; it also had paid workers.
147. This involved the opening up of new branches, the employment of new party workers and additional travel by leaders.
148. Fortunately for him, all the ex-Ministers who were returned apart from himself) were from USNO and the SCA.
149. This included his right not only to choose the persons from UPKO whom he thought suitable, but to appoint them to such positions as he though appropriate. UPKO, on the other hand, argued that it should decide who its own Cabinet members should be, and also insisted that appointments to specific posts should be subject to mutual agreement among the parties.
150. The reasons for his doing so have remained unclear, but it is conceivable that his dedication to his party had been shaken after the election when he realized that he had been "sacrificed" in Bengkoka-Banggi. He had been a Minister in the outgoing Government, and it was very likely that he would have won had he stood in Papar, which many regarded as the obvious constituency for him. But Papar was given to the relatively unknown Fred Sinidol, who was a relative of Stephens, and Richard Yap had been told that UPKO had a wide following in Bengkoka-Banggi and that he would be the best candidate to defeat Mustapha there.
151. Especially when one considers that right up to the very last moment the party was conducting an intensive campaign against USNO.
152. Which would have helped UPKO at least to save face, if not to retain an opportunity to "take over from within".
153. See pp. 241–242.
154. See pp. 290–291.
155. This may well have contributed to the vast expenditure during elections, which is discussed in the next chapter. See also pp. 310–312.
156. Although they constituted only about 22% of the population, the

Chinese in Sabah could have hoped that through their very considerable control of the economy they could acquire more than a proportionate share of political power, or at least be able to manipulate Native politicians. With national political power in the hands of the better disciplined and politically more established Malays of Malaya, however, they were not likely to have the same access to "real" power or even the same influence. As one SCA leader subsequently complained in talking about the future of the Chinese language in Sabah: "How can the SCA fight for Chinese as an official language here when the MCA couldn't get it accepted as an official language in Malaya?"

157. McDougall, *op. cit.*, p. 122.
158. Who by this time had become quite active in directing the course of Chinese politics in East Malaysia.
159. The old NBCA, which had changed its name.
160. *Borneo Times*, (a Chinese daily), 1 April, 1965.
161. See *ibid.*, 14 and 21 April, 1965.
162. *Ibid.*, 18 May 1965.
163. One of the arguments used by the advocates of merger was that some of the more expensive commitments of the original SCA (for example in the field of education) were no longer of the same relevance because government funds had been made available for these purposes. It was also hoped that the new party would take over some of the other functions of the original SCA, for example in resolving differences between Chinese clan associations, but this became difficult because these differences now became more "political", involving competition for control of the party.
164. In the case of UPKO, however, there was continuing friction between the ex-UNKO and ex-PM wings, but the former's overwhelming strength (coupled perhaps with Sundang's reluctance to use his personal wealth for political purposes) discouraged any serious factionalism within the party. Further, although they may have had misgivings about UPKO's policies, the ex-PM stalwarts disliked USNO's policies even more and were aware that divisions among the anti-USNO forces could help no one but the USNO.
165. Significantly, of the various clan associations in the state, only the leadership of the Cantonese Association failed to overlap with that of the SCA when the latter was founded. (McDougall, *op. cit.*, p. 123).
166. In fact, this was openly stated by Khoo Siak Chiew at an Executive Committee meeting of the Sandakan branch of the original SCA before its merger with SANAP in 1965 (See *Borneo Times*, 5 April, 1965).
167. See p. 8 for a discussion of possible reasons for this.
168. It was widely believed that these Independents received financial assistance from certain wealthy Chinese, including some who

were members of the SCA but who resented its policies and power structure.

169. See R. S. Milne and K. J. Ratnam, "Patterns and Peculiarities of Ethnic Voting in Sabah, 1967", *Asian Survey*, Vol. IX, No. 5, (May 1969), pp. 377–8.

170. See, for example, the *Borneo Times* of August and September 1965.

171. *Borneo Times*, 2 September, 1965. Twenty-six of these societies and associations did in fact sign the petition (*ibid.*, 25 September, 1965).

172. *Ibid.*, 13 September, 1965.

173. Which, in setting up Malay as the national language, also guarantees the use, for non-official purposes, of other languages.

174. In Sabah, there was in fact no party outside the Alliance at the time of the 1967 election. In Sarawak, although there were two opposition parties (the SUPP and SNAP) when elections were completed in 1970, both were significantly ambivalent on communal issues and one of them (the SUPP) paid as much attention to ideological as to communal goals. It is also important that SNAP was itself once in the Alliance while the SUPP is now a member of the ruling coalition, with the Alliance.

175. The "formula" refers to the pattern of organization whereby UMNO, MCA and MIC were able to get together to form the Alliance Party while retaining their separate identities. Thus, while the Malayan Alliance is an inter-communal organization committed to multi-racial goals, its component units are communally exclusive and are committed to safeguarding the interests of their respective communities.

For a discussion of the organization and functioning of the Malayan Alliance and its component units, see K. J. Ratnam and R. S. Milne, *op. cit.*, *The Malayan Parliamentary Election of 1964*, pp. 31–43.

176. As pointed out earlier, in some cases the rivalry was based on attempts to gain a dominant position within the Alliance. SNAP, Pesaka and Bumiputera (and before it BARJASA and PANAS) were all involved in this struggle at one time or another in Sarawak. In Sabah the competition was far more straightforward, between USNO and UPKO.

177. Such as those between the various dialect groups among the Chinese, and those which distinguish, even if only vaguely, the indigenous Malays from the more recent immigrants from Indonesia.

178. In Sarawak the cession issue had in fact helped to *split* the Malay Community.

179. Not to mention the sequence in which they were formed: most of the parties, it must be remembered were formed before the Alliance formula was imported; thus many of them started off either by being multi-racial (as in the case of PANAS) or by

being 'friendly competitors' for the same vote (e.g. SNAP and Pesaka, UNKO and USNO.)

180. In Sarawak, for example, there might have been separate units to represent the Ibans, Chinese, Malays, Melanaus and Land Dayaks; in Sabah the main groups requiring separate representations would have been the Kadazans, Bajaus, Chinese and Muruts.
181. In 1969, 23 of the 48 state seats had an Iban majority and 5 an Iban plurality, while only 8 had a Chinese majority and 1 a Chinese plurality.
182. Literally, "Son of the soil".
183. Until Ong Kee Hui's appointment to the Federal Cabinet in 1970, they were also the only two Sarawakians who held such appointments.
184. When Dato Stephens was Minister for Sabah Affairs he also had the not-too-onerous responsibility for Civil Defence.
185. Along with many other ex-UPKO leaders Dato Ganie Gilong subsequently became converted to Islam, as Dato Haji Abdul Ghani Gilong.
186. This is discussed in detail in the next chapter.
187. Although, again, a "compromise candidate", Peter Lo, intervened between the Stephens and Mustapha chief ministerships.
188. Although the Governors (and, before them, the Brookes in Sarawak and the Chartered Company in Sabah) may have symbolized their "nations", there were no national affairs in which the average citizen could become involved. Contact between the administration and the population was confined, by and large, to the district or sub-district level.
189. The growth of parties and the recruitment of traditional elites as candidates and as party leaders at different levels have, however, resulted in some deterioration in the relationship between these elites and their immediate communities.
190. For one thing, it is only natural that these two parties should be better disposed towards a Central Government which is also Muslim-dominated. For another, they are also aware that good relations with the Central Government (and, more particularly, with UMNO which is the dominant partner in the ruling Alliance Party) can enhance their own positions in their respective state Alliance parties.

Chapter 4

1. It should be remembered that direct state elections had not been held previously. For the results of the previous district council elections in Sabah (and also in Sarawak), see K. J. Ratnam and R. S. Milne, *The Malayan Parliamentary Election of 1964*, Chapter X and the Appendix to this Chapter.
2. See pp. 128, 133–134, 140.
3. MacDougall, *op. cit.*, pp. 135–8.

4. The candidate, Richard Yap, the Minister of Health, had apparently gone up to Bengkoka-Banggi before the agreement on the nine seats had been reached. When doubts were raised about his explanation (i.e. that he had received the telegram too late) Stephens stated that the party would inquire into the matter and take disciplinary action against Yap if he had wilfully ignored instructions. Bearing in mind Yap's prominence within the party, it is surprising that another constituency was not reserved for him as there was some doubt about UPKO's intentions in Bengkoka-Banggi. Also puzzling was UPKO's inability to contact him in Bengkoka-Banggi between the date of the initial no-contest agreement and nomination day.
5. It was claimed by some UPKO leaders that they had earlier pretended that their support was declining, when in fact it was increasing, in an attempt to encourage USNO to support early elections. These leaders were now of the opinion that USNO had believed their propaganda.
6. In addition to its determination to prevent USNO from getting a majority, UPKO had its own ambitions of emerging as the dominant party, as shown below.
7. As long as UPKO remained within the Alliance, national leaders could not openly take sides by campaigning for one party and not for the other.
8. There was, however, a precedent because some "friendly contests" had in fact been agreed to in the 1962 district council elections (see Ratnam and Milne, *op. cit.*, pp. 304–5).
9. He never actually took up this appointment, but, in 1968, became High Commissioner to Australia.
10. In one sense support for USNO and the SCA by Malayan Alliance leaders could have been beneficial to UPKO, because it could then have further highlighted its own concern for state autonomy by pointing to the subservience of the other parties. But assistance for USNO and the SCA from the Malayan Alliance would also have meant assistance from the National Government, and the UPKO was keen to portray itself as a party which, while fighting for Sabahan interests, could co-operate with the Central Government to get development funds for the state. Further, there was a reluctance on the part of Donald Stephens to break personal ties with the Tengku and the other leaders of the Central Government, because he considered such ties to be important for the future viability of a state Government controlled by his party, particularly if (as had happened on previous occasions in Sabah and, somewhat more dramatically, in Sarawak) internal rivalries were likely to lead to a situation where mediation by national leaders might become necessary.
11. See pp. 203–207 for a fuller discussion of this.
12. See pp. 312–313.
13. As mentioned earlier, in order to undermine Donald Stephens'

image, especially among the Kadazans, as a fearless champion of Sabahan rights, USNO made it known during the campaign that he had privately accepted his nomination as High Commissioner to Canada. Those who had hoped that, in the event of an UPKO victory, Stephens would contest a by-election and thereafter become the Chief Minister, must have been disappointed by this news, which was not denied.

14. Some of UPKO's candidates, on the other hand, claimed that USNO workers were busily warning Muslims that if UPKO won Muslims would have to give up their religion in order to become Catholics and that some of their taboos—such as the prohibition on pork—would be actively undermined.
15. As pointed out earlier, after the election Mustapha's UPKO opponent, Richard Yap, challenged his election on the grounds of such irregularities, which included an attempt to bribe him so that he would give up his own candidature. This action, however, was withdrawn before the completion of the hearing (See *The Straits Times*, 1, 3 and 9 June, and 9 December, 1967).
16. See pp. 201–202.
17. This group although not organized into a formal party, conducted a co-ordinated campaign and announced its intention to form a rival party (the People's Working Party) after the election.
18. Made from rice.
19. See p. 247.
20. This was the only non-Iban majority seat won by Pesaka.
21. There were, however, some indications that this was considered unsatisfactory, particularly *vis-à-vis* the eleven seats given to the SCA.
22. But some of them had heard it rumoured that Bumiputera was not satisfied with the number of seats given to it and intended taking away three SCA seats.
23. *Vanguard*, 20 March, 1969.
24. See *Ibid.*, 25 February and 11 March, 1969.
25. *Ibid.*, 11 and 14 March, 1969.
26. *Ibid.*, 21 April, 1969.
27. *Ibid.*, 22 April, 1969.
28. *Ibid.*, 17 March, 1969.
29. *Ibid.*, 3 April, 1969.
30. In Sabah, there were no parties which existed outside the Alliance. In Sarawak not only did such parties exist but two of them (SNAP and the SUPP) were each believed to be stronger than any of the component units of the Alliance. Further, Pesaka, as an Iban party, was believed to share common interests with SNAP, and this could have provided a basis for co-operation between them after the election, thereby reducing Pesaka's reliance on its partners.
31. The Sabah Chinese Association had to make a firm choice between the two Native parties, partly because there was no opposition

to the Alliance in the state and there was consequently no possibility of arguing that Alliance unity and co-operation were necessary against common enemies. In Sarawak, on the other hand, the SCA could easily argue that while it had a closer relationship with Bumiputera (at least during the campaign) it was still linked to Pesaka because the Alliance was facing common opponents.

32. Because of its association with communist subversion and because it still had reservations about Malaysia, or at least the terms of Sarawak's entry into Malaysia.
33. One of the SCA-contested seats had a majority of Malay electors, illustrating the links between Bumiputera and the SCA mentioned in Chapter 3. In no seat did Bumiputera and SCA candidates oppose each other.
34. For example land reform, education, health, improved communications, changes in the civil service, etc.
35. For example multi-racialism of one kind or another, and parliamentary democracy.
36. Many voters, of course, could not have benefited from printed manifestoes because they were illiterate.
37. As already pointed out, the SUPP was the only party which was avowedly anti-Malaysia at the time of Sarawak's entry into the new federation. Its continuing intransigence on the issue was, to a large extent, the result of its left wing's refusal to abandon its stand, although the moderate leaders appeared more and more willing to accept Malaysia as a *fait accompli* while pressing for a re-examination of the terms of Sarawak's entry. The conflict between the two wings of the party was discussed in the last chapter; as the election approached it was widely believed that the moderate leaders had obtained a promise from the Central Government that (in contrast to the 1963 district council elections) there would not be any interference in their campaign if they made it clear that they accepted Malaysia and that their only objective in this regard was an alteration of the terms through constitutional means.
38. That is, without the people of Sarawak being given a free say in the matter.
39. *Vanguard,* 28 April, 1969.
40. This was expected to have special appeal among the Ibans and the Chinese who harboured fear of Malay control and tended to have deep reservations about the imposition of Malay as the sole official language and as the medium of education.
41. These workers, although their primary motivation may have been ideological, were often also closely associated with distinctly Chinese causes (such as Chinese education) and had established close rapport with the electorate often through their own tireless efforts on behalf of the party.
42. This was perhaps due to the fact that the party was better

organized and more rigidly articulated in the Chinese areas; it may also have been influenced by the leaders' conviction that a special effort was required to show the Ibans that the party had their interests at heart. Ong Kee Hui and Stephen Yong were well versed in Iban customs and were capable of adapting with ease to an Iban environment; As leaders of the party, they also enjoyed considerable prestige. It must also have been felt that the most active and dedicated party workers, who tended to be Chinese, could not be used appropriately in Iban areas: their deployment to these areas may even have been counter-productive as there was every possibility of their offending Iban sensibilities simply through ignorance of the rules and manners of social intercourse.

43. For a general statement of this view by an SCA politician, see *Vanguard,* 4 May, 1969.
44. They realized that in the event of a SNAP victory this could have invited, rather than discouraged, federal intervention.
45. The only state in Malaya which at that time was under opposition rule. Conflicts between the Central Government and the Government of Kelantan had hampered development in that state since 1959 when the PMIP came to power.
46. *Vanguard,* 14 and 15 April, 1969.
47. In its manifesto, public meetings and party broadcasts, as well as in the numerous letters written by its officials, candidates and supporters to newspapers during the campaign.
48. Although Malays within their own party were singled out as "good" Malays.
49. Particularly for their own community, because communal politics would arouse the hostility of the politically dominant Iban community and might in the long run be detrimental to Malay interests.
50. The fact that they were Melanaus and not Malays was clearly implied in this argument.
51. In order to make sure that he was believed, one SNAP Malay candidate made a large number of photostat copies of the newspaper report which carried this story and distributed them in the villages which he visited during the campaign.
52. Mr. Michael Buma, who had resigned as Director of the Sarawak Council for Adult Education in order to take up this appointment. Mr. Buma had previously been a leader of MACHINDA, a small multi-racial party which existed for about three years between 1964 and 1967.
53. Although SNAP (like the other parties) paid its candidates' deposits and provided a fixed sum for each state and parliamentary candidate, it was common for many of its candidates (especially the more prominent ones) to make their own arrangements for obtaining additional funds from the party's backers.
54. It is conceivable that this calculation was upset as a result of the

suspension of the election. Although a certain amount of informal campaigning continued throughout the one-year period of suspension (and SNAP leaders often claimed that the suspension would in fact help them by further discrediting the Government) the lull in open activity and SNAP's inability to sustain its pace (in expenditure as well as in open propaganda) may have led to some erosion of support during the period of suspension.

55. It also fielded candidates in twenty-three of the twenty-four parliamentary constituencies.
56. In its manifesto Pesaka also "urged" the Government to look into the problems of unemployment, inadequate educational facilities and land shortage, sought to "secure an efficient and honest administration for Sarawak", and "appealed" to the Government to set up more trade and technical schools. There were hardly any references to the achievements of the (Pesaka-dominated) Government. A similar situation had been revealed earlier in Sabah when, during the 1967 election campaign, both UPKO and USNO candidates (including some Ministers) complained about the inadequacies of the previous Government of which they had been a part.
57. But these charges (e.g. subservience to the Central Government) were usually made against the Alliance as a whole and not specifically against Bumiputera and the SCA, although these two parties were sometimes singled out.
58. Although the SUPP had every reason to believe that it would not have much serious competition for the Chinese vote, it was also optimistic about its chances in many non-Chinese areas and spent a great deal of effort (and projected an entirely non-communal image) in these areas. Bumiputera, on the other hand, did not modify its image to the same extent in order to suit local conditions.
59. Some of the banners were obviously brought from West Malaysia because the slogans they contained were written in Malay, Chinese and *Tamil.*
60. Some of the posters printed by the party, for example, had photographs of both the Tengku and Rahman Ya'akub.
61. Such as the section dealing with support for Malaysia.
62. The Alliance Headquarters in fact had accommodation for all three component units. Bumiputera, however, chose to conduct its activities in separate premises which it had acquired for itself, leaving the Alliance building to be shared by Pesaka and the SCA. There was very little liaison between the Bumiputera office and the Alliance office (which was dominated by Pesaka), not only during the campaign but for some time before it. Social relations between Bumiputera and Pesaka leaders were also reduced to a minimum.
63. *Vanguard*, 14 April, 1969.

64. His chief opponent was Ong Kee Hui, the President of the SUPP. The ethnic breakdown of the electorate was as follows: Malay—6,737; Chinese—5,741. Dayaks—258; Others—178. When campaigning among the Malays the SCA candidate himself used every effort to identify himself and his party as ardent supporters "Sukong Tengku" (support Tengku) as his main slogan and made of the Tengku and the Central Government.
65. See, for example, *Vanguard*, 16 April, 1969.
66. In the event, neither these threats nor the general disruption and fears caused by the security operations appeared to have had much influence on the turnout.
67. *Sarawak Tribune,* 24 January, 1970.
68. *Vanguard,* 1 July, 1970.
69. *Sarawak Tribune,* 26 April, 1969. For a similar accusation by an SUPP candidate against another Bumiputera leader, see *Vanguard*, 27 April, 1969.
70. *Sarawak Tribune*, 1 May, 1969.
71. The voting process began all over again in 1970.
72. The State Operations Council was headed by the Federal Secretary in Sarawak and included Temenggong Jugah (*Vanguard*, 15 July, 1969).
73. *Straits Times*, 15 October, 1969.
74. This violence was therefore endemic in nature and was not directly related to the holding of elections.
75. Usually in small numbers because, in the rural areas, not more than a few households could be assembled together conveniently at any given time.
76. Even the Government (in Sarawak as well as in Sabah) had experienced great difficulties in conducting national registration and issuing identity cards because it was not always possible to make arrangements for persons in the more remote parts of the country to be photographed. It was unreasonable in some cases to expect citizens to make long journeys just to have their photographs taken; at the same time, commercial photographers were reluctant to venture off the beaten track because the time and cost of reaching their potential customers would not have been justified by the profits they were likely to make.
77. This information was also broadcast repeatedly over the radio.
78. This was not always an easy thing because many people had never before held a pen or pencil in their hands and did not always know how to put a cross on a piece of paper (some also had to be told which end of the pencil to use in order to write). The ballot paper was also not a familiar object, and people had to be taught its layout and the area where the cross had to be placed.
79. Mock elections were also conducted by the Department of Information in various parts of Sabah, but these, needless to say, were non-partisan.

80. This practice was also followed in Sabah for the parliamentary election completed in 1970.
81. See Ch. 7.
82. Boats were also the chief means of transport in the coastal areas. It was not unusual for candidates from the major parties, in areas where river (or coastal) transport was important, to have five to ten boats at their own disposal during the middle of the campaign.
83. Some aggrieved candidates complained that as a result of this they were unable to transport their supporters to the polling stations. They had made elaborate arrangements to pick up voters at certain points, but were unable to live up to their promises because they were simply unable to rent or purchase boats at the last moment. Their rivals, who had more boats than they "needed", were therefore able to present themselves as saviours even in enemy territory by providing transport, and it was felt that this may have led to some last-minute changes in voting.
84. Only a few exceptional candidates, like Richard Yap of UPKO, appeared willing to sacrifice the comforts of home in order to spend almost the entire period of the campaign roughing it in their constituencies.
85. In one constituency in Sarawak, where the two leading contenders were both extremely wealthy, local accounts had it that boatloads of expensive brands of beer and cigarettes were frequently seen leaving for the interior.
86. Usually on the understanding that after the election these would be used by all the residents in any given area.
87. In one constituency in Sabah, it was widely rumoured that local shopkeepers were having difficulty in finding enough money in small denominations because too many people were producing $50 notes even for minor purchases towards the end of the campaign.
88. That is, in those constituencies which polled last.
89. At a rough guess total expenditures at the Sabah 1967 state election were $4½ million, at the Sarawak 1969–70 state and parliamentary elections, $8 million. For an analysis of the West Malaysian 1964 election, see R. S. Milne and K. J. Ratnam, "Politics and Finance in Malaya", *Journal of Commonwealth Political Studies*, Vol. III, No. 3 (1965), pp. 182–98.
90. These cartoons were abandoned after nomination day, because the cartoonist, who had once been an UPKO member but had had to leave the party after it changed its rules so as to exclude Chinese, stood as an Independent candidate in a constituency where there was also an UPKO candidate.
91. Mr. Leong Ho Yuen, who did not seek re-election in 1969. Mr. Leong had originally belonged to the SUPP and had subsequently become one of the leaders of the short-lived MACHINDA.
92. After the election, the *Vanguard* was in fact successfully sued by

the new Chief Minister, Dato Rahman Ya'akub, for alleged libel during the campaign (See the *Straits Times*, 19 and 29 August, 1970).

93. References to sources and a fuller analysis of the elections may be found in: K. J. Ratnam and R. S. Milne, *The Malayan Parliamentary Election of 1964* (Kuala Lumpur, 1967), Chapter X; R. S. Milne and K. J. Ratnam, "Patterns and Peculiarities of Ethnic Voting in Sabah, 1967", *Asian Survey*, Vol. IX, No. 5 (1969); R. S. Milne and K. J. Ratnam, "The Sarawak Elections of 1970; an Analysis of the Vote", *Journal of Southeast Asian Studies,* Vol. 3, No. 1 (1972); Leigh, *op. cit.*
94. Two seats, both won by USNO, were uncontested. There were other Independents as well as the loosely-grouped Chinese Independents, but the latter won the bulk of the Independent vote.
95. Note, however, that about 7% of the Kadazans are Muslims, and that the Muruts were not pro-UPKO to the same degree as the Kadazans. These factors contributed to the USNO majority among the non-Chinese electors.
96. See p. 73.
97. See Milne and Ratnam, "The Sarawak Elections of 1970", *op. cit.*

Chapter 5

1. "O and E", *Sarawak Gazette*, Vol. XCII, No. 1303 (30 September, 1966), pp. 313–14.
2. *Report of the Land Committee,* 1962 (Kuching, 1963), Chapter III.
3. *Ibid.*, pp. 14–15. There was also *Reserved Land,* land reserved for forestry and other government purposes. Overlaying these other classes were also *Native Customary Land* and *Crown Land.* The Report stated that the Committee had been assured by a very experienced member of the Lands and Surveys Department that nobody outside the department used the correct terminology.
4. *Ibid.*, p. 15. For the delays faced by Chinese in acquiring Mixed Zone Land, see *ibid.*, p. 26. However, the total amount of Mixed Zone Land is not fixed. It is possible to convert Native Area Land to Mixed Zone Land, administratively, through the Department of Lands and Surveys, and such conversions actually take place. The effect of the 1965 land legislation would have been to make procedures simpler, and to increase the possibility of poor Chinese acquiring native land.
5. *Ibid.*, p. 16.
6. Although the Committee was aware of the political implications (*ibid.*, p. 2).
7. The SCA 1963 election manifesto *We Believe in Unity*, made several declarations on land, encouraging to the Chinese, but, understandably, not very specific. See p. 116, above.

   Another political implication arises from the fact that at present the Chinese vote is largely concentrated in urban areas where the number of electors in an average constituency is larger than the number of electors in an average rural constituency. One effect of settling more Chinese on the land would be to increase the "weight" of Chinese votes.

8. For instance, the Minister for Natural Resources stated in December, 1964 that there were nine Land Development schemes in operation. Some of the applications for land in these schemes had not yet been considered, but the total number of Chinese who could have been allocated land in them could not have exceeded 600 or so (*Council Negri Debates, First Meeting of the Third Session* (21 December, 1964), cols. 29–33).
9. Cf. "Some Problems Affecting the Chinese in Sarawak", *Sarawak Gazette*, Vol. LXXXI, No. 1167 (31 May, 1955), pp. 98–9.
10. A. B. Ward, *Rajah's Servant* (Ithaca, New York, 1966), p. 164.
11. There were actually four bills: (1) Land Adjudication Bill; (2) Land (Native Dealings) Bill; (3) Land Acquisition Bill; (4) State Lands and Registration Bill. The texts of all four are in the *Sarawak Government Gazette,* Part III; (1) and (2) in Vol. XX, No. 1, 22 January, 1965; (3) in Vol. XX, No. 2, 6 February, 1965; (4) in Vol. XX, No. 3, 12 February, 1965. These replaced four similar bills published almost a year earlier. Only (2), the Land (Native Dealings) Bill, was contentious, but all four bills were "killed".
12. The word, *Pesaka* (heirloom) is itself suggestive of the principal item which Natives leave to their heirs, land.
13. One BARJASA objection took the form of saying that the bills were based on a "colonial approach, because they followed the lines of the 1962 Land Committee Report".
14. Who left SNAP and joined Pesaka in 1966, and who later replaced Dato Ningkan as Chief Minister.
15. Who had become secretary-general of Pesaka in 1964.
16. The agreement was dated 11 May and signed by over thirty political leaders, including Temenggong Jugah, the President of the new body.
17. In two separate letters, both dated 11 May. They were typed on the same typewriter by the same person, Alfred Mason. Mason had originally been a BARJASA member, appointed as Jugah's political secretary a few months later he joined Pesaka. The BARJASA letter did not specifically mention the land bills. The existence of the Pesaka letter was known to very few, even among the Pesaka leaders.

    Another secret document, addressed to the Governor by twenty-two members of the Council Negri requesting the resignation of the Cabinet (9 May) was never sent. However, a similar technique was used a year later to topple Dato Ningkan.
18. *Straits Times*, 16 May, 1965. The complexities of the situation resulting from the Temenggong's reliance on others for reading

and writing documents are illustrated by Enche Taib's statement: "As for Dato Jugah's charge that I wanted to undermine the unity of the Dayaks in the statement I wrote for him, I have only this to say: the statement was translated to Dato Jugah by Dato Ningkan" (*ibid.*, 18 May, 1965).

19. Later, Taib identified himself with this view: "There was the first crisis—I can speak personally—there was the first crisis where there was an attempt to overthrow the Chief Minister. We tried not to—to effectuate that—because we thought that it would cause unstability; some of our leaders could foresee this. We stopped that" (*Council Negri Debates, First Meeting of the Fifth Session* (13 December, 1966), col. 61). Expatriate pressures in favour of the *status quo* were also based on the desire to preserve stability during the period Confrontation.
20. See Chapter 2, pp. 32–36 and 42–45. The two issues constituted the theme of the Tengku's letter to Dato Ningkan of 28 March, 1966 (see p. 441). The Federal Government's attitude to expatriates was conditioned by the rôle they had played in the 1965 crisis when they had supported Ningkan.
21. *Vanguard*, 20 May, 1966. Tun Razak had also raised the issue during a visit to Kuching.
22. "Native Alliance" proposals did not include SNAP, ostensibly on the ground that, by its constitution, it was open to all races, and that even before the Kuching branch was opened it had some Chinese membership. BARJASA's membership of a Native Alliance did not seem to be impeded by the fact that it had about 500 Chinese members.
23. The most widely-quoted instance of Ningkan's temper in a political context was, according to anti-Ningkan sources, his attempt to "strangle" Mr. Alfred Mason, Temenggong Jugah's political secretary, at a party in Simanggang at which Jugah and others were also present (*Vanguard*, 14 September, 1966). The Ningkan version of the story is that, after having been insulted, he merely placed his hands around Mason's neck; the damage was done by his ability to command occult powers.
24. Cf. Stephen Yong Kuet Tze, *Council Negri Debates, First Meeting of the Fifth Session* (13 December, 1966), cols. 52–3.
25. *Vanguard*, 18 May, 1966.
26. Penghulu Francis Umpau (Pesaka), Tajang Laing (Pesaka) and Awang Hipni (BARJASA). According to Ningkan, the first two of these had been consulted on Taib's dismissal.
27. For tactical reasons it had been decided that it would look better if the move appeared to come from Pesaka, but BARJASA had been sounded out and its leaders were informed about what was going on. The signatures of the fifteen Pesaka members of the Council Negri were collected first, mostly in Sibu; the signatures of the five BARJASA members and one PANAS member were collected later.

28. The twenty-one constituted a majority of the Alliance members of the Council Negri (32) but not of the total membership including the three *ex-officio* members (42, not including the speaker).
29. Penghulu Tawi Sli had been considered for the position of Chief Minister in 1963. Later he switched from SNAP to Pesaka (along with Pengarah Storey). One observer said that his choice as Chief Minister might have been swayed by the fact that Sli's personality was about as different from Ningkan's as possible. Sli was quiet by temperament, had studied theology and had all the "Christian virtues". The range of choice, incidentally, was drastically narrowed by the need to find a Chief Minister who was adequately literate in English.
30. 7 September, 1966.
31. The twenty-one signers of the anti-Ningkan petition had now been joined by one more PANAS member (Abang Haji Abdulrahim bin Haji Moasili) and by the three SCA members. This amounted to twenty-five votes out of forty-two.
32. *Sarawak Tribune,* 12 September, 1966.
33. By the *Emergency (Federal Constitution and Constitution of Sarawak) Act, 1966*. The act was passed by virtue of the "Emergency" provisions of the Constitution of Malaya (Article 150 (1)). See also Leigh, *op. cit.*, p. 199.
34. See p. 227. But see pp. 182–183, 193–194.
35. See pp. 358–359.
36. The other cabinet members were Penghulu Tawi Sli, Chief Minister; Abang Haji Abdulrahim, Local Government; Penghulu Francis Umpau, Lands and Mineral Resources; Awang Hipni, Welfare, Youth and Culture; Tajang Laing, Agriculture.
37. 6 SNAP, 3 SCA, 2 PANAS, 1 MACHINDA, 1 Independent, 5 SUPP, 3 *ex officio*. There was apparently a good chance that the three *ex officio* would vote for "the government", i.e. Dato Ningkan.
38. An illustration of the interlocking activities of Sarawak and Federal politicians during the first crisis is provided by the letter Thomas Kana wrote to the *Straits Times*, correcting a report in that newspaper on the origins of the formation of the Native Alliance. The letter, dated 19 June, 1965, gave as its address "Ministry of Lands and Mines" (in Kuala Lumpur). The Minister of Lands and Mines was then Rahman Ya'akub. The roles of Rahman Ya'akub and his nephew, Taib, add to the problem of finding an adequate definition of "Kuala Lumpur influence". Both were born in Sarawak, and started their political careers in Sarawak; in 1970 the former resumed his political career in Sarawak. Each was also active in Sarawak politics while holding a post as Minister or Assistant Minister in the Federal Government. Should such activities be included under the heading of "Kuala Lumpur influence" or not?

39. *Straits Times*, 4 July, 1966.
40. *Council Negri Debates, First Meeting of the Fifth Session* (13 December, 1966), cols. 62–3 (Taib).
41. The decision not to try to remove Ningkan through action in Sarawak seems to have been the decision of the local coup organizers.
42. *Council Negri Debates, ibid.* (Enche Taib).
43. The sequence is a little reminiscent of coups in Thailand: "... it is characteristic that the incoming group always seeks and receives an amnesty from the throne and legal enactments authorizing ex post facto their actions" (David A. Wilson, *Politics in Thailand* (Ithaca, New York, 1962), p. 257).
44. This is not inconsistent with the fact that, after his brief restoration, Ningkan's government was voted down in the Council Negri. By that time it had been shown that a Tawi Sli government was viable and that the Federal Government was willing to go to the length of changing the Constitution in order to have a Ningkan government removed.
45. And eventually led to the Court decision which returned Dato Ningkan temporarily to office. The legal weakness in the procedure adopted lay in the clause in the Sarawak Constitution which stated: "If the Chief Minister ceases to command the confidence of a majority of the members of the Council Negri, then, unless at his request the Governor dissolves the Council Negri, the Chief Minister shall tender the resignation of the members of the Supreme Council other than the *ex officio* members" (7.(1)). How could it be completely certain that a Chief Minister had lost the confidence of the Council Negri except by being defeated at an actual meeting of the Council Negri, as opposed to the evidence, for example, of a petition? In Sarawak, unlike states with disciplined parties, loyalty to a party was so little to be relied on that a member might quite easily change his allegiance during the few days intervening between signing a petition and attending a Council Negri meeting.
46. There are several parallels to the events in the two Sarawak Cabinet crises in the Western Nigeria crisis in 1962: the use of petitions; attempted buying over of members of the legislature; court cases to determine who was Premier/Chief Minister; Federal Government influence, including the declaration of a state of emergency (John P. Mackintosh, *Nigerian Government and Politics* (London, 1966), pp. 447–58, 516–20). But in Sarawak the conduct of affairs was much more restrained and gentlemanly.
47. References to the two crises will be found in the Sabah press throughout 1964, particularly in February, June, and December.
48. He did not actually resign, and "re-enter politics", until September 1965.
49. See pp. 127–128, above.
50. Other points of difference, which also concerned the Federal

Government, included the rôle of expatriate civil servants and the position of the Federal Secretary (see pp. 32–38, above).

51. In the interim Datu Mustapha's status had been raised. In November, 1964 he was given the (federal) title of "Tun", rarely awarded in Malaysia, and not yet awarded to any other politician in Sabah or Sarawak.
52. Dusing's name was third on the list of "suitable candidates" presented to Stephens. The first two, both Chinese, were according to Stephens, passed over, one because he wanted to stay in his existing post, the other because he was too valuable to be moved from the Treasury (*Straits Times*, 3 December, 1964).
53. *Ibid.*, 14 and 16 December, 1964.
54. See p. 29.
55. This solution has been attributed to Dato Ningkan, one of three Sarawak Alliance members invited by the Sabah Alliance to help to solve the crisis.
56. See pp. 133–134.
57. See pp. 158–162.
58. See pp. 132–133.
59. William H. Riker, *The Theory of Political Coalitions* (New Haven, 1962), p. 47. In a zero-sum game what one player, or coalition of players, gains the other players lose. Side-payments are payments, not necessarily in money, made by some players to induce other players to take part in a coalition. The importance of the size principle is diminished, however, when a number of other considerations which affect coalition formation are taken into account (Charles R. Adrian and Charles Press, "Decision Costs in Coalition Formation", *American Political Science Review*, Vol. LXII, No. 2 (1968), pp. 556–63).
60. Bumiputera 12; Pesaka 9 (one of whom was actually elected as an Independent); SCA 3. The opposition seats were: SNAP 12; SUPP 11. The result of one postponed contest, won by SUPP, was not declared until three weeks afterwards.
61. The appointment was announced only on 7 July. Dato Rahman Ya'akub had resigned as Federal Minister of Education on 3 July. But on 5 July, before the Bumiputera-SUPP negotiations were concluded, Tun Razak had stated that the Alliance would form the next government (*Sarawak Tribune*, 6 July, 1970), and Bumiputera had won more seats than either of the other two Alliance parties.
62. See Chapter 7.
63. See p. 228.
64. On a Tun Razak message to SUPP about the formation of a government, see Leigh, *op. cit.*, p. 250.
65. Although, according to one report, in forming the coalition with Bumiputera, the SUPP leaders understood that Pesaka would also be included.
66. See pp. 84–86.

67. See p. 198.
68. *Sarawak Tribune*, 6 and 7 July 1970 (and by Dato Rahman Ya'akub, *ibid*., 8 July, 1970).
69. *Sarawak Tribune*, 8 July, 1970. Simon Demab anak Maja of Pesaka was later sworn in as Deputy Chief Minister. Both the new Pesaka minister had had reservations about a SUPP-SNAP-Pesaka coalition. Both enjoyed the backing of the Pesaka Youth Section and its leader Sidi Munan, who was soon afterwards appointed political secretary to the new Chief Minister.
70. *Ibid*., 10 July, 1970.
71. *Sunday Tribune*, 12 July, 1970.
72. This does not amount to saying that the original coalition was harmonious from the time of the first Cabinet crisis, June 1964, onwards. See pp. 157–177.
73. *Op. cit*., p. 556.
74. *Op cit*., p. 39.
75. Adrian and Press, *op. cit*., p. 560.
76. With the revival of the Philippine claim to Sabah another factor emerged. The costs of coalition could partly be reckoned as costs in a related "game", the Malaysia-Philippines game (*ibid*., p. 559).
77. See p. 337.
78. *Riker*, op. cit., p. 209.

Chapter 6

1. These numbers have varied over time. Although what in Sabah is called a residency is in Sarawak known as a division, the administrator in charge of each is known by the same title, "Resident".
2. Lord Hailey, *Native Administration in the British African Territories*, Part IV, "General Survey of the System of Native Administration" (London: Colonial Office, 1951), p. 9; Lord Hailey, *An African Survey* (London, 1957), p. 540.
3. This is a broad generalization. The authority of a Kenyah headman, or "chief", was considerable (Charles Hose and William McDougall, *The Pagan Tribes of Borneo* (London, 1912), Vol. I, pp. 67–8). On the other hand among some Melanaus there seems not to have been an indigenous village headman at all. Instead there was a small group of older men of high rank known as a *nyat* (H. S. Morris, *Report on a Melanau Sago Producing Community in Sarawak* (London: H.M.S.O., 1953), pp. 83–7). Ethnic groups also differed in the degree to which succession among their headmen was hereditary. Autocracy in headmen tended to be associated with hereditary succession.
4. W. J. Chater, "Pieces from the Brooke Past—V," *Sarawak Gazette*, Vol. XC, No. 1279 (30 September, 1964), p. 225.
5. At one time the Iban *Penghulu* was known as *Orang Kaya.* The Land Dayak *Orang Kaya Pemancha* was until recently known as

Penghulu. For amplification of the position of headmen and chiefs in different ethnic groups see: Hose and McDougall, *op. cit*., Vol. 1, pp. 64–8, Vol. II, pp. 182, 272–5; Morris, *op. cit*., pp. 83–7; J. D. Freeman, *Iban Agriculture* (London: H.M.S.O., 1955), paras. 20–8; J. D. Freeman, *Family and Kin among the Iban of Sarawak* (Cambridge, England, 1953) (mimeo), pp. 344–56; W. R. Geddes, *The Land Dayaks of Sarawak* (London: H.M.S.O., 1954), pp. 48–51, 105; W. R. Geddes, *Nine Dayak Nights* (Melbourne, 1957), pp. 21–3.

6. Freeman, *Family and Kin among the Iban of Sarawak, op. cit*., pp. 345–8.
7. Geddes, *The Land Dayaks of Sarawak, op. cit*., pp. 50–1.
8. On headmen in various communities, see: K. G. Tregonning, *A History of Modern Sabah* (Kuala Lumpur, 1965), p. 107; Owen Rutter, *The Pagans of North Borneo* (London, 1929), pp. 27–8; M. Glyn-Jones, *The Dusuns of the Penampang Plains in North Borneo* (London, Colonial Office, 1954, pp. 107–11; G. C. Woolley, *The Timoguns* (Jesselton, 1962), p. 3; T. R. Williams, *The Dusun; A North Borneo Society* (New York, 1965), pp. 62–3; Ivor H. N. Evans 'Kadamaian Dusun Headmen of Former Times", *Sarawak Museum Journal*, Vol. 6, nos. 19–21 (1954–5), pp. 248–9; George N. Appel, *The Nature of Social Groupings among the Rungus Dusun of Sabah, Malaysia* (Canberra, A.N.U. Ph.D. thesis, 1965 (microfilmed), pp. 314–19). Among the Dusun in the Keningau-Tambunan area there is a "descent group" leader, or headman, who, in an area containing several villages, "takes precedence over village headmen in all matters, of ritual, ceremony, or adjudication of disputes" (Williams, *op. cit*., p. 50).
9. Tregonning, *op. cit*., p. 113. A variety of factors entered into the Government's appointments. Ability was not the only criterion. A Resident, for example, could fail to support a petition that an able man should be made chief because he felt that the size and interests of his extended family were already too great. (*Resident, Interior, Handing Over Notes*, 28.9.1956).
10. *Ibid*., pp. 113–14.
11. *Ibid*., pp. 115–17; George McT. Kahin, "The State of North Borneo 1881–1946", *Far Eastern Quarterly*, Vol. VII, No. 1 (November, 1947), pp. 49–51; M. H. Baker, *Sabah, the First Ten Years as a Colony 1946–1956* (Singapore, 1965), pp. 55–8, 143; Stephen R. Evans, *Guide for Sabah Native Courts* (Kuching 1967).
12. Mr. J. B. Dusing, Permanent Secretary to the Chief Minister, *Sabah Times*, 16 December, 1967. Previously they had also a tax-collecting function.
13. *Sabah Times*, 31 July, 1968.
14. *Sabah Legislative Assembly Debates*, Vol. III, No. II (31 December, 1968), col. 610.

15. *Minutes of Native Chiefs Conference held at Tawau on the 8th to 12th November, 1966*, pp. 3 and 4.
16. Tregonning, *op. cit.*, pp. 111–12.
17. See pp. 320–322, below.
18. See Chapter 3, above.
19. On a few occasions there have also been elections for *Tuai Rumah*, or the equivalent.
20. Those who were appointed before the 1957 change were exempt from having to contest any elections. They would hold the position until they died or retired.
21. Hose and McDougall, *op. cit.*, Vol. 1, pp. 67–72.
22. *Council Negri Debates, Third Meeting of the Sixth Session* (27 September, 1968), cols. 129–35. *Kapitan China* are now elected, not appointed.
23. Unlike Sarawak, the chiefs in Sabah have never been elected. In September 1967 Peter Mojuntin, commenting on a three-year delay in filling a vacant position for District Chief in Penampang urged that chiefs should be elected. His argument that an election would ensure that chiefs were forward-looking, young, and educated seems to have been very much in terms of Penampang. An election there might have produced a chief with these qualifications. Elections in some other areas would almost certainly not have done so.

    A proposal for the election of chiefs and headmen had been made earlier by Anthony Gibon an UPKO leader who was himself a chief (*Sabah Times*, 29 April, 1964).
24. Philip Woodruff, *The Men Who Ruled India*, Vol. I, *The Founders* (London, 1953), p. 271. On the post-Independence administrative hierarchy in the field, see: S. S. Khera, *District Administration in India* (New Delhi, 1960); *Indian Journal of Public Administration*, Vol. XI, No. 3 (1965) (special issue on the Collector in the 1960s).
25. Owen Rutter, *British North Borneo* (London, 1922), p. 149. On recruitment for Sarawak, see C. P. Cotter, *Some Aspects of the Administrative Development of Sarawak* (Ithaca, 1955) (microfilmed), pp. 46–7.
26. A. B. Ward, *Rajah's Servant* (Ithaca, 1966), p. 54. Ward also quotes an example of his having been put in charge of constructing a section of road without having had any relevant experience of the work. D.O.s were still sometimes asked to perform a "road-making function" over half a century later.
27. Rutter, British North Borneo, *op. cit.*, pp. 150–1. On North Borneo see also Tregonning, *op. cit.*, pp. 75–6. For Sarawak, see Otto Charles Doering III, *The Institutionalization of Personal Rule in Sarawak*, (London School of Economics, M.Sc. thesis, 1965 (mimeo.)), pp. 39–43.
28. See Doering, *op. cit.*, and Tregonning, *op. cit.* The D.O.'s powers are not laid down in any one law or regulation.

29. "Autobiography of J. B. Archer, Part 6, More about Out-stations", *Sunday Tribune*, 5 July, 1964.
30. Some D.O.s have an assistant, sometimes more than one, who in Sabah is known as an Assistant District Officer (A.D.O.), in Sarawak as a Sarawak Administrative Officer (S.A.O.). Occasionally a district is in the charge of an A.D.O. or a S.A.O. rather than a D.O. A fairly typical District Office staff in 1967 (Simunjan, Sarawak) was a D.O., two S.A.O.s, a Chief Clerk, three clerks, four court peons and an outboard driver (*Sarawak Gazette*, Vol. XCIV, No. 1324, 30 June, 1968), p. 137). There are frequent complaints, especially in Sabah, of shortages of administrative staff, particularly, A.D.O.s.
31. *Sabah Times*, 1 November, 1967.
32. On the recruitment of temporary prison staff in Miri, see *Council Negri, Second Report of the Public Accounts Committee* (Kuching, 1966), p. 122).
33. Max Gluckman, "Inter-hierarchical Roles: Professional and Party Ethics in Tribal Areas in South and Central Africa" in *Local-Level Politics: Social and Cultural Perspectives*, Marc J. Swartz, ed. (Chicago, 1968), pp. 70–1.
34. Plus several other committees arising from the D.O.s being Vice-Chairman, Executive Officer and Treasurer of the Ranau District Council.
35. Cotter, *op cit.*, pp. 189–91.
36. Doering, *op. cit.*, pp. 119–20.
37. Source: State Establishment Office, Sarawak and annual *Sarawak Staff Lists.*
38. *The British North Borneo Civil Service List, January 1916* (Sandakan, 1916), pp. 3–7.
39. Source; Sabah State Establishment Office and annual *Sabah Staff Lists.* The main reason why the Sabah technical officers were relatively more numerous than the Sarawak technical officers is that Medical Officers come under the state government in Sabah but are federal in Sarawak. Note: these figures refer to actual civil servants, not to establishments; those officers holding acting rank are not included.
40. "Report by the Resident, Fifth Division, 1963", *Sarawak Gazette*, Vol. XC, No. 1276 (30 June, 1964), p. 149.
41. "Report of the D.O., Kanowit District, Third Division of Sarawak, 1963", *ibid.*, p. 151.
42. "Kapit District Report for the year 1965", *ibid.*, Vol. XCII, No. 1300 (30 June, 1966), p. 211. But see p. 361, below.
43. For 1964 one D.O. reported having travelled only 68 days in the year. Not making any allowance for leave or illness, this was only just over half the new target for travelling (*ibid.*, Vol. XCI, No. 1285 (31 March), p. 88).
44. For example, in Keningau and in Lamag (*Sabah Times*, 23 October, 1967 and 17 September, 1968). See also *Third Legislative*

Assembly, State of Sabah; Sixth Report of the Public Accounts Committee (Kota Kinabalu, L.A. 9 of 1969), cols. 143–4, 155.

45. Cf. Rutter, *British North Borneo*, *op. cit.*, p. 156.
46. Hose and McDougall, *op. cit.*, Vol II, pp. 270–1. Note that the law and order and revenue-collecting functions are placed first.
47. "Griff" (editorial), *Sarawak Gazette*, Vol. XCI, No. 1292, 31 October, 1965, p. 300.
48. *Ibid.*, p. 300.
49. The need to be, and to be seen to be, aloof from politics may be a considerable strain on a Resident. One Resident during the 1967 Sabah state elections had to avoid all his "political" friends even to the extent of excusing himself when asked to play golf with them.
50. "Parish Pump" (editorial), *Sarawak Gazette*, Vol. LXXXIX, No. 1262 (30 April, 1963), p. 73.
51. "Note on Development of Local Government in Sarawak" (1947).
52. Five were set up. Their main function was to assume responsibility for primary education. The "Note" foresaw integration only after some time. It also proposed the "tier" system of District Councils which would elect some members of Divisional Councils, which in turn would elect some members of the Council Negri. This tier system was set up, as was a corresponding system in Sabah. It operated to elect indirectly the Sarawak Council Negri in 1963 and the Sabah Legislative Assembly, 1962–4. But the intermediate Sarawak Divisional Advisory Councils, and their counterparts, the Sabah Residency Councils, never acquired any intrinsic importance as local, or regional, government bodies.
53. Liang Kim Bang, "Sarawak, 1941–1957", in *Singapore Studies on Borneo and Malaya, Number Five* (Singapore, 1964), pp. 30–9.
54. K. J. Ratnam and R. S. Milne, *The Malayan Parliamentary Election of 1964* (Kuala Lumpur), p. 274.
55. $448,238. Of this sum the Council recovered $374,262 in Education Grants-in-aid from the Government. (*Sarawak Local Authority Approved Estimates of Revenue and Expenditure for the Year 1968* (Kuching, 1968), pp. 103–10).
56. *Kuching Municipal Council, Estimates of Revenue and Expenditure Parts I and II, 1969* (Approved by the Governor in Council *vide* Letter MLG/363/6, 20.3.1969), p. 2.
57. *Kuching Municipal Council Annual Report for 1970*), (Kuching, 1971), pp. 13–14.
58. At Bingkor, on the Keningau Plain (Tregonning, *op. cit.*, pp. 126–8).
59. *Address by Hon. G. L. Gray, G.M.G., O.B.E., concurrently Acting Chief Secretary and the Secretary for Local Government for Delivery at the First Meeting of the Tenom District Council on 30th January, 1960* (press release).

60. However, according to the Rural Government Ordinance of 1951, the D.O. would normally be the president of the council. In addition in the Kota Belud Council the deputy assistant district officer, a Native, was Vice-President; "as the authority developed, the president only attended on invitation, and then primarily to answer questions and give advice" (Baker, *op cit.*, p. 51).
61. *Ibid.*, pp. 51–2.
62. *Resident, West Coast, Handing Over Notes, 21.11.1956.*
63. *Town Boards, District Councils, Estimates for the Year 1969* (Kota Kinabalu, 1969), pp. 3–7, 72.
64. See p. 270–272, below. In 1972 responsibility for Sarawak primary education was removed from local councils and taken over by the state government. Factors influencing the decision seem to have included the weakness of some local authorities, a danger of subversion in some Chinese Schools, and preparation for conversion to teaching in Malay, starting in Primary One.
65. Kinabatangan District Council; Labuk and Sugut District Council; Pensiangan District Council.
66. "An appointed member of a Local Authority is a person appointed by the Minister of Local Government on the advice of the Resident and the District Officer to serve as a member of a local Authority, and such appointments are for a period of one year. Such persons are those whom it is considered have sufficient experience and knowledge to be of value to the Local Authority in the conduct of its business" (*Sabah Times*, 26 March, 1964 (answers to questions sent in by members of the public given by the Minister of Local Government, Enche Harris bin Mohd. Salleh, 25 March, 1964, over Radio Malaysia)).
67. The Report of the Local Government Commission (Chairman, Senator Athi Nahappan), 1971, made a recommendation, accepted by the Federal Government, for a freeze in local government elections throughout Malaysia.
68. See pp. 247–249, above.
69. In councils where the membership is wholly appointed, the D.O. is Chairman, not Vice-Chairman.
70. But some councillors have other ideas. In May, 1966 the Sarawak Minister of Local Government blamed the Kuching Rural District Council for extravagance, because in a year it held over a hundred council and committee meetings, at a cost of over $50,000 in allowances (*Vanguard*, 25 May, 1966).
71. *Notes on "Functions of Sandakan Town Board": a Talk to be given by Executive Officer at Civics Assembly on 15 June, 1969* (STB/BUS/94/69 (mimeo)), p. 4.
72. Council Negri, *Seventh Report of the Public Accounts Committee* (Kuching, 1969), pp. 30–40.
73. Although at an early stage this did happen in the Miri District Council ("Miri District Report for 1963", *Sarawak Gazette*, Vol.

XC, No. 1274 (30 April, 1964), p. 88). The councils were also "political" in 1963 in the sense that the council elections were the basis for the system of indirect election to the Council Negri.

74. On the system of grants in aid, designed to help the poorer councils, see *Sarawak Tribune*, 15 and 16 June, 1966.
75. See p. 268, above.
76. Address by Hon. G. L. Gray, *op. cit.*
77. "Lawas District Annual Report, 1964", *Sarawak Gazette*, Vol. XCI, No. 1284 (28 February, 1965), p. 58.
78. See pp. 280–281.
79. *Sarawak Gazette*, Vol. XC, No. 1274 (30 April, 1964), p. 88.
80. *Sarawak by the Week*, 22/66, 22–28 May, 1966.
81. Few cases were actually brought to court. In the absence of court action the only penalty was an interest charge on the amount of rates unpaid. The amount of the charge varied: Kuching Municipal Council charged 12% a year. Labuan Town Board 8%. To pay such rates of interest was often cheaper than borrowing money in other ways.
82. *Third Legislative Assembly, State of Sabah: Sixth Report of the Public Accounts Committee, op. cit.*, cols. 162–5.
83. *Sabah Times,* 10 October, 1967.
84. *Sarawak Gazette*, Vol. XCIV, No. 1322, 30 April, 1968 ("Simanggang District Annual Report, 1967"), p. 87.
85. *Sabah Times*: 7 September, 1967; 8 September, 1967; 10 October, 1967; 8 December, 1967; 16 April, 1968. Their appeal was agreed to by the Rating Appeal Tribunal, a committee of the Sandakan Town Board, and by the Board itself. Their payment was fixed at a low flat rate.
86. The plight of the Matu/Daro District Council (Sarawak) in 1966 was an extreme example of this (Council Negri, *Seventh Report of the Public Accounts Committee, op. cit.*, pp. 139–47).
87. *Kuching Municipal Council Estimates of Revenue and Expenditure Parts I and II*, 1969, *op. cit.*
88. *Sarawak Local Authority Approved Estimates of Revenue and Expenditure for the Year 1968, op. cit.*, pp. 106–8.
89. Until recently this post was sometimes combined with that of Treasurer. In 1968 only one council, Matu/Daro, had a combined Secretary Treasurer.
90. *Sabah Times*, 26 March, 1964 (Harris bin Mohd. Salleh). The last provision, on approval of appointments, is intended to make sure that those appointed are qualified and are not being recommended by the council for personal or party reasons. When the council recommends an appointment it has to send the ministry details of the qualifications and experience not only of the persons recommended but also of the other applicants. Sometimes the ministry will choose a candidate other than the one recommended by the council.
91. *Daily Express*, 30 July, 1965.

92. *Sarawak Annual Report*, 1962 (Kuching, 1963), p. 328 (italics supplied). In point of fact the senior staff appointments are controlled by the Public Service Commission. After seeing the applicants' records the PSC draws up a short list of about three names from which the council must choose. Less senior appointments require the approval of the Resident, which is usually given as a matter of course.
93. *Resident, East Coast, Handing Over Notes, March, 1962.*
94. *Sabah Times*, 24 January, 1967.
95. Italics supplied.
96. *Council Negri Debates, Fourth Meeting of the Sixth Session* (12 November, 1963), cols. 63–70 (Datu Bandar Abang Haji Mustapha and the Minister for Local Government, Dato Dunstan Endawie anak Enchana). See also *Council Negri Debates, First Meeting of the Third Session* (22 November, 1964), cols. 134–5 and 157–8. Councils' minutes go to the Ministry of Local Government only via the D.O. & the Resident.
97. That is, revalue the properties for rating purposes.
98. "Saribas District Annual Report, 1966", *Sarawak Gazette*, Vol. XCIII, No. 10 (30 April, 1967), p. 103.
99. *First Malaysia Plan, 1966–1970* (Kuala Lumpur, 1965), Table 4.1, pp. 69–70.
100. On the national machinery and the machinery in the states of Malaya, see: *First Malaysia Plan, 1966–1970, op. cit.*, pp. 90–94; Gayl D. Ness, *Bureaucracy and Rural Development in Malaysia* (Berkeley and Los Angeles, 1967); Mavis Puthucheary, "The Operations Room in Malaysia as a Technique in Administrative Reform" in *Administrative Reforms in Asia*, Hahn-Been Lee and Abelardo Samonte, eds. (Manila, 1970); Milton J. Esman, *Administration and Development in Malaysia; Institution-Building and Reform in a Plural Society* (Ithaca, 1972), pp. 105–6, 216–26.
101. In 1969 it was suggested that S.D.O.'s functions should not be confined to co-ordination but should be expanded on the economic planning side (Third National Seminar on Agriculture, Kota Kinabalu, reported in *Kinabalu Sabah Times*, 26 March, 1969).
102. *First Malaysia Plan, 1966–1970, op. cit.*, 90–4. See also Ness, *op. cit.*, pp. 144, 150–1.
103. *Sabah Times*, 7 March, 1967, quoting the State Development Officer.
104. SDO/74/2, *Development Instruction* No. 1 (issued on 18 February, 1967).
105. The Chairman or Deputy Chairman of the State Development Planning Committee may appoint additional members.
106. The District Committee Chairman may also invite representatives of departments etc. as required. MARA is represented on the Working Sub-committee of the State Development Planning

Committee and (where applicable) on the District Development Committee.

107. See p. 292.
108. In Malaya, where there are no divisional committees, the district committee includes the State Assemblyman for the district and the Member of Parliament for the constituency of which the district is a part (Puthucheary, *op. cit.*, p. 177).
109. Ness, *op. cit.*, pp. 202–3.
110. *Kinabalu Sabah Times,* 31 October, 1 November, and 6 November, 1969.
111. The distinctive features of development planning in Malaya are well described in Ness, *op. cit.*, Puthucheary, *op. cit.*, and Esman, *op. cit.*, They include the use of Operations Rooms at the level of each committee, equipped with maps and charts to show the progress of development projects. Another feature is the use of the "Red Book", a method of showing the projects for each district on a series of maps and tracings inside a single "book", or binder. These features, however, did not come fully into use in Sarawak and Sabah until three or four years after Malaysia Day. It took time to integrate the existing plans of the two states and their planning machinery with the Malayan Second Five-Year Plan, and the Malayan planning machinery.
112. *Sabah Times*, 13 December, 1966 (State Development Officer, Sabah).
113. "Bintulu District Annual Report", *Sarawak Gazette,* Vol. XCLV, No. 1326 (31 August, 1968), p. 187.
114. See pp. 288–295, below.
115. SDO/651, *Development Instruction No. 2* (*Issued on 3 February, 1967*) (*Revised on 27 November, 1967*).
116. *Sarawak Gazette,* Vol. XCII, No. 1318 (31 December, 1967), p. 310 (Budget speech by the Chief Minister, Dato Tawi Sli).
117. See pp. 292–295, below.
118. Administrative Officers are also responsible for supervising the Scheme Managers of land settlement schemes, although the land settlement function has been taken over by the Sarawak Development Finance Corporation.
119. *Sabah Times*, 17 November, 1967 (the Chief Minister, Tun Datu Mustapha).
120. *Ibid.*, 17 May, 1968 (Tun Mustapha). On the previous day the Acting Director of Community Development had quoted a United Nations definition of the term, based on the "self-help" concept.
    The need for more concentration on *gotong royong* had been mentioned by Tun Razak, speaking in Sabah, as early as May 1966.
121. On the relationship between community development officers and administrative officers in the field, see Peter du Sautoy, "Some Administrative Aspects of Community Development", *Journal of Local Administration Overseas,* Vol. 1, No. 1 (1962).

122. *Sabah Times*, 13 December, 1966 (Sabah State Development Officer).
123. *Ibid.*, 23 September, 1966 (Harris bin Salleh, Finance Minister). However, eighteen months later Harris, remarking on the "slow progress" of development projects, observed that there was a lack of co-ordination and co-operation among government departments (*ibid.*, 20 March, 1968).
124. The Permanent Secretary to the Ministry of Communications and Works, Sarawak, referring to approval for extra expenditure on drainage and irrigation schemes in 1965, said: "It comes from the Director of Public Works to the Ministry, then goes to the State Development Officer, then goes to the Working Sub-Committee, then goes to State Development Planning Committee, then goes to the Federal Ministry, who submits [sic] it to their own department of Drainage and Irrigation, and then way back it comes down again to us and the delay of this is absolutely incredible. We have taken it up with Kuala Lumpur and they have promised us that they will remedy it. In point of fact, on this last bit of $1,180, I think the Director of Public Works is in telephonic communications with this department, so that it is cutting out about ten people" (*Council Negri, Fourth Report of the Public Accounts Committee* (Kuching, 1966), p. 49).
125. *Sunday Times*, 24 July, 1966. Only two-thirds of the amount estimated for Sarawak, 1964–5, was spent; an even smaller percentage was spent in Sabah. In subsequent years underspending was a much less serious problem in both states.
126. Harris, the Finance Minister, made a statement on underspending in Sabah to the Legislative Assembly (*Sabah Times*, 23 September, 1966). He pointed out that Malaya had had a similar underspending problem in 1961.
127. *Ibid.*, 7 March, 1967 (Sabah State Development Officer); *Vanguard*, 30 October, 1968 (Tun Razak).
128. *Council Negri, Fourth Report of the Public Accounts Committee, op. cit.*, pp. 48–51.
129. There were complaints from non-Muslims in Sabah about the relative amount spent on mosques (Peter Mojuntin, *Sabah Times*, 28 June, 1967). Tan Sri Jugah's famous Kapit speech attacked the amount of money spent on mosques (*Vanguard*, 9 October, 1967).
130. As had Tun Mustapha's announcements of projects in Sabah when he was (federal) Minister for Sabah Affairs. Where a hostile state government exists the Federal Government can claim entire credit for Minor Rural Projects, for instance in Kelantan, or until July 1961, in Trengganu (Ness, *op. cit.*, p. 216).
131. These refer to grants from state or federal funds. However, from newspaper accounts these cannot always be distinguished from personal donations. Dato Ling and Dato Rahman Ya'akub were particularly generous in making personal donations, not included in the above calculations.

132. Nine hundred and eighty-seven fire extinguishers were given to the longhouses in the Second Division and only forty to those in the Third, where there are more longhouses (*Council Negri Debates, First Meeting of the Fifth Session* (13 December, 1966), col. 27). SNAP had about half the seats in the Second Division District Councils and only roughly 10% of the seats in the Third Division District Councils.
133. *Sabah Times,* 2 November, 1967. Cf. "The selective areal allocation of public funds and grants for modern amenities (piped water, electricity, hospitals, schools, etc.) and for the development of the country's infrastructure (communications, energy, roads, transportation facilities, etc.) has also been an important instrument of consolidation. In many new states the phenomenon known as the "vanishing opposition" is in large measure explained by the strong pressures placed upon opposition leaders by their constituents to join the governing party and share in this preferential treatment" (James C. Coleman and Carl G. Rosberg, Jr., eds., *Political Parties and National Integration in Tropical Africa* (Berkeley and Los Angeles, 1964), p. 666).
134. Four of these were in the same constituency, Ranau. The others were in Tenom and Keningau.
135. *Kinabalu Sabah Times,* 24 June, 1970.
136. Native Chief Anthony Undan Andulag, *ibid.*, 21 July, 1967. In June, 1966 a Sabah Resident had commented that proposals for rural development tended to be decided on an *ad hoc* basis, for example by ministers on tour (*Resident, West Coast, Handing-over Notes, 18 June, 1966*).
137. *Vanguard*, 9 September, 1967.
138. *Op. cit.*, p. 193. See also Esman, *op. cit.*, pp. 124–8, 132–3.
139. *Sabah Times*, 9 October, 1967.
Cf. on "political interference" in some states in India: Myron Weiner, "India: Two Political Cultures", Lucian W. Pye and Sidney Verba (eds.), *Political Culture and Political Development* (Princeton, 1966), pp. 19 ff.; Richard P. Taub, *Bureaucrats under Stress: Administrators and Administration in an Indian State* (Berkeley and Los Angeles, 1969), p. 201.
140. Puthucheary, *op. cit.*, p. 193.
141. See p. 298, below.
142. The premise was that, if basic democracies succeeded, district administration would disappear. One CSP officer told Richard Gable that he was writing about a corpse (district administration). Another said that district administration would wither away in six or seven years (Richard W. Gable, *Introduction to District Administration* (University of Southern California Public Administration Project, Lahore, 1963 [mimeo]), p. 155).
143. Ronald Wraith, *Local Government in West Africa* (London, 1964), pp. 167–71.

144. Doering, *op. cit.*, p. 160. The Resident's, less assured, future is examined below.
145. There were special reasons for this in some areas. For instance, in the Fifth Division of Sarawak in 1963 the need to put down the revolt which had originated in Brunei gave the law and order function top priority for a time.
146. Gable, *op. cit.*, pp. 121–2.
147. As is done in Malaya, to an A.D.O.
148. Gable, *op. cit.*, p. 122.
149. Alfred Diamant, "Tradition and Innovation in French Administration", *Comparative Political Studies,* Vol. 1, No. 2 (1968), p. 260. Fesler, however, is sceptical about the possibility of a successful co-ordinating rôle. (James W. Fesler, "The Political Role of Field Administration" in Ferrel Heady and Sybil Stokes, eds., *Papers in Comparative Administration* (Ann Arbor, 1962), pp. 121 and 140, fn. 12). On areal co-ordination in Malaya, see Ness, *op. cit.*, pp. 155–71.
150. Gable, *op. cit.*, p. 155.
151. *Development Administration in Malaya, Report to the Government of Malaya*, by John D. Montgomery and Milton J. Esman (Kuala Lumpur, 1966), pp. 13–14. Some short training courses are also given in Sarawak and Sabah.
152. See Noel F. Hall, "The Administrative Staff College", *Public Administration* (Sydney), Vol. XIV, No. 1 (1955); Marshall E. Dimock, "The Administrative Staff College, Executive Development in Government and Industry". *American Political Science Review*, Vol. 1, No. 1 (1956). On the use of the syndicate method in the Philippines see Abelardo G. Samonte, "The Philippine Executive Academy: A University's Response", *Philippine Journal of Public Administration*, Vol. VIII, No. 4 (1964).
153. A. M. A. Muhith, "Political and Administrative Roles in East Pakistan's Districts", *Pacific Affairs* Vol. XL, Nos. 3 and 4 (1967–8), pp. 289–90.
154. See p. 259, above.
155. Other partial reforms are possible, for instance Residents might be abolished, but D.O.s in certain important areas, such as Kota Kinabalu and Sandakan, might be upgraded and given some supervisory functions over adjacent districts.
156. See Muhith, *op. cit.*, p. 290.
157. But only "... provided that sufficiently experienced officers can be found to fill the posts. This is important as almost the main function now (certainly in the West Coast) is that of guidance and mentorship and there is nothing so dangerous as the blind leading the blind" (*Resident, West Coast, Handing Over Notes, 18.6.66*).
158. In Sarawak and Sabah chiefs have never been executive agents of elected councils, as in, for example, "Post-World-War-Two

Kenya and Uganda, outside Buganda" (Lucy Mair, *Primitive Government* (London, 1964), p. 275).

159. See pp. 249–254, above.
160. Cf. the fear of Penghulus Jugah and Sibat that local government was being introduced too precipitately in Sarawak (Malcolm MacDonald, *Borneo People* (Singapore, 1968), pp. 170 and 174).
161. See p. 265, above.
162. The changes in the methods of appointing chiefs and headman announced in Sabah in 1968 may be regarded as constituting a very modest possible first step towards professionalization.
163. Harry J. Friedman, *Administrative Roles in Local Governments* (Comparative Administration Group, ASPA, 1966), p. 11.
164. See pp. 293–295, above.
165. *Sarawak Tribune*, 1 August, 1966.
166. See p. 388, below.

Chapter 7

1. Herbert J. Spiro, *Government by Constitution* (New York, 1959) p. 178.
2. There is a section on violence below; purposive interests are to some extent covered in part of the section on money and in the discussion on bargaining in the next chapter; in a sense law is considered under the heading, "The 'Rules' of Politics"; concentration on immediate goals is well exemplified in the obsession with acquiring timber; ideology, although not prominent in the Borneo states is apparent in the SUPP and, in a rather special nationalist sense, in SNAP.
3. Cf. Sidney Verba, "Conclusion: Comparative Political Culture" in Lucian W. Pye and Sidney Verba (eds.), *Political Culture and Political Development* (Princeton, 1965), p. 545.
4. David B. Truman, *The Governmental Process* (New York, 1951), p. 512. These are Bailey's "normative rules" (F. G. Bailey, *Stratagems and Spoils* (Oxford, 1969) p. 5). Instances of Bailey's "pragmatic rules" may be found below in the various sections on money and under "Constrained Beneficiaries".
5. See pp. 232–233, above.
6. *Sabah Times*, 26 October, 1967.
7. *Sarawak Vanguard*, 6 June, 1968. There is an element of bargaining in such situations. (See pp. 365–366, below.)
8. An editorial in *Sarawak Tribune*, 4 August, 1966, favoured resolving the current crisis outside the Council Negri and within the Alliance machinery. On the other hand, it is possible to discern criticism in the comment that the crises in both states, 1964–6, included a phase of "inter-party haggling, usually carried on outside the parliamentary arena" (C. Paul Bradley, "Communal Politics in Malaysian Borneo"). *The Western Political Quarterly*, Vol. 21, No. 1 (March, 1968), pp. 123–40.

9. Cf. *Sabah Times*, 11 February, 1965. The file, concerning nominated members for district councils, disappeared from an official's desk. When it was returned it contained the names of newly-nominated members, whose appointments had gone through, by-passing the usual channels.
10. This politician was defeated in the 1970 Sarawak election.
11. Lucian W. Pye, *Politics, Personality, and Nation Building: Burma's Search for Identity* (New Haven, 1962), p. 162.
12. Sidney Verba, "Conclusion" in Pye and Verba, *op cit.*, p. 549.
13. *Sabah Times*, 29 December, 1967. Each of the two men draws two or three drops of his own blood, the blood is mixed with water or wine, and each then drinks part of the mixture. A similar ceremony with political implications has been performed in Sarawak.

    The existence of ties in Sabah politics which cut across cleavages is illustrated by the fact that Dato Stephens is said, to have founded the nationalist, non-ethnic, AGABA (Angkatan, Gaya, Baru), and that it was he who suggested the name "USNO".
14. Which tends to invalidate the application of the zero-sum hypothesis in this context (Charles R. Adrian and Charles Press, "Decision Costs in Coalition Formation", *The American Political Science Review*, Vol. LXII, No. 2 (1968), p. 559). See also p. 235 above.
15. Lucian W. Pye, "Party Systems and National Development in Asia" in Joseph La Palombara and Myron Weiner, eds., *Political Parties and Political Development* (Princeton, 1966), p. 389, also p. 421.
16. Pye, *Politics, Personality and Nation Building, op. cit.*, pp. 28–9.
17. See p. 124, above, also: *Borneo Bulletin*, 16 November, 1963; *Press Release* (Sabah Information Service), 22 August, 1964. The original stand was considerably modified later (*Sabah Times*, 20 February, 8 November, and 23 November, 1967). Interestingly, the Constitution of the Society of Kadazans in the opening paragraph after "Kadazan", added "(Note: Kadazan means Dusun)". Dato Stephens had successfully conducted an earlier campaign to have North Borneo given "its old name", Sabah.
18. On the ritual importance of the buffalo, traditionally, see Owen Rutter, *British North Borneo* (London, 1922), p. 274; the buffalo is killed by the Natives only "on feast days and other important occasions, when its blood is used to set the seal upon a solemn oath and buried feud". See also *ibid.*, p. 337.
19. *Sabah Legislative Assembly Debates*, Vol. III, No. 7 (27 December, 1967), col. 363 (Salleh Sulong).

    Sir Charles Jessel had been a director of the British North Borneo Company, but had had no close personal association with North Borneo. When the name of the capital was changed in December 1967, Tun Mustapha announced that there was no intention of changing other European names such as Beaufort or Weston.

20. "Readers' Forum", *Borneo Times*, 15 November, 1967. After the dissolution of UPKO Tun Mustapha acquired shares in the *Sabah Times* and amalgamated it with the *Kinabalu Times* under the title, *Kinabalu Sabah Times.*
21. *Sabah Legislative Assembly Debates, op. cit.* (22 December, 1967), col. 369 (Abdul Momen bin Haji Kalakhan).

    A further exercise in the interpretation of symbols might be stimulated by the statement, attributed to Tun Mustapha that there was only one mountain in Sabah.
22. Arnold J. Heidenheimer, "Comparative Political Finance: Notes on Practices and towards a Theory", *The Journal of Politics*, Vol. 25, No. 4 (1963), pp 807–11.
23. This applies more to the SCA and the USNO than to the UPKO. But several rich Chinese who were bitterly opposed to the SCA, notably Kwan Yui Meng, backed the Chinese Independents and UPKO at the 1967 state elections. How far their "backing" was expressed in money contributions is uncertain. See "British Propertied Bloc Instigates Stephens to Struggle for Power!" *Overseas Chinese Daily News*, 7 April, 1967, quoted pp. 171–174, above.
24. In its initial stages Pasok Momogun was heavily supported with Chinese money.
25. *Sabah Times*, 15 June, 1967. See also, generally, Edwin Lee, *Timber Towkays in Sabah Politics* (Singapore, 1972).
26. *Ibid.*, 5 April and 7 April, 1967; *Press Statement in Sandakan on 12 June, 1966 from the Minister of Natural Resources, the Hon. T. J. Jayasuriya.*
27. Each licence was for approximately 2,500 acres.
28. Interview, Sir William Goode, last Governor of North Borneo, 5 March, 1970.
29. *Sabah Times*, 15 June, 1967. The Tengku expressed concern about concessions to politicians, and said that in West Malaysia Ministers had to declare their assets and give up any profitable or lucrative jobs which they had (*ibid.*, 2 December, 1966).
30. It is impossible to describe in detail the changes in timber policy which occurred. Policy under Dato Stephens aimed at ending the system of annual licences to Chinese (at the same time providing compensation), and at encouraging co-operative schemes (*ibid.*, 15 June, 1967; *Press Statement, SA/6/63/0010, 15 January, 1964,* by the National Council of the Sabah Alliance Party). The policy had the effect of alienating the annual licensees, who then worked against Stephens through the SCA and the USNO. At the same time the co-operative brought little benefit to the ordinary members, as opposed to the promoters. A change in policy was announced in 1969, for the first time allowing individual smallholder settlers to utilize the proceeds from the timber on their land (*Address by Tun Mustapha at USNO General Assembly Kota Kinabalu, 8 March, 1969*, p. 14).

    In 1970 it was announced that the State Government had taken back 3,000 square miles of forest reserves formerly leased to timber companies, and that the timber land would be given to the Sabah Foundation in perpetuity. Three companies were formed, two for timber extraction and selling, respectively, the third a trust management company which would invite adult Malaysian citizens residing in Sabah (anti-national elements and criminals excepted) to apply for one free, non-transferable share each. Part of the profits would be distributed as cash dividends; the remainder would be reinvested in agricultural and commercial projects to earn more revenue for the benefit of the people (Tun Mustapha, *Press Statements* 1 August and 19 September, 1970). The first dividends were paid out in 1971 ($50 for each adult).

31. Applicants for licences used two plausible arguments against a cautious policy emphasizing timber conservation. First, if licences were not given freely, the timber would be lost anyway because of illegal felling by Natives. Second, it was best to take advantage of high timber prices now; it was likely that after Confrontation ended timber from Kalimantan (Indonesian Borneo) would come on the market and cause a price drop.
32. Soon after the State Operations Committee was set up in May 1969, it imposed an effective freeze on large allocations of timber.
33. See pp. 327–330, below. The Niah deal had the added advantage of associating Dato Wee Hood Teck with Pesaka members of the Government, as a contractor.
34. J. M. Gullick, *Indigenous Political Systems of Western Malaya* (London, 1958), p. 131.
35. At a lower level it is suggestive that the Land Dayak equivalent of a *Penghulu* in Sarawak is called *Orang Kaya Pemancha,* and that district chiefs in Sabah are known as *Orang Kaya Kaya* (O.K.K.), "kaya" meaning "rich". Pringle, quoting a reference to an Iban chief in the mid-nineteenth century, said the distinction between him and the lowest of his tribe was not very great, being "rather a difference of riches than of power". (R. M. Pringle, *The Ibans of Sarawak under Brooke Rule 1841–1941* (Ithaca, Cornell Ph.D. thesis, 1967), p. 4).
36. Although it might be argued that their "entry into politics" should be reckoned from the time they entered the hierarchy of native chiefs (Jugah became a *Penghulu* in 1926, Oyong in 1933). On Jugah's early business enterprise see Malcolm MacDonald, *Borneo People* (Singapore, 1968), pp. 202, 205, 363.
37. Cf. Samuel P. Huntington, *Political Order in Changing Societies* (New Haven, 1968), p. 66.
38. *Minutes of Native Chiefs Conference Held at Tawau on the 8th to 12th November 1966*, p. 2. Cf. the proposals in Sarawak that members of school committees and of the Council Negri should have badges (*Council Negri Debates, 1st Meeting of the Second Session* (3 December, 1963), col. 34; (4 December, 1968), col. 54).
39. *Minutes of the Fourteenth Annual Native Chiefs' Conference,*

Held from 16th to 19th November, 1965, at Jesselton, p. 6. The proposal was also raised on other occasions.

There are no corresponding regular meetings of *Penghulus* in Sarawak. But at an *ad hoc* meeting of *Penghulus* from the 3rd division in August 1967 the following resolutions were passed for the attention of the Government: there should be one *Temenggong* per division and one *Pengarah* per district; there should be badges for *Tuai Rumah*; *Tuai Rumah* travelling on official duties should be paid allowances (*Vanguard*, 9 August, 1967).

40. Many prominent Chinese businessmen may commit themselves minimally, because, as one of them observed, "It is best not to join a party but to be friends with everyone. If you join a party you lose business from those who belong to other parties. It is best to support a 'party' only when it is the Government."
41. "Back mountain" equals "influential patron" (Ju-K'ang T'ien, *The Chinese of Sarawak* (London, 1953), pp. 69–70.
42. Although three of the four made a brief incursion into politics in 1963; one of them and one of his "political" brothers, who were not on good terms at the time, each reputedly spread propaganda against the other in the ward he was contesting. Another took a prominent part in talks to form a new Chinese political party which might appeal to Chinese who would not be likely to support the SCA.

    Even in 1972 there was a legal dispute over the management of the Kong Thai Sawmill and political donations made out of its revenues, 1968–9, between "political" and "non-political" Ling brothers.
43. Fred W. Riggs, *Administration in Developing Countries: the Theory of Prismatic Society* (Boston, 1964), pp. 189–93.
44. Ju-Kang T'ien, *op. cit.*, p. 69. See also Craig Lockard, "Leadership and Power within the Chinese Community of Sarawak", *Journal of Southeast Asian Studies*, Vol. II, No. 2 (1971), pp. 195–217.
45. In Sabah the importance of this ministry was quickly recognized; in 1964 the Natural Resources portfolio was given to Thomas Jayasuriya, because at that time he was not a member of any of the constituent member parties of the Sabah Alliance, and could therefore be relied on to be "independent". Later decisions on timber licences became decisions of the whole Cabinet. After Tun Mustapha became Chief Minister these decisions were in effect his decisions, although it is said that some licences which had not received his approval were given out during his absence from the state. In Sarawak politicians were slower in waking up to the potentialities of this ministerial post; by about 1967, however, decisions on timber licences had become Cabinet decisions.
46. To quote one front-line Chinese politician in Sarawak on the importance of prompt information in business: "In business you must learn things the day before your partners or rivals. If they learn the day before you do, you are finished."

47. *Sarawak Tribune*, 9 March, 1968.
48. Riggs, *op. cit.*, p. 143. In the diagram on p. 143 they are perhaps nearer "Introduction" than "Assimilation".
49. Khaw Kai Boh, speaking to Sarawak businessmen (*Sarawak Vanguard*, 6 January, 1969). The truth of this observation was borne out by the Sarawak Government's grant of the Niah concession in 1968. By this concession the balance of economic power was changed, and Dato Ling Beng Siew's influence over the Sarawak Alliance Party was weakened. Tun Tan Siew Sin had already made the same point as Khaw, with reference to Malaya (*Straits Times*, 1 November, 1968).
50. However, quite apart from power or status being esteemed as ends in themselves, they were also useful in protecting property against seizures by officials or ruinous litigation; "... it is clear from our illustrations and from general statistics that money in Ming Ch'ing China was not in itself an ultimate source of power. It had to be translated into official status to make its power fully felt" (Ping-Ti Ho, *The Ladder of Success in Imperial China: Aspects of Social Mobility, 1368–1911* (New York, 1962), p. 51).
51. The symbols of status may be sought before status itself is achieved. One Sarawak anecdote is worth mentioning, not because it is necessarily true, but rather because it was accepted as plausible. A Chinese politician and businessman who had just bought a black Mercedes was believed to be preparing himself for a Cabinet job in the next Government, a black Mercedes being the most conspicuous ministerial status symbol.
52. The Executive Director of the Aurora Hotel, appointed by Dato Ling, also had a political aspect. He was Cheng Yew Kiew, who left the civil service in 1967 and was a member of the group of "Chinese intellectuals" who were reported to be considering forming a separate party. However, instead, Cheng became Chairman of the Kuching Branch of the SCA, and took up work for Dato Ling as Executive Director of the hotel and in several other enterprises. He was a successful SCA candidate for the Council Negri in 1970.
53. Just as Cheng's relationship to Dato Ling was neither purely economic nor purely political. Similar relationships are found in other parties, even the SUPP.

    Similarly, in another terminology, there is often a single market for both political resources and economic resources (Warren F. Ilchman and Norman Thomas Uphoff, *The Political Economy of Change* (Berkeley, 1969)).
54. Each had a "political back mountain" at federal level in the Malaysian Chinese Association; Dato Ling was linked with Tun Tan Siew Sin, Dato Wee with Khaw Kai Boh.
55. "He dropped into our laps like a gift from Heaven."
56. Cf. "Onassis and Niarchos: One-upmanship in the Greek Islands", *The New York Times*, Sunday, 16 March, 1969, p. 2E.

57. Leigh, *op. cit.*, pp. 171–2.
58. His total contribution to the party may have reached $2m. (*Vanguard*, 5 October, 1968; estimated up to $40,000 a month). After he resigned, a letter from his father, Dato Wee Kheng Chiang, was made public which said that he had assumed that his son's relations with Dato Ningkan had been purely social, but that he had recently learned of his son's involvement in politics and its drain on the family fortune. He therefore had asked his son to give up politics. *Vanguard* accurately predicted (5 October, 1966) that he would resign "before the middle of October". The same issue carried the news that Dato Ningkan's appeal to the Privy Council in London against the validity of the Emergency provisions applied to Sarawak had been dismissed. A week later *Vanguard* said that the reasons for Wee's resignation were complicated "but financial could be a good guess" (12 October, 1968).

    Note that, in spite of commitments and competition, there is a limit to the political spending of a rich Chinese in Sarawak or Sabah. Unlike the "big man" of the Tolai he never becomes "committed to ever more and more grandiose and expensive schemes until he finally overreaches himself, and his riches are exhausted" (A. L. Epstein, "Power, Politics, and Leadership: some Central African and Melanesian Contrasts" in Marc J. Swartz (ed.), *Local-Level Politics; Social and Cultural Perspectives* (London, 1969), p. 63).
59. He also supported Ainnie bin Dhoby, who was fighting Dato Rahman Ya'akub in the state constituency of Kuala-Rejang. He associated Dato Rahman Ya'akub with attempts to block the Niah timber concession by the intervention of the, federal, Anti-Corruption Agency.
60. Cf. "The follower who had invested only one-tenth of his political capital with the leader does not stand to lose much if he severs the tie. The man who has invested everything and no longer has channels open to rival leaders is in the opposite position" (Bailey, *op. cit.*, p. 75). Wee wished to remain a prominent member of the Chinese capitalist sector inside the "core combination" (Ilchman and Uphoff, *op. cit.*, pp. 42–4).

    In deciding in their pattern of political investment towkays also have to consider the possibility of *federal* rewards or sanctions. Presumably Dato Wee's ceasing to support SNAP, as a party, made him more eligible to qualify for federal contracts than previously. Some *towkays* may make substantial contributions direct to a federal party, as has Dato Ling Beng Siew to UMNO.
61. Cf. H. H. Gerth and C. Wright Mills (eds.), *From Max Weber: Essays in Sociology* (London, 1948), pp. 296–7.
62. And even on the assumption that they were not given large timber concessions.
63. Huntington, *Political Order in Changing Societies*, *op. cit.*, pp. 59–71.

64. But see the remarks of the Sarawak Federal Secretary (*Vanguard*, 1 May, 1970), alleging that civil servants sometimes authorized payment to contractors for work not performed.
65. M. McMullan, "A Theory of Corruption", *The Sociological Review*, Vol 9, No. 2 (1961), p. 196.
66. See p. 242, above.
67. A few months before the start of the Sarawak election of 1969 an attempt was made through an intermediary, to bring together Dato Ling Beng Siew and Dato Wee Hood Teck to persuade them to cease spending "against" each other. If this attempt had succeeded it would have represented a pact among towkays to to limit their outlays on politicians.
68. Runciman, *op. cit.*, pp. 237–40.
69. *Sarawak Tribune*, 5 July, 1970. An unfortunate by-product of using West Malaysian troops against the terrorists is the possibility of friction between these troops and local residents.

    In 1972, after increased Communist activity, a State of Emergency was declared in the Third Division and later in the First and Second Divisions.
70. K. G. Tregonning, *A History of Modern Sabah, 1881–1963* (Singapore, 1965), p. 197.
71. Cf. T. R. Williams, *The Dusun: A North Borneo Society* (New York, 1965), pp. 66–7.
72. There are problems in comparing statistically "internal violence" or "domestic group violence" elsewhere with comparable violence in Sarawak and Sabah. Various authorities have compared countries on varying definitions of group violence: Bruce M. Russett *et. al.*, *World Handbook of Political and Social Indicators* (New Haven, 1964), pp. 97–100; Raymond Tanter, "Dimensions of Conflict behavior within and between nations, 1959–1960", *Journal of Conflict Resolution*, Vol. X, No. 1 (1966), pp. 41–65; Ivo K. Feierabend and Rosalind L. Feierabend, "Aggressive behaviors within politics, 1948–1962: a cross-national study", *ibid.*, Vol. X, No. 3 (1966), pp. 249–71; Ted Gurr, "A Causal Model of Civil Strife: A Comparative Analysis Using New Indices", *American Political Review*, Vol. LXII, No. 4 (1968), pp. 1104–24. But the dates covered are too early for comparison with the period, 1963–8, in the Borneo States. Also, no separate figures have been issued for deaths resulting from domestic violence (which excludes deaths by murder and execution) in Sarawak and Sabah. The figure was presumably very small for Sabah 1963–8. In Sarawak deaths from "Homicide and operation of war" were higher in 1964 and 1965, when Confrontation was at its peak, than they were in earlier or later years (*Sarawak Annual Yearbook of Statistics, 1968* (Kuching, 1969), Table 5.5, p. 19). But it is not possible to distinguish the "external war" deaths from the "internal", e.g. by CCO action, which would properly count as

deaths from domestic group violence. On the relation between violence and social mobilization, see pp. 385–391, below.

73. The suppression of headhunting among the Muruts has been identified as a possible cause of increased violence within the community (C. H. Ley, "Muruts of Sabah (North Borneo)" in Peter Kunstadter (ed.), *Southeast Asia Tribes, Minorities and Nations* (Princeton, 1967), pp. 356–7).
74. "The Old Man of Baram" by Safri Zaidell, *Sarawak Gazette*, Vol. XCIII, No. 1310 (30 April, 1967), p. 81. He was referring to Brooke rule around 1900.
75. James C. Scott, "An Essay on the Political Functions of Corruption", *Asian Studies*, Vol. V, No. 3 (1967), p. 509.
76. For a diagrammatic representation of possible combinations of coercion, inducements, and legitimacy in securing compliance, see Ilchman and Uphoff, *op. cit.*, p. 83.
77. A combination of constraints and inducements may be used on electors, as opposed to politicians, e.g. in Britain before the 1832 Reform Act or at the Sabah state elections of 1967.
78. *Sabah Times*, 14 November, 1967.
79. *Ibid.*, 31 October, 1967.
80. See p. 224, above.

   Cf. the following account of politics in Western Nigeria in May 1962; "... AG (Action Group) cars had been going out to fetch members of the Western House of Assembly from their constituencies. They are brought to Ibadan and asked to sign a petition to the Governor, Sir Adesoji Aderemi, the Oni of Ife, asking him to dismiss the Premier. Later there were accusations that these members were keenly pressed to sign and that inducements rising as high as £1,000 were offered. Once these members had signed, it was alleged that they were kept in the houses of reliable AG leaders in case the other side tried to approach them" (John P. Mackintosh, *Nigerian Government and Politics* (London, 1966), p. 447).

   Subhash C. Kashyap refers to allegations of kidnapping in India to induce politicians to change sides. However, he does not explicitly mention the combination of financial persuasion and "protection" to prevent defection (*The Politics of Defection* (New Delhi, 1969), pp. 279, 299, 419).
81. E.g. of the three BARJASA members of the Kuching Rural District Council after the 1963 elections in order to protect them from the blandishments of PANAS (Leigh, *op. cit.*, pp. 130–1).

   In 1969 SNAP had made arrangements to protect, or constrain, its winning candidates until the actual formation of a new Government. Allegedly, in 1970 Pesaka failed to restrain Simon Dembab anak Maja from leaving the Kuching hotel where the newly-elected state assemblymen were staying and joining the new Sarawak Government (Goh Teik Cheng, *The May 13th*

Incident and Democracy in Malaysia (Kuala Lumpur and Singapore, 1971), p. 37).

In a broad sense, which did not include actual physical "protection", perhaps the supreme example of a constrained beneficiary was Dato Stephens after the UPKO was dissolved and he became High Commissioner for Australia. Cf. W. Howard Wriggins, *The Ruler's Imperative* (New York, 1969), pp. 171–2 on "exile as an ambassador".

Chapter 8

1. Cf. Samuel P. Huntington, "The Change to Change: Modernization, Development, and Politics", *Comparative Politics*, Vol. 3, No. 3 (1971), pp. 303–4.
2. Gabriel A. Almond and James S. Coleman, *The Politics of the Developing Areas* (Princeton, 1960); Gabriel A. Almond and Sidney Verba, *The Civic Culture* (Boston, 1963); Fred W. Riggs, *Administration in Developing Countries: the Theory of Prismatic Society* (Boston, 1964); Samuel P. Huntington, "Political Development and Political Decay", *World Politics*, Vol. XVII, No. 3 (1965), pp. 386–430; Lucian W. Pye and Sidney Verba (eds.), *Political Culture and Political Development* (Princeton, 1965); Gabriel A. Almond and G. Bingham Powell, Jr., *Comparative Politics: a Developmental Approach* (Boston, 1966); Joseph LaPalombara and Myron Weiner (eds.), *Political Parties and Political Development* (Boston, 1966); Lucian W. Pye, *Aspects of Political Development* (Boston, 1966); Lucian W. Pye (ed.), *Communications and Political Development* (Princeton, 1967); Samuel P. Huntington, *Political Order in Changing Societies* (New Haven, 1968).
3. Almond and Powell, *op. cit.*, pp. 22–5.
4. A recent major work relates five crises or problems, of political development (roughly corresponding to those mentioned on p. 370, below) to three developmental dimensions; equality, capacity, and differentiation (Leonard Binder, James S. Coleman, Joseph LaPalombara, Lucian W. Pye, Sidney Verba, Myron Weiner, *Crises and Sequences in Political Development* (Princeton, 1971)). But the dimension of equality is decidedly ambiguous, and one of the authors notes correctly that there may be some overlap between the crises and the dimensions, "which makes the relation of the one of [sic] the other difficult" (p. 292, fn. 8).
5. Fred W. Riggs, "The Structures of Government and Administrative Reform" in Ralph Braibanti (ed.), *Political and Administrative Development* (Durham, N.C., 1969), p. 234. See also Milton Singer, "Beyond Tradition and Modernity in Madras", *Comparative Studies in Society and History*, Vol. 13, No. 2 (1971); pp. 160–5.
6. Huntington, *Political Order in Changing Societies, op. cit.*, pp. 32

and 39; Daniel Lerner, *The Passing of Traditional Society* (Glencoe, Ill., 1958); Peter Nettl, *Political Mobilization* (London, 1967), pp. 32–3. Note Huntington's distinction between the *state* of modernity, which breeds stability, and the *process* of modernization, which breeds instability (p. 41).

7. See p. 220, above.
8. They agreed with his suggestion, it seems, but enquired plaintively, "Who will organize us?"
9. For his early career, see p. 128.
10. *Sabah Times*, 2 August, 1967. Cf. Dato Stephens' tribute to Tun Mustapha on the occasion of the dissolution of UPKO. "I also thought that Tun Mustapha was selfish and cared for himself. But I was wrong. He has wider vision and has planned well and laid the foundation for a strong Bumiputra party . . . He is a very much stronger leader than I am. Firm and consistent. We tried too much to play to the gallery while he went on working, going towards a firm objective" (*ibid*., 29 December, 1967).
11. See p. 223, above.
12. One of the attractions of military strategy and terminology might be the belief that knowledge of them conferred invulnerability. The invulnerability idea exercises a strong fascination over Natives in both states (Owen Rutter, *The Pagans of North Borneo* (London, 1929), p. 231). In one version it is linked with the widespread deference to "the Government" noted previously. An Opposition politician has been known to boast of his invulnerability, because he has spoken against the Government and yet the all-powerful Government has not arrested him.
13. *Council Negri Debates, First Meeting of the Fifth Session* (13 December, 1966), cols. 60 and 63.
14. A Malay verse form.
15. *Vanguard*, 2 May, 1969 (Pesaka election broadcast). The point had come up because of SNAP allegations that the Alliance had neglected tourism.
16. Tan Sri Jugah's Kapit speech of 7 October, 1967, publicly attacking Taib in the presence of Tun Razak, was a striking exception.
17. Edward Wolfers, *The 1968 Elections-III: Campaigning* (Institute of Current World Affairs, EPW-14, 1968), p. 7.
18. Cf. Ivor H. N. Evans, *Studies in Religion, Folk-Lore, and Custom in British North Borneo and the Malay Peninsula* (Cambridge, England, 1923), p. 4.
19. See pp. 200–202, above.
20. *Sarawak Gazette*, Vol. XC No. 1274. (30 April, 1964), p. 79.
21. *Sabah Development Plan, 1965–1970* (Jesselton, n.d.), p. 1.
22. *Sarawak Tribune*, 27 August, 1967 (Taib).
23. Gunnar Myrdal, *Asian Drama* (New York, 1968), Vol. 1, p. 73.
24. Robert E. Ward and Dankwart A. Rustow (eds.), *Political Modernization in Japan and Turkey* (Princeton, 1964), p. 12.

25. Tom Harrisson, "Tribes, Minorities, and the Central Government in Sarawak, Malaysia" in Peter Kunstadter (ed.), *Southeast Asian Tribes, Minorities and Nations* (Princeton, 1967), pp. 325–6.
26. T. R. Williams, *The Dusun* (New York, 1965), p. 92.
27. Monica Glyn-Jones, *The Dusun of the Penampang Plain in North Borneo* (London, 1955), p. 98. On invulnerability see p. 343, above.
28. "Obituary-Temenggong Koh", *Sarawak Gazette*, Vol. LXXXII, No. 1185 (30 November, 1956), p. 278.
29. *Borneo People* (Singapore, 1968), p. 260.
30. *Kadazan Times*, 12 November, 1966.
31. *Sabah Times*, 11 November, 1966.
32. "Epilogue", *Sarawak Gazette*, Vol. LXXXIX, No. 1261 (31 March, 1963), pp. 51–2. See also Tom Harrisson, "Letter to the Editor", *ibid.*, Vol. LXXXIX, No. 1262 (30 April, 1963), pp. 77–8.
33. "Epilogue", *op cit.*, p. 52; cf. J. D. Freeman, *Iban Agriculture* (London, 1955), para. 21.
34. On changing attitudes to education among Iban *Penghulus* some twenty years ago see MacDonald, *op. cit.*, pp. 161 and 171.
35. George M. Foster, "Peasant Society and the Image of Limited Good", *American Anthropologist*, Vol. 67, No. 2 (1965), pp. 293–315.
36. James C. Scott, *Political Ideology in Malaysia: Reality and the Beliefs of an Elite* (New Haven, 1968), pp. 94–149.
37. *Op. cit.*, p. 119.
38. See pp. 10–11, 214.
39. *Resident, Sandakan, Handing-over Notes, 22.1.64.* See also pp. 281, 332.
40. Perhaps MRP's, in Foster's scheme would be counted as coming from outside the village, and therefore the limited good concept would not be entirely applicable (*op. cit.*, p. 306).
41. See pp. 314–318.
42. Comments on the 1964 Native Chiefs' Conference by a Sabah permanent secretary, 12 March, 1964.
43. A nut used in the manufacture of confectionery. The authors are indebted to Dato Ong Kee Hui for this analogy.
44. Lucian Pye, "Democracy, Modernization and Nationbuilding" in J. Roland Pennock (ed.), *Self-government in Modernizing Nations* (Englewood Cliffs, N. J., 1964), p. 21. Cf. On Malays in West Malaysia, Brien K. Parkinson, "Non-Economic Factors in the Economic Retardation of the Rural Malays", *Modern Asian Studies*, Vol. 1, No. 1 (1967), pp. 38–40.
45. Gayl D. Ness, *Bureaucracy and Rural Development in Malaysia* (Berkeley and Los Angeles, 1967). An output goal refers to "the production of amenities, building up the infrastructure, or providing aids and assistance to rural people". Cultural goals correspond to "community development; changing the values of

the rural people by increasing their participation in their own uplift; reconstructing the rural community". There is also a third category, "Mixed Output-Cultural Goals" (p. 124).

46. *Development Progress, 1964–1967* (Kuching, n.d.), p. 18.
47. In Sarawak the initial emphasis in land settlement schemes was placed on cultural as well as output goals. Each scheme manager was "responsible for the establishment of a community organization and spirit" (*Development Instruction No. 7*, 29 December, 1966). But when the schemes were later put under the newly-created Sarawak Development Finance Corporation (SDFC), the scheme manager was supposed to give more weight to output. "It will become much more a dollars and cents job."
48. Interestingly, for some small projects in Chinese areas, money is provided by the government, the local Chinese add money of their own, and a contractor is hired to do the job. Apparently the goal here is entirely an output one; it is assumed that there is no need to induce cultural changes in the Chinese in that context.
49. See pp. 48–49, 284–286, 388.
50. See p. 285.
51. pp. 71, 142–154.
52. Nettl, *op. cit.*, p. 208, fn.
53. *Sabah Times*, 17 May, 1968 and 16 December, 1967 (Tun Mustapha).
54. *Sabah Legislative Assembly Debates*, Vol. 1, No. 5 (19 December, 1963), cols. 206–7 (Taulani bin Jalaluddin).
55. See p. 45.
56. *Sabah Legislative Assembly Debates*, Vol. III, No. 10 (30 December, 1968), cols. 592–3 (O.K.K. Sakaran bin Dandai).
57. *Council Negri Debates, First Meeting of the Seventh Session* (14 December, 1968), col. 210 (Stephen Yong Kuet Tze).
58. J. F. Guyot, "Bureaucratic Transformation in Burma" in Ralph Braibanti (ed.), *Asian Bureaucratic Systems Emergent from the British Imperial Tradition* (Durham, N.C., 1966), p. 432.
59. See pp. 342–343.
60. These definitions or criteria are among the most common in the literature on political development. See particularly: Almond and Coleman, *op. cit.*; Almond and Powell, op. cit.; Pye, *Aspects of Political Development, op. cit.*; Riggs, *Administration in Developing Countries op. cit.*; Riggs, *Thailand the Modernization of a Bureaucratic Polity* (Honolulu, 1966). No attempt is made here to summarize the entire accounts of political development contained in these books.
61. Almond and Powell, *op cit.*, pp. 22–3 and 30–2. Later (pp. 323–4) the authors say that system capabilities (see pp. 367–388, below) are dependent on the degree of structural differentiation and cultural secularization.

62. Huntington, "Political Development and Political Decay", *op. cit.*, p. 396.
63. R. S. Milne, "Differentiation and Administrative Development", *Journal of Comparative Administration*, Vol. 1, No. 2 (1969).
64. See pp. 424–425, Fn. 3.
65. See pp. 283–284.
66. Milne. "Differentiation and Administrative Development", pp. 220–1; Fred W. Riggs, "Administrative Development: An Elusive Concept" in J. D. Montgomery and W. J. Siffin (eds.), *Approaches to development: Politics, Administration and Change* (New York, 1966), pp. 232–3.
67. Richard W. Gable, *Introduction to District Administration* (Lahore, 1963), p. 155.
68. See p. 269.
69. See pp. 299–300.
70. Amitai Etzioni, *Modern Organizations* (Englewood Cliffs, N. J., 1964), pp. 61–2.
71. Cf. Huntington, "Political Development and Political Decay", *op. cit.*, pp. 399–401.
72. *Local Government Finance in Sarawak; Cmd. 3 of 1966.*
73. R. A. Dahl and C. E. Lindblom, *Politics, Economics and Welfare* (New York, 1953), p. 38.
74. Almond and Powell, *op. cit.*, p. 24. Later the definition is expanded (p. 58), and the concept of bargaining is also introduced (pp. 365–366, below).
75. *Ibid.*, p. 323.
76. See pp. 353–354, above.
77. Almond and Powell, *op. cit.*, p. 33. But, from a personal angle, it is not irrational for an official to stick to the rules as a matter of self-preservation if he knows that a "rational" departure from the rules will be discovered and punished.
78. Cf. Pye on Burma: *Politics, Personality, and Nation Building* (New Haven, 1962), p. 216.
79. Islam as a faith is "progressive and practical", if properly interpreted (Abang Yusuf Puteh, "Thinking Aloud on Cultural Problems of Sarawak Malays", *Development Forum* (Kuala Lumpur), Vol. II, No. 1 (June 1969), p. 44).
80. MacDonald, *op. cit.*, pp. 235–7.
81. Erik Jensen, "The Lemanak Community Development Scheme", *Sarawak Gazette*, Vol. XCII, No. 1302, 31 August, 1966, p. 272.
82. Tom Harrisson, *The Malays of South-West Sarawak Before Malaysia* (London, 1970), pp. 76–9. Cf. Alfred Diamant, "The Temporal Dimension in Models of Administration" in Dwight Waldo (ed.), *Temporal Dimensions of Development Administration* (Durham, N.C., 1969).
83. *Sabah Times,* 1 March, 1966 (Harris bin Mohd, Salleh).
84. Scott, *op. cit.*, pp. 218–19.

85. Cf. pp. 305–312.
86. *Vanguard*, 23 October, 1967. The timber policy which took effect early in 1971 also aimed at achieving long-term prosperity: it increased timber royalties but gave incentives for setting up local timber works and factories (*New Nation*, 15 February, 1971).
87. Almond and Powell, *op. cit*., pp. 57–61.
88. Dahl and Lindblom, *op. cit*., pp. 324 and 326.
89. Chapter 5, especially pp. 234–243.
90. See pp. 305–312.
91. James D. Thompson and Arthur Tuden, "Strategies, Structures, and Processes of Organizational Decision ", in J. D. Thompson (ed.), *Comparative Studies in Administration* (Pittsburgh, 1959), pp. 198 ff.
92. See pp. 157–164, 177–184. Examples of bargaining, between State and Federal Governments, are mentioned in Chapter 2. The process by which the SUPP declared its support for the concept of Malaysia in exchange for being allowed to carry on its 1969 election campaign without hindrance is described in p. 441, Fn. 377.
93. Leonard Binder, *Iran: Political Development in a Changing Society* (Berkeley and Los Angeles, 1964), pp. 44–5, 227–37.
94. Fred W. Riggs, *Administration in Developing Countries, op. cit*., pp. 280–3.
94a. Cf. Almond and Powell, *op. cit*., pp. 47–8.
95. See p. 415, Fn. 52.
96. On the role of Chinese in high political posts, see pp. 322–327, 331, above.
97. See p. 233 above on the choice of the first local Sabah state secretary. Even in August, 1970 the influential Dzulkifli Abdul Hamid, Acting Permanent Secretary to the Chief Minister, in his capacity as President of the *Badan Bahasa Sabah*, wanted the state government to give attention to the difference in the number of Malay and non-Malay (presumably Muslim and non-Muslim) staff in its service (*Straits Times*, 6 August, 1970).
98. Karl Deutsch, *The Nerves of Government* (New York, 1963), pp. 250–3; Almond and Powell, *op. cit*., p. 193. Of course, *indices* of capability should not be confused with capability itself.
99. Gabriel A. Almond, "A Developmental Approach to Political Systems", *World Politics*, Vol. 17, no. 2 (1965), p. 204.
100. Myron Weiner, "Political Integration and Political Development", *The Annals of the American Academy of Political and Social Science*, Vol. 358, No. 1 (1965), p. 54.
101. Almond and Powell, *op. cit*., p. 207; Deutsch, *The Nerves of Government, op. cit*., p. 253; Ilchman and Uphoff, *op. cit*., p. 48 (second definition).
102. Samuel P. Huntington, "Political Development and Political Decay", *op. cit*., p. 394.

103. Where the two characteristics of institutionalization are said to be infusion with value and the capacity to adapt to environmental changes (Samuel P. Huntington, *Some Notes on Political Institutionalization* (I.P.S.A., Salzburg Round Table, 16–20 September, 1968)).
104. Manfred Halpern, "Towards Further Modernization of the Study of New Nations", *World Politics,* Vol. XVII, No. 1 (1964), p. 177; Huntington, *Political Order in Changing Societies, op. cit.*, p. 99. See also Almond and Powell on political elites' reactions to political system challenges (*op. cit.*, pp. 40–1).
105. See pp. 371–373.
106. Almond and Powell, *op. cit.*, pp. 39–40.
107. *Ibid.*, p. 35.
108. Chapter VIII. They later relate differentiation and secularization to these system capabilities (pp. 323ff.).
109. Ilchman and Uphoff, *op. cit.*, p. 209.
110. *Ibid.*, p. 20, fn. 28. See also p. 274.
111. Apart from the emphasis on specificity as opposed to capacity, the four "problem" headings correspond quite closely to the six "capability" headings. In a later article Almond writes about performance rather than about capabilities (Gabriel A. Almond, "Political Development: Analytical and Normative Perspectives", *Comparative Political Studies,* Vol. 1, No. 4 (1969), p. 461).
112. Robert M. Pringle, *Asun's "Rebellion"; the Political Growing Pains of a Tribal Society in Brooke Sarawak* (Paper No. 41, International Conference on Asian History, Kuala Lumpur, 5–10 August, 1968), p. 43; G. V. C. Young, "Does the Law Change in Sarawak?", *Sarawak Gazette*, Vol. XC, No. 1278, 31 August, 1964, pp. 196–7; Otto Charles Doering III, *The Institutionalization of Personal Rule in Sarawak* (London School of Economics, M.Sc. thesis, 1965 (mimeo.), pp. 133–5).
113. Sidney Verba, "Conclusion", Lucian W. Pye and Sidney Verba (eds.), *Political Culture and Political Development, op. cit.*, p. 541.
114. As in Gabriel A. Almond and Sidney Verba, *The Civic Culture, op. cit.*
115. See pp. 332–335, above.
116. See pp. 268–269, above. In the 1930s it was the Sarawak government's clumsy methods of exercising its "extractive capability" (Almond and Powell) that roused Asun to rebellion (Pringle, *The Ibans of Sarawak under Brooke Rule 1841–1941, op. cit.*, p. 569).
117. *Vanguard*, 19 June, 1966.
118. *Sunday Tribune*, 21 April, 1963.
119. Pringle, *The Ibans of Sarawak under Brooke Rule 1841–1941, op. cit.*, p. 574.
120. See pp. 375–378, below.
121. *Op. cit.*, p. 36.
122. See pp. 424–425, Fn. 3, above.
123. Almond and Verba, *op. cit.*, pp. 16–19.

124. The most obvious items distributed by Government are: land, aid in cultivating crops, timber, capital items such as fishing boats, education, town and *kampong* amenities, jobs. The government is blamed if distribution of certain kinds falls, even although it is not responsible for the fall (for instance lower prices for rubber). The costs of distribution are borne by rates and taxes, by contributions from the Federal Government, and, in a broader sense, by those who painfully change their traditional customs or ways of life.
125. Sidney Verba, "Conclusion" in Pye and Verba, *op. cit.*, p. 538. Cf. Almond and Verba, *op. cit.*, pp. 15–26.
126. *Straits Times*, 2 December, 1959.
127. Pringle, "Asun's Rebellion...", *op. cit.*, p. 44. In this context "central authority" would obviously include "state government".
128. See pp. 302–304.
129. *Sabah Legislative Assembly Debates*, Vol 1, No. 5 (19 December, 1963), col. 218.
130. L. W. Jones, *The Population of Borneo: A Study of the Peoples of Sarawak, Sabah and Brunei* (London, 1966). There is, of course, considerable *under-employment* in agriculture.
131. *Sarawak Gazette*, Vol. XC, No. 1278 (31 August, 1964), p. 197.
132. *Vanguard*, 23 October, 1967.
133. Cf. Jones, *op. cit.*, pp. 195–6.
134. *Chinese Daily News,* 14 January, 1969.
135. Cf. in Sabah the announcement of the establishment of the state's first vocational agricultural school (*Kinabalu Sabah Times*, 17 April, 1969). In Sarawak efforts are being made to introduce agriculture and husbandry into the school curriculum, although the opposition criticized the government for not having done enough, and in particular for not having set up first an Agricultural College (*Council Negri Debates, First Meeting of the Seventh Session*, 14 December and 16 December, 1968), cols. 238 and 348, respectively.
136. *Sabah Times*, 7 November, 1967.
137. The Malaysian Head of State.
138. C. S. Whitaker , Jr., *The Politics of Tradition Continuity and Change in Northern Nigeria 1946–1966* (Princeton, 1970), pp. 3–13, 467–8. Cf.: Lloyd I. Rudolph and Susanne Hoeber Rudolph, *The Modernity of Tradition* (Chicago, 1967), "Introduction"; Reinhard Bendix, "Tradition and Modernity Reconsidered", *Comparative Studies in Society and History*, Vol. IX, No. 3 (1967), pp. 293–346.
139. C. S. Whitaker, Jr., "A Dysrhythmic Process of Political Change", *World Politics*, Vol. XIX, No. 2 (1967), pp. 190–217.
140. Huntington, *Political Order in Changing Societies, op. cit.*, p. 132. Cf. Rudolph and Rudolph, *op. cit.*, p. 66; Almond and Powell, *op. cit.*, p. 62; Almond and Verba, *op cit.*, p. 5; Lucian W. Pye, "Introduction", Pye and Verba, *op. cit.*, p. 21.

141. S. Baring-Gould and C. A. Bampfylde, *A History of Sarawak under its Two White Rajahs* (London, 1909), pp. 313–14. Cf. the distinction made by Disraeli between change according to a "national system" or a "philosophic system" (Robert Blake, *Disraeli* (London, 1966), p. 482).
142. K. G. Tregonning, *A History of Modern Sabah, 1881–1963* (Singapore, 1965), p. 103.
143. See pp. 302–304.
144. *The Politics of Tradition Continuity and Change in Northern Nigeria 1946–1966, op. cit.*, pp. 462–5.
145. Lucian W. Pye, *Politics, Personality, and Nation Building, op. cit.*, pp. 30–1. Cf. Lucy Mair, *Primitive Government* (London, 1964), p. 279; on chiefs and slowing down mobilization, see p. 387.
146. See pp. 340–344.
147. *Sabah Times*, 23 April, 1968.
148. MacDonald, *op. cit.*, pp. 168–9.
149. *Ibid.*, p. 169.
150. See p. 360.
151. Francis X. Sutton. "The Problem of Fitness for Self Government", in J. Roland Pennock (ed.), *Self Government in Modernizing Nations, op. cit.*, p. 39.
152. Henry Teune, "The Learning of Integrative Habits:, in Philip E. Jacob and James V. Toscano (eds.), *The Integration of Political Communities* (Philadelphia, 1964), pp. 273–4.
153. Almond and Powell show that they are aware of possible contradictions in their capabilities (e.g. *op. cit.*, pp. 311–31). J. Roland Pennock, whose view of development rests on the provision of political goods, such as security, welfare, justice, and liberty, attempts to meet the point by saying that often such political goods do not conflict ("Political Development, Political Systems, and Political Goods", *World Politics*, Vol. 18, No. 3 (1966), p. 430).
154. See pp. 244–252.
155. See pp. 250–251.
156. See pp. 284–286. On conflict between achievement criteria and presumed nation-building requirements, see pp. 366–377.
157. Recognition of this problem has led to a new research emphasis on political change, as opposed to political development (Huntington, "The Change to Change: Modernization, Development, and Politics", *op. cit.*, pp. 313–22).
158. Huntington, *Political Order in Changing Societies*, p. 5. Institutionalization is the process by which organizations and procedures acquire value and stability. Criteria of political institutionalization are given on pp. 12–24.

This thesis is not universally accepted. See, e.g., on Africa, D. G. Morrison and H. M. Stevenson, "Cultural Pluralism, Modernization and Conflict: An Empirical Analysis of Sources of Political

Instability in African Nations", *Canadian Journal of Political Science*, Vol. V, No. 1 (1972), pp. 82–103.

159. *Ibid*., p. 55.

160 However, Oberschall warns that we should not place too much emphasis on economic factors in accounting for political stability or instability (Anthony R. Oberschall, "Rising Expectations and Political Turmoil", *The Journal of Development Studies*, Vol. 6, No. 1 (1969), pp. 5–22).

161. Some possible indicators of social mobilization in the two states, selected from the data available, were given in Chapter 1, pp. 10–14. For comparative statistical analysis see: Karl W. Deutsch, "Social Mobilization and Political Development", *American Political Science Review*, Vol. LV, No. 3 (1961), pp. 493–514; Bruce M. Russett *et al*., *World Handbook of Political and Social Indicators* (New Haven, 1964); Ivo K. Feierabend and Rosalind K. Feierabend, "Aggressive Behaviors within Politics, 1948–1962: a cross-national study", *Journal of Conflict Resolution,* Vol. X, No. 3 (1966), pp. 249–71.

162. Russett *et al*., *op cit*., p. 303.

163. Almond and Powell, *op. cit*., p. 286.

164. Cf. Huntington, *Political Order in Changing Societies, op. cit*., p. 47.

165. Huntington, "Political Development and Political Decay", *op. cit*., p. 419. Huntington is referring to "political mobilization", but the point also holds good for social mobilization.

166. Parts of the elite in both territories were opposed or indifferent (see, on Sarawak, pp. 19–20, above).

167. See pp. 302–304, above. The proposed new government body in Sabah, mentioned on the next paragraph, would presumably *decrease* confusion among the public, although at the same time it would lessen pressure on ministers.

168. In a sense these extra mechanisms also increase the degree of institutionalization by providing additional institutionalized structures (institutionalization is the next concept discussed below). But the point at issue here is not whether or not particular structures are institutionalized, but the effects of complexity, as opposed to simplicity, of such structures.

169. See p. 303.

170. *Kinabalu Sabah Times*, 6 January, 1969.

171. It was set up on 1st November (*ibid*., 15 November, 1969).

172. Huntington, *Political Order in Changing Societies, op. cit*., pp. 91–2 and 398.

173. Myron Weiner and Joseph LaPalombara, "Conclusion: the Impact of Parties on Political Development" in LaPalombara and Weiner, *op. cit*., p. 403. Cf. the view that an important way of draining off and reducing discontent which may arise from changes in traditional patterns and relationships is perhaps a high level of controlled and manipulated rank-and-file participation

(Seymour Martin Lipset, *Political Man* (New York, 1960), p. 180).

174. But not eliminated. It continues within the USNO, principally in the form of seeking to gain the ear of Tun Mustapha and/or achieving high office in the cabinet, civil service or government-supported organizations.

175. Ch. 7, above. Cf.: Huntington, "Political Development and Political Decay", *op. cit.*, pp. 420–1; F. M. Cornford, *Microcosmographia Academica* (Cambridge, 1953), p. 22 (on ("squaring").

176. Some were originally from Malaya. This extra-legal group is in some ways similar to a French minister's *cabinet*. Alternatively, it might be viewed as making good some of the deficiencies of the actual Cabinet, apparent since the exit of most of its "working ministers" (see p. 359, above).

177. This was the same permanent secretary who had been appointed against Tun Mustapha's wishes (see p. 233, above). He left the service soon afterwards.

178. Cf. Richard P. Taub, *Bureaucrats under Stress: Administrators and Administration in an Indian State* (Berkeley and Los Angeles, 1969), p. 112.

179. This practice had started to spread by 1969. A speech "by" a minister was actually delivered, in Tawau, by a state assemblyman (*Kinabalu Sabah Times*, 17 June, 1969).

180. Guenther Roth, "Personal Rulership, Patrimonialism, and Empire-Building in the New States", *World Politics*, Vol. XX, No. 2 (1968), pp. 202, 203. In other respects the Roth article does not apply closely. It hits off very well the personal aspects of his behaviour, for instance his disregard for what he thinks are unnecessary rules. But the sources of Tun Mustapha's authority are wider than in the Roth typology. Some of the qualities usually subsumed in the misleading term, charisma, belong to Tun Mustapha; some of the loyalty accorded to him is based on his traditional rôle of Suluk chief.

Cf. F. G. Bailey, *Stratagems and Spoils* (Oxford, 1969), pp. 83–4. Tun Mustapha's leadership uses "moral", "transactional" and "bureaucratic" principles.

181. Huntington, *Political Order in Changing Societies, op. cit.*, p. 410.

182. See pp. 45, 61, above.

183. Cf. the committees being set up for community service development, for liaison between the government and the public, and for the rehabilitation of refugees (*Sarawak Tribune*, 5 December, 1970).

184. This was the only State Operations Council in Malaysia not headed by the State's Chief Minister (see pp. 38, 57, above). State Operations Councils were abolished when parliamentary government was restored in 1971.

Bibliography

APPELL, G. N. "Ethnography of Northern Borneo: Critical Review of some Recent Publications", *Oceania*, Vol. XXXVII, No. 3 (1967).

——, *The Nature of Social Groupings among the Rungus Dusun of Sabah, Malaysia* (Canberra, 1965; Ph.D. thesis, Australian National University).

BAKER, M. H., *North Borneo, The First Ten Years, 1946–1956* (Singapore, 1965).

BARING-GOULD, S., and C. A. BAMPFYLDE, *A History of Sarawak under its Two White Rajahs* (London, 1909).

DICKSON, M. G., *Sarawak and its People* (Kuching, 1954).

1867–1967, Council Negri Centenary (Kuching, 1967).

EVANS, IVOR H. N., *Among Primitive Peoples in Borneo* (London, 1924).

First Malaysia Plan, 1966–1970 (Kuala Lumpur, 1965).

FORTIER, DAVID H., *Cultural Change among Chinese Agricultural Settlers in British North Borneo* (New York, 1964).

FREEMAN, J. D., *Family and Kin among the Iban of Sarawak* (Cambridge, 1954; Ph.D. thesis, Cambridge University).

——, *Iban Agriculture* (London, 1955).

——, *Report on the Iban of Sarawak* (Kuching, 1955).

GEDDES, W. R., *The Land Dayaks of Sarawak* (London, 1954).

GLYN-JONES, MONICA, *The Dusun of the Penampang Plains in North Borneo.* (London, 1955).

HARRIS, GEORGE L., *et al.* (eds.), *Human Relations Area Files, North Borneo, Brunei, Sarawak (British North Borneo)* (New Haven, 1956).

HARRISSON, TOM, "Tribes, Minorities, and the Central Government in Sarawak, Malaysia", in Peter Kunstadter (ed.), *Southeast Asian Tribes, Minorities, and Nations* (Princeton, 1967).

——, *The Malays of South-West Sarawak Before Malaysia* (London, 1970).

——, (ed.), *The Peoples of Sarawak* (Kuching, 1959).

HAYWARD, N., *Sarawak, Brunei and North Borneo* (Singapore, 1963).

HOSE, C., and W. MCDOUGALL, *The Pagan Tribes of Borneo* (London, 1912).

JACKSON, JAMES C., *Sarawak: A Geographical Survey of a Developing State* (London, 1968).

JONES, L. W., *North Borneo: Report on the Census of Population taken on 10th August, 1960* (Kuching, 1962).

——, *Sarawak: Report on the Census of Population* (Kuching, 1962).

——, *The Population of Borneo* (London, 1966)

JU-K'ANG T'IEN, *The Chinese of Sarawak* (London, 1953).
KAHIN, G. MCT., "The State of North Borneo, 1881–1946", *Far Eastern Quarterly,* Vol. .VII, No. 1 (1947).
LEACH, E. R., *Social Science Research in Sarawak* (London, 1950).
LEE YONG-LENG, *North Borneo (Sabah): a study in Settlement Geography* (Singapore, 1965).
——, *Population and Settlement in Sarawak* (Singapore, 1970).
——, *Settlements and House Types in British Borneo* (Singapore, 1958; M.A. thesis, University of Malaya).
——, "The Development of Resources in British Borneo and its Impact on Settlement", *Sarawak Museum Journal*, Vol. X, Nos 19–20 (New Series) (1962).
LEIGH, MICHAEL B., *The Chinese Community of Sarawak. A Study of Communal Relations* (Singapore, 1964).
——, *The Development of Political Organization and Leadership in Sarawak, East Malaysia* (Ithaca, 1971; Ph.D. thesis, Cornell University).
LIANG KIM BANG, "Sarawak, 1941–1957" and Lee, Edwin, "Sarawak in the Early Sixties" in *Number Five: Singapore Studies on Borneo and Malaya* (Singapore, 1964).
LING, ROTH, HENRY, *The Natives of Sarawak and North Borneo* (Kuala Lumpur, 1968).
MACDONALD, MALCOLM, *Borneo People* (Singapore, 1968).
MCDOUGALL, J. A., *Shared Burdens: A Study of Communal Discrimination by the Political Parties of Malaysia and Singapore* (Cambridge, 1968; Ph.D. thesis, Harvard University).
MEANS, GORDON P., *Malaysian Politics* (London, 1970).
Mid-term Review of the First Malaysia Plan, 1966–1970 (Kuala Lumpur, 1969).
MORRIS, H. S., *Report on a Melanau Sago Producing Community in Sarawak* (London, 1953).
MORRISON, HEDDA, *Life in a Longhouse* (Kuching, 1962).
ONGKILI, J. P., *The Borneo Response to Malaysia, 1961–1963* (Singapore, 1967).
POLE-EVANS, R. J., "The Supreme Council, Sarawak", *Sarawak Museum Journal,* Vol. VII, No. 7, New Series (1956), pp. 89–108.
PURCELL, VICTOR, *The Chinese in Southeast Asia* (London, 1965).
Report of the Commission of Enquiry, North Borneo and Sarawak (Kuala Lumpur, 1962) (the "Cobbold Report").
Report on the Economic Aspects of Malaysia by a Mission of the International Bank for Reconstruction and Development (Kuala Lumpur, 1963).
RUNCIMAN, STEVEN, *The White Rajahs* (Cambridge, 1960).
RUTTER, OWEN, *The Pagans of North Borneo* (London, 1929).
——, *British North Borneo* (London, 1922).
Sabah Since Malaysia, 1963–1968 (Kota Kinabalu, 1969).
Sabah Development Plan, 1965–1970 (Jesselton, 1965).
Sabah's Revolution for Progress (Kota Kinabalu, 1971).

Second Malaysia Plan 1971–1975 (Kuala Lumpur, 1971).
SANDIN, BENEDICT, *The Sea Dayaks of Borneo Before White Rajah Rule* (East Lansing, 1968).
Sarawak Development Plan, 1964–1968 (Kuching, 1963).
Sarawak Development Progress, 1964–1967 (Kuching, n.d.).
SILCOCK, T. H., *The Commonwealth Economy in Southeast Asia* (Durham, N. C., 1959).
TREGONNING, K. G., *A History of Modern Sabah (North Borneo) 1881–1963* (Singapore, 1965).
United Nations Malaysia Mission Report (Kuala Lumpur, 1963).
WARD, A. B., *Rajah's Servant* (Ithaca, 1966).
WILLIAMS, THOMAS RHYS, *The Dusun: a North Borneo Society* (New York, 1965).

West Malaysia (Malaya)

ENLOE, CYNTHIA, "Issues and Integration in Malaysia", *Pacific Affairs,* Vol. 41, No. 3 (1968).
GULLICK, J. M., *Malaya* (London, 1969).
MILNE, R. S., *Government and Politics in Malaysia* (Boston, 1967).
NESS, G. D., *Bureaucracy and Rural Development in Malaysia* (Berkeley and Los Angeles, 1967).
RATNAM, K. J., *Communalism and the Political Process in Malaya* (Kuala Lumpur, 1965).
——, and R. S. MILNE, *The Malayan Parliamentary Election of 1964* (Kuala Lumpur, 1967).
SILCOCK, T. H. and E. K. FISK (eds.), *The Political Economy of Independent Malaya* (Canberra, 1963).
The May 13 Tragedy, a report by the National Operations Council (Kuala Lumpur, 1969).
TILMAN, R. O., *Bureaucratic Transition in Malaya* (Durham, N. C., 1964).
WANG GUNGWU, *Malaysia, a Survey* (New York, 1964).

Indonesian Confrontation and the Philippine Claim to Sabah

BOYCE, PETER, *Malaysia and Singapore in International Diplomacy; Documents and Commentaries* (Sydney, 1968).
BRACKMAN, ARNOLD C., *Southeast Asia's Second Front: the Power Struggle in the Malay Archipelago* (New York, 1966).
GORDON, BERNARD K., *Dimensions of Conflict in Southeast Asia* (Englewood Cliffs, N.J., 1966).
KAHIN, GEORGE MCT., "Malaysia and Indonesia", *Pacific Affairs,* Vol. 37, No. 3 (1964).
LEIFER, MICHAEL, *The Philippine Claim to Sabah* (Hull, 1968).
Malaya-Indonesian Relations (Kuala Lumpur, 1963).
Malaya-Philippines Relations (Kuala Lumpur, 1963).

MEADOWS, MARTIN, "The Philippine Claim to North Borneo", *Political Science Quarterly,* Vol. LXXVII, No. 3, 1962.

ORTIZ, PACIFICO A., "Legal Aspects of the North Borneo Question", *Philippine Studies,* Vol. II, No. 1 (1963).

TREGONNING, K. G., "The Claim for North Borneo by the Philippines", *Australian Outlook,* Vol. XVI, No. 3 (1962).

WRIGHT, LEIGH R., "Historical Notes on the North Borneo Dispute", *Journal of Asian Studies,* Vol. XXIV, No. 3 (1966).

The following newspapers and periodicals in English will be found useful:

SARAWAK

Sarawak Tribune
Vanguard
Sarawak Gazette
Sarawak Museum Journal

SABAH

Daily Express
Kinabalu Times
Sabah Times
} in 1969 merged to form *Kinabalu Sabah Times.*

Among official publications in Sarawak reports on the Council Negri Debates will be found particularly useful, although they are sometimes issued two or three years in arrears. Reports of the Public Accounts Committee are also valuable. Reports of Sabah Legislative Assembly Debates are also usually available only after an interval of a year or two. Reports of the Sabah Public Accounts Committee are not obtainable by the public.

Malaysian Information Services, Sarawak, issue a *Sarawak Who's Who* giving brief biographies of politicians and some civil servants, which is updated quite frequently. There is no exact equivalent of this in Sabah, but a pamphlet, *Biographical Notes on Ministers* was issued by the Information Department in 1965.

When Sabah was still North Borneo the Government produced several *Native Affairs Bulletins*, dealing with customs among various ethnic groups. More recently the Lands and Surveys Department, Sabah, has produced a series of *Town Planning Bulletins*, some of which are based on data obtained by means of questionnaires.

The Borneo Literature Bureau has also issued a wide range of publications on both states.

Index

DORSET INSTITUTE OF HIGHER EDUCATION
LEARNING RESOURCES CENTRE